Time Bomb 2000

Selected Titles from the

YOURDON PRESS COMPUTING SERIES

Ed Yourdon, *Advisor*

ANDREWS AND LEVENTHAL Fusion: Integrating IE, CASE, and JAD
ANDREWS AND STALICK Business Reengineering: The Survival Guide
AUGUST Joint Application Design
BODDIE The Information Asset: Rational DP Funding and Other Radical Notions
BOULDIN Agents of Change: Managing the Introduction of Automated Tools
BRILL Building Controls into Structured Systems
COAD AND NICOLA Object-Oriented Programming
COAD AND YOURDON Object-Oriented Analysis, 2/E
COAD AND YOURDON Object-Oriented Design
COAD, MAYFIELD, AND KERN Java Design: Building Better Apps and Applets, 2/E
COAD WITH NORTH AND MAYFIELD Object Models: Strategies, Patterns, and Applications, 2/E
CONNELL AND SHAFER Object-Oriented Rapid Prototyping
CONNELL AND SHAFER Structured Rapid Prototyping
CONSTANTINE Constantine on Peopleware
CONSTANTINE AND YOURDON Structured Design
DEGRACE AND STAHL Wicked Problems, Righteous Solutions
DeMARCO Controlling Software Projects
DeMARCO Structured Analysis and System Specification
EMBLEY, KURTZ, AND WOODFIELD Object-Oriented Systems Analysis
FOURNIER A Methodology for Client/Server and Web Application Development
GARMUS AND HERRON Measuring the Software Process: A Practical Guide to Functional Measurements
GLASS Software Conflict: Essays on the Art and Science of Software Engineering
GROCHOW Information Overload: Creating Value with the New Information Systems Technology
HAYES AND ULRICH The Year 2000 Software Crisis: The Continuing Challenge
JONES Assessment and Control of Software Risks
KING Project Management Made Simple
McMENAMIN AND PALMER Essential System Design
MOSLEY The Handbook of MIS Application Software Testing
PAGE-JONES Practical Guide to Structured Systems Design, 2/E
PUTMAN AND MYERS Measures for Excellence: Reliable Software on Time within Budget
RODGERS Oracle: A Database Developer's Guide, 2/E
RUBLE Practical Analysis and Design for Client/Server and GUI Systems
SHLAER AND MELLOR Object Lifecycles: Modeling the World in States
SHLAER AND MELLOR Object-Oriented Systems Analysis: Modeling the World in Data
STARR How to Build Shlaer-Mellor Object Models
THOMSETT Third Wave Project Management
ULRICH AND HAYES The Year 2000 Software Crisis: Challenge of the Century
YOURDON Death March: The Complete Software Developer's Guide to Surviving "Mission Impossible" Projects
YOURDON Decline and Fall of the American Programmer
YOURDON Rise and Resurrection of the American Programmer
YOURDON Managing the Structured Techniques, 4/E
YOURDON Managing the System Life-Cycle, 2/E
YOURDON Modern Structured Analysis
YOURDON Object-Oriented Systems Design
YOURDON Techniques of Program Structure and Design
YOURDON Time Bomb 2000: What the Year 2000 Computer Crisis Means to You, 2/E
YOURDON AND ARGILA Case Studies in Object-Oriented Analysis and Design
YOURDON, WHITEHEAD, THOMANN, OPPEL, AND NEVERMANN Mainstream Objects: An Analysis and Design Approach for Business
YOURDON INC. YOURDON Systems Method: Model-Driven Systems Development

Time Bomb 2000

What the Year 2000 Computer Crisis Means to You!

2nd Edition

Edward Yourdon
and
Jennifer Yourdon

Prentice Hall PTR
Upper Saddle River, New Jersey 07458
http://www.phptr.com

Library of Congress Cataloging-in-Publication Data

Yourdon, Edward.

Time bomb 2000: what the year 2000 computer crisis means to you! / by Edward Yourdon and Jennifer Yourdon. -- 2nd ed.

p. cm.

Includes bibliographical references and index.

ISBN 0-13-020519-2

1. Year 2000 date conversion (Computer systems) I. Yourdon, Jennifer. II. Title.

QA76.76.S64Y68 1998b

363.34'97--dc21 98-55447

CIP

Editorial/production supervision: *Kathleen M. Caren*
Compositor: *Scott Disanno*
Cover design director: *Jerry Votta*
Cover design: *Scott Weiss*
Back cover photo: *Charlie Samuels*
Manufacturing manager: *Alexis R. Heydt*
Acquisitions editor: *Jeffrey M. Pepper*
Marketing manager: *Dan Rush*
Editorial assistant: *Linda Ramagnano*

Prentice-Hall, Inc.
Upper Saddle River, New Jersey 07458

Prentice Hall books are widely used by corporations and government agencies for training, marketing, and resale.

The publisher offers discounts on this book when ordered in bulk quantities. For more information, contact Corporate Sales Department, Phone: 800-382-3419; FAX: 201-236-7141; Email: corpsales@prenhall.ocm

Printed in the United States of America
10 9 8 7 6 5 4 3 2 1

ISBN: 0-13-020519-2

Prentice-Hall International (UK) Limited, *London*
Prentice-Hall of Australia Pty. Limited, *Sydney*
Prentice-Hall Canada Inc., *Toronto*
Prentice-Hall Hispanoamericana, S.A., *Mexico*
Prentice-Hall of India Private Limited, *New Delhi*
Prentice-Hall of Japan, Inc., *Tokyo*
Simon & Schuster Asia Pte. Ltd., *Singapore*
Editora Prentice-Hall do Brasil, Ltda., *Rio de Janeiro*

To my family, in the hope that this book will help us muddle through the Year-2000 problem together. And most of all, to my wife, Toni, whose love and support make it possible for me to face the Year-2000 problem with strength and hope for the future.

Ed Yourdon

To the people I feel so lucky to call my family and friends.

Jennifer Yourdon

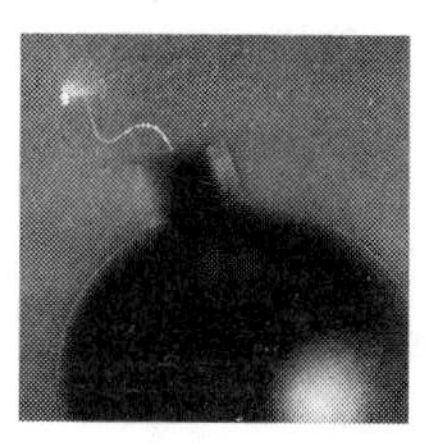

Contents

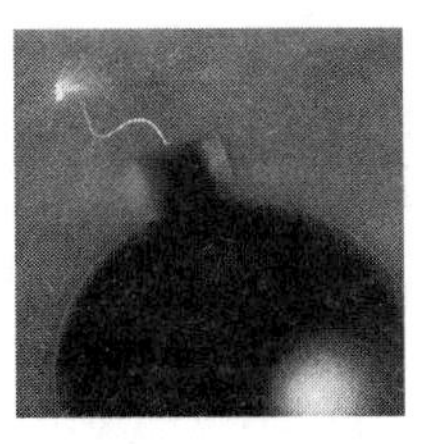

Preface to the Second Edition

I came here today because I wanted to stress the urgency of the [Y2000] challenge to people who are not in this room... With millions of hours needed to rewrite billions of lines of code and hundreds of thousands of interdependent organizations, this is clearly one of the most complex management challenges in history.

President Bill Clinton, Speech at the National Academy of Sciences, *July 14, 1998*

By now, the average citizen has been bombarded by countless newspaper articles and magazine reports concerning the so-called "Millennium Bug." Of course, there are still some who aren't sure what it means, or why it's relevant, or how it might affect their lives; if you're one of these people, you'll find a more traditional introduction and explanation in the preface to the original first edition of the book, which follows immediately after this material.

But for those who already have a general understanding of the Y2000 problem, and especially for those who read the first edition of *Time Bomb 2000*, a brief update is in order. We've maintained the same basic organization of the book in this second edition, but we've updated virtually all of the references, footnotes, links, and examples to reflect the most recent Y2000-related events. We've also added a chapter on the international ramifications of Y2000, as well as a new appendix that provides a bibliography of books, articles, and Internet sites.

Unfortunately, we have *not* been able to provide the one thing that many of our readers and colleagues have asked for: an unequivocal, black-and-white answer to the question "How bad will the Y2000 problem be?" To be perfectly honest, we don't know—and neither does anyone else. It's about time we all admitted that, notwithstanding our predictions and estimates and guesses and wishes, we really don't know what will happen on January 1, 2000. Commentators, experts, gurus, business executives, and government leaders may *think* they know what's going to happen, and they may construct an eloquent and appealing argument to support their prediction. Chances are that if it appeals to your predisposed opinion about Y2000, you'll like it; otherwise, it will make you angry.

Many people who have contacted us are obviously frustrated by this state of affairs. "What good are all these experts," one college student complained to us, "if they can't tell us what's really going to happen?" Another email correspondent said "I don't have time to read all of the hundreds of articles, books, Web sites, and newsgroup forums about Y2000. Can't you just summarize it for me, and give me a simple answer: Is it going to be a disaster, or can I stop worrying?"

But if someone summarizes, abstracts, and filters the hundreds of disparate articles about Y2000 for you, then you're going to get that person's bias or prejudice mixed in with the summary. And if that person has an "agenda" or a particular "spin" that he wants to put on the Y2000 phenomenon, you're going to get that, too. This may sound cynical, but do you really expect the Federal Reserve system and the banking community to give us a pessimistic outlook on their Y2000 progress, even if the situation really *is* pessimistic? For that matter, it's simply not realistic to expect *any* senior business executive to stand up and say, "We've missed every milestone on our Y2000 project, and we underestimated the cost by a factor of five. Our programmers are burned out and demoralized; they've formed a conga line, and they're dancing out the door with their last burst of energy... and the CIO just quit. There is no way on earth we're going to finish even our mission-critical systems in time. We're doomed; you might as well sell your stock now."

But beyond this obvious point, there's something more important: People seem to want a crystal-ball prediction expressed in terms of an "either-or" outcome. They want someone to say, "Either Y2000 is going to be the end of the world (TEOTWAWKI), or it's going to be a non-event. I'm convinced it's going to be a non-event, and here are the 27 reasons why..." But this is an overly simplistic way of looking at the future, and it doesn't help us make effective plans for coping with what, at this point, remains unknown.

Here's a metaphor. Suppose you plan to drive your car from your home to the office, and you want us to predict the outcome. We could say to you, "One of two things will happen: Either you'll either arrive safely, or you'll be killed in a fatal accident. We think you'll arrive safely, and here are the 27 reasons why..." For a 200-word newspaper article, or a 2-minute TV report that's absolutely obsessed with reducing everything down to a black-and-white sound-bite, this might be an acceptable way to summarize the situation—and that's what seems to be happening with much of the media reporting of the Y2000 situation.

But there are obviously a number of other outcomes in our automobile example, and it would be much more helpful if we could say to you, "The most likely outcome is that you'll arrive at your office without any problems. But there's a moderate chance—perhaps 1 in 10—that you'll be involved in a minor fender-bender accident along the way, in which nobody is injured, but a few hundred dollars of damage is inflicted upon your car. There's a smaller chance—perhaps 1 in 100—that you'll be involved in an accident in which you or the other driver will sustain minor injuries. And there's an even smaller chance—perhaps 1 in 1,000—that you'll get involved in a really serious accident, in which your car will be destroyed, and one or more drivers or passengers will be sent to the hospital with major injuries. And, unfortunately, there is a tiny chance—perhaps 1 in 10,000—that you'll be involved in a fatal accident that will kill you."

Armed with that information, you could then ask yourself the obvious questions: *How much risk am I willing to tolerate? What should I do to reduce the risk?* A teenager might ignore all of this information, and drive a convertible with no seat-belts, no airbag, no insurance, and no auto registration. A more conservative person would consider the risk-reward tradeoff of a seat-belt and an air-bag so obvious that he would happily spend the extra time and money to reduce his risk. Some might eschew a convertible, and drive a Volvo instead. And a few might be so fearful of the risks, especially in urban centers like New York or Los Angeles, that they would decide not to drive at all.

The big problem with Y2000, of course, is that we don't know how to quantify the various risk scenarios; we don't have the benefit of 50 years of statistics about automobile accidents and fatalities. That's unfortunate and frustrating, but it's not an excuse to ignore the problem. After all, we deal with uncertainty in our lives all the time, and we do the best we can to make an intelligent decision that's compatible with our level of risk-tolerance. When we get in our car, we don't have precise statistical data about accidents and fatalities for my neighborhood; we have a "gut feeling" that incorporates not only the general information about traffic accidents, but also up-to-the-minute impressions about the weather, the road conditions, and unusual circumstances (e.g., it's New Year's Eve, and there may be a lot of drunk drivers on the road). We go through a similar risk-evaluation process when we consider taking a stroll through a potentially dangerous neighborhood in a strange city, or when we respond to an invitation to go hang-gliding or sky-diving or bungee-jumping.

When it comes to Y2000, most of us will agree that the "non-event" scenario is relatively unlikely; there's a reasonably good chance that we'll experience one or more minor disruptions, at the very least. Beyond that, we each have to do our own risk assessment: How likely is it that the disruptions might last a couple days, or a month, or a year, or longer? And how much are we willing to gamble that our assessment might turn out to be wrong? *All* of these scenarios need to be considered and evaluated, not just the two extremes of non-event and TEOTWAWKI.

One last point about the crystal-ball assessment, and the decisions we make: They deserve to be private. We're tired of newspaper reporters and TV journalists asking us, in the midst of an interview, "How much food have you stockpiled in your house? How much cash have you taken out of the bank? How many Kruggerands have you bought?" The proper answer, we believe, is: *None of your business!* After all, nobody asks us how much money we have in our savings accounts, or what percentage of our annual income is set aside for savings and retirement; nobody asks us how much auto insurance we have, or how much life insurance we're providing for our families. At least in North American society, those questions are considered an invasion of privacy. But why do we bother with a savings account or insurance policies, if not to provide a "nest egg" for a rainy day? How is that any different from the decision that a few folks are making to stockpile some extra food in their pantry to cope with possible Y2000 disruptions? While there might be emotional criticism about "hoarding" of food and supplies in December 1999 if everyone decides to rush to the grocery store at the same time, stockpiling ought to be a personal and private decision in late 1998 and early 1999—just like the decision to divert some of our disposable income to savings, rather than consumption.

The concerns about Y2000 that we expressed when we wrote the first edition of our book in 1997 have been validated and supported by a growing number of conservative, reputable politicians, industry officials, and corporate executives. When the President of the United States and the Prime Minister of England describe Y2000 as a serious problem, as they both did during 1998 speeches, it suggests that the subject should not be casually dismissed as an alarmist exaggeration. It requires only a modest effort to search the Internet to find somber warnings and/or dire predictions about Y2000 from the Chairman of the Federal Reserve System (Alan Greenspan), a former Secretary of Defense (Caspar Weinberger), and numerous Congressmen and Senators. Of course, none of the statements made by these officials constitutes proof that our assessment of Y2000 is completely correct—but it does suggest that it's a legitimate topic of discussion and concern, rather than something reserved for the lunatic fringe.

Though we can't forecast the outcome of the Y2000 problem with absolute accuracy, we certainly can argue that the past year has been plagued with procrastination. Procrastination seems to be most severe in the small businesses, and in the small towns. Optimists may sincerely believe that the *Fortune 500* companies will finish their Y2000 projects on time, and that the Federal government will manage to at least finish the mission-critical systems in the most critical agencies. But recent surveys indicate that approximately 75 percent of small businesses *around the world* have not yet begun working on Y2000; here in the U.S., surveys indicate that approximately 40 percent of the small companies don't plan to spend any time or money on Y2000 until the year 2000 itself, at which point they'll see what's broken. Similarly, recent surveys have indicated that approximately 55 percent of the mayors of local towns and communities believe that Y2000 won't impact them; therefore, they're doing nothing about it.

A year of procrastination and delay may be tolerable for long-term problems like global warming or the destruction of rain forests, but it's likely to be fatal for Y2000. Even 1997 was too late for most companies to start their Y2000 project with much hope for success; a company starting in 1998 has no choice but to use a triage strategy in order to keep at least its mission-critical systems running. Meanwhile, Wall Street remains, for the most part, sound asleep, despite the risks associated with Y2000 disruptions within corporate America, not to mention the risks associated with disruptions within the financial institutions themselves.

One other dramatic change has taken place during the past year, and it bodes ill for Y2000: The financial crisis engulfing Russia, Korea, Indonesia, and several other parts of the world. Russia, known to some as Bangladesh With Missiles, has an official Y2000 budget of *zero*. The country has no money for Y2000; it has no money for anything these days. Reports in late October 1998 indicated that food supplies had fallen to approximately a two-three week level, and that fuel stockpiles were also falling; chances are that Russian bureaucrats, business leaders, and citizens are far more concerned about the lack of food and fuel, as winter approaches, than they are about fixing a pesky computer bug whose consequences won't be felt for another several months (by which time they may be dead anyway). Similar problems confront the government and businesses throughout several Asian countries; it doesn't give us much hope that Y2000 projects will be given a high priority throughout the region.

What about the optimistic reports from U.S. agencies like the IRS and FAA? What about the reports from the banking community that the vast majority of its members are making good progress, and expect to be finished on time? In short, what about the *good* news? To paraphrase former President Ronald Reagan when asked if he trusted the Russians to live up to their promises after the nuclear disarmament treaty was signed, "Trust, but verify." With few, if any, exceptions, all of the optimistic news about Y2000 has been *self-reported* status information; even if the people who tell us the good news are honest, sincere, and competent (an assumption we all have to evaluate for ourselves), they may still be wrong. Ask anyone who has worked on large, complex software projects: Things often seem great until the system testing and integration begins. Even if dozens of serious bugs are discovered during testing, the project team and the project manager will exude confidence that the deadline will be met—right up until the day before the deadline, they'll earnestly tell you that the system-killer bug they just found is absolutely, positively, the *last* bug. Serious testing—end-to-end testing, and integration testing involving multiple firms, and multiple combinations of "supply chain" interfaces—has not yet begun in any of the key industry sectors. All we know for sure is that 1999 will be The Year of Testing Dangerously.

We expect that there will be several "trigger events" during 1999 when we'll get a preview of just how good or bad the Y2000 situation will be; the most significant events are likely to occur on April 1, July 1, and October 1, 1999 for the simple reason that large numbers of government agencies and private-sector organizations will begin their 1999-2000 fiscal year on those dates. We may also get an advance indicator of the severity of Y2000 on April 9, 1999 (the 99th day of the 99th year); and on August 22, 1999 (the date that the GPS satellite system "rolls over" to zero); and on September 9, 1999 (a date that some computer systems will interpret as 9/9/99, which may signify "end of process" or "end of file"). But we won't really know for sure what will happen until we reach midnight on December 31, 1999.

In the meantime, we all have to make our own assessment of the situation, and act accordingly. Optimists with great faith in the ability of organizations around the world to fix the problem may decide to do nothing at all; those who are somewhat more pessimistic will implement varying degrees of contingency plans—ranging from modest plans for putting a few extra dollars of cash in their wallet to more ambitious plans to stockpile food, water, and other essentials. We can't tell you just how optimistic or pessimistic you should be; what we can do is provide you with as much information as possible, so that you'll be able to make an informed judgment on your own.

If you have questions or comments about the Y2000 situation as you go through your planning process, please feel free to send us an email message at ed@yourdon.com or jennifer@yourdon.com. We wish you the best of luck in your plans and preparations for Y2000, whatever they may be.

Edward Yourdon
Jennifer Yourdon
New Mexico and New York, December, 1998

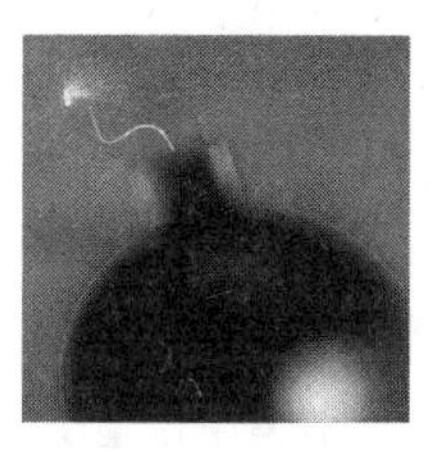

Preface

The day the world ends, no one will be there, just as no one was there when it began. This is a scandal. Such a scandal for the human race that it is indeed capable collectively, out of spite, of hastening the end of the world by all means just so it can enjoy the show.

Jean Baudrillard, Cool Memories, Chapter 5 *(1987)*

Saturday morning, 11:00 AM

Your head throbs as you roll out of bed. It was quite a celebration last night—the celebration of a lifetime—and you've slept through your alarm clock. But now it's Saturday morning, and you always call your dear old mom in North Carolina every Saturday morning. So you shuffle past the kitchen, pause briefly to snarl at the coffee machine that failed to brew your morning coffee as usual, and slump into the living room sofa to conduct the weekly hi-Mom-howya-doin' ritual. You pick up the phone, and after a moment, snarl again—there is no dial tone.

Shuffling back to the bedroom, it becomes obvious why you didn't hear the alarm clock—there's no electricity. And, when you step into the shower to wash away the headache, there is no hot water. You're in a worse mood when you step out again. Snarls have given way to soft curses, but you realize that you need to sound pleasant and cheerful when you talk to Mom, so you force a smile onto your face as you head for the living room again. You pick up the phone again, and after another moment of silence, all attempts at civility vanish—still no dial tone. You hold the phone in front of your face and curse in loud, angry terms at the telephone company.

There's still no dial tone at 1 PM, and the coffee maker still won't work. To make matters worse, the refrigerator has stopped too, and the freezer is now leaking water onto the floor. You've gotten dressed in the interim, and even though you've frequently criticized the coffee at the corner deli, you now decide that it's better than no coffee at all. As you reach the front door of the apartment building, you remember that you ran out of cash during the celebrations last night, so you stop at the bank on the corner to get a few dollars out of the ATM machine—but the machine gobbles up your bank card and refuses to give you any cash at all. When you reach the deli on the corner, you find it even more curious that *their* phone is also out of service, and that they're operating without electricity. And when you return to your apartment, you still find silence rather than a dial tone when you pick up the phone.

More silence on Sunday, and again on Monday. It's now been three days since you've had working telephone service, and it's no longer funny. Not only have you been unable to reach Mom in North Carolina, but you haven't been able to communicate with any of your friends and business associates. Indeed, the whole point of staying home on Monday (January 3) was that you were expecting a *very* important call from a prospective employer who had been trying to lure you away from your current job with a possibility of a 50 percent salary increase—but only if the negotiations could be finalized by January 3.

We won't continue the vignette any further—you get the point. If your phone was out of service for three days, it would be somewhat annoying, and there could possibly be some important consequences. But suppose that it wasn't just your phone that was inoperable, but every phone in your building... in your neighborhood... in your city... in your state... in the entire country? Suppose that nobody could call anybody else for three days? Would civilization come to a screeching halt? Not likely—but there would be a lot of grumpy people, and there would inevitably be some financial consequences.

Let's make this vignette more serious: suppose the phone outage persisted not just for three days, but for a full month. No phone calls for the entire month of January; nobody has a dial tone. Don't just nod your head when you read this sentence: *think about it*. Suppose you couldn't call anyone, and no one could call you because nobody in your city had a working phone, and as far as you could tell, nobody in North America, Europe, or anywhere else where phones were taken for granted had viable telephone service. (It's worth noting, by the way, that approximately 50% of the human race, particularly in large sections of China and Africa, has *never* made a phone call, so not everyone would be affected!)

Obviously, a month without telephone service would be pretty serious—but what if it was a full year? Could your employer survive for a full year, let alone a month, without phone service? Could your city? Could the national government of whatever country you live in? And if you think a year is bad, what about a decade? A century ago, *all* of what was then considered "modern society" functioned quite well without telephones—but would that be possible today?

Lest you think that we're concocting stories to pick on the phone company, remember the other events in the vignette above: your bank's ATM machine doesn't work and the lights are out. And, let's expand our vignette a bit: What about your car? Suppose you turned the key in the ignition and nothing happened? Or, to put things into the proper perspective: Suppose you were driving home a little early from the New Year's Eve festivities, and just at the stroke of midnight, all the red lights and alarm signals on the dashboard begun to flash and beep at you? Now what?

Welcome to the Year-2000 problem. No, this is not a joke, and it's probably not an exaggeration. It won't happen to you on *this* New Year's Eve... but the next New Year's Eve that falls on a Friday will be December 31, 1999. And when the clock strikes midnight on that very special Friday night, every computer system in the world will encounter a "rollover" phenomenon that may or may not be fatal. In the best of cases, your phone will still work on Saturday morning, January 1, 2000 (indeed, the major telephone companies assure us this will be the case), and so will your car, the electric utility company, and all of the other machines and devices that you've come to depend on, often without even realizing that there's a computer inside.

But in the worst of all cases, the rollover phenomenon that occurs when 1999 changes to 2000 could cause consequences that make the vignettes above seem quite tame by comparison. The computer industry is planning to spend between $300-600 *billion* over the next two to three years in an attempt to avoid this problem, and some experts[1] are already warning that this estimate is too low. But as we write this book in late 1997, it's becoming increasingly clear that the vast complex of computer systems will *not* be completely modified and upgraded to deal with what has come to be known as the as "Year-2000" or "Y2K" software problem.

Because of the magnitude of the Year-2000 problem, hundreds of technical articles have already been published in computer journals, and dozens of computer conferences have been held to offer advice to computer professionals and managers. Numerous articles have appeared in *Fortune*, *Forbes,* the *Wall Street Journal*, the *Economist*, and other business publications to warn senior managers of the impact of the problem. Articles have even appeared on the front pages of the *New York Times*, the *Boston Globe,* and *Newsweek*. And, several technically-oriented Year-2000[2] books have been published—with more on the way.

But this is not a book aimed at computer professionals, even though that's the area in which one of the authors makes his living. This book is aimed at computer users, including our family, our neighbors, our friends, and all the millions of people who *use* computers without really understanding or caring about how they work. The technical books and articles warn the computer professionals: "The Year-2000 problem could be really serious if we don't do something about it. We need to get started right now in order to avoid a major disaster!" But this book asks the question: *What if the computer industry doesn't manage to fix the Year-2000 problem successfully?* How serious a problem could it be, and what should your fallback plan be? What would be the economic consequences of a telephone outage for a day, or a month, or a year, or a decade? The telephone, of course, is only one form of communication; what if we didn't have FedEx, the Post Office, or the Internet available? What if the Year-2000 problem knocks out electricity for three days, or the water supply for a month, or access to your bank account for a year, or regular Social Security checks for a decade? Then there's the field of transportation: What are the *personal* consequences of failures with cars, buses, trains, and airplanes? What about credit cards and the stock market? What about newspapers, radio, and television? Hospitals, access to medicine, access to doctors? Food supplies? Welfare? The Internal Revenue Service? The Defense Department? Schools and universities? Oh yes, one last question: What about your job?

If you've never heard of the Year-2000 problem before, the notion that every aspect of our social infrastructure could shut down for even a single day seems preposterous. And when it's presented in such simplistic terms, it *is* preposterous; Year-2000 problems won't happen in the same way, at the same time, in all of these areas. It's highly likely, for example, that when you pick up the phone on January 1, 2000, you *will* get a dial tone—because it's one of the most fundamental, obvious, high-priority aspects of telephone service that AT&T, MCI, Sprint, and the regional Bell operating companies are working on. However, we're far less confident about all of the tiny telephone companies that have sprung up since the telecommunications industry decentralized; indeed, we're not even sure that the larger phone companies will succeed in converting the other aspects of their operational systems. What happens, for example, if you get a phone bill on January 31, 2000 for $325,914,166.14? What happens if every telephone customer in your city gets an equally preposterous bill? What happens when every customer tries to call the phone company's Customer Service department, on the same day, to complain about his or her bill? What happens when the phone company's computer systems decide to cancel everyone's service because of non-payment of his or her bill?

Why do we think something like this could happen? Not because we think the phone company is incompetent, but because the effort to fix the software is a massive job with a very immovable deadline. Most of the large telephone companies have a "portfolio" of computer programs and systems with a total of some 300-400 *million* program instructions that need to be examined for possible corrections for proper operation after January 1, 2000. Banks are dealing with equally large numbers, and as we'll see later in the book, the federal government is dealing with an even larger software portfolio. Unfortunately, the computer industry has been notorious for being substantially behind schedule and over budget, even on projects that are a hundred times smaller than the Year-2000 project. Not only that, programmers have a notorious record for innocently injecting "bugs" into the complex software systems they create. If the statistics about the error-prone nature of "normal" software development is any indication, Year-2000 project teams will still be fixing their mistakes in 2005.

For those who are curious about the details, we explain in Appendix A how this problem came about and what kind of corrections are necessary for Year-2000 projects. In Appendix B, we discuss the "domino effect" problem that can occur if a relatively simple error in, say, the computer systems of banks "ripple" into the credit card systems, and then into the Wall Street stock market systems, etc. This is a variation on the "chaos theory" argument that says a butterfly flapping its wings in Tokyo could cause a tornado in Wichita, Kansas.

If you're not interested in the technical computer details, or if you've already heard the basic explanations of the Year-2000 software problem, feel free to skip the appendices. The "meat" of this book is a discussion of the consequences of Year-2000 failures in our personal lives, and the contingency plans we should be making. As we'll discuss in Chapter 1, one aspect of this contingency planning is to assign reasonable levels of probability to different levels of "severity" of Year-2000 problems. Do you think the most likely scenario is a rash of Year-2000 problems that will last for two or three days? Or, do you think the most likely scenario is a massive decade-long collapse reminiscent of the Great Depression of the 1930s? We personally believe that a majority of the Year-2000 problems will be of the minor variety, though there could well be some "minor" problems that render such critical systems as banking, telecommunications, and utilities inoperable for a few days. We also believe that a significant minority of the Year-2000 problems—perhaps as great as 25-35%—will be of the "moderate" variety, causing failures that will take a month to solve; invoicing and billing systems within business organizations are a prime example of this category.

Unfortunately, we also think that a small percentage—perhaps in the range of 5-10%—of the Year-2000 problems could be of the "serious" variety, i.e., requiring a year to repair. In many cases, this will occur because the "cleanup" process can be time-consuming and tedious. A hurricane usually lasts for only a day, but the hurricane *recovery* can easily take a year if the damage is extensive; we believe the same situation will occur with a small percentage of the Year-2000 software bugs.

Here's an example: Your local bank runs afoul of the Year-2000 problem and begins generating wildly incorrect banking statements. Panicked customers begin withdrawing their cash, and after a few days of attempting to cope with the crisis, the bank has to shut down operations. Assuming that you have a standard bank account (as opposed to uninsured certificates of deposits), and assuming your balance is less than $100,000, your account is insured by the Federal Deposit Insurance Company (FDIC). Assuming that several banks have the same problem, and that all of their banking records are corrupted by Year-2000 bugs, how long do you think it will be before the FDIC gives you your money? Many of us would be grateful indeed if it only took a year—but attempting to carry out our day-to-day business without the funds in that frozen account could be a problem indeed.

Finally, we think that a very small percentage of Year-2000 problems could be sufficiently devastating that it could take a decade to recover. A decade, by the way, is approximately the length of the Great Depression; we won't try to draw any parallels between the events of 1929 and 1999 at this point, but we do want to emphasize that not all problems can be fixed or forgotten overnight. Our primary concerns in this area are the massive government agencies and systems that are in shaky condition already. Two that come to mind are the Internal Revenue Service (IRS) and Social Security Agency (SSA), though several other federal agencies were experiencing Year-2000 difficulties as this book went to press in late 1997. We'll discuss in Chapter 10 why we think it's possible that the political fall-out of the Year-2000 problem could lead to both the IRS and SSA being abolished in their present form, and being replaced by something fundamentally different. For those who have based their life's plans on the assumption that income and savings would be taxed in a certain way, or that retirement funds would be available at a certain age, it could well take a decade to recover from such a shock.

With this kind of framework—minor, moderate, serious, and devastating failures—we'll begin examining each of the major aspects of society mentioned up to this point: communications, utilities, transportation, banking and finance, news broadcasting, travel, medicine, social services, education, government, and employment. Chances are that you'll ignore certain categories. Parents of school-age children, for example, might be thrilled at the prospect of television disappearing from their lives for a year. But, there are likely to be a few categories that represent life-and-death risks. If you're a diabetes patient, the notion that insulin might be unavailable for a month is not a joking matter.

Of course, a far more pleasant Year-2000 scenario would be to assume that nothing will go wrong at all. In the best of all worlds, $300-600 billion will be spent by the world's government agencies and private corporations, the computer problems will be quietly taken care of, and we'll all enjoy New Year's Eve in 1999 with nary a hiccup. Another scenario you're likely to hear is: "Well, it may be a problem for a few of the big companies with those old-fashioned mainframe computers, but it won't be a problem for small companies with their modern PCs; and in any case, most individuals don't depend very much on computers for their day-to-day lives." Perhaps this will turn out to be true, in which case we'll be justifiably criticized for needless scare-mongering. But even though both authors are optimists in our day-to-day lives, our investigation of the Year-2000 situation leads us to believe that it's *very* unlikely that we'll escape serious problems so easily.

Thus, one of our tasks in the chapters ahead is to explain some of the reasons why the Year-2000 rollover could cause significant problems in the various aspects of society that affect all of us. If nothing else, the issues raised in this book may lead you to ask the appropriate officials—i.e., the spokespeople and managers of the various organizations that provide critical services—whether they can confidently promise that their organizations *will* be Year-2000-compliant. When Senator Alphonse D'Amato asked this question of the Federal Reserve Bank, in his capacity as head of the Senate Banking and Finance Committee, the answer he got was, "No comment." A common variation, which we received from several large organizations while researching this book, was,

"We don't know what you're talking about, but whatever it is, don't worry about it." What will you do if you get that answer from *your* bank… or *your* phone company… or *your* automobile manufacturer... or *your* local doctor and hospital?

What most people will do, in the final analysis, is *nothing*. After all, the prospect of a moderate, serious, or devastating collapse of the nation's socio-economic system is too awful for many people to accept. And the actions that would be required to protect oneself from such a disaster would require too much of a sacrifice for most people to accept in advance. This is rather puzzling, because our society has long accepted the notion of paying for insurance associated with crises it hopes will never occur. We pay hundreds of dollars per year for automobile insurance, but nobody wants an auto accident. We pay for medical insurance, and then hope that we won't have to use it for operations or serious illness. And even though each of us must accept the inevitability of our eventual death, we certainly don't expect it to happen next month or next year—yet most of us realize that it's important to plan for it by purchasing life insurance. The Year-2000 planning that we discuss in this book is, in a sense, just another form of insurance; unfortunately, we aren't very optimistic that most people will see it that way.

As we wrote this book during the summer and fall of 1997, we posted draft chapters on our Internet Web site. As a result, we received feedback and comments via email from literally hundreds of people around the world. In addition to pointing out factual errors and making numerous suggestions for improvements, we found a wide range of opinions about the ultimate impact of the Year-2000 problem. Some of our readers and reviewers pleaded with us to take a stand: "If you really think it's going to cause another Great Depression, put yourself on the line and say so." And a few readers criticized us for alarmist exaggerations, implying that perhaps we were doing it in an attempt to generate more sales of the book. Especially when communicating with non-computer-savvy readers, we consider scare-mongering to be the moral equivalent of shouting "Fire!" in a crowded theater—and we did our best to avoid it. But if an occupant of such a theater smells smoke, there's a moral obligation to say so. And if the theater is constructed of wood and other flammable materials, we also think it's appropriate to shout, "There are no smoke detectors or fire sprinklers in this building!" and then let people draw their own conclusions.

We don't *know* what's going to happen when the clock strikes midnight on December 31, 1999; nobody else does either. Some have suggested to us that by making the decision to write a book, we have created an obligation for ourselves to find out, so that we could state the future with certainty. Instead, we've tried to describe plausible scenarios to allow you to evaluate the likelihood of their occurrence, and then we offer some suggestions for responding to those scenarios. We don't have the "answer" to the Year-2000 problem, and given the complexity of the problem, we think it's pretentious for anyone to suggest that he or she does. Instead of presenting answers, we've focused on raising what we think are responsible questions that you should be asking yourselves.

Ultimately, what we think, and what other people think or do, is not your problem. What *you* do is the real issue—in the final analysis, you're responsible for your own actions and for the health and happiness of your family and loved ones. The issues we're writing about in this book are of direct concern to our family, and it forms the basis for our own plans for the Year-2000. We can only hope that we've made a modest contribution to society by articulating the issues for your consideration.

Edward Yourdon
Jennifer Yourdon
New York City, 1997

Endnotes

1. Paul A. Strassmann, "Numbers Add Up to a Bigger Year 2000 Disaster," *Computerworld*, June 13, 1997.
2. See, for example, William M. Ulrich and Ian S. Hayes, *The Year 2000 Software Crisis: Challenge of the Century* (Prentice Hall, 1997).

Year-2000 Planning Overview

Every business should assess its exposure, ask vendors and suppliers to be ready as well, and develop contingency plans, as we are, in case critical systems or systems of vendors fail as we move into the year 2000.

President Bill Clinton, Speech at the National Academy of Sciences, *July 14, 1998.*

Planning ahead is a measure of class. The rich and even the middle class plan for future generations, but the poor can plan ahead only a few weeks or days.

Gloria Steinem, "The Time Factor," Outrageous Acts and Everyday Rebellions, *1983.*

Introduction

"So what?"

That's the question you should be ready to ask by now. If you've read the brief vignettes in the preface, you should have some awareness that the Y2000 phenomenon *might* be a problem for you. Indeed, you may have been aware of the problem already, for it's been widely discussed in magazines and newspapers for the past couple of years.

When informed of the Y2000 problem, most people—including, ironically, many computer professionals—shrug their shoulders and say, "Well, I guess it *could* be a problem. I sure hope they're working on it..." *They* are the computer programmers who are methodically scanning through hundreds of millions of program instructions, replacing two-digit representations of the year with four-digit years in computer systems. We've convinced many of our friends and colleagues that there aren't enough programmers available, and that this massive task probably won't be finished in time—there's simply too much to do, it's an error-prone process, and most companies have gotten started far too late. Our friends shrug their shoulders again, and refer to a different category of "they": politicians, corporate managers, disaster relief agencies, and other civic leaders, who will be expected to organize and plan an appropriate response to whatever goes wrong.

If you're willing to put your fate in the hands of "they," you can skip the remainder of this book. But keep in mind that the Y2000 problem is unlike other disasters, such as normal hurricanes and blizzards, which can be anticipated days or weeks in advance, so that citizens can be warned to take shelter, board up their windows, or evacuate. With Y2000, we can anticipate *when* the problem will begin occurring, but we don't know whether it will be the equivalent of a Force-5 hurricane or a mild spring breeze. It's never happened before, and there are no well-practiced contingency plans to draw upon.

Even with the "familiar" forms of disaster, there are agonizing delays before recovery and relief operations spring into action. As the residents of Florida can testify from repeated experience, it often takes two to three days for state and federal relief agencies to respond to a massive hurricane. And as the residents of Grand Forks, North Dakota can testify with some bitterness after the disastrous spring flood of 1997, it can take well over a month for Congress to stop bickering about allocating relief funds and actually take action. Situations like these involve *one* hurricane or *one* flood; what happens if something of this magnitude hits every part of the country (including the government itself!) at the same time?[1]

It's comforting to think that the government will take care of things when there's a problem, and that organizations like the Red Cross will help with real emergencies. Government's ability to deal with even familiar disasters is certainly less than perfect, though perhaps it's the best that can be expected. But when it comes to Y2000, we're far less impressed: As we'll see in Chapter 10, the city, state and federal government agencies are generally much farther behind in converting their own computer systems than private industry. Directly or indirectly, the actions, operations, and policies of dozens of government agencies at the city, county, state, and federal levels affect every citizen of this country. If a substantial number of these agencies fail or go into a tailspin because of Y2000 bugs, then government becomes part of the problem, not part of the solution.

Obviously, this is not a black-and-white issue; we're not trying to suggest that government is evil or malicious, nor that it's hopelessly and utterly incompetent. Assuming that our leaders are concerned about the welfare of the country, and assuming that they'll respond to serious disasters, then it's reasonable to expect that government will eventually help organize and direct the appropriate recovery process from Y2000 failures. But, there's ample evidence from governmental responses to crises over the past century to suggest that it could be sluggish, disorganized, misguided, and downright harmful to some individual members of society.[2]

Back to the question at the beginning of this chapter: *So what?* We have some detailed answers to that question in the next several chapters, for the "so what?" question depends on whether you're concerned about the loss of basic utilities (electricity, water), or food supplies, communication (phone, fax, and mail), or your job. Before we plunge into the details, though, we want to set a framework for developing your own "fallback" plan. This involves the notion of "risk management," and it also requires you to think about the *duration* of a Y2000 problem.

Risk Management

Though the Y2000 problem itself is unique, the notion of planning and preparing for future problems is not. Engineers, planners, and (ironically) managers of computer projects routinely practice *risk management* prior to, and throughout the conduct of, any important and/or expensive project in which something might conceivably go wrong.

We don't have room in this book to provide you with a comprehensive treatment of the subject of risk management; if the idea appeals to you, there are numerous textbooks available.[3] But the basic concepts are straightforward, and we've summarized them below:

- *Identification of risks:* It's hard to anticipate or plan for a risk if you don't have any idea of what it might be. It might not have occurred to you before you glanced at the table of contents of this book that your bank account or your job were at risk because of Y2000; but once you've identified the risk, you can begin making plans to deal with it. Risk identification is one of the primary objectives of this book. We may not have covered everything that could possibly go wrong, but we'll discuss the major Y2000 risk areas in the next several chapters, and this should be enough to help you begin thinking about any others that might be relevant.

- *Evaluation and assessment of risk likelihood and risk impact:* You probably don't spend much time worrying about the risk of being struck by a bolt of lightning, because the odds are infinitesimally small; on the other hand, if such an event were to occur, the consequences would probably be fatal. Automobile accidents can also be fatal, and the odds of such an incident are considerably higher; that's why you wear seatbelts and buy automobile insurance. You manage your day-to-day affairs in this fashion, developing both offensive and defensive plans based on your assessment of the likelihood of unpleasant events (illness, unemployment, violent crime, and so forth) and the impact of those events. You need to do the same thing for Y2000 risks: how likely is it, for example, that the stock market will shut down—and what are the consequences if it does? We can make some general observations about this, based on our knowledge of both the computer situation and the overall economic impact of various Y2000-related failures; however, this is something you'll need to assess very carefully on your own. Some people, for example, have no stock market investments and would not be impacted if Wall Street ground to a halt; other people have invested their life savings and their retirement portfolio in stocks and bonds, and would be devastated if the market crashed.

- *Regular monitoring of risks:* In most situations, risk is not static: it ebbs and flows, and it increases and decreases over a period of days, weeks, months, and years. The Y2000 problem is *not* going to be a one-shot affair that occurs precisely at the stroke of midnight on December 31, 1999; ramifications of the problem will begin occurring in 1999, and will last well into the next decade. Depending on the efforts of the computer programmers, the risk of Y2000 problems within specific companies will hopefully decrease over during the remaining months of the decade; but depending on the tendency of corporate management to procrastinate and delay a serious commitment of resources to Y2000 projects, the risk of failure will increase sharply between now and January 1, 2000.[4] More important, the "ripple effect" problem discussed in Appendix B will cause Y2000 problems to ebb and flow throughout the entire socioeconomic system of not only the United States, but all the other countries around the world as well. This is something you'll need to monitor both before and after January 1, 2000, and it's not something we can do for you in this book. If, for example, your bank provides you with convincing evidence in 1999 that all of its computer systems are Y2000-compliant, then perhaps you don't need to withdraw all your funds. But if you learn in Marc, 2000 that your bank has made massive loans to a large corporation that has just defaulted on its repayments because of its own Y2000 problems, then perhaps you should hustle down to the bank and transfer your money before the bank collapses.

- *Proactive planning to eliminate risks in advance:* In most cases, the best way to deal with a risk is to "head it off at the pass" and eliminate it before it even occurs. Depending on your situation, as well as on your degree of involvement and dependency on computer systems, this may or may not be practical. If you believe, for example, that the Y2000 problem will create a severe disruption of social services within your metropolitan area, perhaps you should move to a smaller community now, while it's still relatively easy. If you believe that your company or industry will be severely affected, then you have a couple years to begin finding a "fallback" job or a new career.[5]

- *Reactive planning to minimize the impact of risks that materialize:* Proactive planning is sometimes expensive, and it may involve some unpleasant sacrifices: Not everyone is willing to change jobs or move out of the city, and not everyone can install a solar-panel energy system for their home. Indeed, it may be utterly impractical in some situations; it's hard to imagine spending the next few years trying to learn to live without the telephone, just because we think the Y2000 problem might cause a disruption. Similarly, many people are unable or unwilling to take the proactive step of moving out of geographic regions with a frequent occurrence of hurricanes; but they *do* have a reactive plan that essentially says, "If a big storm hits, get into the basement as quickly as possible, because that's the best way to minimize the likelihood of being seriously injured. And get some candles in case we have a power failure for a couple days."

There are two additional items to keep in mind: First, because of the unique, unfamiliar nature of the Y2000 problem, none of us will be able to fully anticipate all of the risks. To some extent, this is the same situation we face in other aspects of our life: We don't really know whether, at some point, we're going to be faced with a serious illness, or long-term unemployment, or a massive fire that burns our home to the ground. That's why most people try to set aside a "nest egg" or "rainy day fund"; that's why most of us have insurance policies. The more of a buffer and reserve that we have, the more we're able to absorb the impact of an unexpected problem. And the more "liquid" we are financially, without the encumbrance of heavy debt, the more flexible we can be if unexpected problems occur.

Ironically, the institutions that we've depended on to help us in this area may be among those at risk. We tend to keep our nest egg account in a bank or brokerage company; we tend to establish insurance policies with trusted, stable insurance companies. As we've already implied in this book, institutions like these are heavily dependent on computer systems that will fail on January 1, 2000 unless they're fixed. So, one of the aspects of risk management that you'll need to worry about is whether your bank, insurance agent, and/or stock broker are part of the problem or part of the solution.

But the larger problem is that many American families have no nest egg at all. This is particularly true of young adults, especially those with new families and savings that consist of equity in their house. As numerous books and magazine articles have informed us over the past few decades, ours is a consumption-oriented society with a very low savings rate. To put it more bluntly, many families live from paycheck to paycheck, with a substantial amount of credit-card debt. They may have a positive net worth, from an accounting perspective, but only because of the contribution of the equity in their home. A home is a highly illiquid asset, unless one considers home-equity loans that are readily available today. But in a Y2000 crisis, such loans may be much more difficult to obtain. Not only that, the amount of equity in a home is largely a function of the market value of the home; if that drops substantially because of a Y2000-induced recession, many American families would find that they have a negative net worth.

The lack of a liquid, fungible nest egg is the bad news. The good news is that some people will be able to profit from the Y2000 crisis because they'll be better prepared and better able to take advantage of risks that others are trying to avoid. By analogy: Not everyone went bankrupt during the Great Depression, and a few people actually prospered. We offer no specific stock market advice in this book, but we note that a Y2000-induced stock market crash is certainly a possibility. If you believed that was likely, and if you liquidated your stock-market investments during the record-high levels of early 1998, you might be in a very good position to pick up bargain-priced stocks in the early years of the next decade.

We won't pursue this notion of aggressive, opportunistic planning for profits or advantages that might be achieved as a result of the Y2000 problem. It's easy enough to talk about it now, but if a serious Y2000 crisis does occur, such behavior will generally be described as profiteering, hoarding, or scalping. In any case, we think that most people will have enough trouble surviving the Y2000 problem without even thinking about how to profit from it.

Severity of the Problem (Day, Month, Year, Decade)

Assessing the impact of a Y2000 risk involves (among other things) an assessment of the pervasiveness of the risk, and also the duration of the risk. By pervasiveness, we mean this: Is the problem localized within your neighborhood or town, or is everyone facing the same problem throughout the country? If your town is serviced by a small, independent phone company that collapses because of a Y2000 problem, it will be very inconvenient for you and your neighbors. But if the major metropolitan areas survive with uninterrupted phone service because of the successful Y2000 conversion efforts of AT&T, MCI, and Sprint, then your town's plight will get nothing more than a few minutes' sympathetic coverage on the evening news. On the other hand, if the IRS collapses and a new tax collection scheme is imposed, it will affect everyone. The same is likely to be true if we experience massive Y2000 failure in several of the other federal government agencies such as the Federal Aviation Agency (FAA), or Medicare.

Regarding duration, we have found it useful to identify four distinct time periods: two to three days, a month, a year, and a decade. Each of the time periods we've chosen is approximately ten times longer than the one before; because of that, each time-duration is likely to require a *qualitatively* different risk-management approach. Also, each "level" of time duration has a different degree of likelihood: You might decide, for example, that your local phone company is so well-organized that if something does go wrong, they'll surely have it fixed within two to three days. But your personal risk-management assessment might lead you to conclude that your bank is so screwed up, even under normal circumstances, that if it encounters a Y2000 problem, it will be at least a month before things are back to normal.

To see the impact of these different durations of time, consider a non-computer metaphor: Think back to when you were a kid, and your friends and siblings had a tendency to "dunk" one another underwater in the neighborhood swimming pool. If you knew that you were about to be dunked for two to three minutes, what would you do? Assuming that you couldn't avoid the experience by swimming away quickly, the answer is simple: Hold your breath. The best you can hope for is that you have a moment to prepare, so that you can take a deep breath before your head goes under water.

But, what would happen if you knew that you were going to be held underwater for two to three hours by the neighborhood bully? Unless you had superhuman powers, there is no way that you could hold your breath for three hours; the three-minute risk-management strategy simply cannot be "extended" to deal with this new situation. Admittedly, the possibility of being subjected to this kind of treatment is pretty small, but if you *did* have to plan for it, the answer might be to get some scuba gear and make sure the compressed-air tanks are full. If you had more time to prepare, it might even be worth taking some scuba-diving lessons. You might also take a proactive risk-avoidance strategy: Leaving the swimming pool when the bully jumps in, or advising your parents of the imminent danger you face.

What if the underwater dunking lasted for two to three days? Obviously, a completely different riskmanagement strategy would be required: Any commercially available scuba gear is going to run out of air in a few hours. In addition, you've got to figure out how to sleep and how to get the required food and liquid nutrition to keep you going for three days.

What if the situation persisted for a year, or a decade? We won't try to imagine possible solutions, but you see the point. And while you might argue that the example is ridiculously unlikely beyond the three-minute dunking, we can assure you that it's not so unlikely with regard to the Y2000 problem. You shouldn't have too much trouble imagining a scenario in which the effects of a Y2000-related problem last for a few days or a month; and, your risk-management strategy should take that into account.

Is a one-year timeframe unrealistic? If the Y2000 problem does lead to a nationwide (or worldwide) recession, then unemployment will go up sharply. And if the Y2000 problem causes your employer to go bankrupt, then you may not be able to find a replacement job in two to three days or a month. Those who were laid off during the recession of the early 1990s will tell you that it can easily take 6-12 months, or more, to find a job.

Similarly, if the FAA is unsucessful at repairing, upgrading, and testing all of its systems by December 31, 1999—and if the problem is further compounded by Y2000 disruptions in the airports, airplanes, and airline companies—it's likely to be more than a few days, or even a month, before things are back to normal. A total shutdown of the world's air-traffic system might only last for a few days, but ongoing difficulties in all of these computer systems could force a 50 percent reduction in commercial air service for 6-12 months, or a quarantine of those regions and airports deemed unsafe.

As for the prospect of a decade-long Y2000 impact—as we noted in the Preface, it's not beyond the realm of possibility that major federal agencies like the IRS or SSA could go belly-up because of the political repercussions of a massive Y2000 failure. Not only would this have long-term repercussions for taxpayers and retired citizens, it would also have serious consequences for those whose jobs and careers have depended on the *existing* IRS/SSA environment. If you're a tax attorney whose past 20 years of employment have depended on your expertise at deciphering arcane IRS rulings, how long will it take you to readjust your life in a world where the IRS tax labyrinth has been replaced with a simple flat tax?

Of course, there's one other Y2000 scenario: Maybe there won't be any Y2000 problems at all. Maybe every company and every government agency around the world will finish repairing all of their mission-critical computer systems in time, and maybe they won't make any mistakes. Maybe we'll all wake up on January 1, 2000 and find that aside from a few niggling, insignificant problems, all the computers continue humming along as usual. Maybe we authors will be accused of behaving like the boy who cried "Wolf!" in the fairy tale. If so, it will be deeply embarrassing to us—but that's a small price to pay! Like everyone else in American society, we authors have jobs, bank accounts, telephones, and credit cards. Our lives will be considerably less complicated if we don't have to face disruptions in these areas, even if it does mean spending the first year of the new millennium apologizing to everyone for a problem that never occurred.

Even in the unhappy event that we're correct about the severity of Y2000 problems, it won't be the end of Western civilization. We're *not* suggesting that Americans will wake up on January 1 and collectively say, "Oh my goodness, our computers have stopped working! Let's all commit suicide!" Nor do we suggest that the entire population will passively sit in their homes, waiting for legions of programmers to belatedly fix the computer problems and save the day. Life will go on, one way or another; many of the computer systems *will* work on January 1, and people will eventually find a way to compensate for the failures of the other ones. As one computer scientist remarked to us, World War II was fought without computers—and all of world society survived in a more-or-less reasonable fashion prior to the advent of computers in the early 1950s. We could do it again, if necessary, especially because it would be only a matter of days, weeks, or months before most of the Y2000 bugs were fixed, and the computers restored to their normal operation.

But one could make the same kind of upbeat, rosy assessment of the Crash of 1929 and the decade-long Great Depression that followed. It wasn't the end of the world; life went on. The banking system didn't disappear, the U.S. government didn't fall, and 75 percent of the work force continued to hold jobs. But on the other hand, 25 percent of the work force was unemployed, some 9,000 banks failed, many people lost their life savings, and some other governments (including Germany) did fall. It may not have been the end of the world, but it was a very unpleasant period of time for a number of individuals. Obviously, the Y2000 situation is quite different than the events that led to the Depression; and just as obviously, we hope that the consequences will be far less significant. But just as a few prescient individuals anticipated the 1929 Crash and thus avoided some of the subsequent problems, we believe that some early planning could reduce the impact of whatever Y2000 problems might occur.

"Bottom Line" Advice

Chances are that 90 percent of the population of the U.S. will never hear about this book, and 99 percent will never read it. Even if 1 percent do read the book (which would make it a phenomenal bestseller!), the majority won't take any action. They may worry about some of the scenarios we've outlined, and perhaps even lose a couple nights' sleep. And while it's understandable that very few people will have the determination and stamina to prepare for a year-long or decade-long disaster, it's sad to realize that the relatively easy preparation for two to three days or a month of disruption will also be ignored.

What you *should* do, in our opinion, is read through each of the remaining chapters in this book and make your own assessment of the likely impact of Y2000 problems in the various areas that could affect you. As you do this, you may find yourself frustrated that our descriptions of possible Y2000 scenarios are not more precise. Even if we were capable of confidently stating, "There is a 75 percent chance that Bank XYZ will fail because of Y2000 problems, and a 90 percent chance that the IRS will be unable to *ever* get its computer systems working correctly," our assessment would be based on the information available to us in mid-1998, when the second edition of this book was being prepared. We expect the situation to change dramatically—hopefully for the better, but possibly for the worse—during 1999, as private-sector and public-sector organizations stop talking about the Y2000 problem and start *doing* the repair work. By mid-1999, if not earlier, it should be abundantly clear to you and everyone else whether the IRS and Bank XYZ will be ready or not.[6] However, it will be crucial for you to have made your own contingency plans in advance, so that you can take whatever action is appropriate without any further delays. And if those contingency plans involve substantial purchase—such as a diesel generator or a six month supply of food—you should consider doing it as early as possible, in order to avoid finding yourself at the end of a very long line of others who have the same idea.

If you need to boil it all down to a few simple guidelines, consider the following recommendations:

- *The majority of Year-2000 problems are likely to be of the kind that will last two to three days.* This scenario is the bare minimum of risk management contingency planning you should be doing—indeed, it's so simple and inexpensive that it's extremely shortsighted *not* to do so. You should prepare in much the way you would prepare for a major blizzard or hurricane that knocks out all public services for a few days. That means a few days' worth of spare food, water, candles, and cash. It means that your office might close down for a few days, and you might lose your salary for that period. It means that you might lose access to the convenience of phone, television, and ATM machines for a few days. Preparing for this is not a difficult task at all, and the financial investment is modest indeed. People who live in areas of the country subject to extreme weather conditions do this already. But, people who live in major urban areas like New York, Chicago, and Los Angeles generally don't.

- *A significant percentage of the Y2000 problems will be serious enough to last for a month.* You'll have to decide whether you're cautious enough to prepare for such a contingency, but in our opinion, this is where you should be doing most of your planning and serious thinking. One of us, for example, is a self-employed consultant who has already concluded that the Y2000 disruptions probably means there will be no clients and no revenue for at least the month of January 2000, and perhaps for much of the ensuing year. Planning for this in mid-1998 is not a problem; coping with it unexpectedly in January 2000, when our family was counting on that month's income, would have been a problem. Stockpiling a month's worth of cash, in anticipation of a bank failure, is difficult but not impossible; stockpiling a month's worth of food, if you're an urban dweller in a cramped apartment, may turn out to be far more difficult. In the unlikely but nevertheless possible occurrences of situations like this—e.g., food shortages in urban centers—you should plan for a temporary escape, such as a month-long vacation to visit relatives in the countryside.

- *A minority of the Y2000 problems will have year-long consequences.* The primary things we're worried about here are loss of employment and long-term disruption of banks, public institutions, and social services. People raised during the Great Depression advised their children to amass a nest egg that would last them for at least six months of unemployment, but few of today's families are in that position. At this point, there may not be enough time left before January 1, 2000 for the average middle-class family to save a year's living expenses. If you're in such a position, the one thing you *can* do is begin cutting back on your level of spending, and begin preparing yourself psychologically for the possibility of a *major* reduction in lifestyle. Don't take on any long-term financial commitments; do try to eliminate as much short-term, credit card-oriented debt as possible. If you have friends or colleagues who were downsized, outsourced, or laid off during the recession of the early 1990s, ask them what strategies they used to get themselves through a year or two of difficult times.

The key point to remember here is that a serious plan for a yearlong Y2000 disruption is almost certain to require a change in life-style, in contrast to the preparations for a one month or two day disruption. Whether it's changing your job, changing the place where you live, or changing your spending habits, it will require a much more serious psychological commitment than that associated with stockpiling a few day's worth of food. But if you make such a decision in late 1998 or early 1999, you can incorporate such changes into the rest of your family plans, career plans, and lifestyle plans without panicking and making costly sacrifices; that probably won't be possible if you procrastinate until late 1999.

- *Finally, there is the possibility of a few Y2000-induced disasters that could take a decade to resolve.* One example of such a disaster would be a complete collapse of the nation's financial system, and its replacement with a new financial system (and new currency) that would effectively wipe out the accumulated wealth of the nation's citizens. It's important to emphasize that the nation's banks, financial institutions, and appropriate government agencies are working quite hard to ensure such a

> nightmare won't occur—but if it did, the consequences would be felt for a number of years. A more likely disaster scenario is a collapse of one or more of the major federal government agencies, such as the IRS, Medicare, or Social Security. If the political reaction to such a collapse was to eliminate the social services provided by those agencies, or to change the nation's taxation system entirely, it could well take a decade to adapt and adjust. Since we have no idea exactly how the Y2000 situation will unfold, there's no way that we can make any plausible, detailed predictions about the situation in 2005 or 2010; all we can say is that whatever long-term assumptions you've made (many of which are implicit and subconscious) may turn out to be invalid.

If you think such a situation is entirely impossible, consider the citizens of the former Soviet Union. How many of them would have predicted the complete collapse of the Communist economic system prior to Gorbachev's resignation in 1991? And, how many of them are coping adequately with a transition period—including a 75 percent decline in the Russian stock market during 1998—that will last far more than a single decade before a new equilibrium emerges? The only thing we can advise for a situation like this is an emphasis on flexibility and adaptability; beyond that, any semblance of traditional planning is likely to be futile. If the Y2000 problem leads to something equivalent to the collapse of the Soviet Union—unlikely, perhaps, but not impossible—then all bets are off. It will be a whole new ball game.

Endnotes

1. This is a key point: the disaster-relief strategy in most government agencies and charitable organizations is predicated on "single-point" disasters. The January 1998 ice-storm in eastern Canada, for example, resulted in the largest peace-time effort in history by the Canadian military forces, as equipment and personnel were brought in from all over the country to help the civilian population cope with the loss of electricity; a number of U.S. relief agencies also participated in the effort. But if the loss of electricity had been caused by Y2K instead of an ice storm, it probably would have affected the rest of Canada and the U.S., too, and the relief forces would have been busy tending to their own problems.
2. The relative lack of attention and concern by state and federal governments that we've observed in 1997 and 1998 may be compounding the Y2K problem, for it means that there is almost no contingency planning and preparedness on the part of the civilian population. Governments around the world could be stockpiling food, blankets, emergency supplies of water, etc; but thus far, we've seen no evidence of such preparations, nor have we seen any government authorities recommending such actions. Read, for example, President Clinton's Y2K speech on July 14th (which is available on the Internet at http://www.whitehouse.gov/WH/New/html/19980714-5571.html); while he does suggest that businesses should be making contingency plans for potential Y2K failures, he offers no such advice to private citizens.
3. See, for example, Robert N. Charette, *Software Engineering Risk Analysis and Management*, (McGraw-Hill, 1989) or Capers Jones, *Assessment and Control of Software Risks*, (Prentice Hall, 1994).
4. As the second edition of this book was being prepared, industry surveys indicated that approximately 75 percent of small businesses around the world had not begun *any* Y2000 preparations. Some intend to look into the situation in 1999, but approximately

half of the small businesses have no intention to do anything unless they experience a failure on January 1, 2000.

5. Another example: one of the authors installed a solar-panel energy system on the roof of his house in August 1998, and replaced the refrigerator and light-bulbs throughout the house with energy-efficient versions that consume *10 times* less electricity. The solar-panel system is now the *primary* source of electricity, with the traditional electric utility company serving merely as a backup; an additional backup consists of a small, but highly efficient, windmill installed on the roof to generate power at night, and on windy, cloudy days. Ignoring the Y2000 problem, the investment of approximately $10,000 in the solar-panel system will be recouped over the next 8-10 years because of the elimination of the usual monthly electric bill. And of course, if there *is* a serious Y2000 problem, the electrical appliances will continue to operate without interruption.
6. This is not a casual statement. It turns out that the governments of Canada and Japan, as well as the state of New York, operate on a fiscal year that begins April 1st; thus, on April 1, 1999 these government organizations will begin their 1999-2000 fiscal year, and their computer systems will either be ready or not. On April 6th, the government of England (as well as many private-sector UK organizations) begins its new fiscal year; on July 1st, the government of Australia, and another 46 U.S. states begin their fiscal year. And on October 1, 1999, the U.S. federal government begins its 1999-2000 fiscal year. None of these dates involve embedded systems, so we still face the prospect of a large number of failures on January 1, 2000—but if we make it through these "dress rehearsals" without serious difficulties, it will be a very positive sign.

Y2000 Impact on Jobs

...we need literally an army of programmers and information technology experts to finish the [Y2K] task... I'm pleased to announce that the Department of Labor will expand its jobs bank and talent bank to help to meet this challenge. And I thank Secretary Herman and Deputy Secretary Higgins for that.

President Bill Clinton, Speech at the National Academy of Sciences, *July 14, 1998*

A tremendous number of people in America work very hard at something that bores them. Even a rich man thinks he has to go down to the office everyday. Not because he likes it but because he can't think of anything else to do.

W. H. Auden, The Table Talk of W. H. Auden, *November 16, 1946.*

The greatest analgesic, soporific, stimulant, tranquilizer, narcotic, and to some extent even antibiotic—in short, the closest thing to a genuine panacea—known to medical science is work.

Thomas Szasz, The Second Sin, *"Medicine" (1973).*

Introduction

Capers Jones, a software expert in the Y2000 field, estimates that five to seven percent of U.S. businesses will go bankrupt as a result of Y2000 failures.[1] If those companies happen to be somewhere else—a remote region of the Appalachians, or a manufacturing plant on the other side of the country—then you're likely to shake your head sympathetically, and carry on with your own life. But what if it's your company? What if several of the companies in your industry, or in your region of the country, go bankrupt as a result of the Y2000 crisis?

As with other aspects of the Y2000 phenomenon, it may be difficult to accept the possibility that such a thing could happen. And indeed, it may not be a "permanent" phenomenon; maybe your office will only shut down for two or three days. But it might be out of operation for a month, in a fashion analogous to the aftermath of a major hurricane. And if your employer does shut down permanently, it's conceivable that it could take a year to find a replacement job.

The Y2000 problem threatens three of the most important economic goals of politicians and economic policy makers: full employment, price stability, and economic growth. Why are these goals so important to politicians? Because they're also the most important to the voters: Most of us want steady employment so that we can feed our families, pay the rent, buy necessities, and occasionally buy some treats for ourselves. We want to be confident that the dollars we receive today will be sufficient to cover our needs tomorrow; in other words, we don't want to worry that inflation will erode the value of our savings accounts. In the U.S., inflation has rarely been above 10 percent in this century, but we all have read and heard about hyperinflation in countries like Germany and Brazil.[2] Such inflation can lead to widespread social discontent, speculative investments, and efforts to convert one's money into a more stable currency.[3] In the news lately, a sharp decline in the value of the ruble, and the fear of subsequent inflation, has led to lines forming outside of Russian banks, with people pushing and fighting to enter the building, and exchange their rapidly declining rubles for U.S. dollars and German marks. As for the third goal, steady economic growth leads to improved living standards, and usually greater labor productivity, which is accompanied by increased income. Not only is this desirable, it's something that we've come to expect during our lifetimes, if only because we constantly hear our leaders promising they can deliver it to us.

This chapter focuses on U.S. unemployment, and exactly what happens when it rises—whether because of a Y2000-related problem or any other reason. If you're in your 20s or early 30s, then you probably weren't in the labor force when unemployment was last near 10 percent, during the 1981-82 recession. Indeed, some of us have been in the labor force for only a few years, and have thus enjoyed the good fortune of experiencing a "tight" labor market during the current economic boom. Unemployment is one of the most widely followed economic indicators, most commonly expressed by the unemployment rate (the number of people unemployed divided by the number of people in the labor force, or people actively seeking work). High unemployment can cause severe social discontent; our parents and grandparents still remember the marches and strikes during the Great Depression, when the unemployment rate peaked near 25 percent. More recently, look to France where unemployment has only declined modestly to just under 12 percent when we were writing the second edition of this book, from 13 percent in the spring of 1997 when we wrote the first edition. It is disappointing to many in France that their unemployment rate fell so little in a time when markets were booming, and general prosperity was rising through the summer of 1998. The following chart shows how U.S. unemployment has varied over the past 50 years; it illustrates graphically that we have very little experience with high unemployment rates since the end of World War II.

U.S. Unemployment Rate
January 1948-August 1998

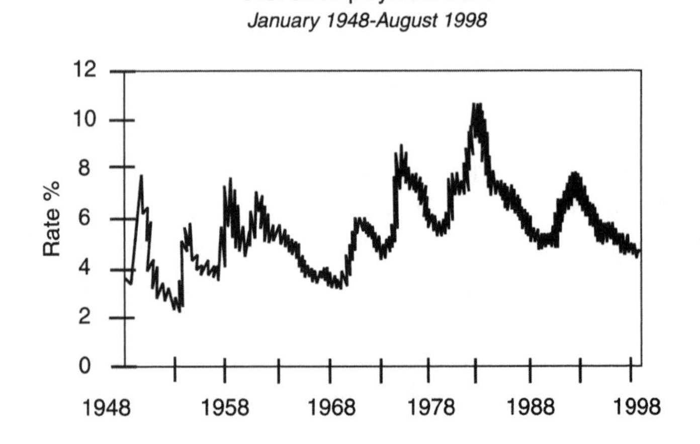

As we update this book in the summer and fall of 1998 for the second edition, the U.S. has an unemployment rate of 4.5 percent, inflation of less than 2 percent, and an economic expansion in its sixth year. Domestically, conditions inside the United States had improved in the year since we first started writing this book, and the U.S. is still at, or near, what economists call "full employment." Some minimal level of unemployment will always exist because in a dynamic economy, even in the best of times, workers change jobs and adapt to shifting market conditions, or are unemployed because of "seasonal" factors (the ski bum that looks for work in the summer), or because of "frictional" factors (the family that moves to the West Coast to enjoy nicer weather and then looks for new jobs). This minimal level of unemployment is called the "full employment level." So what happens if circumstances—whether politics, international competition, or Y2000 problems—cause unemployment to rise?

On the simplest level, when unemployment increases, people lose their "wage income." As the phrase suggests, wage income is what is earned on the job—and for most workers in the United States, it is the only source of income. Non-wage income is income earned from sources outside the job, e.g., interest and investment income, or rental income. What would happen if wage income were lost for two or three days? Well, honestly, not too much. Think of it from your own perspective: If you were to lose two or three days pay, you probably wouldn't be thrilled, but you could survive, and pay your rent—and you probably would enjoy your few days off.

But what would happen if wage income was lost for a month? This could be a quite serious problem for many people. Many members of the labor force don't have enough savings to survive for a month without pay. Many young people, and many lower-income workers, would be forced to go on unemployment for a month, and/or look for another job, and/or seek other benefits. Some would be lucky enough to be able to borrow from friends or family. Most young workers and low-income laborers, however, would change their lifestyle by cutting down on their consumption spending. These workers would eliminate any "luxury" items from their budget, perhaps substitute lower-cost items for higher-cost goods, and cut down on any entertainment expenses. This reduction in consumption spending would have a slight dampening effect on the economy, but if workers were only out of work for a month, the effect would probably be visible but relatively slight.

Things obviously become much more serious if people lose their jobs for a year. A very small percentage of these unfortunate workers would exit the labor force completely, based on their assessment that they didn't really need to work anyway. A much larger percentage would begin looking for another job, and would begin collecting unemployment. A small percentage would also begin collecting welfare. In this instance, the effect on consumption spending would be much more marked. A moment of personal introspection will confirm this: How would you change your spending habits if you were out of work for a year? All "frivolous" expenses-vacations, dinners out, movies, unnecessary clothing, and so forth-would be eliminated.

U.S. Saving Habits

When people lose their jobs, they begin depleting their savings by spending the money in their savings account. That can be quite a problem, because the U.S. is a nation that saves very little by international standards: The savings rate (savings as a percent of disposable income) was a meager 0.3 percent in August 1998. This issue got a lot of attention in the 1980s when the U.S. savings rate dipped to about 3 percent. A low savings rate can become an important political issue: When savings are low, there is less money in banks to be lent out for new plants and equipment, and can thus reduce the future potential output of the economy. When the saving rate is low, there are also less funds available for U.S. government borrowing, and the government is forced to borrow from abroad.

Why do Americans save so little? One reason is that interest rates on long-term (30 year maturity) government bonds are currently at a historic low in the United States, so people don't earn much when they just put money in the bank-and the stock market has performed very well in recent years, so there are attractive alternatives. Another reason is that in the U.S., interest income is taxed (unlike some other countries), creating yet another disincentive. A final possible explanation is that U.S. consumers are generally very confident about the future, and about their upcoming job prospects. American consumers feel that if they lose their jobs, they will be able to get another one relatively easily, so they do not have to save too much. This is somewhat borne out by the available economic data: Consumer confidence and the savings rate are negatively correlated, which means that when consumer confidence is high, savings is low. This correlation has become even more negative in recent years;[4] thus, during this decade, there has been even less of an inclination for Americans to save as long as their confidence in the economy remains high.

Consumer Confidence

As shown in the following chart, consumer confidence can be a sensitive indicator of recessions and other macroeconomic shocks. Most recently, consumer confidence plunged during the Iraqi invasion of Kuwait, reflecting the concerns of consumers about the implications of the invasion. Consumer confidence may be an indicator to watch in the months immediately before and after January 1, 2000, to see how broad-based the effect on the economy will be. If consumer confidence drops sharply because of the various Y2000 problems discussed in this book, the savings rate would be expected to increase—but this is only relevant if the majority of people have jobs that provide sufficient earnings with which to accomplish their savings activity. If we look at what has happened to consumer confidence between the summer of 1997 and the summer of 1998, we can see that consumers generally remain confident, despite the troubles of President Clinton, and despite international terrorist acts. We fear that the more time passes without Year 2000 becoming a more widespread topic of discussion, the more severe the decline in consumer confidence will be when Year 2000 does come to the forefront. With a more severe decline in consumer confidence will likely come a more severe drop in consumer spending.

U.S. Consumer Confidence
January 1978-August 1998

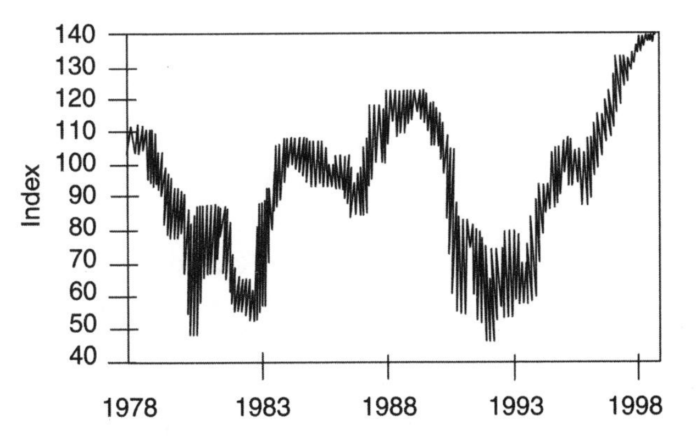

Savings Statistics

And this raises an interesting question: What kind of savings do Americans indulge in? It is difficult to pinpoint this precisely, but there are some data available. We can obtain figures from the Federal Reserve, but reading that there is over $1 trillion in currency, demand deposits, NOW accounts, credit unions, and non-bank travelers checks is not very useful. We found it more useful to look at U.S. Census Bureau data: As of 1993, 11 percent of all households had a zero or negative household net worth, while 14 percent had a household net worth of between $1 and $4,999. So in total, 25 percent of U.S. households have a net worth of less than $5,000. Depending on monthly living expenses and the number of people in the household, 25 percent of U.S. households could be in serious trouble if work was lost for a month. It is also possible, of course, that this definition of "household net worth" includes some items that are not liquid, i.e., they can't be readily turned into cash.

Fallout Ripple Effect

What does this all mean? Well, if people are out of work for two or three days, it doesn't mean very much. If people are out of work for a month, however, some people's savings could be seriously depleted. Many young workers who have been in the labor force only a few years have very little savings, have started families, perhaps have taken on mortgages, borrowed money for down payments on houses, and have credit card debt to boot! Related to the statistics detailed above, 15 percent of married-couple households under 35 years old have a zero to negative net household worth. A further 19 percent of married-couple households in that same age group have a net worth of between $1 and $4,999. For these households, and many more, a month out of work will be extremely difficult. This month out of work will depress consumption for more than that month, however—because when workers do return to work, they will work on building up their savings in case they ever have to face the same problem again, and will keep consumption spending down for a period of time.

Personal Level

As the length of time out of work increases, the younger and older members of the labor force become more and more at risk. The youngest members of the labor force are at risk because they have the least amount of savings, and often have debt they need to pay off. Older workers are also at risk because they are at the end of their income-earning cycle, and have begun to decrease their budgets. They are also the least flexible members of the workforce, and will find it difficult to get new jobs. A year out of work for either of these groups would almost certainly be a very severe problem; those who do have enough savings to last a year will do so, but will do so frugally. They will cut down on consumption spending, collect unemployment if possible, and try to limit the depletion of their savings account. The inevitable reduction in consumption spending will be a damper for the U.S. economy. And those who don't have enough savings to last a year, and don't have any investments, will liquidate their savings and then be forced to rely on other sources of income.

National Level

If Y2000 problems throw people out of work for a month, then some may be forced to withdraw a portion of their mutual fund investments, or funds from their 401K retirement plans. This will be a drag on the stock market, and could cause a small correction, depending on the amount of money that is withdrawn. Obviously, a year's loss of employment could lead to significant withdrawals from stocks and mutual funds, as individuals liquidate investments to support themselves. Also, for that year, those same employees will no longer be contributing to their 401K plans, nor will they be contributing any money on their own to mutual funds or the stock market.

This could lead to a serious drop in the stock market, which could make matters worse. A decline in share prices can cause a "negative wealth effect." What does this mean? First, declines in share prices decreases the "paper" value of people's investments, or their wealth. Seasoned veterans of the stock market, with millions of dollars of disposable income, might be able to survive such a decline without losing much sleep; but the great majority of middle-class investors will "feel poorer" and will cut back on their spending. This decrease in consumption demand, depending on its severity, will cause companies to cut back on production, and perhaps staff. This could lead to more layoffs, which will only make the cycle begin again. As we write the second edition of this book, companies are announcing declines and disappointments in earnings, in part because of decreased demand from abroad. The drop in demand from foreigners, especially in Asia, has come about because of the financial market turmoil in that region. Second, a decline in the share price of some companies will reduce the net worth of their companies. Companies, too, feel poorer; it curtails their ability to make investments, and acquire other companies; and it can lead to further layoffs. This is already happening in the summer and fall of 1998, as companies, especially banks, have begun to announce layoffs amidst sharp declines in their stock prices.

Government Level

An increase in unemployment will also reduce government revenues. As might be expected, this is a negligible factor if people are out of work for only a day or two (though there have been extraordinarily few cases where the entire population has been unemployed for a day or two, since the U.S. is not prone to the kind of national strikes one occasionally sees in Europe). But if people are out of work for a month, the loss in income tax revenue is more substantial, especially if large numbers of people are involved. Workers idle for a year will mean quite serious losses in income tax revenue. That, coupled with increased government spending on unemployment, welfare, and other benefits will increase the government deficit, if only temporarily.

Global Level

A drop in the stock market could also have international ramifications, as the U.S. stock market is the benchmark and leader for global stock markets. In the financial community, it's often said that,

"When the U.S. gets a sniffle, Europe gets a cold," which seems applicable both to the strength of the U.S. dollar and also the equity market. When the U.S. stock market fell by 29 percent in 1987, the Australian stock market fell by 25 percent, the Japanese stock market fell by 15 percent, and the stock market in the United Kingdom lost over 21 percent of its value. More recently, the U.S. stock market fell by approximately 15 percent in August of 1998, and the British stock market fell by 9.6 percent and the Japanese stock market fell by 13.9 percent. We stress these numbers because of their potential impact on the global job market, and the potential for a global recession.

It's useful to see what has actually happened in the past when the unemployment rate has risen. As the following chart indicates, there is a very high correlation between unemployment rate and the average weeks spent unemployed. This makes sense: When jobs are harder to find (as evidenced by a higher unemployment rate), people tend to stay out of work longer. The strength of this relationship has deteriorated a bit over time, though even recently it still has some statistical significance. What it tells us, quite simply, is that if we see a doubling in the unemployment rate because of the Y2000 problems (or any other problems, for that matter), average weeks of unemployment are likely to increase quite dramatically. In the past, a doubling in the unemployment rate led to an 80-percent increase in the average weeks unemployed. This means that if the unemployment rate increases from its current level of approximately 5 percent to a new level of 10 percent (a "doubling" phenomenon that was last experienced during the 1981-82 recession), people will, on average, be unemployed for 24 weeks. An average is, of course, an average, so unfortunately some people will be unemployed for longer than 24 weeks. That's an awfully long time to be without a paycheck.

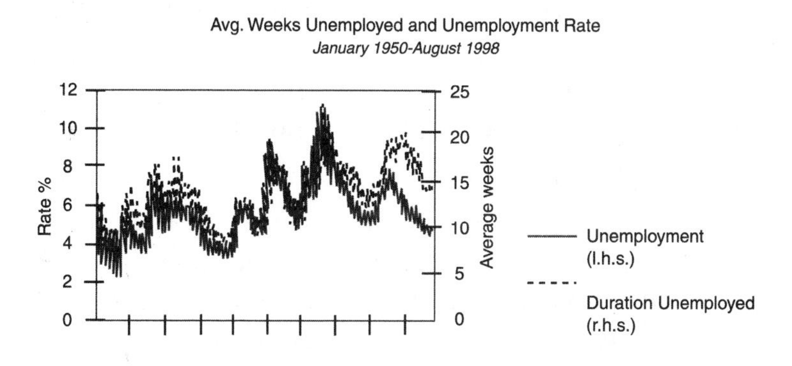

Another consequence of an increase in the unemployment rate is a loss in employment tax revenues for the government. Obviously, if people are out of work for a day or two, the loss in tax revenues will be negligible—but if people are out of work for a month, the loss in income tax revenue is more substantial. Workers idle for a year will mean quite serious losses in income tax revenue. Since 1982, the correlation between government employment tax receipts and the unemployment rate is -0.64—suggesting the strength of the statistical relationship between income tax revenue and the unemployment rate. The U.S. Treasury has averaged approximately $40 billion per month in employment taxes since the beginning of 1995. It is difficult to accurately predict what the decline in employment tax receipts will be if there is a rise in the unemployment rate, given the different tax regimes and the effect of inflation over time. However, the strength of the historical statistical relationship between the two data series suggests that a doubling in the unemployment rate could translate into a loss of several billion dollars every month. This means, of course, that the government will have less money to spend at the exact time when the U.S. economy would need an extra boost from government spending.

On a nationwide basis, an increase in unemployment will depress the economy: More people out of work will mean less demand. As demand decreases, manufacturers will cut their production, and this, by definition will mean a decrease in the nation's economic output. Gross Domestic Product (GDP), which consists of all output produced within the United States, is a common measure of economic output. It is not, however, a measure to watch carefully as the Y2000 deadline approaches because the GDP figures are "old news" when they are released a month after the end of a financial quarter. Instead, you should watch more current indicators like unemployment, consumer confidence, industrial production, and retail sales (all of which are regularly reported in the major newspapers throughout the U.S.) to gauge how the economy is being affected.

As in most of our examples, if people are out of work for a few days, there should be little impact on GDP. However, if even a small percentage of people are out of work for a month, there can be a noticeable impact on GDP. In the first edition of our book, we used the GM strike of 1996 as a good illustration of the ripple effects of extended time out of work. That 17-day strike resulted in a decline of 0.5 percent of U.S. GDP in the first quarter of 1996. For our second edition, we will focus on the GM strike of 1998, as it is more recent, and could provide a more realistic example for our readers.

Case Study—GM Strike of 1998

In early June of 1998, 3,400 United Auto Workers (UAW) members who make hoods, fenders, and other parts went on strike, resulting in the closing of six GM assembly plants in three U.S. states and Canada, and the idling of 16,500 GM workers within five days. The strike took place in Flint, Michigan where GM employs 34,000 people, making it the largest employer. In the early days of the strike, Lear Corp., North America's third-largest auto parts supplier, closed two seating plants in Michigan as production slowed down resulting from the newly begun strike. In 1997, General Motors accounted for approximately 27 percent of Lear's $2.4 billion revenue. On the sixth day of the strike, GM shut down its seventh vehicle assembly plant, this one a truck factory in New Jersey, idling another 1,000 workers. Two days later, GM closed an eighth assembly plant, and laid off workers at a truck and van plant in Missouri, and sent home workers from a number of different parts plants. Strikes then halted production at its auto parts unit Delphi Automotive Systems in Chihuahua and Reynosa, Mexico, idling 3,400 workers. According to press reports, Adelphi is Mexico's largest private employer with 72,000 workers in 53 plants. GM was then struck with another parts-plant strike by the UAW, this one at the GM Delphi plant in Flint, Michigan, where 5,800 workers walked out of work. The GM Delphi plant in Flint makes spark plugs and other parts for almost all of GM's car and truck plants. Layoffs at this point reached 50,900 workers for General Motors alone, resulting in an estimated reduction of $480 million in pretax profits. Meanwhile, workers at truck plants in Indiana, Michigan, and Wisconsin were sent home after their plants ran out of fenders and hoods.

The strike then halted production at American Isuzu Motors Inc. on most of the company's trucks and light trucks assembled in the U.S. General Motors owns 37.5 percent of Isuzu, and has supplied truck parts to Isuzu since 1994.

This trend continued, with GM's most profitable plants being forced to shut down as they ran out of parts. Towards the end of the strike, almost 95 percent of GM's North American vehicle production had been stopped. This strike affected plants and auto-parts suppliers in the U.S., Canada, Mexico, and Brazil as well as Canadian railroad companies who relied on GM vehicle and parts shipment for some of its profits. Delis and restaurants, small businesses and auto dealers in the surrounding areas of the closed plants were beginning to suffer because of the strike. The owner of a sandwich store, Baldino's Subs in Doraville, Georgia, where GM workers come for food, was quoted as saying that his business was down about 10 percent every day the workers were idled. A bartender at a bar called Timothy's Pub in Flint, across the street from the Delphi plant where 5,800 workers were on strike, said business was down by about one third from where it was when the strike started. Lear Corp., the auto parts supplier we mentioned earlier, ended up closing 10 seat plants, and one interior-components plant idling about 2,800 workers in New Jersey, Ohio, Texas, Virginia, Missouri, Michigan, Delaware, and certain areas in Canada. As the strike was nearing its 30th day, there were news reports that GM was contacting television networks, magazines, and newspapers about pulling commercials and ads for the next six weeks. We were unable to find any confirmation of this by GM officials, though the possibility would be enough to make any of the sellers of ad space in the media nervous.

All told, the strike ended up lasting for two months and costing GM an estimate $3 billion in second quarter 1998 profits. Near the end of the strike, over 160,000 GM workers were idled, and 26 of 29 North American assembly plants were closed, resulting in a 95-percent shutdown in production. It was estimated that it would take approximately 10 days to get assembly plants up and running again. Our purpose here is not to pick on GM or the UAW. But we believe these events bear striking similarities to the ripple effects Y2000 problems could have, and they show how severe the economic consequences of a shutdown of a key U.S. industry can be. We can easily imagine a scenario in which Plant A in XYZ company cannot produce its goods because of a Y2000 problem, and so Plants B, C, and D must temporarily shut down because they rely on the output of Plant A. And that's only intra-company. What if Plant E in 123 company relies on the output of Plant B of XYZ company? Or, what if you run a deli that relies on the lunch crowd from company ABC for a large share of your business, and company ABC is shut down for a month? What if you supply parts to company XYZ and they are shut down for six months, and they are a major percentage of your annual revenues? You get our point; your vulnerability lies not only in how well prepared your company is for Y2K, but how well prepared your customers and suppliers are as well.

If unemployment increases significantly and the economy begins a downturn, as we expect, what will the authorities do? If the decline, or expected decline, in GDP is significant enough, the Federal Reserve will lower interest rates in order to stimulate the economy. The Alan Greenspan-led Federal Reserve has been quite successful in taking a "forward-looking" approach to monetary policy. For example, in the beginning of 1994, the Fed raised interest rates before actual signs of inflation had emerged. This was quite different from U.S. central bank policy in the 1970s and 80s, when the Fed typically voted to raise rates only after inflation indicators had become too high. Likewise, the Fed would vote to lower rates when the economy was already in a recession. This policy often caused what is known as "overshooting"—when the Fed would lower rates so much that the economy would overheat and begin a boom cycle with inflation; subsequently the Fed would raise interest rates so much that the economy would turn down into a recession.

This overshooting occurred because of the lag of monetary policy: economists believe that it takes 6 to 18 months for the impact of interest rate changes to be felt on the economy. In the past, the Fed would continue lowering rates as long as economic indicators remained weak even though effects of past interest rate cuts were yet to be felt.[5] A new era began in 1994, when Alan Greenspan decided that interest rate changes should be made based on forecasts of where the economy would be a year in the future. That way, if the economy was expected to be weak in 12 months, the Federal Reserve would begin cutting interest rates now. In 1998, the Fed and Alan Greenspan are looking towards the future again, and cutting official short-term interest rates by 0.25 percent, primarily because of concerns about international economies, and how they could affect the U.S. in the next 6 to 12 months.

While this may all sound rather academic to the average worker, there may be some very real consequences in the coming years. It will be very interesting, for example, to see whether the Fed will include the Y2000 problem in its forecasts during its 1999 policy meetings. How would the Federal Reserve quantify those problems? Unless the potential economic ramifications of the Y2000 problem become clearer by then, it would seem difficult for the Fed to assess the magnitude of the Y2000 problem in its forecasts. The Fed has made numerous comments about the year 2000, but few of them have involved a discussion about the economic consequences of the problem. Rather, they have focused on the risk of transaction failure, and what that would mean for banks and the banking system as a whole. We suspect that that trend may start changing soon. In testimony to the Committee on Banking and Financial Services in the U.S. House of Representatives, Federal Reserve Governor Edward W. Kelley said:

> *The Year 2000 problem will touch much more than just our financial systems and could temporarily have adverse effects on the performance of the overall U.S. economy as well as the economies of many, or all, nations if not corrected. As I said last April in testimony before the Senate Committee on Commerce, Science, and Transportation, some of the more adverse scenarios are not without a certain plausibility, if this challenge were being ignored. But it is not being ignored. While it is impossible today to precisely forecast the impact of this event, and the range of possibilities runs from minimal to extremely serious, an enormous amount of work is being done in anticipation of the rollover of the millennium, and I am optimistic that this work will pay off.*

Fed Governor Kelley went on to make interesting and informative remarks in the rest of his testimony, though there was no further mention of the potential economic impact of the Year 2000 problem. In an April 1998 speech, Fed Governor Kelley said U.S. GDP could be reduced by 0.1 percentage points in 1998 and 1999 because of the Year 2000 problem. He added that its unlikely that disruptions associated with the Year 2000 would cause a recession, though offered no hard facts. In January of 1998, Federal Reserve Bank President William McDonough said the following in a speech to the Bankers' Association for Foreign Trade:

> *Getting Year 2000 programs right is critical for every organization...Failure to get it right could affect the integrity of the payments system and the performance of the U.S. and global economies.*

Comments like these are the extent of what we have seen from the Federal Reserve on the potential economic impact of the Year 2000 problem. To put it very simply, declines and interruptions in supply and demand related to Year 2000 problems are likely to cause layoffs prior to and after the Year 2000. We do not know the extent of the layoffs, nor do we know what sector or geographic area they will be most concentrated in, but we do our best to explore the topic, and reach some relatively logical conclusions.

If, in the beginning of the Year 2000, substantial jobs are lost and the economy contracts sharply, it's highly likely the Fed will begin lowering interest rates with little or no delay. Unfortunately, the economic impact of the lower interest rates won't be felt until the year 2001 or later; indeed, some of the economists who have studied the government's economic policy in the years immediately following the Great Crash of 1929 argue that traditional tools of monetary policy (such as raising or lowering key interest rates) may not be sufficient to cope with a severe economic downturn.

We can look to Japan for a more recent example of how difficult it can be to revive an extremely depressed and structurally weak economy: The once-envied Japanese economy has been wallowing since 1990, despite official short-term interest rates that have been reduced to an historic low of 0.25 percent. The Japanese government has implemented numerous tax incentive schemes and fiscal stimulus plans, yet in the second quarter of 1998, Japanese GDP fell by an annualized 3.8 percent, fully ensconcing the economy in recession. In the year that has passed between the first and second editions of this book, more Japanese banks have failed, more Japanese people are unemployed, and the Japanese economy has sunk deeper into recession. Sometimes, like in recent years in Japan, the bulk of economic problems are structural and will not be solved by simply lowering interest rates.

Lower interest rates, or borrowing costs, may not help companies who are grappling with Y2000 problems—companies may not need to borrow money at low interest rates, and might instead prefer a large supply of Jolt Cola to encourage their computer programmers to work 72 hours per day. Similarly, if the lower interest rates are introduced at the same time that consumer confidence is eroding because of pervasive Y2000 difficulties, then as we noted previously, consumers are likely to spend less and save more, to the extent they are able to do so. The lack of a classical response to lower interest rates could extend the slowdown.

Another impact of a downturn in the U.S. economy would be the ripple effects on other countries, especially our neighbors and biggest trading partners, Canada and Mexico. Canada, for example, relies on the United States for roughly 75 percent of its exports. If the U.S. economy slows down, there will be less domestic demand for Canadian goods, and this will have a negative impact on international economies. In addition to our closest trading partners, the economies of western Europe and Japan will also be affected negatively; meanwhile, these same countries will be dealing with their own Y2000-induced unemployment problems. We have devoted more time to the international aspects of the Year 2000 problem in Chapter 14.

How Could the Y2000 Problem Cause All of This?

Our fundamental argument should be familiar to you by now: Any business that's highly dependent on computer systems, which in turn are highly dependent upon the ability to calculate dates correctly, may be vulnerable to serious problems after December 31, 1999. If Y2000-sensitive computers control the electronic locks, or the lights, or the phone systems, or other equipment, it may not be possible for employees to function at all. If computers are essential for entering orders, scheduling the activities of people and manufacturing equipment, generating invoices, and other "mission-critical" operations, then a Y2000 failure could make it impossible to carry on "business as usual" until the problem is fixed.

While these kinds of "direct" consequences are probably fairly easy to understand if you look closely at the activities within your company, the "indirect" consequences of Y2000 failures may be more subtle and surprising. As we explain in more detail in Appendix B, every individual, and also every company, depends to a greater or lesser extent on a complex web of services and products provided by other individuals and organizations. Even if your company has worked diligently to ensure that all of its computers are Y2000-compliant, it will be hard to carry on business if the lights go out and the phones don't work. If your critical subcontractors or suppliers disappear, it may be difficult to manufacture your products; if your distributors, wholesalers, and independent sales agents can't contact you, then you can't sell your product. And for a retail business, it may be even more obvious: What if your customers can't contact you because of failures in the communication system or the transportation system?

In some cases, the situation could be deceptively simple: Your cousin Vinnie, for example, operates a small pizza stand, with two part-time high-school kids and no computer. Why should he (or, for that matter, his high-school assistants) worry about the Y2000 problem? Very simple: The pizza stand is located in the Wall Street area, and 95 percent of its business consists of serving a slice-and-a-Coke to busy stockbrokers. If Wall Street is closed for a month, it's highly unlikely that the stockbrokers will make a special trip to enjoy Vinnie's pepperoni pizza. A variation on this theme occurred in 1987, after the famous stock market crash: A number of limousine drivers found that their fat-cat customers weren't so fat any more, and had been reduced in status (particularly in the area of expense-account perks) to the point where they had to ride the bus or subway to work—assuming they had a job at all. As a result, many of the limo drivers quickly found themselves unemployed.

We're describing this in terms of generalities, without having any way of knowing whether it's relevant for your business. Our studies indicate that Wall Street firms, banks, insurance companies, and telemarketing-based firms, among others, are highly vulnerable; small businesses, farmers, and proprietors of small neighborhood stores, delis, and pizza parlors may be less vulnerable. It's up to you to examine the company you work for, and the environment you work in. If it's a large company, with lots of computer systems, then track down the appropriate computer experts and managers and ask them. If you get a blank look when you ask the question, our advice is to grab your paycheck, cash in your stock options, and get out as fast as you can.

And watch out for the computer manager who pats you on the shoulder and says, "Don't you worry yourself about something like that. It's too complicated to explain to you, but we've got the problem under control." Yes, the technical details of fixing the software may be difficult to understand if you're not in the computer field, but the overall "scorecard" is pretty straightforward. How many programmers within the organization are working on the problem? How large is the "portfolio" of computer systems, and how much of it has already been converted to ensure Y2000 compliance? If there's not enough time, and not enough resources, to finish the job by December 31, 1999 (which is almost certain to be the case), what kind of triage of computer systems has been carried out? Which computer systems have been judged non-critical (and thus likely to be abandoned), and what impact will the failure of those systems have on the organization? What steps have been taken to ensure that the "end-user" programs—e.g., spreadsheets developed in Lotus or Excel, desktop databases developed with Microsoft Access, Foxpro, and dBase IV—have been identified for Y2000 compliance? You don't have to be a rocket scientist to ask questions like these, and you don't have to be a rocket scientist to understand the answers. If you can't get straight answers to these questions, or if it appears that the relevant computer managers in your organization haven't begun thinking about them, then—to paraphrase the Stephen King novels—be afraid. Be very afraid.

And this is just the beginning. If you get adequate answers concerning the planning for direct Y2000 failures, then you need to show Figure B.5 (from Appendix B) to your computer managers, and ask them whether they've planned for non-compliant computer systems feeding input to your company's computers, and accepting output from your company's computers. What if your largest customer begins sending computerized orders to your company that are non-Y2000-compliant? What if the bank and the IRS rejects your loan payments and tax payments after January 1st, because your computers are sending Y2000-compliant transactions, but their computers aren't working correctly? Any computer manager who has thought about this possibility for more than a few minutes realizes that there will be a period of time when your company's computers will have to be capable of coping—somehow—with a mixture of both compliant and non-compliant computer systems in other companies.

Interestingly, that's about as far as the typical computer manager is likely to extend his thinking. You'll have to talk to your senior business managers about the consequences of outright failure (e.g., bankruptcy) on the part of the suppliers, subcontractors, customers, and other entities illustrated in Figure B.5. What are the chances of survival if your three top customers go bankrupt? How long can the business survive if the company's bank scrambles its computers and refuses to provide any revolving-credit or line-of-credit loans for six months? How long would it take to find a replacement if the company's chief supplier of "raw materials" (which could be anything from pizza dough to iron ore) went bankrupt?

Y2K Already Causing Problems

There was a recent news story about complications that occurred at a firm when systems were in the process of being fixed and replaced, which shows how Year 2000 complications could cause companies problems even if they are using their best efforts to be ready on time. In late September 1998, the shares of a company called Quaker Fabric, which makes woven upholstery fabrics for the furniture industry, fell 45 percent after an earnings warning was made. The company announced that employees were slowed down by computer system updates that were designed to solve Year 2000 problems. This slowdown resulted in a decline in production, and an expected decline in third- and fourth-quarter earnings. The CFO of the company, Paul Kelly, said that employees who had been insufficiently trained were entering months of data onto new systems. The CFO continued, "Ultimately, our purchasing people had no idea what level of inventory we had on hand, or what level of raw materials were on hand." The company went on to say that it was re-training employees, and that it expected production to be below expectations for the remainder of the year.[6]

As far as we know, Quaker Fabric did not announce any layoffs because of the service-related decline in production. There are many interesting aspects of the company's story, though: first, the company's business (upholstery) is not directly heavily dependent on technology, yet Year 2000 system remediation efforts resulted in a decline in production (and this company was attempting to make system changes in 1998!!). The earnings warning issued by the company led to a steep decline in its share price. Finally, the mess caused by the errors in data entry will limit production for the next several months. It is easy to imagine how problems like these (at a generic company, not Quaker Fabric), where production declines, systems are interrupted, and there is a sharp decline in the company's share price could result in layoffs. It is even easier to imagine that possibility with a company more heavily dependent on computers, with more widespread systems, during a time when the economy is weak, and when many other firms are having Y2K troubles.

The questions that you can ask at your own company can go on and on, and our experience is that most senior managers will become increasingly frustrated if you continue asking. If they were honest, most of them would tell you they've made no contingency plans for such disasters. But their official statement is more likely to be, "These scare-story scenarios you're inventing are so preposterous that they're not worth talking about in a serious way." And the blunt reality is that if some of these events did occur, there would be no practical way to recover. Your company would shut down—period, full stop, end of story. Small startup companies often have to contemplate such possibilities even in normal times, and it's not considered a heresy to raise such questions. But large, established companies, with a noble history of decades or centuries, have a culture that finds it virtually impossible to consider its own demise. If you ask too many blunt questions, you're likely to be branded a heretic and rabble-rouser; so be discreet and indirect, if necessary. But don't fall into the same "denial of reality" trap that your company may be suffering—just because your management is behaving in ostrich-like fashion and your company goes bankrupt doesn't necessarily mean that you have to behave in the same way. If you do work in a large company, you will have the opportunity to share ideas with a larger number of colleagues than if you were in a small company. Doing a little research is relatively easy inside a large company, and you may be able to find others that you work with who have similar concerns. If you can do that, it is possible to approach problems and senior management as a group, perhaps taking the pressure off the individual somewhat. In addition, it is a great opportunity to share ideas and opinions with people who are very familiar with the types of risks you may face because of the Year 2000 at work.

Keep in mind that even if the Y2000 problems are severe in your company, it doesn't necessarily mean that things will abruptly shut down on January 2nd. If the company can't get access to its customers or the funds in its corporate bank account, it may still be able to limp along for a month or two before it closes the doors. If it can't process orders and invoices properly because of Y2000 problems, it could find itself bleeding to death over a period of six months to a year. And it's quite possible, of course, that through the heroic efforts of both computer people and business people throughout the organization, all of the problems and computer screw-ups that emerge after January 1, 2000 might be corrected before they become fatal. If you're a loyal employee with a vested interest in keeping the company alive, you may very well want to offer every possible bit of support.

But be very careful if you find yourself in this position. It's one thing to work 16-hour days for a few months to help put your company's accounting records back together. It's one thing to suffer through a few months of no heat, no air-conditioning, and no phone systems in the office because the company's "process control" computers fell apart. But when the company tells you that it will be a couple of months before anyone can be paid, and that there's some question about the status of your company-funded 401K retirement plan, then you have crossed the line between loyal employee and lender/investor in the company. If you really love your company, perhaps you'll be willing to risk a few months of your salary; it's obviously inappropriate for us to tell you where you should draw the line. But at least we can remind you to think carefully about what you're doing; after the stroke of midnight of December 31, 1999, we'll be entering perilous times, where the usual corporate promises and assurances are likely to be worth very little.

Fallback Advice: The Two-Day Shutdown

Will anyone bother making special plans to cope with a two-day work shutdown caused by a Y2000 problem? Probably not; for most, it will seem like an unplanned holiday, much the same as the blizzard or tornado or hurricane that occasionally shuts down the schools and keeps prudent parents and workers at home.

A particularly benevolent employer would treat this as a crisis beyond the control of the employee, and continue to provide a salary for the missed day or two at work. If the potential loss of a couple days' pay concerns you, it would be a good idea to check with your boss, or with the Human Resource Department in your company. As noted earlier, the Y2000 policy should be much the same as for other kinds of natural disasters. If yours is the kind of company that does not pay for such missed days, then you should see whether you can use sick-days, vacation-days, or other mechanisms to avoid a reduction in your next paycheck.

Ironically, there are likely to be a few situations where the employee wants to stay home (perhaps because of concern about the safety of transportation, which we'll discuss in Chapter 4), but where the employer desperately needs the services of the employee. Doctors and nurses are one obvious example; and there are a variety of other jobs where the employee is supposed to show up, come hell or high water... or Y2000 breakdown.

If yours is a job that falls into this category, the best thing we can advise is to have a calm, rational discussion with your employer now, before any crisis occurs. The most likely date for Y2000 problems may be January 1st, 2nd, and 3rd of the Y2000—but there will inevitably be problems both before and after these dates. You may need to find alternative ways of getting to and from work; you may also want to think about the circumstances that are beyond the reasonable call of duty. You may already have some experience about dealing with the demands of your job when blizzards or hurricanes are involved; but none of us have yet experienced a Y2000 shutdown.

Fallback Advice: The One-Month Shutdown

This is where things get serious: For whatever reason, your office or factory or place of work shuts down for a month... or maybe two months, or three. The interesting thing here is that your employer may not be able to give you a firm date for resuming normal operations. Again, since nobody has experienced the kind of software problems associated with the Y2000 bug before, it's very difficult to offer a precise estimate of the time that will be required to get past the crisis stage.

There's one important exception: the situation where the office has been shut down because of the "clean up" effort required after a Y2000 problem. This could happen in almost any kind of company where the day-to-day operations are highly dependent on computer-generated plans, schedules, and the like. Let's take a simple, hypothetical case: You work as a teller in a major bank, and your primary job is to process deposits and withdrawals at the teller window for those customers who don't use the ubiquitous ATM machine. It's easy to imagine that you might have far more customers to deal with than normal, in the event of a Y2000-based failure in the ATM machines; but even ignoring this potential problem, you may find that your employer tells you to stay home for a month.

Why? Because a Y2000 bug causes the kind of problem discussed in more detail in Appendix A: During the normal overnight processing of checks, payments, deposits, and so forth, an erroneous computer program scrambles every customer's database record, thus making it impossible to tell what any customer's true balance is. Let's make the optimistic assumption that the problem occurs on January 1st, when everyone is likely to be especially alert for such a problem. And let's assume that the programmers scurry into the office on January 2nd (which happens to be a Sunday) to fix the bug. Unfortunately, even though the bug has been fixed (so that any subsequent processing of checks and deposits will be handled correctly), the damage has been done. What now awaits the computer department within the bank is a massive cleanup job: The pre-January customer balances and associated information have to be restored, and the erroneous processing has to be re-run (correctly, this time). It's like cleaning up after a serious tornado: The tornado itself might only have lasted for a few moments, but the cleanup can easily take weeks.

In any event, if you've been told not to come into the office for a month, chances are that you won't be paid during the idle period (we'll ignore the additional complication that it might not be possible to run the payroll system or deposit your check in the bank anyway, though it's precisely this kind of compounded "ripple effect" that we're most concerned about with regard to the overall Y2000 situation). The bottom line is: If your company is shut down for a month because of a Y2000 problem, you're probably going to lose a month's income.

Don't count on your insurance company to make up the difference, either. Again, there is the ripple-effect problem to worry about: Your insurance company is likely to be hard-hit with its own Y2000 problems, and won't be sending its agents out in Boy-Scout fashion, the way it would with a fire or weather-related danger. But aside from that, the simple fact is that you don't have Y2000 insurance; take a look at your insurance policy to confirm it for yourself. You may be covered for fire, flood, earthquakes, meteor showers, theft, plagues of locusts, and a variety of other familiar problems, but chances are that there's also an explicit clause that absolves the company of any responsibility for damages associated with hang-gliding, parachute-jumping, wars, and a catch-all phrase known as "acts of God." The Y2000 problem is definitely an act of Man; but under the circumstances, it defies credulity to assume that a typical insurance company would send you a check for a month's lost wages because of a computer programming bug.

What does all of this mean? You'll have to make your own judgment about the likelihood that a Y2000 bug could keep you from earning your normal paycheck for a month. But if you think it's a reasonable possibility, then you have two choices: Find a job that's guaranteed not to suffer Y2000 problems and do so before New Year's Eve, 1999 (we might add here that we think it is practically impossible to find such a job). Or, your other choice is to make sure that you've got a month's worth of living expenses available. The first option is a bit extreme, and we'll discuss it in more detail for the more serious possibility of a one-year loss of income.

But the second option is perfectly sensible. After all, even without the bizarre phenomenon of a Y2000-induced loss of income, today's turbulent economy could put any one of us out of work for a month. Even civil servants have learned this sobering fact, when the political squabble between Republicans and Democrats effectively shut down the Federal Government for two weeks in early 1996. As noted earlier, the generation that grew up during the Depression era would find it odd that we even bother to talk about this: Of course, they would say, you have to assume that you might have to go a month or two without income because your company has closed its doors for a while.

The authors of this book represent two generations, one of whom was born at the end of World War II, when the common advice was to make sure that one always had 6-12 months living expenses in the bank in case of unforeseen economic difficulties. This generation heard this from their Depression-age parents, for whom it was very real indeed; but since Baby Boomers had not experienced the Depression personally, the advice wasn't always followed. Successive generations, including the Generation-X represented by the other author of this book, sometimes watched their Boomer parents suffer from episodes of corporate downsizing and reengineering, but they were even further removed from the experiences of their grandparents in the Depression.

Such experiences are only a part of today's economic situation; but the overall situation is grim indeed, if one imagines the consequences of a one-month loss of income occurring both randomly and pervasively across the U.S. landscape. Our strong advice: Take a look at your savings account today. You still have almost one full year to put yourself in a position where you could survive a one-month lapse in income without any serious repercussions. This may seem like a daunting task in the first few months of 1999, but even modest savings every week will help to accomplish this goal.

By the way, beware the usual reaction from today's middle-class consumer: Charging things on a credit card, and then "catching up" later on, may not be an option. This was a common trick of the Wall Street yuppies who were caught unexpectedly by the 1987 stock market crash. One of the authors was applying for a home mortgage during this period, and was astounded by the stories from loan officers about the practice of upper-middle-class New York residents to run up credit limits of $25,000 or more on each of half a dozen credit cards while looking for a new job.

If the banks manage to avoid the Y2000 problem, and if the MasterCards, Visas, and American Expresses of the world are equally successful in avoiding problems in this area, and if merchants and suppliers are willing to accept credit-card charges as a form of payment, then maybe you can get away with charging a month's worth of living expenses while you cope with the loss of income. But it seems to us that this is a greater risk than any prudent person should take. It's far more realistic to assume that you won't be able to live on credit for the first few months (if not longer) of the next decade, while the Y2000 problems are being sorted out.

Indeed, you may not even be able to depend on the normal functioning of the banking system during the early days or weeks of the next decade. One advantage of growing up as a child of Depression-era parents is that one hears, first-hand, of the experience of the "bank holiday" that took place in the United States during the early days of the FDR administration. The word "holiday" conjures up an image of a day or two of gaiety and celebration—but it's worth remembering that many of the banks in the U.S. were closed for ten days in March 1933. It's even more sobering to realize that more than 4,000 banks failed during this period; whether we'll suffer this level of crisis is something we'll discuss further in Chapter 5.

Thus, if you're feeling somewhat paranoid about all of this, our advice is to have a month's living expenses in cash, outside your normal bank. You'll lose a month's interest, but interest rates are so low in 1998-99 that the loss of interest income for most people is literally a couple of dollars.[7] It should be noted that withdrawing a month's income now, and hiding it under your mattress (or wherever you hide such valuables) is unlikely to have any effect on the nation's economy, especially as only a tiny percentage of U.S. citizens were worrying about such things in early 1998. However, if it suddenly occurs to a substantial percentage of the population to behave in this fashion in late 1999, then we'll have an old-fashioned run on the banks. We haven't seen this phenomenon since the days of the Depression; it's unclear whether the population or the banking officials or the government is capable of dealing with such a phenomenon in a rational fashion today. If you're concerned about this sort of thing, we recommend early action for obvious reasons.

Indeed, Fed officials recognize that a bank run is a possibility: Clyde Farnsworth, director of the Federal Reserve's bank operations and payment systems, said: "We are increasing the inventory [of cash] as a precautionary measure in case there is extra demand for currency as a result of the rollover into new year."[8] In fact, the Fed has planned to increase its cash holdings by 33 percent to $200 billion, up from its regular $150 billion holding. This is something we discuss in greater detail in Chapter 5. In a study done by the Gartner Group, 38 percent of information technology professionals said they may withdraw personal assets from banks and investment companies prior to the Year 2000.[9] The implications of that survey are straightforward.

Indeed, if you're really paranoid, you might wonder whether the dollar bills stuffed under your mattress will be worth anything. In Chapter 5, we'll briefly discuss the impact of Y2000 bugs on the overall banking system. Depending on the details of the situation, we could find the national economy faced with either a sudden, acute deflation or an equally sudden, government-initiated inflation. The primary experience of the Depression era in the United States was a substantial deflation, including falling prices in almost every sector of the economy. However, the experience in 1920s-vintage Germany and Austria, 1970s-vintage Brazil and Argentina, and now possible 1998 Russia, has been that of massive hyperinflation. Both scenarios might be a problem for those who wish to store their life's savings under their mattress, as we'll see in Chapter 5.

Fallback Advice: The One-Year Shutdown

Now the situation becomes much more serious: Suppose that the Y2000 problem is sufficiently serious that you're without work for a year? This is a good example of the point that we stressed in the previous chapter: There are qualitative differences as one increases the dimension of the Y2000 problem by an order of magnitude.

If a Y2000 problem causes your office to shut down for a month, and thereby causes a loss of income for a month, the natural instinct is to respond, "Well, it's a serious, annoying problem, but not one that requires me to change my life style." In the best of cases, you've got a month's income stuffed under the mattress; in a reasonable scenario, you can borrow money from a credit-card lender, or from sympathetic neighbors, friends, or parents; in the worst case, you simply accept some level of deprivation for a month.

But when the problem extends to a year, things are different. Parents may be willing to take their children back into the house for a year; after all, that has been a common experience with Generation-X children in recent times. But it's much more difficult to live off the generosity of friends and parents for a year; and it's extremely difficult to imagine living off a credit card for a year. What would you do if you were without income for a year?

Let's put this in the proper context. It's highly unlikely that your boss will come to you on January 3, 2000 and say, "Gee, we have a serious Y2000 problem, and we won't be able to employ you for quite a while—check back with us next year, and we should have everything back to normal by then." It's conceivable, we suppose, that a Y2000-induced problem could drag on from one month to the next, until a full year had transpired. But the most likely scenario is fairly simple: Your current employer shuts down unexpectedly, and it takes you a year to find a replacement job in the same industry. This could happen not only in the Y2000-sensitive industries like banking and insurance, but in any industry that suddenly discovers that it is highly dependent on other industries that have been bankrupted by Y2000 problems.

Such a scenario could result from a conscious decision, reached during the "triage" planning described earlier, to shut down a part of the business for which Y2000 repairs could not be scheduled. This kind of planning is beginning to take place in 1997 and 1998, and could even lead some organizations to shut these non-compliant parts of the company down, in an orderly fashion, a few weeks or months prior to December 31, 1999.

For those lucky enough to earn upper middle-class salaries in these Y2000-related (computerized) industries, the prospect of switching fields is probably not attractive; the 32-year-old Wall Street investment banker who enjoys a million-dollar salary probably doesn't want to trade it in for a modest $20,000 income running an antique shop. But the 45-year-old investment banker who has managed to stash away a large nest egg (the vulnerability of which is a separate topic, in Chapter 5), and who has grown weary of the pressure and the politics of a high-stress job, might want to take the opportunity to change his life style in 1998 or 1999, before things go awry. And the vast numbers of people who hold less-glamorous clerical, administrative, and service-oriented jobs—jobs that are nevertheless vulnerable to Y2000 failures—might have even less hesitation about finding an alternative life style.

Our advice: Take a look at your industry now, and make appropriate changes before it's too late. Some of the changes may be industry-related. You might decide that it's not a good idea to be a bank teller or an insurance agent as the century comes to an end. But it's also likely that the problems will be geographical: The situation could be more serious in banking communities like New York City. Ironically, Washington may turn out to be one of the best places to live and work, for even if all the government computers shut down for a year, the civil-service bureaucrats will still show up and sit at their desks. It has sometimes been difficult to tell if they were doing anything useful, and one could even make a plausible argument that they'll cause less trouble if they don't have access to their computers.

Washington has another interesting feature: It's the home of the Treasury Department, where fresh money can be printed if necessary. Obviously, the situation is more complex than just asking the Treasury Department to print some new dollar bills for all the government workers; but the fact remains, as we'll discuss in more detail in Chapter 5, that the federal government controls the currency and thus maintains some benevolent power over its employees (as well as various other groups towards whom it may feel benevolent). But state governments may not fare so well. A confluence of Y2000-related problems (including massive shortfalls in tax collections, for example) might exhaust the state treasuries and leave the legislators with no choice but to furlough large numbers of its employees. So it may well turn out that cities like Sacramento and Albany, Trenton and Austin are not the place to be, from a job-hunting perspective.

There's a further irony to all of this: One job category that probably will remain in high demand for several years after January 1, 2000 is that of computer programming. Whether or not you blame this group for having caused the Y2000 problem in the first place (most of them would tell you it was their predecessors' fault, or their bosses' fault), the fact remains that many organizations will be critically dependent on programmers, systems analysts, database-designers, networking and telecommunication experts, and various other specialties. Not only are these people considered valuable in today's good times (there was an estimated shortage of approximately 300,000 software specialists in the U.S. as this book was being written), but it's quite likely that an even larger number will be required for the post-Y2000 cleanup activities. Thus, if you don't mind walking into the eye of the storm, as it were, this might be a good time to consider getting a two-year degree, or some other credentials, in computer programming.

One last piece of advice: Make sure your resume is updated, and that you've printed or photocopied an adequate number of "hard" copies. It would be an irony of the worst kind if your resume was locked within your company's non-Y2000-compliant computer.

Fallback Advice: The Ten-Year Shutdown

Though the notion of being without work for a decade is incomprehensible for the vast majority of Americans, it bears noting that an unfortunate minority is already grimly familiar with the experience. The welfare class, the terminally unemployable, and the handicapped probably have a lot to tell the rest of us about the ordeal of going year after year without a real paycheck. Yet another irony: A Y2000 failure in the unemployment and welfare payment systems (including such things as food stamps) could create a particularly volatile situation for unemployed/welfare people who have no other financial resources at all.

If there should be such a Y2000 failure in these government-sponsored payment systems, we don't think it will last longer than a month or two; the political pressures for finding some remedy—any remedy—will be too great. Indeed, a minor version of this problem occurred years ago when computer systems of the U.S. Veterans' Administration collapsed. Because the problem could not be fixed quickly, and because the constituency was politically vocal, matters reached the point where administrators of the government agency began handwriting checks in whatever amount they thought appropriate. The subsequent "cleanup" operation to straighten out the accounting records was horrendous indeed.

It's conceivable, of course, that a massive Y2000 failure might cause one or more social welfare systems to be shut down completely. It's hard to predict in advance what the political mood of the country is going to be in the post-Y2000 years, but the current political climate in Washington and many state governments is already oriented towards cutbacks in the social services.

In any case, our primary concern here—notwithstanding the desire to provide care for the unemployed and welfare recipients who need it—is with the working-class majority. As we've already suggested in this chapter, most of the work-related problems are likely to involve minor disruptions of a couple days, or moderate disruptions of a month. A disruption of a year is serious indeed, but most of the victims of this level of Y2000-induced problem are probably not going to change careers, even though we've suggested that it could be a good idea. Instead, they'll seek other jobs in the same field. If you've been a bank teller for 10 years, there's a good chance that you'll want to continue your career as a bank teller. If your own bank shuts down, then you'll apply for a job at another bank—even if it means moving to a different city.

But what if the entire industry disappears? What if your profession vanishes? We hasten to note that banking is unlikely to disappear, no matter how serious the Y2000 problem turns out to be. Greenbacks might be printed in a different color; old banks might be replaced by new banks; but money and banking have survived for thousands of years, and will continue to exist in some form. The day-to-day operational activities of a bank teller might change, but it's reasonable to assume that someone who performs competently today in this profession will be able to adjust to the newly-defined bank-teller jobs that might emerge a few years hence.

We can't be so confident about the future prospects of other job categories—e.g., tax attorneys, especially those who specialize in dealing with the IRS. What if a Y2000 catastrophe brings about the downfall of the IRS and the entire hodgepodge of tax regulations, all of which is replaced with a simple flat-tax mechanism that can be calculated by any third-grade school child? The highly paid tax attorney may well find that there is no requirement for his expertise at all, nor will there be for another decade, until the inevitable tendency of bureaucrats to add exceptions and loopholes to the flat tax eventually brings about the need for a new generation of tax attorneys.

In recent years, there has been much political debate about the long-term disappearance of jobs and professions in the U.S. because of political agreements like NAFTA, and the gradual globalization of industry. But over the past 200 years, since the beginning of the Industrial Revolution, a much larger threat to many jobs and professions has been automation; and in the past 50 years, much of that automation has involved computers. Indeed, it has been argued that the major reason for massive layoffs of middle-level managers in the last recession was the realization that desktop computers had eliminated the need for human managers to process and refine raw data from the bottom-level workers, and then manually pass that data upward to senior managers.

In any case, it's almost a tautology that the workers in companies most vulnerable to Y2000 failures are those who are computer literate, to one degree or another. Why should we expect that any of their jobs might go away as a result of a massive Y2000 failure? The reason is that many of the computer-supported activities within organizations exist to provide a service that society has deemed necessary or desirable; if society changes its mind about such matters, then the service may no longer be needed, and the organization will cease to provide it.

This is particularly true of services that are imposed by government regulation, and that no organization would ever bother carrying out if not forced to. Take a look at the Human Resource Department in your company. The reason it's no longer called the Payroll Department is that it spends much of its time collecting data about the age, gender, nationality, race, and other details of its work force, in order to file appropriate reports with EEOC, OSHA, IRS, SSA, and various other government agencies. As noted earlier, it's hard to predict the political mood of the country if the Y2000 problem turns out to be as serious as we think it might be. But it's not impossible to imagine one or more government agencies collapsing (especially if they were incompetent, disorganized, on the verge of collapse before the Y2000 problem came along, and propped up almost entirely by their computer systems), along with the associated bureaucracy—both in the government and in the private-industry organizations who have been forced to submit to that bureaucracy.

A bizarre example will illustrate this point: One of the authors happened to be in South Africa in the early 1990s, when that country's government was taking its first steps to dismantle apartheid prior to Nelson Mandela's release. One of the government actions was to eliminate the racial classification scheme that had existed for decades, a scheme that defined each citizen as being a member of one of seven racial classifications (the consequences of which, throughout the rest of that citizen's life, were profoundly negative unless the classification was "white"). The decision was given front-page coverage in all the newspapers, as one might imagine, and one of the Johannesburg papers also carried a sarcastic editorial. What should be done, the newspaper asked, with the large group of government bureaucrats who had spent their entire professional life classifying humans into such categories? What industry could possibly use the skills these individuals had developed? Perhaps, said the editorial writer, the local South African mines could use people who could divide rocks into different colors, so that gold and diamonds might be more easily recognized; but that was ultimately rejected, and the editorial concluded by noting, with grim satisfaction, that these government bureaucrats had no useful role to play in society ever again.

Fortunately, we have no bureaucrats in the U.S. government with such offensive duties; but we do have bureaucrats, and many of them enforce regulations, make policies, and generally fill up their day with activities that might—in the lucid moments following a Y2000 crisis—be judged no longer necessary or appropriate. And the key point to remember here is that it's not just the government bureaucrats who are affected by the dismantling of such activities—it's all the people in private industry who have built careers around such activities. When Prohibition was ended in the 1930s, for example, how many jobs were lost?

It's also possible that certain careers or professions will vanish because of sharp changes in the fashion, taste, mood, or hobbies of society, following a massive Y2000 failure. Maybe we'll abandon baseball as the national hobby—a change that will not only be catastrophic for today's highly paid athletes, but also for those who sell peanuts and beer in the baseball stadium. Obviously, things like this are difficult, if not impossible, to predict; we merely wish to point out that such changes could occur.

Given that it's possible, what should we do about it? There's not much chance that you'll convince a highly paid baseball star to abandon his career, and take up farming; nor would such advice have any impact on the seller of peanuts and beer. We might advise the baseball star to start socking away most of his money in conservative investments, rather than spending it wildly; but the peanut-seller is probably operating on such a tight budget that he wouldn't listen to such advice. Indeed, it would be hard enough to persuade anyone in the middle-class or lower-middle-class to put away a month's expenses in cash, and a year's expenses in a savings account; suggesting that a 10-year nest egg should be squirreled away would be rejected as sheer lunacy.

Only the very affluent can consider a 10-year nest egg, and these individuals have the ironic problem of wondering where and how they can store their nest egg without running into Y2000 problems. Those of us who enjoy middle-class incomes may have to worry about the danger of losing a one-year nest egg if the local bank collapses, but that's a more manageable problem. As for the problem of a decade-long collapse in our chosen career or profession: The only intelligent thing we can recommend is flexibility. Certain professions may be safe (prostitutes, for example, will continue to flourish!), but given the pervasive impact of computers on society, most of us have no guarantee at all that our current experience or credentials will be worth much at all in the post-Y2000 years.

It's a sobering thought, but one that is beginning to be discussed independently of the Y2000 problem. Jim Taylor and Watts Wacker, for example, offer the following advice in their intriguing new book, *The 500 Year Delta*:[10]

> *How do you plan for the inevitability of disaster? By taking the blinders off. By seeing the world as it is. By counting on the certainty of uncertainty, rather than the certainty of certainty. Not by trying to wish the bad away, but by acknowledging that things are going to happen soon to you and your business—things that by all your current reasoning schemes are any-*

> *thing but reasonable. Here's an exercise that we have our clients do: Take out a sheet of paper. Write down the 10 worst things that could happen to your business in the next 500 days, the next 500 weeks, and then start acting as if they will happen, because in a chaos world they or something very similar will.*

Even more sobering is the impact that a pervasive Y2000 problem is likely to have on different generations. Just as the Great Depression had a different impact upon the generation of children, young adults, middle-aged people, and the elderly, we're likely to see a similar range of reactions to the Y2000 crisis. Freedom, as one of the folk songs of the 1960s lamented, means you've got nothing left to lose; and a younger generation with no savings and no mortgage and no retirement plan may well find a Y2000 crisis refreshingly liberating. An older generation is likely to have more to lose, and is likely to find it far more difficult to abandon a lifetime career because a Year-2000 bug has rendered it useless. The generational issues are indeed profound; we have neither the space nor the expertise to pursue the topic further in this book, but we strongly encourage you to study an eloquent and thought-provoking discussion in *The Fourth Turning*,[11] by William Strauss and Neil How. The Year-2000 crisis, in our opinion, is likely to be the formative event that will unleash what Strauss and Howe call a "fourth turning," the last example of which was the great stock market crash of October, 1929.

Jobs will certainly be at risk if the Y2000 bug causes such a "fourth turning," but that will be just the beginning. In the next chapter, we'll look at the impact on utilities: what happens if the lights don't work, and we have no oil or gas.

Endnotes

1. Capers Jones, quoted in "The Day The World Shuts Down," *Newsweek* magazine, June 2, 1997. Also, see Capers Jones, *The Global Impact of the Y2000 Software Problem* (Reading, MA: Addison-Wesley, 1998).
2. One of the authors visited Brazil annually during the late 1980s and early 1990s; inflation was so bad that a new currency was introduced on at least two occasions, thereby rendering the left-over currency one had from the previous year's visit entirely use-less. The Brazilians joked that you could tell how bad inflation was by watching to see whether people took buses or taxis; in one case, the fare determined at the beginning of the ride, but in the other case the fare is determined at the end of the ride—by which time it might have gone up!
3. One of the authors had the opportunity to visit Venezuela in 1994, during a prolonged period of high inflation and widespread dis-trust of the major banks. It was amazing to see that even the most modest of white-collar workers, including secretaries and clerks, all had U.S. dollar accounts in Miami-based U.S. banks. The stan-dard practice was to immediately convert one's paycheck into dol-lars and deposit it in the U.S. bank. Small amounts of cash, sufficient to cover a day's normal expenses, would then be with-drawn on a daily basis and converted back into the local currency.
4. For statisticians and economists, we note that the correlation between consumer confidence and the savings rate has been -0.31 since 1978, and -0.45 since 1990.
5. Note that this involves the concept of system dynamics, which we discuss in more detail in Appendix B. The U.S. economic system is indeed a highly dynamic system, and if one wants to manipulate it successfully, it's crucial to have a sense of the time-delay and feedback loops associated with actions being contemplated.
6. As reported by Bloomberg Business News on September 25, 1998.
7. Let's say, for the sake of argument, that your normal monthly liv-ing expenses are $3,000. If you kept that amount of money in a savings account for a year, at today's typical savings-account

interest rate of 3.25%, the interest earnings would be $97.50; that's roughly $8 per month, or a quarter a day.

8. As reported by Bloomberg Business News on August 19, 1998.
9. *Business Week*, January 26, 1998: "Will Your Bank Live to See the Millennium?"
10. Jim Taylor and Watts Wacker, *The 500 Year Delta: What Happens After What Comes Next?* (HarperCollins Publishers, 1997).
11. William Strauss and Neil Howe, *The Fourth Turning: What the Cycles of History Tell Us About America's Next Rendezvous With History* (New York: Broadway Books/Bantam Doubleday Dell, 1997).

Y2000 Impact on Utilities

Some people have asked why we are starting our hearings with the power industry. The answer is brutally simple: Without electricity nothing else works... Quite honestly, I think we're no longer at the point of asking whether or not there will be any power disruptions, but we are now forced to ask how severe the disruptions are going to be.

Senator Christopher J. Dodd, Vice-Chairman of the Special Senate Committee on the Year 2000, from his opening statement at the *June 12, 1998* hearings on the power industry.[1]

We have just on this platform representative people from utilities, from transportation, from finance, from telecommunications, and from small business. And this really is a joint effort we are all making.

President Bill Clinton, speech at the National Academy of Sciences, *July 14, 1998*

Introduction

Most Americans, except those in dire economic straits, take a number of comforts for granted. Among these are the common utilities: electricity, running water, gas for cooking, and either gas, oil, or electricity for heating and cooling. Like so many other comforts, we can do without them for a few days—indeed, we sometimes do so willingly, when camping or hiking. But take all this away for a month, and we would be a cold, odiferous, grumpy, miserable lot. Take them away for a year, and American society would be thrown backward a century, to the candle-lit days of the mid-19th century.

It's not a prospect that anyone relishes. Indeed, it's so unthinkable that it's easier not to think about it at all—but that's what we'll do in this chapter. Our primary focus is the possibility of Y2000-induced failures in the electrical utility industry. A similar investigation could be made of gas,[2] oil, and water—but it would be largely repetitious, so we've skipped it, in order to focus instead on suggesting some measures for coping with such a failure.

How Could Such Failures Happen?

The first thing to realize is that such failures already *have* happened, on numerous occasions—but they weren't caused by Y2000 bugs, and most of them have been relatively brief. Throughout the United States, we've all seen temporary failures in the delivery or supply of electricity, gas, oil, and even water. Most of the examples have been weather-related—e.g., a tornado in the south, or a blizzard in the north, knocks down power lines and cuts off electricity for a period of a couple days up to a week. Floods and problems in a city's sewage system or water supply have occasionally deprived communities of potable water for a few days. Industrial strikes, bad weather, and other problems have sometimes prevented delivery of heating oil. The list goes on...

The second thing to realize is that Y2000 problems can easily become "systemic," because of the ripple effect phenomenon. A local power outage in a small suburban town won't merit a mention on the national TV news. But if the entire city of New York or Chicago or Los Angeles suddenly has the lights turned off, then it *will* get some attention. And if it spreads beyond that ... well, if you're old enough, you may remember the chaos surrounding the 1965 blackout that shut down much of the Northeast; that was followed, a decade later, by the blackout in the summer of 1977. If you're too young to remember those events, think back to July 3, 1996, when a power outage knocked out electricity in parts of eight western states and two Canadian provinces; we'll discuss it in more detail below. More recently, a severe ice storm disrupted power in parts of eastern Canada, upstate New York, and Maine for several weeks.

The third thing to keep in mind, as you begin planning for all of this is that there are two fundamentally distinct aspects of a Y2000 problem with utilities: One has to do with the physical delivery of the utility to your home, and the other has to do with the business computer systems, operated by the utility companies, that determine whether they *should* deliver the utility service. We'll comment on both aspects below, but the latter one is fairly obvious: If the electric company (or the gas company, or the oil company ...) decides that you owe them $357 million and that you haven't paid your bill for six months, it could decide to shut off your power even if the generators are working just fine.

The Electrical System

With little doubt, electricity is one of the fundamental linch-pins of modern society: If power shuts down, a great deal of the rest of society shuts down with it.[3] And as noted previously, the nation's electrical generating system is definitely an area where ripple-effect problems can occur. Within the U.S., there are approximately 7,800 electrical generating units, of which approximately 110 are nuclear plants. They're all linked together in a grid—and even with redundancy and fail-safe mechanisms (which was improved after the 1965 and 1977 experiences), it's still possible for a problem in one part of the system to ripple elsewhere.

A good example of this is the outage that occurred on July 3, 1996. We've excerpted and condensed one of the news reports that was filed shortly after the outage; it will give you an idea of how massive the problem can be.

> *Across the West, a power outage knocked out electricity and phone service Tuesday to 1.5 million customers on a day of record heat above 100 in some places. The blackout shut down elevators, air conditioners and subway cars, and briefly darkened flashy casinos. The sporadic outages in at least eight states from California to Colorado, and into Canada,*

didn't last long — from 1 to 1 1/2 hours. But it was enough to reveal the vulnerability of the region's linked power grid.

Utility officials prepared today to investigate the outages, which came amid heavy usage in the heat wave. "Having an interconnected system really makes for more efficient use of our natural resources and keeps the cost down" said Lynn Baker, spokeswoman for Bonneville Power Administration, which oversees the power grid in the Pacific Northwest. "But it means when something goes wrong, it can cascade through the system."

At the center of the outage were three 500-kilovolt transmission lines that extend from the hydroelectric dams in the Northwest down to the Southwest. All three lines, which can supply up to 2.2 million homes, were knocked out at one point. Authorities were unsure whether the lines caused the outages or were affected by a problem elsewhere.

Elsewhere in California, hundreds of thousands lost power. Thrill seekers at the Del Mar Fair outside San Diego were surprised when the rides suddenly shut down. Subway cars in San Francisco's Bay Area Rapid Transit system stopped in their tracks. Los Angeles briefly shut down seven of its giant water pumps.

Some stores, banks and restaurants closed; others operated without cash registers, computers, lights and refrigeration. In northern Nevada, police in Reno and Sparks reported so many traffic lights out of service that they ran out of temporary stop signs. Casinos in Reno briefly lost power. Las Vegas was unaffected.

Most hospitals and emergency services were able to switch to auxiliary power. Federal Aviation Administration officials in Seattle said air traffic controllers were able to use backup power generators. Elevators were knocked out for about two hours at the 19-story Ambassador East condominiums in Denver.

The outage touched parts of Oregon, California, Idaho, Utah, Wyoming, Colorado, Arizona, and Nevada as well as the Canadian provinces of Alberta and British Columbia. At least 700,000 people lost power in northern Nevada, eastern Oregon and southern Idaho, and at least 500,000 customers were blacked out in California, utility officials said. In Boise, Idaho, most offices and state agencies sent workers home and banks locked their doors during a two-hour outage.

All of this from a power outage that lasted only one to two hours; think what the consequences would be if the outage lasted for the time periods we've focused on in this book: a few days, a month, a year, or a decade. It's quite unreasonable to assume that electricity would disappear from our lives for a decade; in the worst of all cases, the nation would rebuild its electrical infrastructure from scratch, if it had to. The most likely scenario, in our opinion, is the blackout that lasts for a couple days; a less likely scenario, but one we feel should not be ignored, is the one-month blackout. Why? Because it could take that long to fix whatever Y2000 problems are discovered in the hours after midnight on December 31, 1999; and it could take that long to restart the system. While most of us would agree that a two-three day blackout could be tolerated with only moderate discomfort, the prospect of a one-month failure obviously needs to be taken more seriously.

One of the things we must continue reminding ourselves about in discussions of this kind is the "ripple effect" phenomenon: Even if a utility company's Y2000 computers are *all* Y2000-compliant, is this enough? The North American Energy Reliability Council (NERC) summarized the problem in a June 12, 1998 report entitled "Y2K Coordination Plan for the Electricity Production and Delivery Systems of North America, Phase 1: June-September 1998 Initial Assessment and Coordination":[4]

> *The electric systems of North America are connected within four large Interconnections. The largest, the Eastern Interconnection, covers the eastern two-thirds of North America, including the United States and Canada. The second largest, the Western Interconnection, covers the western one-third of the U.S. and Canada, as well as a portion of the Baja California Norte region of Mexico. The other two Interconnections include 1) most of the state of Texas—also known as the ERCOT Region—and 2) the Quebec Interconnection, which covers the province of Quebec, Canada.*
>
> *Each of these four Interconnections is a highly connected network. A major disturbance within one part of an Interconnection will rapidly have an impact throughout the Interconnection and has the potential to cascade the effect to the entire Interconnection. The four Interconnections are for the most part independent from each other, because they are connected by comparatively small high voltage direct current (HVDC) electrical ties and do not interconnect synchronously. The one notable exception is the major HVDC tie lines from Hydro-Quebec into the Northeastern United States. Loss of these facilities and the*

power supply from Quebec can have a substantial impact on power delivery systems in the Northeastern portion of the United States.

Within each Interconnection, power production and delivery systems are highly interdependent. In general, systems are operated such that the loss of one facility, or in some cases two or three facilities, will not cause cascading outages. Y2K poses the threat that common mode failures (such as all generator protection relays of a particular model failing simultaneously) or the coincident loss of multiple failures may result in stressing the electric system to the point of a cascading outage over a large area.

This high level of interdependence within an Interconnection means that the robustness of the overall system needs to be tested against this new "contingency." An individualistic approach to the problem may not cover all potential problem areas, e.g., coordination with neighboring utilities, and, thus, could adversely affect operations within an Interconnection. An individual electric utility that invests tens of millions of dollars in solving Y2K problems could be affected in a major way by an outage initiated in neighboring systems that have not been as diligent. Therefore, preparation of the electricity power production and delivery systems in North America must be a coordinated team effort by those entities responsible for system reliability. All preventive programs do not have to be the same, but they do have to be coordinated. The industry will succeed or fail together in its readiness for Y2K.

Similarly, consider the dilemma faced by utilities that depend on coal, oil, or natural gas for the generation of their power: What happens if the raw materials are not available? Martyn Emery, a UK-based Y2000 expert, provided the following note as a sobering reminder of how interconnected everything seems to be:

> *In the UK, 8 miles from my home is a chemical / petroleum plant that processes UK oil requirements, it requires a crude oil tanker delivery every day, and within 2 days this has been refined and delivered to petrol stations. They really have no more than 4-5 days buffer. Directly next to the refinery is a power station that produces electricity for the region using the refined oil. Water companies can not operate without power.*
>
> *At a recent presentation by a petroleum company they estimated that 17% of all computer systems on a tanker were Non-y2k compliant, and they have a fleet of over 100 tankers. Changing and testing all the systems is impossible in the next 18 months, they simply do not have the dry dock facilities or labor resource. So they will not be able to get the approval from the Marine Safety Agency to issue seaworthy licenses and hence they will not be able to obtain insurance from 1.1.1999. The business impact is very significant.*

In the case of coal-, gas-, or oil-powered generators, perhaps all of this still will fall into the "nuisance" category. An expensive, serious, annoying nuisance, to be sure—but probably not life-threatening. But there's another source of electrical power, one we've learned to treat carefully after the famous incident at Three Mile Island in 1979: *nuclear* power generation. Interestingly, there's an entire government bureaucracy devoted to this area: the Nuclear Regulatory Commission. After first issuing a lengthy, but non-binding set of Y2K recommendations to the nuclear plants in December 1996 (NRC Notice 96-70[5]), the NRC followed up with a series of guidelines and workshops throughout 1997, culminating in a more detailed set of requirements published in May 1998, which we have excerpted on the following several pages.[6]

UNITED STATES NUCLEAR REGULATORY COMMISSION
OFFICE OF NUCLEAR REACTOR REGULATION
WASHINGTON, D.C. 20555-0001
May 11, 1998
NRC GENERIC LETTER NO. 98-01:
YEAR 2000 READINESS OF COMPUTER SYSTEMS AT NUCLEAR POWER PLANTS

Addressees

All holders of operating licenses for nuclear power plants, except those who have permanently ceased operations and have certified that fuel has been permanently removed from the reactor vessel.

Purpose

The U.S. Nuclear Regulatory Commission (NRC) is issuing this generic letter to require that all addressees provide the following information regarding their programs, planned or implemented, to address the year 2000 (Y2K) problem in computer systems at their facilities: (1) written confirmation of implementation of the programs and (2) written certification that the facilities are Y2K ready with regard to compliance with the terms and conditions of their licenses and NRC regulations.

Description of Circumstances

Simply stated, the Y2K computer problem pertains to the potential for date-related problems that may be experienced by a system or an application. These problems include not representing the year properly, not recognizing leap years, and improper date calculations. An example of a date-related problem is the potential misreading of "00" as the year 1900 rather than 2000. These problems can result in the inability of computer systems to function properly by providing erroneous data or failing to operate at all. The Y2K problem has the potential of interfering with the proper operation of computer systems, hardware that is microprocessor-based (embedded software), and software or databases relied upon at nuclear power plants. Consequently, the Y2K problem could result in a plant trip and subsequent complications on tracking post-shutdown plant status and recovery due to a loss of emergency data collection.

The Y2K problem is urgent because it has a fixed deadline. It requires priority attention because of the limited time remaining, the uncertain risk that the problem presents, the technical challenges presented, and the scarcity of resources available to correct the problem.

Existing reporting requirements under 10 CFR Part 21, 10 CFR 50.72, and 10 CFR 50.73 provide for notification to the NRC staff of deficiencies and non-conformances, and failures, such as some of those which could result from the Y2K problem in safety-related systems. To date, the NRC staff has not identified or received notification from licensees or vendors that a Y2K problem exists with safety-related initiation and actuation systems. However, problems have been identified in non-safety, but important, computer-based systems. Such systems, primarily databases and data collection processes necessary to satisfy license conditions, technical specifications, and NRC regulations that are date driven, may need to be modified for Y2K compliance.

Some examples of systems and computer equipment that may be affected by Y2K problems follow:

Security computers

Plant process (data scan, log, and alarm and safety parameter display system) computers

Radiation monitoring systems

Dosimeters and readers

Plant simulators

Engineering programs

Communication systems

Inventory control systems

Surveillance and maintenance tracking systems

Control systems

To alert nuclear power plant licensees to the Y2K problem, the NRC issued Information Notice (IN) 96-70, "Year 2000 Effect on Computer System Software," on December 24, 1996. In IN 96-70, the NRC staff described the potential problems that nuclear power plant computer systems and software may encounter as a result of the change to the new century and how the Y2K issue may affect NRC licensees. In IN 96-70, the NRC staff encouraged licensees to examine their uses of computer systems and software well before the turn of the century and suggested that licensees consider appropriate actions for examining and evaluating their computer systems for Y2K vulnerabilities. The NRC staff also incorporated recognition of the Y2K concern in the updated Standard Review Plan, NUREG-0800, Chapter 7, "Instrumentation and Control," dated August 1997, which contains guidance for the NRC staff's review of computer-based instrumentation and control systems.

At the Nuclear Utilities Software Management Group (NUSMG) Year 2000 Workshop, an industry workshop held in July 1997, some nuclear power plant licensees described their Y2K programs and gave examples of areas in which they had addressed Y2K issues in order to ensure the safety and operability of their plants on and after January 1, 2000. Some of the issues discussed were (1) the evaluation of the impact of the Y2K problem on plant equipment, (2) the assessment process involved in the identification of Y2K-affected components, vendors, and interfaces, (3) the development of Y2K testing strategies, and (4) the identification of budget needs to address the Y2K problem.

The Nuclear Energy Institute (NEI) met with NUSMG and nuclear plant utility representatives in August 1997 to formulate an industry-wide plan to address the Y2K issue. On October 7, 1997, representatives of NEI and NUSMG met with the NRC staff to discuss the actions NEI was taking to help utilities make their plants "Year 2000 ready." NEI presented a framework document that provides guidance for utilities to use in readying for the Year 2000. The framework document makes a distinction in terminology between "Y2K ready" and "Y2K compliant." "Y2K compliant" is defined as computer systems or applications that accurately process date/time data (including but not limited to calculating, comparing, and sequencing) from, into, and between the 20th and 21st centuries, the years 1999 and 2000, and leap-year calculations. "Y2K ready" is defined as a computer system or application that has been determined to be suitable for continued use into the year 2000 even though the computer system or application is not fully Y2K compliant. (These definitions have been adopted by the NRC for purposes of this generic letter.)

NEI/NUSMG issued the framework document NEI/ NUSMG 97-07, "Nuclear Utility Year 2000 Readiness," to all licensees in November 1997. The document recommends methods for nuclear utilities to attain Y2K readiness and thereby ensure that their facilities remain safe and continue to operate within the requirements of their license. The scope of NEI/ NUSMG 97-07 includes software, or software-based systems or interfaces, whose failure (due to the Y2K problem) would (1) prevent the performance of the safety function of a structure, system, or component or (2) degrade, impair, or prevent compliance with the nuclear facility license and NRC regulations.

Discussion

Diverse concerns are associated with the potential impact of the Y2K problem on nuclear power plants because of the variety and types of computer systems in use. The concerns result from licensees' reliance upon (1) software to schedule maintenance and technical specification surveillance, (2) programmable logic controllers and other commercial off-the-shelf software and hardware, (3) digital process control systems, (4) software to support facility operation, (5) digital systems for collection of operating data, and (6) digital systems to monitor post-accident plant conditions. The scope of NEI/NUSMG 97-07 includes the broad range of computers and software-based systems in a nuclear power plant. However, NRC Y2K concerns are limited to safety-related systems and other systems required by the nuclear power plant license or NRC regulations.

One application that is common to all power reactor licensees is the link between plant computers and the NRC's Emergency Response Data System (ERDS). This application performs the communication and data transmission functions that provide near real-time data availability to NRC and State incident response personnel during declared emergencies. The NRC is currently performing Y2K-related upgrades to ERDS, which will maintain the same communication protocol as the current system, with the exception that either 2-digit- or 4-digit-year fields will be accepted.

Those licensees that anticipate changes to their ERDS link should allow time in their schedules for retesting their systems. NRC contractors will support requests for testing on a "first-come, first-served" basis.

NEI/NUSMG 97-07 suggests a strategy for developing and implementing a nuclear utility Y2K program. The strategy recognizes management, implementation, quality assurance (QA) measures, regulatory considerations, and documentation as the fundamental elements of a successful Y2K project. The document contains examples currently in use by licensees and also recommends that the Y2K program be administered using standard project management techniques.

The recommended components for management planning are management awareness, sponsorship, project leadership, project objectives, the project management team, the management plan, project reports, interfaces, resources, oversight, and QA. The suggested phases of implementation are awareness, initial assessment (which includes inventory, categorization, classification, prioritization, and analysis of initial assessment), detailed assessment (including vendor evaluation, utility-owned or utility-supported software evaluation, interface evaluation, and remedial planning), remediation, Y2K testing and validation, and notification.

The QA measures specified in NEI/NUSMG 97-07 apply to project management QA and implementation QA. Regulatory considerations include the performance of appropriate reviews, reporting requirements, and documentation. Documentation of Y2K program activities and results includes documentation requirements, project management documentation, vendor documentation, inventory lists, checklists for initial and detailed assessments, and record retention. NEI/NUSMG 97-07 also contains examples of various plans and checklists as appendices, which may be used or modified to meet the licensee's specific needs and/or requirements.

It should be recognized that NEI/NUSMG 97-07 is programmatic and does not fully address all the elements of a comprehensive Y2K program. In particular, augmented guidance in the area of risk management, business continuity and contingency planning, and remediation of embedded systems is needed to fully address some Y2K issues that may arise in licensee program implementation. The NRC staff believes that the guidance in NEI/NUSMG 97-07, when properly augmented and implemented, presents an example of one possible approach for licensees when addressing the Y2K problem at nuclear power plant facilities.

Another document that provides a useful overview of the elements of an effective Y2K program is a guide issued by the Accounting and Information Management Division (AIMD), U.S. General Accounting Office (GAO), GAO/AIMD-10.1.14, "Year 2000 Computing Crisis: An Assessment Guide," September 1997. This guide is a distillation of the best practices of the Government and the private sector for dealing with the Y2K problem.

It should be noted that the guidance in NEI/NUSMG 97-07 and GAO/AMID-10.1.14 provides a framework only. Any Y2K program employed at a nuclear facility must be tailored to meet the specific needs and requirements of that facility and should, in general, be composed of the following phases: awareness, assessment, remediation, validation, and implementation. Completion of the Y2K program means the attainment of the program objectives, which could range from all computer systems and applications, including embedded systems, being Y2K compliant, to some being Y2K compliant and the remaining retired or with permanent and/or temporary compensatory measures or work-arounds in place. Also to be considered are the future maintenance requirements for keeping the systems and applications Y2K ready, for example, when the 'fixed date window' approach is used.

It is recognized that in spite of every reasonable effort by licensees to identify and correct Y2K computer system problems at their facilities, some software, applications, equipment, and systems may remain susceptible to the problem. Additionally, software, data, and systems external to the facility could potentially affect the facility adversely. Therefore, to ensure continued safe operation of the facility into the Year 2000 and beyond, contingency plans should be formulated for affected systems and equipment. The concept of Y2K readiness includes the planning, development, and implementation of appropriate contingency plans or compensatory actions for items that are not expected to be Y2K compliant or ready and to address the possible impact of unidentified items and their effect on safe plant operation.

Because of the limited time remaining in which to address the Y2K problem, at some facilities it may be necessary that some remediation and implementation activities be performed during normally scheduled plant outages in order to avoid additional outages to effect these activities. Hence, licensees should plan for this work accordingly. The NRC staff notes that unless the majority of the Y2K program remediation, validation, and implementation activities are completed at a facility by mid-1999, leaving only a few such activities scheduled for the third and fourth quarters of 1999, the facility may not be Y2K ready by the year 2000.

In the course of implementing the Y2K program, problems could be identified that potentially affect the licensing basis of the plants. In certain cases, license amendments may be needed to address the problem resolution. Licensees should plan to submit such license amendments to the NRC on a timely basis. The utility Y2K programs and schedules should have the flexibility to accommodate such an eventuality. In addition, licensees are reminded that any changes to their facilities that affect their current licensing basis must be reviewed in accordance with existing NRC requirements and the change properly documented. Finally, we strongly encourage licensees to share information regarding identified remediation and implementation activities in order to maintain the likelihood that all Y2K problems are identified. We understand that Owners' Groups are implementing this and we encourage this effort.

Required Response

In order to gain the necessary assurance that addressees are effectively addressing the Y2K problem with regard to compliance with the terms and conditions of their licenses and NRC regulations, the NRC staff requires that all addressees submit a written response to this generic letter as follows:

(1) Within 90 days of the date of this generic letter, submit a written response indicating

whether or not you have pursued and are continuing to pursue a Y2K program such as, or similar to, that outlined in NEI/NUSMG 97-07, augmented appropriately in the areas of risk management, contingency planning, and remediation of embedded systems. If your program significantly differs from the NEI/NUSMG guidance, present a brief description of the programs that have already been completed, are being conducted, or are planned to ensure Y2K readiness of the computer systems at your facility(ies). This response must address the program's scope, assessment process, plans for corrective actions (including testing and schedules), QA measures, contingency plans, and regulatory compliance.

(2) Upon completing your Y2K program or, in any event, no later than July 1, 1999, submit a written response confirming that your facility is Y2K ready, or will be Y2K ready, by the year 2000 with regard to compliance with the terms and conditions of your license(s) and NRC regulations. If your program is incomplete as of that date, your response must contain a status report, including completion schedules, of work remaining to be done to confirm your facility is/will be Y2K ready by the year 2000.

Address the written reports to the U.S. Nuclear Regulatory Commission, Attention: Document Control Desk, Washington, D.C. 20555-0001, under oath or affirmation under the provisions of Section 182a, Atomic Energy Act 1954, as amended, and 10 CFR 50.54(f). In addition, submit a copy to the appropriate regional administrator.

To get a sense of why the NRC *should* be monitoring the nuclear plants, consider the following snippet from the March 31, 1998 issue of the *Augusta Chronicle:*[7]

> *Savannah River Site could be punished with a funding cut for failing to fix its Year 2000 problem in time for a federal deadline, says an agency tracking the government's massive computer conversion project. . . .*
>
> *SRS has 494 systems that control nuclear waste processes and other critical work that must run smoothly to ensure the safety of workers, surrounding communities and the environment. Of those, all but five will have been fixed a year from today, plant officials say.*
>
> *They should be fixed by the end of October 1999.*
>
> *"That still gives us 60 days," Mr. Giusti said. . . .*

Nuclear plants are not the only ones with Y2K schedules extending into the summer or fall of 1999. For example, California's Pacific Gas and Electric utility posted the following on its Web site:[8]

> *Pacific Gas and Electric Company has established a dedicated team of business and technical experts to address the potential impacts of this problem. Currently, we are focusing our efforts to be Year 2000 ready on those software and embedded systems, which are critical to our business. We expect to complete remediation of the critical software systems by the end of 1998 and to complete testing of these systems by the third quarter of 1999.*
>
> *PG&E has recently completed an enterprise-wide inventory of all embedded systems to assess the degree of Year 2000 compliance. We expect to complete assessment of all critical embedded systems and to repair or replace those systems found to be non-compliant by the fourth quarter of 1999.*

And Chicago's Commonwealth Edison also plans to be finished in the fourth quarter of 1999, according to a September 15, 1998 article in Reuters-C/NET:[9]

> *Chicago-based electric utility Commonwealth Edison said yesterday that it planned to spend a total of $60 million toward making its systems Year 2000 compliant and was in the second quartile of electric utilities in terms of progress on the project. . . .*
>
> *... "mission critical" systems will be fully compliant by the second quarter of 1999 and the entire project will be complete by the fourth quarter of 1999. . . .*
>
> *The utility has 3.4 million customers in the northern fifth of Illinois.*

Whether these examples are the exceptions or the norm continues to be a matter of intense debate throughout the power industry, the press, and the community of Y2K consultants. On September 17, 1998, the North American Electric Reliability Council (NERC) presented a report[10] to the Department of Energy that provided an upbeat conclusion, based on an extensive survey of the U.S. power industry:

> *The initial findings of this report are that the impacts of Y2K on electrical systems appear to be less than first anticipated. With continued work toward finding and fixing components that may be Y2K deficient and with properly coordinated contingency planning, the operating risks presented by Y2K can be effectively mitigated to achieve reliable and sustained operation of electric systems into the Year 2000.*

But industry consultant Dick Mills observed, in a subsequent critique of the report,[11] that

> *Neither assertion is substantiated by the data in the report. The first assertion amounts to little more than hand waving. The report does not*

> *say how many faults were expected, how many were found, or what the basis of the expectations was. In this suspicious era, it sounds like prevarication.*
>
> *The second comment is presumably substantiated by the survey results but it is not. Rational people can look at those results and conclude almost anything. In my opinion, the results don't substantiate any conclusions period. If there is any analysis in the report that bridges the gap between the surveys and this conclusion, I can't find it.*

Meanwhile, industry consultant Rick Cowles provided a more detailed critique of the NERC report:[12]

> *Only 64 percent of the "bulk power entities" under the NERC umbrella have a written Y2K plan. It's impossible to develop metrics in the absence of a plan, schedules, and goals with which to measure progress against. A rhetorical question emerges: How can any company even begin to provide metrics to a survey as extensive as NERC's without a plan to measure against? The implication is that 36% of the responding companies were literally flying by the seat of their pants in providing response to the NERC survey. Additionally, there has been no qualitative assessment of the existing plans. . . .*
>
> *Seventy-four of the survey respondents reported that their Y2K inventories were between 90 and 100 percent complete. In reality, the Y2K inventory process is an ongoing endeavor for the life of the project, and will most likely never be completed in a large enterprise. Even accepting the reported percentage of 74%, this is a troubling statistic when put in the frame of 26% of the "bulk power entities" that are still actively engaged in the first stage of a Y2K program. . . .*

Thirty-seven have not progressed beyond 50 percent assessment. Next to remediation and testing, assessment is the most resource intensive phase of the program. Much time must be spent in verifying component level Y2K compliance with vendors (if available) and verification / validation testing for mission critical components and systems (vendor statements of compliance not withstanding). NERC recommends completion of this phase within the next six weeks. This is not merely an aggressive goal, it's simply unrealistic. Again, this recommendation underscores a basic misunderstanding of both the real world dynamics and organizational nature of the Y2K issue.

More than half (52 percent) of the "bulk power entities" are less than 30 percent complete on remediation / testing. (It's also important to note that remediation and testing efforts can not be lumped together. "Testing" needs to be completed on a component level basis (for business / process critical items), and then conducted in an integrated manner at a system level). Various Y2K program management case studies have concluded that testing is clearly 60 to 70 percent of the total Y2K program effort. . . .

And Senator Robert Bennett, the Chairman of the Senate Y2000 Committee, characterized the NERC report as a combination of "good news/bad news":[13]

. . . Before we get started, I would like to take a moment to follow up on our June 12th utilities hearing. As you may recall, we were unable to determine at that hearing whether "the lights will stay on" because there had been no industry-wide Year 2000 assessment of the industry. I am pleased to report that the North American Electric Reliability Council ("NERC") plans to re-

> *lease its industry assessment today. My reading of advance results suggests that there is both "good news" and "bad news."*
>
> *The good news is that this is the most comprehensive Year 2000 assessment the Committee has seen to date in any industry sector. Such assessments are needed desperately in other industry sectors. NERC should be commended for this monumental undertaking. The bad news is that progress continues to be slow. One third of the electric utility companies have still not completed assessment of their computers and embedded devices—a task that should have been completed a year ago. The hard part—fixing, testing, and implementing—is yet to come. Nevertheless, the NERC study represents an excellent starting point with which to monitor Year 2000 progress over the next critical months. I assure you that this Committee will be watching closely.*

By the way, disruptions in the electrical system are typically exacerbated by extreme weather conditions; the July 3, 1996 failure described above was partially caused by a massive 100-degree heat wave that blanketed much of the western United States. The Year-2000 problem begins, of course, on January 1st; if it happens to be a cold winter, much of the middle and northern U.S. could be drawing large loads of electricity for heating purposes. And as if that wasn't enough, it turns out that the year 2000 will also be a period of intense solar flares, which have been a cause of severe electrical disruptions in the past. The subject of solar flares, as you might imagine, is far beyond the expertise of the authors of this book; however, if you have access to the Internet, we invite you to browse http://www.sel.

noaa.gov/info/Cycle23.html to see the U.S. government's summary of flare activity in 2000-2005; you should also browse http://www.pathfinder.com/@@yQsh2AUABc4RMSCY/time/magazine/domestic/1996/960909/space.html to see an article in the September 9, 1996 issue of *Time* that warns about the impact of flare activity on the nation's electrical system.[14]

How Can You Tell How Your Utility Company Is Doing?

It's important to know how the utility industry as a whole is faring, because the problems of one utility company can have a ripple-effect problem on other parts of the electric power grid. But for obvious reasons, most of us are more concerned about the progress and Y2000 status of our own *local* utility company than the fate of a utility company 3,000 miles away. Thus, the average citizen might mutter to himself, "It's very interesting to hear Senator Bennett's assessment of the overall industry, but how can I tell what's happening in my own back yard?"

The first step, of course, is to contact your utility company and ask them to describe their Y2000 status. Call the main telephone number and ask for the Y2K or Y2000 department. If there is no such department, then ask for the public relations department. If you find that nobody knows what you're talking about, or that nobody is willing to talk to you, it doesn't necessarily mean that they're ignoring the Y2000 problem; it probably means that the utility company has simply decided to "stonewall" you, rather than exposing itself to potential legal problems by making a statement about Y2000 compliance that turns out not to be true. In addition, the utility may have decided that it lacks the resources to spend a substantial amount of time discussing the Y2000 problem with thousands, or even tens of thousands, of customers. If this strikes you as a poor marketing approach, remember: The utility company is a monopoly, and they know that you have nowhere else to take your business.

If you can't get any answers on your own, then look for help. Find, or create, a Y2000 community-awareness group in your local area; contact your town, county, or state elected officials and ask them to make inquiries on behalf of the entire community. Contact your local bank, Chamber of Commerce, or other business organizations—after all, they should have a vested interest, just as you do, in determining whether electric power will still be available on January 1, 2000. The utility company may be able to ignore, or stonewall, an individual; but it can't easily stonewall an entire community.

If you can persuade a representative from the utility company to attend a community meeting, the chances are that you'll get a statement something like this:[15]

> *Pacific Gas and Electric Company has established a dedicated team of business and technical experts to address the potential impacts of this problem. Currently, we are focusing our ef-*

> *forts to be Year 2000 ready on those software and embedded systems, which are critical to our business.*
>
> *We expect to complete remediation of the critical software systems by the end of 1998 and to complete testing of these systems by the third quarter of 1999. PG&E has recently completed an enterprise-wide inventory of all embedded systems to assess the degree of Year 2000 compliance. We expect to complete assessment of all critical embedded systems and to repair or replace those systems found to be non-compliant by the fourth quarter of 1999.*
>
> *Also, we are developing contingency plans to be implemented if PG&E, or any significant third party on whom PG&E relies in operating its business, fails to achieve Year 2000 compliance.*

On the surface, a statement like this looks perfectly reasonable; in essence, it says "we're aware of the problem, we're working on it, and we expect to be finished in time." However, as Y2K consultant Roleigh Martin[16] has observed, there are some interesting questions that one can ask in order to get a better assessment of whether the utility *will* finish in time:

Have you finished the inventory of your software and embedded systems? Note that PG&E's statement indicates that they have done so. A utility company that cannot say "yes" to this question is in no position to express confidence that they'll finish their task in time—for they don't know how much work needs to be done. If you really want to test the credibility of the utility company, you might also ask, "May we see a copy of your inventory report?" An individual consumer who asks such a question will be politely stonewalled, of course, but it might be more difficult to do so if the question comes from a state legislator or regulatory authority.

Have you finished the assessment of your software and embedded systems, in order to determine which ones are compliant and which ones are not? Note that the PG&E statement, which we downloaded from the company's Web site on October 27, 1998, implies that the assessment of "critical software systems" has been finished (because the overall remediation work on those systems is scheduled to finish by the end of 1998), but that the assessment of "critical embedded systems" was *not* finished. If the assessment has not been completed, then the organization doesn't accurately know how many systems need to be repaired or replaced; this calls into question the credibility of the schedule and completion-date promised by the organization.

Have you placed orders for those embedded systems that need to be replaced?

Have you received firm delivery orders from the manufacturers of those embedded systems that need to be replaced?

These last two questions are perhaps the most crucial ones. By early 1999, almost all utilities will be able to honestly answer "yes" to the questions about inventory and assessment of their embedded systems. But if they haven't placed their orders, and if they haven't received a firm delivery date, they may find that their entire Y2000 schedule is in jeopardy—simply because the Y2000-induced demand for replacement parts is *much* higher than what the "parts" industry is capable of supplying under normal conditions. To illustrate this point, consider this excerpt from an October 18, 1998 newspaper article describing Y2000 activities in upstate New York:

> *Niagara Mohawk Power Corp. has already identified digital control units at some of its generating stations that must be replaced if the facilities are to continue running in 2000. Some of the new devices will not arrive until mid-1999, because just about every utility in the country has placed a similar order, NiMo spokesman Gerald Rockower said.*[17]

Additional Y2000 Problems for Utility Companies

Everything we've discussed so far is concerned with the actual creation and distribution of electrical power. But as noted above, problems could also occur even if this part of the utility industry completely avoids Y2000 software bugs. Electricity—and, in a similar fashion, oil and gas and water—are delivered to customers for a price; we all get a monthly bill, and the utility company expects us to pay that bill in a timely fashion. We may be given various payment options (e.g., spreading payments over a period of months, in order to reduce the impact of high usage during summer months), and we may have occasional interactions with the utility when we move into a new home, or switch from oil heat to gas heat. All of this, of course, involves interactions with the business computer systems within the utility company; and these computers are obviously vulnerable to the kind of software problems discussed in Appendix A.

One of our concerns involves billing: A faulty utility computer might send you a multi-million dollar bill, or it might come to the conclusion that you're a deadbeat who never pays his bills. But any number of other problems could occur: An aberrant computer could accidentally delete your database record, so that the utility company doesn't even know that you exist; or it could come to the mistaken conclusion that you asked to have your service terminated.

If problems of this kind occur, the important question is: Will the decision to shut off your service be made by a human or a computer? In the case of a large utility company—e.g., the gas/electric utility for a metropolitan area—it's easy to imagine that all of this has been automated, because the numbers are too large for humans in the utility's Customer Service department to deal with. Thus, we might expect a wave of automated service shut-offs in the event of a Y2000 problem; but the hue and outcry associated with such an action would probably be large enough that most utilities would be forced to quickly program an "over-ride" into their system to disregard any such actions. (However, even this could take a few days or weeks to program and test and install within the computer system.)

In today's normal operating conditions, we don't know whether the decision to shut off electric, gas, or water service is made automatically or manually in our own city, let alone yours. You might want to call your Customer Service department to find out; we attempted to do so in New York City, but (as is common with calls to the customer-service department of banks, automobile companies, and many other large firms these days), our call was answered by a puzzled representative who had never heard of the Y2000 problem, and who forwarded us on to another representative who was equally puzzled, who forwarded us to another department, where an automated voice-mail system recorded our question and never got back to us. C'est la vie.

Our real concern is the smaller utility services, in the suburban and rural areas. Even in these cases, the electric and gas utilities are somewhat centralized; but other utilities—especially the delivery of heating oil, for example—are likely to be in the hands of smaller companies, who service a limited number of customers. These companies are likely to have far less sophisticated computer systems, and are likely to encounter far more serious Y2000 problems—indeed, it's far more likely that in mid-1998, as this book is being revised, they're completely unaware of the problem. The local oil-heating distributor is more likely to have a human involved in any decision to shut off your deliveries, and one might expect more humane decisions to be made in the event of a Y2000-induced billing mistake. On the other hand, the delivery schedules in such companies are also computerized; a Y2000 bug could easily cause your house, and a hundred others, to be left off the list for regularly scheduled deliveries of winter heating oil.

Fallback Advice: The Two-Day Failure

Two or three days with no heat or electricity is manageable, right? Indeed, if you knew exactly when the problem would occur, you could plan ahead for it: Empty out the freezer, stock up on candles and batteries, make plans to eat out, and so forth. Unfortunately, if a minor Y2000-related utility problem does occur, there's no guarantee that it will happen at the stroke of midnight on New Year's Eve, 1999. Depending on the nature of the problem, it could occur at almost any point during the year; for example, a shut-down caused by a Y2000-related billing problem might occur on January 31st or February 29th; a problem with delivery of your heating oil could occur in the middle of January, or in the middle of February.

Nevertheless, the basic precautions mentioned above do make sense. Suburban and rural residents are already aware of the desirability of having candles and batteries, as well as some extra wood for the fireplace, in the event of a short-term utility outage. The Canadian/New England ice storm of early 1998 also emphasized the usefulness of a modestly priced generator, with sufficient fuel to power the basic appliances in the home for a few days. Unfortunately, it's the city-dwellers who are likely to be the least prepared; after all, the lights *never* go out in New York City... except in 1965, and 1977, and perhaps in 2000.

A small point to keep in mind: If problems with the electrical industry are at all widespread, then you should be prepared for brownouts, “spikes,” and voltage fluctuations in the power supply, quite possibly for several weeks after the initial problems. A colleague of ours lives in northern Nevada, and works as an independent computer consultant; when the July 3, 1996 power outage occurred, it zapped three of his desktop and laptop computers, despite the surge suppresser in the “power strip” he had purchased in the local hardware store.

Along those same lines, we got an email note from Rob Jones, who reviewed a draft of the first edition of this book and commented:

> *...surge protectors/transient suppressors (the kind the hardware store typically sell) should be replaced about once a year. Many people are surprised when suddenly their equipment is damaged. But often these devises have been taking a beating and saving the equipment far more often than they might realize. These are not like fuses (in serial with the equipment) but are a bypass for spikes (in parallel)... So when they wear out, instead of preventing the equipment from running (like a fuse or circuit breaker) they simple cease to provide a bypass for future spikes. They silently stop working. I think a lot of people are putting more faith in old surge suppressors than they should. It doesn’t take Y2K outages to destroy your electronics, a good thunder-storm will do.*

Fallback Advice: The One-Month Failure

If the lights go out or the gas gets shut off for a month, it’s more likely to be the result of a major disagreement with the billing department of your utility than a Chernobyl-style meltdown. The distinction may sound academic: A month without utilities would be unpleasant, regardless of the reason it happens.

But if the problem is that a faulty computer thinks you owe seven zillion dollars for last month's electric power, it's possible you can rectify the problem by dealing with a human being. If you're concerned about the possibility of this kind of Y2000-induced failure, then one of the most important things you can do is ensure that you have not only the current utility bill, and a canceled check to confirm that it was paid, but also the appropriate bills and payment records for the last several months. You may need to show all of this to an intelligent, sympathetic clerk at the gas company or electric company, and confirm that you're an honest bill-paying citizen, in order to get your utilities restored. There's nothing complicated about this, of course, but it's amazing how many people throw away the bills once they're paid, and manage to lose all of their canceled checks. Forewarned is forearmed.

The notion of actually speaking to a utility company clerk, face-to-face, may not seem strange to suburbanites, or residents of small towns; but it's unlikely that any city-dweller has ever done such a thing. For most of us, a call to a utility company—or, for that matter, the bank or the phone company or any other large institution—means that we interact with a confusing series of voice-response messages ("if you're calling about a problem with your bill, press 1; if you want to discontinue your service, press 2") before ever talking to a human. And if we do speak with a human, we never learn his or her name—and it's never the same person we spoke to last time we called. In some cases, large organizations deliberately design their customer-service systems this way: If you ask the customer service person for their name, they'll tell you that they're not allowed to give you that information. Even if you do find that you're discussing your billing problem with Joe Shmoe, you'll discover that it's impossible to call the customer service department and ask to speak specifically with Joe. You'll be told—typically by another automated voice-response system—that you can only speak with "the next available representative," whoever that turns out to be.

If that's the way things work in your utility company, we offer our sympathy—it works that way in New York City, where one of us lives, too. But it's worth testing the system to see how it works, and whether the automated anonymity can be circumvented. The point of all this discussion is that it may turn out to be *very* valuable to have a direct, human contact within these vast organizations, should there be a Y2000-related problem that causes your utility service to be disrupted. Sometime in the middle of 1999, we suggest that you nurture a personal relationship with someone at your electric company, gas company, and oil-heating company. Call someone to get an explanation of your bill in mid-1999 (even if you understand your bill completely), and then send a thank-you note to the customer-service representative to show how much you appreciate the assistance. Send a note to his or her supervisor, send a birthday card, send a box of candy, send... well, you get the idea.

All of this may or may not help in the event of a month-long shutdown of utility services. As for other strategies: well, stockpiling may or may not be relevant, depending on your situation. You can't stockpile electricity or gas, but you may be able to stockpile oil to some minor extent. Make sure the tank is completely full toward the end of December 31, 1999 and then try to get it topped off every time it falls to the halfway mark.[18] Batteries and candles may be worth stockpiling, too, though it's doubtful that many of us will be willing to put up with reading by candle light for more than a month.

Indeed, this is the real question: When do we reach the point where we decide that we can't stand it any more—and what options do we have at that point? As you can imagine, it's extremely unlikely that anyone is going to make a proactive decision to move to a different location in mid-1999 because of the possibility of a utility company failure in the post-2000 era. After all, who's to say whether such failures are more likely in a big city like New York or a small city like Boise? Who can really say whether the suburban residents of Long Island, New York are more vulnerable than the ranchers in Montana? Wherever we happen to live, we're likely to stay put—as long as utility-company failures are the only form of Y2000 disasters we're concerned about.

It's also unclear whether we'll be able to tell that we're entering a month-long failure at the outset. If there's a physical failure in an electrical generating facility (e.g., a generator burns out because of an errant computer or, God forbid, a radiation leak occurs in a nuclear power facility), then perhaps you'll see an official announcement that power won't be restored for a certain number of weeks or months. But if the disruption is caused by a billing system that erroneously decides to terminate your service because of non-payment, you could be faced with a day-to-day battle with the customer service representatives to get things restored. Keep in mind that you won't be the only one dealing with such a problem; everyone else in your neighborhood or city may complaining about it, too, which may keep the Customer Service department from fixing *your* problem for quite a while.

Bottom line: If a problem of this magnitude occurs, you're not going to be able to do much about it. Depending on where you live, what the weather is like, and how much you're able to stockpile, you may be able to survive a few weeks of utility service disruption. We figure that a month is about the most that anyone can be expected to put up with before some drastic action needs to be taken; it could happen even sooner if an entire city is without heat or electricity. But there is the possibility that banks and businesses and government agencies will be able to maintain operations, while a miserable 10 percent of the population carries on a battle with the utility company to restore their service.

In any case, if it comes to this, you should be prepared to leave town until the situation is resolved. Make sure that your network of relatives, college roommates, and other friends is intact; you may need to move in with them for a few weeks. Make sure that you've got enough money—in cash, or in whatever bank is functioning in the post-2000 era—so that you can afford to leave town without hitch-hiking.

Fallback Advice: The One-Year Failure

A one-year failure, in our opinion, is *not* likely to be the result of the billing mixup we described earlier. If a situation like this persisted for more than a month or two—especially if it's fairly pervasive, so that large segments of the population are affected—is likely to result in drastic action by the utility companies themselves, or by government regulation. One can almost imagine Congress passing the Electrical Relief Act of 2001, decreeing that all citizens are entitled to electric power regardless of the status of their bills.

So a problem of this magnitude—which we think is unlikely, but nevertheless minimally possible—would almost certainly be associated with a physical/mechanical shutdown of the utility provider in the affected area. If there are massive power failures throughout the entire national grid, for example, then it's conceivable that the repair effort could be so expensive and time-consuming that certain rural areas will be put at the bottom of the priority list. If the distribution network itself is damaged or rendered inoperable, then it may be impossible to switch electrical power from a region that has escaped Y2000 problems to one whose local generation capability has collapsed because of a Y2000 failure.

One option worth considering is the installation of a "permanent" form of alternative energy, such as a windmill or solar-panel system. Interestingly, the state of California has made this option particularly attractive, by subsidizing 50 percent of the cost of such systems as part of an overall plan to deregulate the power industry within the state. The California Energy Commission summarized the plan as follows:[19]

> *On March 20, 1998, California consumers and small businesses began reserving money to help them install renewable energy equipment—and also saving up to half the cost.*
>
> *As a part of deregulating the state's electricity industry, $54 million was set aside by the California legislature to help homeowners and other electricity users install what are called "emerging renewable technologies." The first $10.5 million of that fund became available March 20, 1998, from the California Energy Commission on a first-come, first-served basis.*
>
> *The California Emerging Renewables Buy-Down Program will initially pay 50 percent of the system cost or three dollars a watt (whichever is less) for the installation of eligible renewable energy generation equipment to primarily offset the customer's electric load. Any excess power can be sent back into the power grid...*
>
> *Remote, self-contained energy systems that are not grid-connected do not qualify. The offer is good only for systems installed in the service territories of the state's largest three investor-owned utilities—PG&E, SCE and SDG&E.*

Four types of renewable power generation qualify for funding under the program, including:

- *Fuel cells that convert renewable fuels into electricity.*
- *Photovoltaic systems—also called PVs—that directly convert sunlight to electricity.*
- *Solar thermal electric technology, that converts sunlight into heat to power an electrical generator.*
- *Wind turbines of 10 kilowatts or less.*

For those living in urban centers across the country, the "alternative energy" option is unlikely to be available. Thus, in the unlikely event of a one-year outage, the "escape" option mentioned earlier will be even more necessary. Indeed, the real question is whether things will still be intact when you return. Think, for a moment, about the plans you make when leaving your house behind for a one-month vacation, versus the plans you would have to make if you were leaving the country for a year. And think about how much more difficult such planning would be if you had to assume the absence of heat, light, water, or gas during that absence. Now factor in the likelihood that your neighbors will be gone, too; at some point, for example, you might have to worry about the possibility of looting or break-ins.

One thing is for certain: The people who rent are going to be in much better shape than the people who own, in a scenario like this. Those who rent have the option—in the worst case—of piling themselves and their family and their most precious possessions into the car and driving away; if they default on their rent and lose the rest of their household possessions, it won't be a severe disaster. Those who own their homes can also drive away in the family car, but they leave behind the largest part of their financial equity. If they return a year later and find that the house has been ransacked, trashed, or burned to the ground, it will be that much more difficult to recover.

Is anything like this even remotely possible? That depends on your opinion about two things: first, the likelihood of a Y2000 breakdown; and second, your opinion about the possibility of a social breakdown following a Y2000 breakdown. As we've said, we think it's highly unlikely that we'll see a one-year disruption of utility services; and we think it's particularly unlikely in the urban areas, if for no other reason than the political pressure that will be imposed to restore such services. On the other hand, if Y2000-induced utility breakdowns are compounded by breakdowns in banking, communications, and other areas discussed in this book, then the social reaction—especially in the urban areas!—could deteriorate rather quickly. A month without power, in the middle of winter, is not something that the residents of New York City, Boston, Chicago, or any of the other northern cities of the US are likely to accept with good humor and civic spirit. The residents of these cities are already understandably grumpy about the circumstances in which they live; a three-month, or six-month, or nine-month utility disruption could easily lead to rioting in the streets.

Endnotes

1. The full text of Senator Dodd's remarks are available on the Internet at http://www.senate.gov/~dodd/2000/980612.html.
2. If you're concerned about Y2K problems in the natural gas industry, you should visit the web site of the American Gas Association (http://www.aga.com/gio/july98amgas/ag7y2k.html), where a July 1998 posting said, in part, "A utility's gas distribution function relies on countless numbers of microcode, firmware and real-time operating systems—all sending out a wide variety of signals, instructions and data. And to complicate matters even further, checking the Y2K compliance of these functions might necessitate shutting down operations entirely."
3. Several people who reviewed an early draft of the first edition of this book argued that *water* is even more fundamental. For most citizens, especially those living in urban centers, a supply of fresh water also depends on electricity and Y2K-compliant computers. Water travels to most consumers through a vast, complex network of rivers, lakes, reservoirs, and aqueducts, which use computers to regulate the flow. Once in the general vicinity where it will be consumed, the water must pass through a purification process (computer-controlled), and then pumped into a holding tank, from which it can be released into the consumer's faucet.
4. See http://www.nerc.com/y2k/y2kplan.html for the full report.
5. You can find this information on the Internet at http://ftp.fedworld.gov/pub/nrc-gc/in96070.txt and, as you'll see in the NRC document, you can visit their Web site and subscribe to an Internet mailing list for updates.
6. The document is also available on the Internet at http://www.nrc.gov/NRC/GENACT/GC/GL/1998/gl98001.html .
7. See http://augustachronicle.com/stories/033198/tec_124-2873.shtml for the text of the article.
8. See http://www.pge.com/resources/compliance/ for more details.
9. See http://www.news.com/News/Item/0,4,26141,00.html?st.ne.87.head for details.
10. See ftp://ftp.nerc.com/pub/sys/all_updl/docs/y2k/y2kreport-doe.pdf for the full report.
11. See http://y2ktimebomb.com/PP/RC/dm9838.htm for the full text of Mr. Mills' comments.
12. See http://www.y2ktoday.com/modules/news/newsdetail.asp?feature=true&id=326 for the text of Cowles' remarks.

13. See http://www.senate.gov/~y2k/statements/091798bennett.html for the text of Senator Bennett's remarks.
14. See also "Geomagnetic Storms Can Threaten Electric Power Grid," by John G. Kappenman, Minnesota Power, Duluth, Minn.; Lawrence J. Zanetti, Johns Hopkins University, Applied Physics Laboratory, Laurel, Md.; and William A. Radasky, Metatech, Goleta, Calif. *Earth in Space*, Vol. 9, No. 7, March 1997, pp.9-11. You can find this on the Internet at http://www.agu.org/sci_soc/eiskappenman.html.
15. This verbiage comes from the Y2000 section of California's Pacific Gas & Electric (PG&E) web site at http://www.pge.com/resources/compliance/.
16. See Martin's web site at http://ourworld.compuserve.com/homepages/roleigh_martin/ for more details of his assessment of the Y2000 status in the electric power industry.
17. See "Businesses' lives depend onY2K factor: Not everything will be fixed in time," by Tim Knauss, *Syracuse Online*, Oct 18, 1998; available on the Internet at http://www.syracuse.com/news/stsunday/19981018_ahnyk.html.
18. But keep in mind that the pilot light on your oil furnace is probably powered by electricity—so that if the electricity fails, you may also be without heat.
19. For more details, see http://www.energy.ca.gov/greengrid/index.html.

Y2000 Impact on Transportation

As machines become more and more efficient and perfect, so it will become clear that imperfection is the greatness of man.

Ernst Fischer, The Necessity of Art, *Chapter 5 (1959).*

The Bottom Line

Among the "scare stories" that consumers sometimes hear about the Y2000 problem is that airplanes might fall out of the sky, or that cars might explode while driving down the highway at midnight on December 31, 1999. Before we get into the details of how Y2000 will impact transportation, we'll summarize the "bottom line":

- Airplanes will *not* fall out of the sky, though there's a distinct possibility they may not even get into the sky. In addition to the much-publicized problems of the Federal Aviation Agency (FAA) in the U.S., there are also concerns about the safety of air-traffic control systems in other parts of the world, especially in the so-called Third World countries. In addition, there are Y2000 risks in the commercial airline companies,[1] in the airports, in the airplanes, and in the willingness of the large insurance companies to provide adequate insurance to both the airlines and the passengers[2] to keep everything operating.

- Automobiles will *not* explode at midnight on December 31, 1999, and it's unlikely that any of them will suffer any significant problems. However, there are several *thousand* combinations of make, model, and vintage-year of automobile on the highways today, and it's not beyond the realm of possibility that a few of these combinations will suffer Y2000 problems. It's more likely that we'll see problems in tractors, trucks, fire engines, buses, and other "high-end" industrial vehicles. Meanwhile, the far larger question is whether the major automobile companies will be able to operate their manufacturing plants.

- Rail transportation may be disrupted, but the status of the rail industry is not well enough known at this point to make any definitive statements. In addition to potential embedded-system problems in the locomotives, there are also concerns about the computerized switching in the railroad yards, as well as the risk of Y2000 problems within the scheduling and logistics systems of the railroads.

- Maritime shipping may be badly disrupted, because of Y2000 problems in the embedded systems on ships and tankers[3] as well as Y2000 problems in the government systems that handle duties, taxes, and other paperwork at the shipping ports.[4] 95 percent of the export tonnage from the U.S. goes by ship, so problems in this area could have a major impact on global trade; the problem is compounded by the fact that the maritime industry has been one of the laggards in dealing with Y2000.

- Bicycles, horses, and roller-skates will continue to be Y2000-compliant. Walking is safe, too.

Introduction

In the hilarious movie *Planes, Trains, and Automobiles*, actors Steve Martin and the late John Candy demonstrated that when things go wrong, it requires almost superhuman effort to travel from New York to Chicago in time to be home for the holidays. While the movie-based predicament has nothing to do with Y2000 problems, it does provide a rough idea of how difficult things could be if the Millennium Bug disrupts the transportation system.

While perhaps somewhat less important than electric power and the telephone, the transportation system is obviously crucial to the nation's economy—not to mention our own individual lives. Many of us think nothing of hopping in our car each morning for a 50-mile ride to the office, completely forgetting that 50 miles was often a day's journey in the mid-19th century. Others ride to work each day on a complex network of trains, buses, subways, ferries, and other carefully synchronized devices. Even more amazing is the practice of business executives, some of whom fly from the East Coast to the West Coast for a one-hour meeting, then zoom cross-country at 35,000 feet, back to the East Coast in time for David Letterman and Jay Leno on the late-night TV.

Of course, it doesn't always work perfectly: Everyone has experienced automobile breakdowns, delays in the train schedules, or canceled airline flights. Indeed, that was the whole point of *Planes, Trains, and Automobiles*: What should have been a straightforward two-hour flight to Chicago, at the end of a business meeting in New York City, turned out to be a marathon experience of one disaster after another.

While it sometimes seems that these travel-related problems are occurring more frequently than they were in the "good old days" (whenever that might have been), a realistic appraisal would have to conclude that overall, transportation works pretty well. But a similar appraisal would conclude that the Y2000 bug could wreak havoc upon all of this. We're not predicting that American society will retreat back to the horse-and-buggy days, but for reasons that should be familiar to you by this stage in the book, we *do* believe that there will be a significant number of minor transportation problems that persist for two or three days. There will be some that last a month, with moderately serious consequences; and, yes, there could be one or two problems that create transportation hardships that take a year to undo.

Automobiles

We begin our discussion with automobiles, which have two salient characteristics: First, there are a lot of them;[5] and second, they operate under the personal control of the owner. As this book was being written, there were nearly 100 million automobiles on the highways and byways of the United States, many of which were manufactured during the current decade.

The last statistic is relevant, because it has only been the past five years or so that we've begun to see a significant increase in the number of microprocessors embedded within typical consumer automobiles. The numbers vary from model to model, and from manufacturer to manufacturer, but the typical car has about 50 microprocessors—i.e., tiny embedded computers. Some of these computers are relatively passive: They provide readout displays of the current temperature (in both Centigrade and Fahrenheit, just to show how clever they are), or the average mileage since the car was last powered on. But some of the computers provide *control* functions: They regulate the mixture of air and fuel in the carburetor, they provide "intelligent" braking and suspension capabilities, and so forth. Under the appropriate circumstances, they can signal alarms, reminders, or flashing lights on the driver's dashboard—or they can initiate more serious actions, such as inflating the air-bags in the event of a crash.

What happens if one or more of these computer systems fail? In some cases, the results are merely annoying: Perhaps you won't see a display of the outside air temperature, or a display telling you your average mileage and speed on this trip. Lack of information could be more serious, though, if there's a failure in the microcomputer that controls the digital display on the entire dashboard in front of the driver. And there is, of course, the possibility of more serious trouble: Faulty braking, faulty suspension, faulty fuel mixture, and so forth.

Obviously, the relevant question is: How dependent are these systems on Y2000-related date logic? At first glance, one would think the answer is "not at all." We can't recall ever having seen a calendar in any car we've ever driven, so why worry about a "rollover" program on New Year's Eve in 1999? The problem has to do with the nature of "embedded systems" in general. In general, the problem is that the computerized chips that form the core of the embedded systems are now generic commodities, and they often contain functions that the end-user (in this case, the manufacturer of the automobile) has no interest in. By analogy, take a look at the digital wrist-watch you're wearing: How many of its embedded functions are you using? Almost all of them have a stop-watch, a timer, and other simple functions; and many of them can record a hundred telephone numbers, and even carry out mathematical functions. Since you paid only $19.95 for the watch, it doesn't bother you that there's a lot of unused functionality buried within it—all you want is the basic task of keeping the time-of-day.

That's not a fully satisfactory answer for our automobile situation; after all, why would an auto manufacturer buy a generic chip with date-calculation capabilities, in order to display the car's temperature and gas mileage? The answer is simple: Even though a car may not need to know the calendar date, it *does* have to know about the passage of time-intervals. The microcomputer that controls your carburetor has to recalculate the fuel mixture several times a second; the microcomputer that displays your average gas-mileage on this trip probably recalculates its figures once a second. Calculating a time-interval is indeed a "generic" piece of computerized functionality; the fact that the chip-manufacturer (e.g., Intel, Texas Instruments, Motorola, AMD, or a dozen others) enlarged upon that functionality to keep track of the day-of-year is probably not something the auto manufacturer stopped to think about.[6]

A more likely example of a date-related problem is the embedded computer system that keeps track of the elapsed time and/or mileage since the car was last serviced. These computers are normally reset by the technician each time a car is brought in for servicing, so that it can begin "counting down" again. When the counter reaches zero, an audible alarm is sounded, or a red light is flashed on the dashboard.

While this is obviously not a fatal problem, it could take a driver by surprise if it occurs at the stroke of midnight on December 31, 1999; it could also lead to a number of unnecessary visits to the auto service centers to fix the problem.

Note that such a mechanism could be implemented in a very simple fashion that does not appear to involve any awareness of specific dates. If the computer has a counter that can be set to an integer value—e.g., 100—then with each passing day, the computer can decrement the counter, until it reaches zero. However, even this simple approach requires that the computer be able to keep track of the passage of a day, which may rely upon some hardware logic that *is* date-sensitive, and therefore Y2000-sensitive. On the other hand, if the counter is tracking the car's mileage, then no dates are involved at all: Every time the odometer clicks up a mile, the time-for-service counter clicks down a mile. The simplest solution to this problem is to ask your service technician if any of his diagnostic tools allow him to set a date *anywhere* within the car; if so, ask him to certify (in writing) that the relevant computer systems are Y2000-compliant. Chances are that he won't be willing or able to do so; in that case, ask him to set the date back several years.

We'll discuss the issue of embedded systems in more detail in Chapter 11; as you can appreciate, such a problem could also occur in household appliances, factory devices, and an enormous variety of other man-made gadgets that now have computer chips embedded in them. For now, we'll simply summarize: Some percentage of the on-board automobile microcomputers could conceivably be date-sensitive, and some percentage of the "sensitive" computers might carry out "mission-critical" functions (e.g., fuel mixture) for which a sudden failure could have life-threatening consequences. We don't know which cars might be subject to such a problem; for what it's worth, very few of the major automobile companies anywhere in the world have yet published any warranty guarantee, or even informal assurances that their automobiles *are* Year-2000 compliant.[7]

The good news, if one can call it that, is that the vast majority of Y2000 problems in these embedded automobile systems will occur right at the stroke of midnight on December 31, 1999. After all, there are no business-oriented billing systems in an automobile, and no databases to corrupt. If something goes wrong, it's likely to go wrong right away. Regardless of whatever assurances or warranties the automobile manufacturers may eventually publish, we think that simple prudence dictates that you stay off the highway at midnight on that fateful New Year's Eve. In the best of cases, your car will work, and so will all the other automobiles on the road. In the more plausible situation, one or two of the cars on the highway (and hopefully not yours!) will experience some kind of malfunction, which could cause them to behave erratically. And in the worst of cases, it could be *your* car that suddenly shuts down while you're hurtling down the highway at 60 mph.

The bad news about a Y2000 automobile problem is that it could lead to an automobile "recall" situation unlike anything the auto industry has ever seen. The auto manufacturers will almost certainly be facing their own problems, dealing with the logistics of continuing to manufacture new cars in the face of Y2000 problems. If they also have to repair millions upon millions of faulty cars that are already on the highway, it will compound their problem enormously. And as a practical matter, the chances of getting your car fixed quickly are relatively small. There may be only one or two chips that need to be replaced, but the waiting list for such repairs will be horrendous.

Let's assume for the moment that we've gotten past this category of "immediate" problem with Y2000-sensitive automobile systems. What else do we need to worry about? The details will vary from person to person, but the two obvious categories are:

- *Gas, oil, and other supplies*—You can't get very far in your car if you can't refill the gas tank. Sooner or later, you'll need to change the oil, replace the spark plugs, and repair anything else that breaks down. Putting gas in your car requires that (a) the distributors have managed to deliver adequate supplies to your gas station, (b) the gas station has electrical power, (c) panic hoarding, of the kind we saw during the oil crisis of the late 70s, hasn't occurred, and (d) your credit card works, or you have adequate cash, to pay for the gas.

- *Bridges, tunnels, and other parts of the highway system*—Bridges and tunnels are likely to be controlled, to some extent, by computers; it's another variation on the embedded system problem. Not only that, many parts of the country charge tolls for access to the bridges and tunnels. That means the tolls collectors have to be in place, and all of their computerized support systems have to be somewhat operational. The latter problem could be ignored in an emergency, of course; an appropriate government decree could allow free access. But if bridges can't be raised or lowered, and if tunnels can't have carbon monoxide exhaust fumes pumped away, then we've got a problem.

We find it interesting to see how often the subject of Y2000 automobile risks comes up in Internet discussion groups, and also how spirited and emotional the arguments often become. Several people claim to have personal expertise in the inner workings of automobiles, or to be married or related to someone with expertise; and many seem to believe that it's almost unpatriotic to even suggest that automobiles might have such a basic flaw. We believe that there are four basic questions you should ask yourself about the Y2000-compliance of your automobile, or any other expensive, sophisticated product you might happen to own:

- *To whom should questions of Y2000 compliance be directed?* Before you base your decisions on the information we've provided you, remember that (a) neither author is an automobile mechanic, and (b) neither of us are likely to be available to chat with you about the situation on January 1, 2000. For similar reasons, we think it's risky to make a decision about a $20,000 automobile based on the casual opinion of your cousin Vinnie or someone who expresses an opinion on an Internet newsgroup—remember, there are over a thousand different combinations of make, model, and vintage automobile on the road, and it's highly unlikely that any one individual can be an expert in all of them. Get a firm, specific statement in writing, on letterhead stationery, from a responsible official at your auto dealer, about *your* car.

- *What kind of a priori assumptions should you make about the credibility of the answer you'll receive?* It's a cliché to suggest that a "used car salesman" can't be trusted—but would you really expect a thoughtful, well-informed, legally binding assurance about the Y2000 compliance of a car that such a salesman is discussing with you in the auto showroom? By contrast, if you discuss the same issue with the Chief Legal Officer of the auto company, you're likely to make an a priori decision that he or she is telling the truth.

- *What are the consequences if the answer is wrong?* If you believe that a non-compliant car could cause life-threatening risks while your spouse and children are in the car, you'll take the situation much more seriously than if the consequences are simply a defective alarm light on the dashboard. This notion of *failure mode analysis* is a crucial part of the Y2000 "contingency planning" within many large companies today; the question that needs to be asked is: "If it turns out that your product is *not* compliant, what's the worst thing that could happen?" The answer to that question is likely to influence your decision; similarly, a vendor's inability or unwillingness to discuss such a question should make you think twice.

- *How can you minimize the risks or dangers if you do receive an incorrect answer?* The obvious strategy, as we discussed earlier, is not to be on the highway, driving at 60 mph, as the clock strikes midnight on December 31, 1999. But here's another example: One of the authors acquired a new automobile in early 1998. But rather than purchasing the car, he negotiated a two-year lease, which expires in February 2000. Thus, if the car turns out to be completely inoperable on January 1, 2000 and if the auto dealer is unwilling or unable to rectify the situation, the maximum "exposure" consists of two months of contested lease payments.

Public Transportation: Trains and Buses

From a Y2000 perspective, trains and buses are significantly different than automobiles: There are fewer of them, they carry more passengers, and their operations are *scheduled*. Because of their size and complexity, they're likely to have more micro-computers than a standard automobile; and those computers may, of course, have the same possibility of Y2000 problems. We've found no written indications yet that such computers have been tested for Y2000 compliance, nor have we found any formal assurances from public transportation companies that they'll indeed carry out such testing before December 31, 1999. Common sense says that such testing *will* be done, but as the American humorist Will Rogers once remarked, "Common sense isn't common." It's up to you to decide whether you want to be riding a bus or train at the stroke of midnight on that particular New Year's Eve.

Assuming that such testing is done, and that any Y2000 problems associated with the embedded systems have been fixed, there's a separate issue that must be dealt with: scheduling. Whether it's a city bus, a Trailways/Greyhound bus, or an Amtrak Metroliner between New York and Washington, it's virtually certain that a computerized scheduling system will be used to determine departure times, scheduled arrival times, frequency of service, and so forth. Those systems are typical of the business-oriented computer systems we discussed earlier in the book; there are numerous opportunities for Y2000-related bugs in such systems. In the case of a bus, it may mean that the standard 7 AM bus that you ride to work on Monday morning, January 3rd, doesn't arrive. Or perhaps two buses will arrive; or some other bizarre scheduling mishap could occur.

In the case of buses, none of this is likely to have life-threatening consequences; in the case of trains, there's a more serious problem to worry about: Two trains could be scheduled to operate on the same section of track at the same time. Assuming that the conductors are alert, and assuming that mechanical fail-safe mechanisms operate correctly, such a double-scheduling snafu should be detected and dealt with before the trains crash into each other. On the other hand, more and more of the information used by conductors and dispatchers throughout the rail system are computerized; and more and more of the fail-safe mechanisms themselves are computerized. Train collisions occur a few times a year, throughout the United States, even when things are supposedly operating in a normal fashion; the risk of such a failure is arguably higher given the possible of Y2000 computer glitches.

Planes

Commercial airplanes are similar to trains and buses, in the sense that (a) there are far fewer of them than automobiles, (b) they carry many more passengers than automobiles, and (c) they operate on a scheduled basis. But unlike buses or trains, Y2000 problems in mid-air run a more serious risk of fatal injuries. On the other hand, it's also fair to say that the airlines are operated by more highly skilled and trained personnel (i.e., pilots, navigators, and so forth) than is the case with buses.[8]

Commercial airplanes are also, to put it mildly, *much* more complex pieces of equipment than a car, bus, or train. Not only does a Boeing 767 or a McDonnell-Douglas MD-11 represent $100+ million worth of engines, wings, and chassis, but it's also much more heavily computerized; Boeing's latest aircraft, the 777, has been described by some in the software industry as "two and a half million lines of Ada code flying in close formation—not so much an airplane as a complex software system packaged and shipped in an airframe."[9] One of the authors had the experience last year of listening to an airline pilot brag to all the passengers on his flight that the airplane they were riding on contained some 500 computers. Some of these, as with the automobile, are performing functions whose failure would be nothing more than annoying—perhaps the onboard movie wouldn't work, perhaps the airline meals would be even more badly cooked than normal. Obviously, what we're concerned about is the "control" systems that produce all the displays (most of which are now digital) on the cockpit instrument panel, as well as assisting the pilot and copilot with takeoff, landing, collision detection, navigation, communication with air traffic controllers, and numerous other functions.

Are all of those systems Y2000 compliant? The largest U.S. aircraft manufacturer, Boeing, claims that except for "nuisance effects," its planes will be Y2000-compliant by December 31, 1998; the company has posted a reasonably detailed description of its Y2000 efforts on the Internet at http://www.boeng.com/comercial/aeromagazine/textonly/sy01txt.html. There are, of course, numerous other aircraft manufacturers, and it stands to reason that they too are working on whatever Y2000 issues may be involved in their planes; it also stands to reason that the commercial airlines and air-traffic authorities will engage in independent testing to ensure the equipment is safe before allowing flights on January 1, 2000.

Then there is the Federal Aviation Administration (FAA), the central government authority that defines, develops, and coordinates the air traffic control systems throughout the United States. The FAA air-traffic control systems is one of the nation's largest and most complex computer systems; it's also one of the oldest, and has been the subject of a major redesign and redevelopment for the past several years. In a nutshell: The current FAA software is *not* Y2000 compliant as the second edition of this book was being prepared, there was significant controversy about the agency's status, progress, and likelihood of finishing critical Y2000 work in time. In an August 6, 1998 hearing before the House technology subcommittee, Ray Long, the FAA Year 2000 project director, testified that he believes there is enough time to fix all of the FAA's critical systems. Long reported that the agency plans to fix all systems by June 30, 1999, which he feels would leave "ample time" for testing and detection of errors before Jan. 1, 2000.[10] And on September 29, 1998, FAA administrator Jane Garvey reported that the FAA would have 99 percent of its systems renovated by the following day— September 30th.[11]

But officials and auditors from the OMB and GAO have disputed these optimistic reports; at the same House subcommittee hearing, John L. Meche, Deputy Assistant Inspector General for Financial, Economic, and Information Technology, at the U.S. Department of Transportation, presented a report that included the following observations:[12]

> *FAA is reporting that it is on schedule to achieve the next major OMB milestone—fixing all known Year-2000 problems by September 30, 1998. Significant progress was reported in the last 2 weeks of July. With less than 60 days to go, FAA still has to complete repairs on 53 mission-critical systems, 11 of which are complex Air Traffic Control systems. There are three areas where FAA needs more attention. First, FAA needs better documentation to support the completeness of the renovation work, especially with replacement parts and system interfaces. Second, FAA needs to determine whether six of the new systems under development are Year-2000 compliant. And third, FAA needs to begin testing the systems.*
>
> *With about 500 days to the Year 2000, FAA still has significant challenges ahead. For example, 102 of FAA's mission-critical systems will not be*

tested and implemented by OMB's milestone date of March 31, 1999. This includes 19 percent of the mission-critical systems for air traffic control. We have been urging FAA since October 1997 to accelerate its implementation schedule. While a great deal of progress has been made, FAA's current schedule, in our opinion, is still cutting it too close. It is imperative that FAA make a concerted effort to accelerate implementation of the 102 systems to March 31, 1999, or as soon thereafter as possible. This would provide for a cushion if problems are identified when fielding these systems, and allow FAA time to go through the repair and testing process again before the end of 1999.

Of more concern in the same report by Mr. Meche was the suggestion that FAA may have been exaggerating or misstating its Y2000 progress:

FAA recently disclosed it had not determined interfacing requirements for 38 mission-critical systems, 9 of which were reported as fully renovated. Based on our work, some of the systems may not have been completely fixed and reported in accordance with departmental guidance. We are currently working with FAA management to determine whether repair work has been completed for all required elements—i.e., code modification, system replacement, and interfaces.

At the same House hearing, GAO's Joel Willemssen added his own pessimistic assessment of the FAA situation:[13]

On July 31 [1998], FAA announced that 67 percent of its mission-critical systems in need of repair were renovated, exceeding its goal of 60 percent. However, FAA's July 31 projections for completing renovation, validation, and implementation of the 159 mission-critical systems it is repairing will not meet the Office of Manage-

ment and Budget's (OMB) September 1998 and January and March 1999 milestones, respectively. In addition to these 159 systems, another 44 systems are being replaced. Of these, 38 are not scheduled to be replaced until June 30, 1999, according to FAA's schedules. These replacement systems, too, must be validated and implemented. FAA Year 2000 program officials stated that these replacement dates may not be accurate and that they will be reassessing them in the near future. . . .

. . . while FAA projects that 99 percent (157 systems) of the 159 systems will meet OMB's renovation deadline of September 30, 1998, it expects only 79 percent (126 systems) to meet the January 1999 validation deadline, and just 61 percent (97 systems) to meet the March 1999 implementation deadline. FAA plans to complete implementation by June 30, 1999.

Moreover, these projections are based on very optimistic schedules that may not prove to be realistic. One reason is that officials are counting on a steep rise in the pace of completion activity. For example, currently 106 of the 159 systems have been renovated, 9 more are set to be renovated by the end of this month, and a total of 157 by September of this year; this means that 42 systems will have to complete renovation within 1 month.

Validation and implementation also show ambitious schedules. As of July 31, sixteen systems had been validated; by November, that number is set to be 67; by December, 118; and by next January, 126. Finally, as of July 31, just 4 systems out of 159 had been implemented. FAA projects that this number will climb to 46 by next February and, 1 month later—in March 1999—reach 97. According to the Year 2000 program manager, FAA is now reassessing its schedule.

> *Another reason for uncertainty about FAA's projected milestones is that, according to the Year 2000 program manager, after solutions are tested and validated at FAA's technical centers (scheduled to be completed by March 31, 1999), many must then be tested and implemented at scores of field sites across the country. A task of this complexity—concurrently rolling out numerous system changes to many sites—will likely be time-consuming and filled with difficult implementation challenges, yet FAA projects full implementation by June 30, 1999—only 3 months later. As a comparison, an FAA official responsible for maintaining the Host Computer System stated that it generally takes 4 to 6 weeks to test and implement a single modification once it has been deployed to the en route centers. Multiple concurrent changes would likely prolong this process.*

Let's move on beyond the embedded systems within the airplanes, and the FAA's air traffic control systems (as well as the various information systems and business systems that the FAA needs to operate properly). What else is required to avoid a significant Y2000 impact upon airline transportation? A May 1998 report from the International Air Traffic Association (IATA) summarized the key Y2000 issues facing the airlines:

> *The year 2000 will have an impact on any company which makes significant use of computer systems; however, the airline industry has a number of specific characteristics which make it somewhat special. These include: Major use of automated systems: the airlines have always been at the forefront of using computers to support their business functions, starting with the introduction of the first high-performance reser-*

vations systems in the 1960s. Since then the application of IT has pervaded every area of the company, providing essential support to the entire business, ensuring high levels of customer service and providing the means for introducing new strategic initiatives. Highly integrated industry: to function effectively the airlines rely heavily on the exchange of information to support their business processes. The industry has much higher interaction between individual companies' systems (e.g., for reservations, check-in, baggage, etc.) than most other sectors. This places an additional level of complexity on efforts to address the year 2000 problem and means that a key component will be ensuring that all the standards for interchanging such data are examined to determine what action is required with regard to dates. World-wide, round-the-clock operations: By the nature of the industry, critical airline systems need to be operational 24 hours a day, every day of the year. Even short interruptions to system availability can cause major inconvenience to customers; longer "outages" would have serious business implications. High-profile: Airlines are generally considered as "high-profile" companies which receive considerably more interest and media attention than some other business sectors. Speculation on the impact of the year 2000 on the airlines is much more "sensational" than for other industries.[14]

Here are the problems that appear most significant to us:

- *Aircraft maintenance and repair*—FAA establishes the regulations for scheduled maintenance and repairs, and carries out appropriate investigations to ensure that it's done properly; in addition, the aircraft manufacturers establish guidelines and recommendations for maintenance and replacement of engines, tires, and other parts of the plane. But it's the *airlines* that carry out the maintenance, from an operational perspective; if you're a passenger on XYZ Airlines, you're more concerned that XYZ's maintenance-scheduling computer systems are working in the days and weeks after January 1, 2000 than you are about the well-established guidelines and policies of the aircraft manufacturers and the FAA.

- *Scheduling of pilots, crew, and flight attendants*—This is fairly obvious: No crew means no flight. If you've done any amount of flying on commercial airlines, you're probably already aware that this is a fairly complex business; it's not uncommon to see flights delayed because the flight crew was stuck in another city because of bad weather. The bad news, of course, is that Y2000 problems could thoroughly scramble these elaborate, computer-generated schedules; the good news is that there are very strict regulations that prevent the airlines from responding to such problems in a fashion that might otherwise occur—i.e., politely, but firmly, asking the crew to work additional hours to compensate for scheduling mistakes. Again, if you're a veteran flyer, you've probably seen this already: After a certain number of hours of continuous service, the crews walk off the plane in order to avoid operating a flight when they're too tired to perform properly.

- *Airline reservation systems*—Arguably, this is not a life-and-death issue, but the absence of today's highly sophisticated, world-wide reservation systems would throw the airline industry into a state of utter chaos until things were resolved. "Shuttle" flights, like the ones between New York and Washington, would be fine; but anyone who needed a confirmed reservation for a cross-country flight, or an intercontinental flight, would be out of luck. Obviously, if such a situation persisted for any length of time, the airlines could fall back to the kind of manual systems that existed prior to the 1960s; but it would be *extremely* costly, chaotic, and painful. (Note, by the way, that this problem essentially doesn't exist with trains and buses. You show up at the terminal and get on.)

- *Airport infrastructure systems*. The 550 airports[15] across the United States (and several thousand more around the world) are small cities unto themselves; they have upwards of 10,000 employees, and they have a transient population that sometimes numbers in the hundreds of thousands. There are dozens, if not hundreds, of shops and restaurants; acres upon acres of parking lots; intricate schedules of shuttle buses; and a complex traffic control network to ensure that the ebb and flow of passengers doesn't screech to a halt. Again, computers are heavily involved in all of this; and on top of that, we've got the electrical, oil, gas, and telephone services discussed in other chapters of this book. A reasonable subset of this vast infrastructure has to work in order to avoid Y2000 problems in order for the airport to stay open. (A similar statement could be made about bus and train stations, but it's on a much smaller scale; indeed, many such facilities are so antiquated that it appears nothing has changed since the 1940s, prior to the appearance of the modern computer!) Scattered reports through the spring and summer of 1998 suggest that Y2000 repair work is just beginning at such major airports at Atlanta,[16] Denver,[17] and Dallas;[18] that leaves a large number of airports whose status is simply unknown at this point.

Another Transportation Problem: GPS Rollover Failures in 1999

While most of the problems discussed in this chapter are directly attributable to the Y2000 "rollover" problem, there's another rollover problem that will occur approximately six months earlier—specifically, on August 22, 1999. The problem involves the Global Positioning System, a set of satellites installed by the U.S. Navy to provide navigational data for ships, planes, and missiles. The system is not only used by the Defense Department, but by an estimated *10 million* commercial planes and ships.

The problem with the GPS system will sound familiar to anyone who has become involved in the Y2000 crisis: The GPS satellites record the time of day, with remarkably accurate atomic clocks. The time is recorded in terms of seconds, minutes, hours, days, and *weeks* since the inception of the system on January 5, 1980; unfortunately, the computer memory assigned to keep track of the "week number" is only 12 "bits" long, which means that it will roll over after 1,024 consecutive weeks of operation; as luck would have it, that will occur on August 22, 1999. Lest you think we're making this up, here's the official announcement from the US Navy:[19]

> *The GPS Week Number count began at approximately midnight on the evening of 05 January 1980 / morning of 06 January 1980. Since that time, the count has been incremented by 1 each week, and broadcast as part of the GPS message. The GPS Week Number field is modulo 1024. This means that at the comple-*

tion of week 1023, the GPS week number will rollover to 0 on midnight of the evening of 21 August 1999 / morning of 22 August 1999.

Week beginning at 0000 GPS Time on	GPS Week Number broadcast by satellites
08 Aug 1999	1022
15 Aug 1999	1023
22 Aug 1999	0
29 Aug 1999	1

Once the rollover has occurred, it is the responsibility of the user (i.e., user equipment or software) to account for the previous 1024 weeks.

Depending upon the manufacturer of your GPS receiver, you may or may not be affected by the GPS Week Number Rollover on 22 August 1999. Some receivers may display inaccurate date information, some may also calculate incorrect navigation solutions.

Contact the manufacturer of your GPS receiver to determine if you will be affected by the GPS week number rollover.

The problem is a serious one indeed, especially since it affects guided missiles, bombers, and commercial airlines, as well as the weekend hobbyist who has just installed a fancy new navigation system in his boat. We're not sure whether it's a good thing or bad thing that the GPS problem will occur approximately four months before the Y2000 problem; it would be ironic indeed if the Y2000 problem became irrelevant because all of our GPS-sensitive transportation vehicles were grounded several months before New Year's Eve, 1999.

One last irony: The GPS system is widely used not only to help vehicles determine where they are at any given time, but it's also used by many *non*-transportation systems (including many of the major banks in the U.S.) as a standard mechanism for recording the time of day. Because the accuracy of the GPS atomic clocks is among the highest in the world, and because it can be accessed by anyone with a GPS receiver, thousands of financial systems use GPS for their time calculations; they need the accuracy of GPS, because interest calculations on multi-billion dollar loans is sometimes calculated to the nearest millisecond. Thus, in addition to all of the other banking problems that we'll be discussing in Chapter 5, there is the additional problem that some of the banks may lose track of which week it is, beginning in late August, 1999.

Fallback Advice: Two-Day Problems

Like most of the other areas discussed in this book, a two-day loss of transportation services is something that you can probably tolerate with only minor inconvenience. Note that we're probably dealing with failures in the public-sector forms of travel here—i.e., bus, train, or air travel. If something goes wrong with your car, it's more likely that (a) it will be a minor problem (e.g., an incorrect readout of the outside air temperature) that you can ignore, or (b) a problem that requires sending your car to the repair shop, where you're likely to wait for a month or two before the replacement "chip" arrives.

If a problem does occur with any form of transportation, it's likely to occur at the stroke of midnight on December 31st, when the Y2000-sensitive embedded systems fail. Thus, if you're concerned about this level of failure, the obvious precaution is not to count heavily on public-sector travel during the first few days of January. January 1st and 2nd are, respectively, a holiday and a Sunday; most people will be home relaxing, celebrating, or recuperating anyway. By January 3rd, it will be widely known whether the planes are flying, and whether the public transportation system is operating on schedule—i.e., you'll know whether it's safe. But if you're scheduling a business trip for January 2000, and if you have any flexibility at all, schedule it for the middle of the month.

There's a corollary to this advice: Don't travel in, or on, anything more sophisticated than a bicycle or horse-and-buggy at midnight on December 31, 1999—unless you're the type who enjoys Russian Roulette as a pastime. As noted already, few (if any) of the companies who manufacture transportation devices (cars, planes, trains, and buses) are in a position in mid-1998, when the second edition of this book was being written, to unconditionally guarantee that their products are Y2000 compliant. It's quite possible that one or more of these companies *will* make such a claim in 1999, which you may or may not find credible.[20] But even if you're confident that your car is Y2000 compliant, it doesn't necessarily mean that all other cars on the highway are Y2000 compliant. All it takes is one malfunctioning car, perhaps compounded by one inebriated driver, to cause a major traffic accident.

Fallback Advice: One-Month Problems

The one-month problems could occur for a number of reasons: Your car malfunctions, and it take a month to get a replacement chip for the carburetor or the braking system or some other critical component. The bus company finds that its database of drivers has been destroyed, and has no idea which drivers should be assigned to which routes; union-management disagreements compound the problem, and nobody shows up to drive the buses for a month. The commuter train company finds that its database of train schedules has been clobbered, and it can't figure out which trains should occupy which tracks at which time. The airline that you depend on for your business flights has discovered that its maintenance/repair systems are misbehaving—and the FAA discovers that airplanes are disappearing off the radar scopes at the air-traffic control centers.

Aside from the automobile recall problem, most of the other scenarios described here could occur at random times during the first few months of 2000; just because we reach January 5th without problems doesn't necessarily mean that we can rule out the possibility of Y2000 bugs. The transportation companies could run into problems as a result of computer processing that they carry out on January 31st, or February 29th (which the computers might not recognize as a legitimate leap-year), and so forth.

In any case, what will you do if this level of disruption occurs in the transportation systems you depend on? Here are some possibilities:

- Avoid scheduling any personal or business trips requiring air transport for the month of January. January is a slow month for many businesses anyway, as people recover from the holidays and winter vacations; but such a scheduling delay will obviously create hardships for some. Consider video conferencing as an alternative; schedule your trips for December 1999 instead of January 2000.

- Plan ahead for backup travel arrangements. If the trains aren't working, perhaps you can take the bus—or vice versa. If your car doesn't work, perhaps your neighbor's does; since your neighbor is faced with the same potential Y2000 problem, perhaps you can make advance arrangements to car-pool to your respective offices in the event that either of your cars malfunctions.

- Investigate "personal" transportation mechanisms—e.g., walking or bicycling to the office. If the problems actually begin in January, 2000, then this won't be a pleasant option for those living in the northern half of the country; but it might be an acceptable option for those living in Florida, Arizona, and most of California.

Fallback Advice: One-Year Problems

Like most of the other topics discussed in this book, the prospect of a one-year disruption in transportation service is difficult to imagine. However, even though we might judge such a scenario as highly unlikely, it *is* possible: Worse-than-expected problems in the FAA air traffic control system could conceivably ground the nation's airlines for a year; larger-than-expected automobile recalls might mean a one-year delay in getting your car repaired; and so forth.

In the case of individual transportation systems—e.g., a car—the straightforward advice is: Make sure you have sufficient funds to get a replacement, Y2000-compliant transportation system. It's an expensive, unpleasant option; and it presumes that not all automobiles will be subject to fatal Y2000 problems. But for those who depend heavily on their car, there may not be a viable alternative.

As for the public transportation systems, there's not much we can suggest besides looking for backup alternatives. If the airlines are grounded for a year, we'll become a nation of train-riders once again, which might even have a positive impact on the aging, decrepit, poorly serviced train infrastructure. If the trains break down for a year, we'll eventually get used to riding Greyhound and Trailways once again.

For the few who are inclined towards proactive planning, here's a thought: This might be a good time to move to an area where you're not so dependent on public transportation systems or even an automobile. Many of us today live in congested urban centers where the transportation infrastructure barely works even without a Y2000 problem. Indeed, some of us have already begun asking ourselves why we put up with a daily commute of two or three hours, and whether it really makes sense to live in an area where highway congestion, or weather-related breakdowns in the trains and bus system, sometimes extend that commute time to four or five hours. Changing one's job or residence is not a casual decision, but even today there are some who make such a decision based on the inconvenience and unpredictability of transportation. If such thoughts have occurred to you, then you should re-examine the situation in 1998 or early 1999, before the Y2000-related travel difficulties occur.

Fallback Advice: Ten-Year Problems

The only aspect of transportation where we can imagine the possibility of a severe Y2000-related software crisis extending beyond a year is the FAA air-traffic control system. As noted earlier, the FAA is well aware of the problem, has set up an organizational structure to deal with it, and has already begun committing resources to fix its software. Unfortunately, the existing hardware/software complex is so aged and overloaded that it has been on the verge of collapse for several years. And the project to replace the existing system with a new-generation system has been mired in such political controversy and technological confusion that it's years behind schedule. Thus, while we would like to believe that the FAA will have all its Y2000 problems fixed before December 31, 1999, the age and intrinsic complexity of its systems, coupled with a less than stellar track record in the past few years, makes us somewhat more pessimistic.

And the worst-case situation for the FAA is likely to be *much* worse than would be the case for Amtrak or Greyhound Bus Lines. If the entire FAA computer infrastructure collapses and has to be replaced from scratch, it will be a massive undertaking. Rome wasn't built in a day, and the existing FAA system certainly wasn't built in a year; building a completely new FAA system could easily take three-five years, and with the political bureaucracy that seems to surround most FAA activity, it wouldn't be surprising to see such a project drag on for five-seven years. Whether there would still be an airline industry at the end of such a long period is an interesting question to contemplate.

In the meantime, society would muddle along somehow: We don't expect 250 million Americans to commit mass suicide simply because United Airlines is unable to fly the friendly skies between Chicago and New York. But while most of us *would* muddle along in some fashion, such a long-term disruption in air travel could indeed turn out to have permanent, tragic consequences for anyone whose business or profession depends critically on being able to travel between New York and Chicago (or any other such pairs of cities) on a daily basis. We can't predict the likelihood of such a situation, though we do believe it to be quite small; as with the other aspects of society we explore in this book, the possibility of a 10-year disruption essentially changes life as we now know it.

Endnotes

1. As an example, United Airlines reports that it has 40,000 computer programs, of which it estimates that 11,000 are non-compliant and thus need to be repaired or replaced. See "Y2K solutions expensive; pervasiveness annoying," by Charles Slack, *Richmond Times-Dispatch*, May 24, 1998; available on the Internet at http://www.gatewayva.com/rtd/special/year2000/y2ktran.html.
2. There have been several reports throughout 1998 of tentative decisions by insurance companies to curtail insurance or incorporate Y2K exclusions in their policies. See, for example, "Air travellers may bear bug risk," by Stan Beer, *Australian Financial Review*, August 26, 1998; available on the Internet at http://www.afr.com.au/content/980826/inform/inform2.html.
3. Tankers and freighters might each have more than 100 chips running engine rooms, navigation and communications and managing cargo. A recent report from London's Entropy Management Ltd., indicated that up to 20 percent of these chips could fail because of millennium problems. See "Shipping full-speed ahead to beat millennium bomb," *Reuters News Service* , June 16, 1998, available on the Internet at http://www.nando.net/newsroom/ntn/info/061698/info19_9529_noframes.html.
4. If you want to track the Y2K issues in the maritime industry, a good web site to watch is http://www.tm-online.com/Ship2000.nsf/d9e352160e6d9dcf802565a0005739d1?OpenView.
5. Not only are there many *units* of automobiles on the road, but also many makes, models, and vintages. Even if we worry about 10 automobile manufacturers, each of whom has produced 10 different models for each of the past 10 years, that's still 1,000 different combinations. With 20 manufacturers, 20 models, and 20 years (i.e., cars dating back to 1979-80), we have 8,000 different combinations.
6. There is enormous debate about this point, and we received email messages from several software engineers who responded to the

early drafts of the first edition of this book with emphatic statements that the embedded computer systems are *not* date-sensitive. They may be right, but unless your auto company is willing and able to guarantee it in writing, you're putting yourself at risk. Some embedded computers, for example, are designed so that when they they're first activated, they set the year to an "epoch date" (which, in one case, turns out to be the birth-year of the founder of the engineering company that builds the chip). Thus, if the "epoch date" is 1980, then it will experience a "roll-over," with possibly unpredictable behavior, after 20 years of operation; if you bought your car in 1985, then you won't have a problem until 2005.

7. One auto company that *has* provided a reassurance that its cars are compliant is Saturn. At its Web site at http://www.saturn.com/communication/index3.html, the company says, "The year 2000 will pose no difficulties for the computer or Powertrain Control Module (PCM) in your Saturn. The need to adapt to the turn of the century was taken into account by Saturn engineers."
8. We haven't focused on the charter airlines or the small airplanes piloted by individual "amateurs." The equipment involved here is obviously smaller and simpler, but still capable of experiencing severe Y2000 problems. The risk of massive fatalities is presumably smaller, though the training and supervision of the pilots is generally less strenuous.
9. See "Scaling up Management," by Larry Constantine, *Software Development*, November 1998, p. 79.
10. See "FAA May Run Out of Time To Fix Y2K Bug, GAO Says Agency Disputes Expert's Assessment," by Stephen Barr, *Washington Post*, August 7, 1998; Page A23; available on the Internet at http://www.washingtonpost.com/wp-srv/WPlate/1998-08/07/0661-080798-idx.html.
11. See "FAA flying through its Y2K computer renovations," by Cassandra Burrell; available on the Internet at http://www.foxnews.com/nav/wires_news.sml.
12. See http://www.house.gov/science/meche_08-06.htm for the text of this report.
13. See http://www.house.gov/science/willemssen_08-06.htm for the text of the report.
14. See "Year 2000—Countdown to chaos?" by Barry Tate —Senior Manager Industry Operations, available on the Internet at http://www.iata.org/y2k/articles.htm.

15. This statistic comes from "Airlines Battle the 2000 Bug," by Chris Stamper, *ABCNEWS.com*, May 7, 1998; the article also points out that there are 290 U.S. airlines, and an aggregate of 17,000 suppliers to the airline industry. See http://www.abcnews.com/sections/tech/DailyNews/fly2k980429.html for more details.
16. See "Airport computers far from ready," by Shade Elam, *Atlanta Business Chronicle*, May 17, 1998; available on the Internet at http://www.amcity.com/atlanta/stories/051898/story4.html.
17. See "DIA flunks Year 2000 compliance test: task force counting computer fix toll," by Rebecca Landwehr, *Denver Business Journal*, April 20, 1998, available on the Internet at http://www.amcity.com/denver/stories/042098/story1.html.
18. See "D/FW Airport aims to swat computer bug before 2000: Boardapproves spending $1.3 million to correct glitch," by Todd Bensman, *The Dallas Morning News*, March 7, 1998. Available for downloading from the newspaper's web site at http://archive.dallasnews.com/.
19. "GPS Week Number Rollover Approaches," located on the Internet at http://tycho.usno.navy.mil/gps_week.html.
20. We'll discuss the credibility of such claims of Y2000 compliance in more detail in Chapter 11, when we examine the broader issue of embedded systems.

Y2000 Impact on Banking/Finance

Money is a singular thing. It ranks with love as man's greatest source of joy. And with death as his greatest source of anxiety. Over all history it has oppressed nearly all people in one of two ways: either it has been abundant and very unreliable, or reliable and very scarce.

John Kenneth Galbraith,
The Age of Uncertainty, *Chapter 6*

Introduction

By now, it should be no surprise when we suggest that your bank account, your credit cards, and your stocks and bonds might be vulnerable to Y2000-induced computer failures. Indeed, the only reason you might be surprised at all is that American society has been so trusting of its financial institutions for the past several decades. Notwithstanding the occasional stock market slump, or the savings and loan "crisis" of the 1980s (a phenomenon the average citizen would be hard-pressed to plain in any detail), or the occasional story of credit-card fraud, the prevailing opinion in this country is that the dollar is stable and the institutions in which we store our dollars are equally stable.

Yet the elder generation—those who were young children or young adults on October 29, 1929—still recall an era in which thousands of banks failed. And any study of economic history[1] over the past 300 years will illustrate numerous panics, depressions, bank runs, and crises in which people discovered that the money they had deposited in their local bank was gone, or that their money had become worthless, or both. The proximate causes of these crises have varied from war to speculation (as in the case of 1929) to corruption and malfeasance on the part of bankers and government officials. While none of these unpleasant forces have vanished from the earth, they are not the focus of this chapter. Indeed, in the fall of 1998 when we are writing the second edition of this book, there is a near crisis occurring in the financial markets. Financial institutions are under immense pressure in the United States, as a result of exposure to emerging markets and hedge funds. The current state of financial institutions in late 1998 does not bode well for the potential impact of Y2K in 1999 and 2000. In this chapter, we'll worry about the impact of a unique technological failure upon our financial institutions during a time when they are already under other pressures.

Ironically, it's conceivable that speculation, malfeasance, and corruption could further aggravate a Y2000-induced financial crisis. While some investors seek profits from rising stock prices, others sell short if they anticipate a decline; there are already investors and analysts on Wall Street who are looking for ways to profit from the Y2000 difficulties, and some would argue that the stock price of Y2000-related computer vendors borders on speculative fantasy. We find it surprising, however, how little the interest in Year 2000 has picked up in the financial community in the 16 months that have passed since we wrote the first edition of this book. Just as unscrupulous business people and charlatans prey on the hopes of AIDS victims by promising a miracle cure, we should not be surprised to see wild schemes emerging in 1999 whose purpose is to relieve nervous citizens of their life savings in return for a phony scheme to protect those savings.

In this chapter, we'll discuss three primary components of the financial institutions with which most of us have some day-to-day contact: the banks that provide checking and savings accounts, the credit card companies that fill our wallets with plastic, and the stock-market industry that provide innumerable ways in which to invest our funds. As usual, we'll then conclude with some advice for coping with minor, moderate, serious, and catastrophic failures in these institutions.

Y2000 and the Banking System

Appendix A of this book provides the technical details of a simple example of a Y2000-related banking problem: Erroneous date arithmetic could cause a bank's computer system to go awry, or to generate hysterically incorrect results, when computing the interest on your car loan or your home mortgage. The fundamental problem is that nearly every computer system within a bank is concerned with "transactions," and those transactions have dates attached to them. Whether it's a deposit transaction, or a withdrawal transaction, or a transaction describing the transfer of funds from your checking account to your savings account, they're all vulnerable.

One of the most common questions we are asked is what progress has been made on Y2K since we were writing the first edition of this book in the spring of 1997. This is a relevant question for all topics and industries, not just banking and finance. With regards to banks, we wanted to address this question in the beginning of the chapter. We cannot provide much of an update here, as banks are forbidden from disclosing much on their Y2K progress, and Y2K ratings given out by the Fed are top secret. We strongly believe that disclosure, research, and information-providing should be integral to dealing with Y2K, which is not how the government is choosing to handle Y2K with respect to banks. This is from a May 13, 1998 FFIEC bulletin:

> *Depository institutions are reminded that they may not disclose publicly the contents of federal supervisory agency examination reports or reviews of the institution or any service provider or software vendor, including the confidential Year 2000 summary ratings contained therein. Thus, in designing their Year 2000 public awareness plans and efforts, institutions should be careful not to violate this prohibition. Moreover, they should avoid any statements that indicate or im-*

ply that the institution's readiness has been approved or certified by a supervising agency with regard to its Year 2000 plan.

Conclusion

Financial institutions should develop a pragmatic strategy for responding to customer inquiries about their institution's Year 2000 readiness. The guidance in this interagency statement is designed to assist financial institutions in developing their programs. Each institution may choose to tailor its customer awareness program based on its own business environment, but ultimately, it is essential that each institution develop a program to address customer questions and concerns about the status of Year 2000 readiness.

Below, we show a filing from the FDIC Web site, which clearly states its policy on disclosing Y2K assessment information. We believe it is very important to include these postings to make it clear that the reason why we don't have much information on banks is because we are not allowed to get it.

FIL-74-98 July 8, 1998 YEAR 2000 ASSESSMENT RATING

TO: CHIEF EXECUTIVE OFFICER

SUBJECT: Confidentiality of Year 2000 Assessment Rating

The Federal Deposit Insurance Corporation (FDIC), in partnership with state banking regulators, recently completed initial on-site Year 2000 assessments of all state non-member banks. A number of insured financial institutions have asked whether they may disclose to the public the rating assigned to their institution. FDIC regulations strictly prohibit such a disclosure.

Information from Year 2000 assessments are governed by the same rules of confidentiality that apply to FDIC examinations for safety and soundness, compliance, information systems, and trust activities. Under Part 309 of the FDIC's rules and regulations, disclosure of reports of examination, or any information contained in them, is strictly prohibited. Accordingly, institutions may not disclose results from Year 2000 assessments just as they may not disclose other types of examination information.

Moreover, disclosure of such information to third parties such as financial ratings firms or fidelity bond carriers is likewise prohibited. Requests from such entities are not authorized by the FDIC or any other banking regulator. In light of the blanket prohibition on disclosing ratings, compilations of Year 2000 ratings by such firms are necessarily incomplete and unreliable.

While the disclosure of Year 2000 assessment information is prohibited, the FDIC strongly encourages financial institutions to publicly disclose the steps they have taken to address Year 2000 issues, including their own evaluation of their compliance with Year 2000 guidance issued by the Federal Financial Institutions Examination Council (FFIEC). Such disclosures are an effective method for institutions to inform customers of their Year 2000 readiness, and are recommended by the FDIC. In FIL-52-98, "Year 2000 Customer Awareness Guidance" issued on May 13, 1998, the FDIC emphasized the importance of effective communication between institutions and their customers. In FIL-24-98, "Discussion of Year 2000 Issues in Annual Disclosures" issued on February 27, 1998, the FDIC highlighted the Securities and Exchange Commission's (SEC) Year 2000 disclosure requirements for publicly traded institutions. The FDIC also encouraged other institutions not subject to SEC requirements to use the SEC guidance as the basis for voluntary public disclosure about Year 2000 readiness.

The FDIC, in conjunction with the other federal banking agencies, also assesses the Year 2000 readiness of the majority of service providers and selected software vendors.

The FDIC and the other federal banking agencies disclose the assessment information of such service providers, and those software vendors who consent to disclosure, to their insured financial institution customers. However, under the same disclosure rules that apply to financial institutions, service providers and software vendors are not authorized to disclose their Year 2000 assessment information. Likewise, insured financial institution customers may not disclose the assessment information of their service providers or software vendors. The FDIC does not "certify" Year 2000 compliance of service providers or software vendors, nor does it rank their Year 2000 readiness efforts. Like insured financial institutions, service providers and software vendors are encouraged to share with their customers the steps they have taken to address Year 2000 issues.

For further information, please contact your Division of Supervision regional office.

Nicholas J. Ketcha Jr.

Director

Lest you think this discussion of banking problems is academic or reserved for public officials, take a look at the news report summarized below, which appeared in *Business Week* when we were preparing this chapter for the second edition of our book in the fall of 1998:

01/26/98

WILL YOUR BANK LIVE TO SEE THE MILLENNIUM? The Year 2000 glitch could sink lots of smaller techno-laggards.

Business is booming for John McIsaac, a consultant who helps small banks with Year 2000 issues. But his life could get a lot more hectic. Recently, McIsaac, the CEO of Market Partners Inc. in West Chester, Pa., was approached by executives of a midsize regional bank with $20 billion in assets that had not started its program to fix its computer coding. The bank had hired a consulting firm, but the contract fell apart when the firm "found a more attractive financial deal." Says McIsaac. "In this industry, there's more work than consulting companies can handle."

McIsaac may take the assignment, but he's not optimistic. "No matter how much money they put on the table, we may find there is nothing anyone can do to help them," he says. "They were too slow to start, and now it may be too late."

The Year 2000 problem—computer systems that will read 1900 instead of 2000 on Jan. 1, 2000—is bedeviling thousands of businesses. But financial institutions, especially banks, have the most to worry about. They all deal with funds with dates attached. Banks are linked in an intricate financial web so that each bank depends on the accuracy of other banks' computer systems, including the Federal Reserve Bank. If computers can't read the date 2000, the best-case scenario is that computers just won't work. Worst-case, they miscalculate all types of numbers, from mortgage payments to stock prices.

Most major banks are well on their way to fixing their systems. But more than a fair number are lagging behind, especially midsize and small banks. Says George R. Juncker, vice-president of the Federal Reserve Bank of New York: "I think definitely... some just won't be open for business on Jan. 3, 2000."

BROKEN KNEECAPS? For now, banks are being subjected to extraordinary scrutiny by regulators and scrambling to pass stiff audits that started last spring. The Federal Reserve Board already ordered one case-and-desist last November on three affiliated banks in Georgia for their lack of preparedness. Expect more. "We anticipate to take whatever supervisory action is needed," says Mark L. O'Dell, director of the bank technology division at the Office of the Comptroller of the Currency (OCC). "And if it involves taking formal enforcement action, we will do it." Edward E. Yardeni, chief economist for Deutsche Morgan Grenfell Inc., says, "There have been pretty explicit threats from the Fed they'll break kneecaps to get banks ready for this." Still, Yardeni predicts that from 5% to 20% of banks will fail as a direct result of Year 2000.

Fixing the problem is a costly, labor intensive task. At San Francisco-based Bank of America, the fifth largest U.S. bank, a thousand people are working full-time examining 200 million lines of code. Currently, only 35% of the code is fixed. Estimated price tag for the job: $250 million.

While Bank of America's problems are complex, it has an edge over smaller banks in that it has the resources to throw at the project, even if costs rise. Already, some fairly large banks—such as CoreStates, Boatmen's Bancshares, U.S. Bancorp, and Barnett Banks—have put themselves up for sale over the past year-and-a-half, citing as factor spiraling technology costs. A significant portion of that increase is due to Year 2000. Over the next six months, many more banks are expected to seek partners.

Midsize banks, which range in assets from $5 billion to $35 billion, are particularly vulnerable. "There could be a number of midsize size banks [that are] going to have trouble," says Merrill Lynch & Co. analyst Sandra J. Flannigan. "I don't think they are as far along with this as the big guys." For starters, these banks have higher expense-to-revenues ratios than the top 20 banks. While software costs can be similar for both large and midsize banks, big banks can spread the costs over more customers.

Plus, midsize banks don't have the same clout as large banks when it comes to recruiting programmers. "They have the problems of the big banks, with all their customized software," says Joe McIsaac, chief information officer at Market Partners. "But they have many of the same limitations of the smaller banks, with limited budgets and technical capabilities."

Austin A. Adams agrees about the resource problem. He heads up technology for First Union Corp., the sixth-largest bank in the U.S. with $155 billion in assets. Its Year 2000 program is considered one of the industry's most advanced. But recently Adams asked a colleague at a bank with $30 billion in assets what his biggest Year 2000 concerns were. The response: "I think I've got a solid plan...but if I run into problems and need resources, I'm behind the guys like Chase {Manhattan] or NationsBank in getting help from consultants."

"There's no question small banks are further down the food chain," says Hal Schroeder, an analyst at Keefe, Bruyette & Woods Inc. in New York. The problem is code-fixing can entail unforeseen snafus. Even software packages certified as Year 2000 compliant may not be bug-less. At Wachovia Bank in Winston-Salem, N.C., which has $60 billion in assets, every piece of software that was "supposedly compliant had at

least some minor date problems," says Betsy Harris, Wachovia's vice-president for the Year 2000 project. "Vendor certification needs to be examined very carefully."

That's a crucial issue for small banks that outsource much of their operations and are at the mercy of service providers to make sure software is sent on time. Software vendors that are late delivering compliant software can put banks at risk. For instance, last summer in a letter to BankTec Inc., one of the largest software providers to community banks, a group of banks complained that BancTec Year 2000 compliant software had been delayed. BancTec says its lateness was caused by another computer firm, which had delays in making its own servers compliant. The software still has not been delivered.

CUSTOMER JITTERS. Eugene A. Ludwig, head of the OCC, expressed concern in July that small community banks, with 16% of national bank assets, were behind on their 2000 programs. According to the OCC, 20% were just starting to address the issue.

Then there's the customer perspective: "There may be movement to the high ground as we move closer to 2000. Meaning...if you are heavily reliant upon a [smaller] bank, you might want to have a relationship with a major player," says Steve Sheinheit, a senior vice-president and head of corporate systems and architecture at Chase Manhattan Bank, the nation's largest.

But even large banks may pay a price. In one study, 38% of information-technology professionals surveyed by Gartner Group Inc., a technology consulting firm, said they may withdraw personal assets from banks and investment companies just prior to 2000.

> *If the pros become sufficiently concerned about banks' ability to operate, ordinary citizens may follow suit, says Schroeder, "It could turn into an It's a Wonderful Life scenario with depositors demanding the withdrawal of large sums of money, whereby banks have to liquidate assets to have sufficient cash." Unfortunately, when it comes to easing customers' concerns, most bankers are no Jimmy Stewart.*

A second fundamental problem is that banking (along with insurance companies and government agencies) were one of the first industries to begin automating their operations in the 1950s. Thus, unlike many small companies that only began computerizing when the price of desktop computers fell below $2,000, banks have accumulated 30-40 years of old "legacy" computer programs. Obviously, some of the old programs have been replaced by newer programs; the newer programs (e.g., those that are only, say, 10 years old) may also have Y2000 software problems, but they're likely to be written in more familiar programming languages, with some vestiges of useful documentation with which the programmers can figure out where the corrections need to be made.

Along with ancient age of these legacy programs, there's also the problem of magnitude: Banks have vast amounts of software that has to be fixed. Citibank and Chase, two of the country's largest and most visible banks, are widely reported to have roughly 400 million and 200 million program instructions, respectively, in their "portfolio" of computer applications; one can expect similar numbers at Bank of America, Wells Fargo, First Bank of Chicago, and the rest of the top 50-100 banks.[2] (The numbers for Citibank do not reflect its recent merger with Travelers, and its new name, Citigroup.) Indeed, it would be rare to find a bank of any significant size—i.e., a bank with branches in more than one locality—that has a portfolio of less than 100 million program instructions.

These numbers are more mind-boggling than you might realize. Despite the fact that we might only have a few hundred dollars in our personal bank account, we tend to be blasé about the notion that banks wheel and deal with hundreds of millions, if not billions, of dollars. We're also blasé about the numbers associated with computer hardware: A desktop computer can carry out a million calculations a second, it can store a billion characters of data on its hard disk, and so forth. But the program instructions that comprise the bank's software were written by hand, one instruction at a time; the typical productivity of programmers creating such software is about 20-30 tested, debugged program instructions per day. The process of examining all those instructions, repairing the ones that have faulty Y2000 date-arithmetic, and testing the modified programs, can be greatly assisted by computerized tools (which explains the sudden prominence of software vendors who provide such tools)—but there is still an enormous amount of manual labor involved. A bank with 100 million program instructions can expect to devote approximately 8-12 *thousand* person-months of effort, and approximately $100-150 million to fix the problem.[3] In the spring of 1998, Citibank revised upwards its estimate of Y2K spending to $650 million from $600 million, and Chase now plans on spending $300 million on Y2K, rather than the $250 million it originally anticipated spending.

If it were merely a question of time and money, society would shrug its collective shoulders—few of us, if any, will lose any sleep worrying about the big banks spending some of their accumulated profits. On the other hand, it's quite possible that such expenses could be the straw that breaks the camel's bank for the marginal banks. And it could easily turn out that the diversion of resources (i.e., the assignment of programmers to Y2000 projects who would otherwise have been working on "new" development projects) will further erode the competitiveness of those marginal banks. And there's a further point to keep in mind, something we learned when we saw how the banks responded to their problematic real-estate and Third-World loans in the 1980s: To recoup their Y2000 expenses, the banks will raise the fees and interest charges they levy upon individuals and small companies.

Still, this is not what really troubles us. Our concern is that computer software is notoriously complex in even the best of cases, and computer development projects are notorious for being substantially behind schedule (as well as being over budget, which merely aggravates the problem described above). *The typical large business-oriented software project is 100 percent over budget and one year late.*[4] There were over 9,500 main offices of separate, discrete, FDIC-insured commercial banking institutions in the U. S. at the end of 1996; every one of them will be—indeed, already *are*—working on the problem. Thus, in terms of typical software-industry statistics, about 25 percent of them will be late finishing the job, and an embarrassingly large minority will be substantially late (and this ignores the normal industry behavior of canceling 24 percent of all development projects before they finish!).

There are more than 55,000 branch offices of these commercial banks, and of course the computer systems of each individual branch must be Y2000 compliant. These commercial banks have over $4 trillion in assets. There are also over 600 savings bank that are insured by various other agencies that are regulated by the FDIC, and these banks have almost $300 billion in deposits. There are also a few thousand thrifts, credit unions, and other savings institutions. For reasons discussed below, most banks are trying to finish their Y2000 conversion projects by December 31, 1998; thus, if they're only a year late, they may wrap things up just before the New Year's Eve party at the end of the decade. But some banks will not finish the task in time for the inexorable deadline; the only question is whether it will be your bank, or our bank, or some other hapless soul's bank.

As mentioned above, computer software is notoriously complex; that is, programmers have a very difficult time ascertaining whether their programs will behave correctly under all the possible conditions and scenarios to which it might be subjected. For a tiny computer program of, say, 100 instructions, it's possible to construct a mathematical proof of correctness; by the time one reaches the size of 1,000 instructions, such an effort is sufficient to gain a Ph.D. degree in our best universities. As one might imagine, such an effort is far beyond the ability of the most brilliant programmer—or team of programmers—when dealing with computer programs of 100,000 instructions or more. Obviously, most computer programmers are intelligent people, and they don't make a lot of mistakes; but the chances for error are much greater when (a) working under extreme pressure, (b) modifying a computer program written by someone else, (c) working in a programming language with which one is not particularly familiar or experienced, and (d) working on a program for which there is no current documentation. These four conditions are exactly what most Y2000 projects face.

The remedy, such as it is, consists of *testing*: massive testing to ensure correct behavior of the computer programs under every condition that the programmers can imagine. That's why the banks want to finish the main part of their work by December 31, 1998: They need to test "normal" conditions, end-of-month conditions, leap-year conditions, and as many other scenarios as possible during the full year of 1999. Indeed, the Federal Reserve system, as we'll see below, has strongly recommended a more aggressive stance: Banks should have finished their planning efforts by the September, 1997, so that they can spend 1998 converting and testing their own (internal) systems, and 1999 testing the *inter*-bank scenarios.

We assume that all of this will be done by intelligent, dedicated, energetic people; indeed, it's fortunate that the software industry is populated by people who are relatively young and energetic, and who are already accustomed to working massive amounts of overtime. But no matter how intelligent, and no matter how industrious they may be, the reality is that they will make mistakes. Not many, but more than you might suppose. One of the most depressing statistics about the computer software industry is that its professional practitioners deliver allegedly well-tested software to their customers with an average of approximately one defect (often referred to as a "bug") for every *hundred* program instructions. With good discipline, sophisticated tools, and sufficient resources, an average IS/IT organization within a typical American company can reduce the defect levels by approximately two orders of magnitude—i.e., to the level of one bug for every 10,000 program instructions. The "best of the best" organizations—e.g., organizations like Lucent (formerly Bell Laboratories) and Motorola and the NASA Space Shuttle software group—can improve upon this by another two orders of magnitude, thus achieving a minuscule one bug for every million program instructions.

The layman may well find these figures so appalling as to be unbelievable; indeed, it raises the obvious question: How on earth have we ever managed to get today's computer systems to work at all? The answer is: with great difficulty, at great cost, and with frequent embarrassment along the way, over a period of 30-40 years. The defects mentioned above are the ones that are discovered in operation, e.g., when the computer abruptly halts, or when it produces incorrect output. The problem is then repaired, the programmers congratulate themselves on having found what they assume is the "last" bug, and the computer system is put back into operation again. Thus, what's really significant about the legacy banking systems is that the banks have had 30-40 years to shake almost all of the defects out of their computer systems. Even today, under normal circumstances, there will be the occasional hiccup; interest payments will sometimes be incorrect, deposits or withdrawals will be double-booked, and so forth.

Consequently, the real problem with the Y2000 projects in the nation's banks (and, in a similar vein, the other banks around the world) is that all of the software will be investigated, corrected to eliminate Y2000 problems, and tested as thoroughly as possible until time runs out on New Year's Eve, 1999—*but there will still be residual errors that will gradually become evident during the first few years of the new decade.* A bank whose portfolio of computer applications contains 100 million program instructions, and whose programmers are geniuses on a par with the very best in the world may wrap up their work at the very end of the decade with only a hundred residual bugs. But the typical bank will have 10,000 such bugs, and the worst will have as many as a million defects.

Let's assume that your bank is one of the average ones, and that it marches bravely into the new millennium with hastily-modified software containing some 10,000 bugs.[5] The majority of these bugs will be nothing more than minor annoyances—e.g., an expanded date field on your monthly banking statement will chop off the first two characters of your name. But a few of the bugs are likely to have more serious consequences, such as:

- Incorrect statements, with erroneous information about deposits, withdrawals, transfers, and balances.

- An inability to withdraw money, or to credit deposits and payments properly.

- An inability to provide loans, mortgages, letters of credit, and other financial instruments.

- An inability to support normal banking operations via ATM machines, thereby requiring a retreat back to a practice long abandoned by many individuals: waiting in line to deal with a human bank teller.

These, and many other similar problems, are all internal and localized—that is, they involve the internal consequences of the bank's Y2000 computer problems. But a potentially larger problem exists when banks communicate with one another—e.g., when your employer gives you a paycheck drawn on ABC bank, and you deposit it in your account at XYZ bank, the two banks have to communicate in order to accomplish the shift of funds from ABC to XYZ. Even if all of the computer software in ABC is Y2000-compliant, problems could occur if XYZ's software is *not* Y2000 compliant. And since we're dealing with two different organizations, finger-pointing and accusations will be the typical response when a Y2000 problem emerges; the bugs that remain in the software of both banks after January 1, 2000 will most likely be the subtle, obscure bugs (the obvious ones will have been found and removed by then), so it may not be at all evident which of the banks is responsible for the Y2000 problem if your paycheck mysteriously disappears in transit between ABC and XYZ.

In some cases, the communication (and thus the "system interfaces," as computer people like to call them) exist in a more-or-less straightforward fashion between two banks, as implied above. But the country's banks have become remarkably sophisticated and complex during the past hundred years, and even something as simple as the clearing of a check written on ABC and deposited into XYZ is likely to involve several other financial institutions that operate in a manner invisible to the average citizen, but nevertheless highly dependent on computers.

The country's check-clearing system actually operates in a couple of different ways. To illustrate the most common approach, imagine that Joe Consumer writes a check from his checking account at Bank A to Joe Merchant who sells him/her some merchandise. The merchant physically brings the check to his bank (Bank B) and deposits it—but because the consumer's check is not drawn on an account at the same bank, Bank B must collect from another institution. Bank B begins the funds collection process by physically presenting the check to the bank on which it was written. Before these funds are collected, the merchant can't access them, and the bank puts them in a separate account, usually labeled Cash Items in the Process of Circulation (CIPC). When the funds become available, the CIPC account is reduced by the amount of the check, and the bank's reserves are increased. The funds, of course, are now available to the merchant. It doesn't seem like there will be many unique Year 2000 problems here because this mechanism involves physical, tangible paper (i.e., the checks themselves) being transferred between banks. The most likely Year 2000 problems that would arise in this kind of processing mechanism would be in the banks' own internal systems—and presumably these will also arise along with other functions the bank performs. Smaller banks would be more likely to use this traditional approach to check-clearing than any of the largest banks in the country. The Federal Reserve also operates an air courier service to transfer checks between member banks across the country, which could conceivably suffer its own

Y2000 problems, if there are transportation problems of the nature discussed in Chapter 4.

In addition to this traditional check-clearing mechanism, there are public and private electronic payments systems, the former being the Federal Reserve and the latter being bank clearinghouses and the CHIPS international payment system. In the example above, if an electronic payments system is used, Bank B will deposit the check from the customer into its own account at its regional Federal Reserve Bank branch. The Fed will then transfer funds electronically from Bank A's reserve account to that of Bank B. The Fed then sends the check to Bank A, and it is subtracted from the customer's account. This assumes that there are sufficient funds in the account to cover the check. Indeed, most checks do have sufficient funds, so the Federal Reserve performs this funds transferring service for checks drawn on banks in other Federal Reserve districts. Fedwire is the Federal Reserve System's bank wire transfer system. It is used by 11,600 institutions and is available on-line to 7,000 of these institutions. This same function is performed by clearinghouses.

And the problems here, of course, are compounded by the sheer volume of transactions, and the magnitude of money involved. Bank B communicates not only with Bank A and the Fed, but (directly or indirectly) with thousands of other banks; it processes not just your paycheck and the others within your company, but millions of deposits and withdrawals made by its various account-holders. The *daily* volume of "clearing" activity, including public and private payments systems, is more than $2 trillion in payments and electronic securities transactions.

This electronic payments system is where we believe most check-clearing related Year 2000 problems could occur. The payments system can be endangered by an institution defaulting on payments to other institutions or if liquidity decreases sharply. These problems arise if an institution has no more assets it can transfer to others for cash. For example, a liquidity crisis occurred in 1985, when the Bank of New York encountered a computer malfunction that enabled it to continue buying government securities, but prevented it from selling those securities. The Bank kept buying government securities, and was quickly running out of cash. This did not result in a crisis because the Bank was able to borrow from the Federal Reserve—and it did so to the tune of more than $20 billion on an overnight basis. The Bank was therefore able to meet its outgoing payment commitments until the computers were fixed. This was by far the largest one-day borrowing from the Federal Reserve's discount window (the facility by which credit is extended to eligible institutions).

Private clearinghouses sometimes argue that they can clear checks more efficiently (on a cost and time basis) than the Federal Reserve. The Federal Reserve is, however, the only institution that can *guarantee* payments, and can cause money to be created. Thus, the Fed is able to safeguard the payments system, but in doing so, also assumes payment systems risk.

In order to reduce that risk, the Fed has instituted certain rules that include a limit on how much banks can overdraw on their reserves account during the day. (Banks are required by the Fed to keep a certain percentage of their customer deposits on reserve with the central bank. These reserves can be in the form of cash held in the banks' vaults or in accounts held at the Federal Reserve.) This rule was implemented because the Fed wanted to ensure that the bank would be able to replenish their reserves account by the end of the day. When a bank is overdrawn, it must either stop payments temporarily until it has received more deposits, or it must borrow additional reserves from other banks (in the Fed Funds market).

Thus, a Year 2000 problem could hamper the check-clearing system, and could indeed start a severe liquidity crisis. Computer glitches can also hamper all of the steps outlined in the above paragraph—borrowing reserves in the Fed Funds market and monitoring reserves accounts are all done electronically. Unlike in the Bank of New York example above, though, Year 2000 computer problems would be very unlikely to be fixed in a day or two. Imagine, for the example, how serious the problem would be if Citigroup or BankAmerica or Chase found itself in a position where it could pay out funds, but not receive any because of computer glitches.

However, it's important to keep in mind that the Fed can create money, and is the protector of the payments systems. Thus, we would expect the Fed to provide unlimited liquidity if needed, much like in October 1987, when the stock market crashed. Indeed, official statements from the Federal Reserve show they are well aware of all the potential risks, and are letting us know that they intend to act as the lender of last resort. This was indicated in testimony made by Federal Reserve Governor Edward W. Kelley, Jr. to the U.S. Senate on July 30, 1997, which we've excerpted below:

> *We already have arrangements in place to assist financial institutions in the event they are unable to access their own systems. For example, we are able to provide financial institutions with access to Federal Reserve computer terminals on a limited basis for the processing of critical funds transfers. This contingency arrangement has proven highly effective when used from time to time by depository institutions experiencing major hardware / software outages or that have had their operations disrupted due to natural disasters such as the Los Ángeles earthquake, hurricane Hugo in the Carolinas, and hurricane Andrew in south Florida. In these cases we worked closely with financial institutions to ensure that adequate supplies of cash were available to the community and also arranged for our operations to function virtually without interruptions for 24 hours a day during the crisis period. We feel the experience gained from such crises will prove very helpful in the event of similar problems triggered by century date change. We are also beginning to formulate responses for augmenting certain functions, such as computer help desk services and off-line fund transfers, to respond to short-term needs for these services...*
>
> *We recognize, nonetheless, that despite their best efforts, some depository institutions may experience operating difficulties, either as a result of their own computer problems or those of their*

customers, counterparties, or others. These problems could be manifested in a number of ways and would not necessarily involve funding shortfalls. Nevertheless, the Federal Reserve is always prepared to provide information to depository institutions on the balances in their accounts with us throughout the day, so that they can identify shortfalls and seek funding in the market. The Federal Reserve will be prepared to lend in appropriate circumstances and with adequate collateral to depository institutions when market sources of funding are not reasonably available. The terms and conditions of such lending may depend upon the circumstances giving rise to the liquidity shortfall.

Unfortunately, Y2000 differs from the natural disasters outlined above. Y2000 will not occur in one geographic area... it will occur at the same time, everywhere, and to everyone, in every country around the world that has a banking system. We believe that there is likely to be delays in the clearing of some checks, and this we think would be the main ramification of Year 2000 problems in the check-clearing system.

Kelley spoke on February 11, 1998 to the Florida International Bankers Association, and the tone of his speech was more serious:

The stakes are enormous, actually, nothing less than the preservation of a safe and sound financial system that can continue to operate in an orderly manner when the clock rolls over at midnight on New Year's Eve and the millennium arrives on the scene. And even the government can not declare an extension!

So much has already been written about the difficulties ascribed to the Year 2000 challenge that the subject is becoming almost commonplace in most conversational circles. By now, almost everyone's familiar with the basic issue—specifically, that information generated on computer may be miscalculated and conveyed to others, or possibly programs may be terminated because they cannot recognize dates shown as 00. The problem is even the brunt of jokes contained in the monologues of late night TV comics, one of whom laughs that he'll know when midnight, New Year's Eve, 2000 arrives because his pace maker will start to play Auld Lang Syne. Whether you think the problem funny or not, it is quite real.

From the Federal Reserve's perspective as the central bank of the United States and a bank supervisor, we have been working intensively to address the issues faced by the industry and formulate an effective supervisory program tailored to those issues. To start with, it has taken an enormous effort simply to elevate the industry's senior management awareness of the seriousness and magnitude of the problem which sounds at first like a modest technical issue that's easy to fix and not terribly significant. But, if programming logic misinterprets the two-digit 00 representation of 2000 to be 1900, automated operating systems across the entire breadth of the world's economy are likely to miscalculate date-sensitive information or simply cease to operate. One reads in the press about the possibility of catastrophic failures in such vital systems as air traffic control, telecommunications, and the utilities that make up the power grid. Society depends on these vital systems to operate dependably, as it also depends on the financial systems to do likewise. And they are interdependent. Those responsible for every critical service need to review their Year 2000 plans to be sure they will be compliant in a timely manner so that, among other obvious reasons, the financial services industry can rely on them. In turn, we in the financial services industry are determined, to the very best of our ability, to be part of the solution and not part of the problem.

In the context of our banking environment, calculations based on a span of time such as interest earned, interest due, settlement dates and many others, may result in the generation of misinformation and errors that would be labor intensive, slow and costly to identify and correct after the fact. In the extreme, if the problem doesn't get fixed ahead of time, a bank or securities trading firm may find itself unable to depend on the information provided by its general ledger including its funding position and the account balances of its depositors and trading customers. Obviously, a bank's inability to understand and manage its funding and liquidity positions could have disastrous consequences for the organization, its customers and its counterparties.

The Federal Reserve has been involved with contingency planning and dealing with various types of emergencies for many years. Today is no different in many respects, but the need for Year 2000 readiness raises new concerns that are applicable to all banks, foreign or domestic. One is the risk of contagion. Operating problems at individual banks must not be allowed to spread and become systemic.

Another concern of the Federal Reserve is the extent to which the industry is so heavily dependent on vendors. As I noted earlier in discussing the most recent advisory to the industry, banks are ultimately responsible for their own operations despite their reliance on third-party service providers. There are many thousands of information systems vendors of one form or another that provide services to federally insured depositories, and obtaining meaningful information on vendor plans and status has proven difficult for the industry and the regulators. If they have not already done so, vendors need to provide very soon their program to renovate and support a product relied on by banks. With sufficient information on vendor plans, banks can prepare their testing strategies.

Hopefully, when the century date change arrives, we will be ready, everything will work effectively, and we will all celebrate the new millennium in a relaxed and unreserved manner.

More Serious Banking Problems

That Y2000 software bugs could cause problems in the nation's banking system is hardly in doubt; the real question is how many such problems will occur, and how serious they'll be. If the problems were confined to one bank, and if they were resolved within a matter of days, it would be annoying for those involved, but not a matter of serious national concern. Similarly, if your paycheck is the only item lost among the millions of transfers between banks ABC and XYZ, it won't make you feel any better, but the programming staff at both banks will feel they've done a pretty good job. Sooner or later, your paycheck will be found (or the check will be canceled, and a new one issued) and life will go on.

A study of economic history reminds us, unfortunately, that things can occasionally be much worse: At intervals of approximately 20-30 years prior to the legislation associated with the New Deal era, there have been waves of bank runs, bank failures, and currency collapse. As noted earlier, many of these acute problems have been caused by war, massive speculation, or corruption; and while today's banking laws may be adequate for dealing with those issues, they may not be sufficient to cope with a "systemic" Y2000-induced banking crisis.

One of the classic problems is that of a "run" on the bank, caused by a real or imaginary fear on the part of depositors that their funds have vanished, or that the bank is in imminent danger of being shut down. There is an interesting paradox here, one that exists not only in the modern American banking system, but that has been true since banks were first created. In recounting the history of banking in Amsterdam, for example, Galbraith notes that:

> *In 1672, when the armies of Louis XIV approached Amsterdam, there was grave alarm. Merchants besieged the Bank, some in the suspicion that their wealth might not be there. All who sought their money were paid, and when they found this to be so, they did not want payment. As was often to be observed in the future, however desperately people want their money from a bank, when they are assured they can get it, they no longer want it.*[6]
>
> *Unfortunately, the converse is also true: When depositors are no longer confident, their natural instinct is to withdraw their money as quickly as possible. Given the nature of banking, this almost always causes problems even when the bank is fundamentally sound and operating in a conservative fashion—because only a fraction of the aggregate funds of depositors is actually lodged within the bank. The rest has been loaned out to individuals, corporations, other banks, and even governments.*

> *Federally chartered banks (i.e., those that belong to the Federal Reserve Banking system) are required to maintain 10 percent of their demand deposits (checking and others from which transfers can be made to third parties) "in reserve," but are not required to maintain any reserve for time deposits. This "fractional reserve" system is designed to ensure that if you want your money, it will be there.*

While carrying out the research for this book, we found a Dallas-based software company, Carreker Antinori (http://www.carreker.com), whose software product makes it possible for banks to "sweep" funds from accounts with reserve requirements, to those without reserve requirements. This software, and similar software developed internally at banks, uses "artificial intelligence" to determine what the optimal amount of funds is to leave in the account from which funds are being swept. In other words, banks are sweeping money out of accounts from which checks are paid and funds are withdrawn, to accounts that cannot readily have funds withdrawn, and that are not subject to reserve requirements. This practice is permitted by the Federal Reserve as long as the number of transfers per month is limited. It thus permits banks, as a practical matter, to carry fewer reserves than the 10 percent required by law. This practice is used more than we might have thought: Our source at Carreker Antinori informed us that most of the top 200 banks use this process, and that approximately $80 billion has been "restructured" using this process. We find this alarming, given the potential problems banks face entering the new millennium.

Unfortunately, even a conservative reserve policy may be insufficient to stop a true panic: If a substantial majority of the bank's depositors demand to liquidate their account and withdraw their cash, it's virtually certain that the bank will be unable to honor the demands—unless, of course, it can borrow funds from other banks or from the "lender of last resort," the Federal Reserve. It was the lack of such a backup system that was largely responsible for the bank failures at the beginning of the Great Depression. For those of the current generation who may have slept through their high-school civics class when this topic was being discussed, a brief summary of the statistics may be useful:

> *In 1929, 659 banks failed, a fair number after the crash. In 1930, 1352 went under and in 1931, 2294. Failures were still the most numerous among the small non-member banks of the old compromise. But now, when the rumours spread and the lines formed, no bank was safe... By the end of 1933, nearly half of all the nation's banks had disappeared.*
>
> *...The [Reconstruction Finance Corporation] notwithstanding, the runs continued. And by late 1932 and early 1933, they had ceased to involve individual banks and small banks and now spread over whole communities and even states. They also extended into the principal financial centres and to the big banks. The remedy that now occurred to the authorities, as the runs became pandemic, was to close up all the banks in the community before their depositors close them up anyway. At the end of October 1932, all the Nevada banks were thus placed on vacation...when Roosevelt was inaugurated, only the banks in the Northeast were still doing business. On 6 March 1933, by Executive Order*

deriving its authority from the Trading with the Enemy Act of the First World War, the holiday was made nationwide.[7]

Sobering though these statistics might be, the common reaction from both layman and expert in today's society is, "Such a thing could never happen again." And perhaps the strongest reason for this faith in today's banking system comes from one of the final legacies of the banking debacle in 1933: the creation of the Federal Deposit Insurance Corporation, known to most citizens simply as the FDIC. As Galbraith puts it:

In the banking legislation passed in 1933, there was one provision that was opposed by conservatives and the new Administration alike. This was written by Representative Henry B. Steagall of Alabama, who had a reputation for eccentricity, even crankiness, where money was concerned, and by Senator Arthur Vandenberg of Michigan; it provided for the insurance of bank deposits. A special corporation, the Federal Deposit Insurance Corporation, would be chartered and capitalized by the Treasury and the Federal Reserve Banks. Insurance would be available to the depositors of all banks—state or national, members or nonmembers of the Federal Reserve—which chose to join...

In all American monetary history no legislative action brought such a change as this. Not since, to this writing, have the lines formed outside one bank and then spread ineluctably to the others in the town. Almost never have the lines formed at all. Nor was there reason why they should. A government insurance fund was now back of the deposits; no matter what happened to the bank, the depositors would get theirs.[8]

There is only one problem with this noble scheme: The FDIC is based on the same "fractional" reserve system as the banks themselves. Its officers and supporters would doubtless prefer to describe the situation in some other terms, but as noted by Professor Galbraith in the comments above, FDIC is first and foremost an *insurance* entity; thus, its existence is predicated on the statistical probability that only a small number of its member banks (and their respective depositors) will need assistance at any given time. The FDIC can bail out a single bank, or even a handful; but it lacks the reserves to bail them all out at once, nor can it realistically handle a large wave of simultaneous bank failures. This sobering reality came to light during the 1980s, when the failure of several smaller banks in the so-called "savings and loans" scandals sorely tested the financial resources of the FDIC. As a result, we think it's useful to look at why and how the FDIC was created, and the history of bank failures, and why they have arisen—for it may give us a better understanding of the possible impact of a systemic Y2000-induced jolt to the system.

After the stock market crash of 1929 and the failure of many banks and corporations, the Banking Act of 1933 established the Federal Deposit Insurance Corporation (FDIC), and some faith returned to the banking system. The FDIC was created as an independent federal agency responsible for the regulation of federally insured savings banks, the Bank Insurance fund, and the Savings Association Insurance Fund (SAIF). The FDIC works much like a medical insurance company, in that it charges premiums to its members based on the probabilities of bank failures and depositors it might have to pay off. Unlike a medical insurance company, however, the FDIC has actually returned premiums when it has had surpluses at the end of the year.

Obviously, anyone but the most fanatical extremist devoutly hopes that the FDIC will never be called upon to handle more than a few Y2000-induced bank collapses. The authors of this book have modest savings accounts, too, and those accounts are just as vulnerable as the accounts of readers of this book. But wishful thinking and collective optimism may not be enough to prevent a serious problem: If indeed there does turn out to be a banking crisis on the scale of the Great Depression, we believe that it's almost inevitable that government legislation and regulation will be created to cope with it. The risk of Year 2000-related bank withdrawals has already been publicly addressed by the Federal Reserve: The Fed has already announced that they plan on increasing the amount of cash in circulation to deal with possible bank runs. The Fed announced that they would hold $200 billion in bills in inventory next year, rather than the usual $150 billion. While this increase (33 percent) does not seem terribly significant, we think it is important to note that this announcement was made in August of 1998, so it is possible we could see further increases to that number throughout next year.

A recent survey done by the Gartner Group showed that out of 1,100 IT professionals surveyed worldwide, 38 percent said they may withdraw personal assets from banks and investment companies before the Year 2000. A survey in CIO magazine showed that 25 percent of 643 professionals surveyed said they would withdraw assets from financial institutions in mid-1999 if it looked like there would be problems related to Y2K. If the people who are working on the Y2K problem are concerned about their assets, its reasonable to assume that others will be too... and that maybe we all should be.

Another risk, of course, is the Year 2000 compliance of the FDIC itself, the status of which was called into question in February 1998. The Associated Press reported that in a letter to FDIC Chairman Andrew Hove, Representative Jim Leach (R-Iowa), chairman of the House Banking Committee, wrote:

> *It now appears that the FDIC may not itself have met the standards it has set for financial institutions.*

And this, according to the FDIC itself:

> *The FDIC has a total of 39 mission critical systems. Of these, 10 systems are Year 2000 ready and have been fully tested and implemented. Of the remaining 29 systems, 24 mission critical systems have been renovated and 5 mission critical systems are being replaced.*
>
> *Testing on renovated systems will be completed by January 31, 1999 and implementation will be completed by March 31, 1999.*

About 380 of our information technology systems are currently scheduled to continue beyond January 1, 2000. Of these 380 systems, 101 (28 percent) are Year 2000 ready and have been tested and implemented. Seventy-five systems (19 percent) are currently being tested. The remaining 204 systems (53 percent) have been renovated and are awaiting testing. Test plans are being developed for each application and testing is scheduled to occur between now and January 1999. Testing will be completed by January 31, 1999 and the implementation of systems will be completed by the end of March 1999.

The FDIC has over 1,800 purchased products supporting its operations, including commercial off-the-shelf software, mainframe operating systems and associated software, and vendor provided hardware components, including personal computers and telephones. We contacted vendors and requested Year 2000 readiness information on each of these 1,800 products. We have responses from many of these vendors and are validating the information. In addition, we have identified upgrades that are necessary for our telephone equipment to be Year 2000 ready, and will complete the upgrades this year. We also have identified personal computers and other equipment, such as facsimile machines, that are not currently Year 2000 ready. We plan to replace this equipment in 1998 and 1999 and these efforts are on schedule.

We believe that our strong project management efforts will enable us to continue business as usual after January 1, 2000. Nonetheless, as recommended by the U.S. General Accounting Office and the FDIC's Office of Inspector General, the FDIC is preparing a business continuity plan outlining how the agency would resume normal business operations for each of the FDIC's core business processes in the event that unforeseen Year 2000 problems cause disrup-

> *tions. We also have developed contingency plans for each of our mission critical systems to ensure continuity of core business processes.*

It's impossible to tell, at this point, precisely what kind of action will be taken; the only certainty is that it will be surrounded by massive partisan, political debate and that it will be enacted months or years after the crisis begins. Though history rarely, if ever, repeats itself with precision, we can't help wondering how many parallels there may be between the Great Depression of the 1930s and the potential crisis caused by Y2000-induced banking failures. It's worth noting, in this context, that three years, four months, and seven days elapsed between the stock market crash of October 29, 1929 and Franklin Delano Roosevelt's declaration of a national banking holiday on March 6, 1933.

One of the shortcomings of the creation of the FDIC was that it created a "moral hazard" problem. People just assumed that if their bank offered federally sponsored insurance, then it was a safe bank. This gets to the heart of what could be quite serious problems in the financial sector because of the Year 2000: Our banking, financial markets, and economy are built on confidence. A sharp drop in confidence in U.S. financial institutions will cause a multiplier effect, where individuals will only want their money under their mattress. Despite our confidence-reliant banking system, federally insured banks are subject to frequent examinations, including the CAMEL (Capital adequacy, Asset quality, Management competence and control, Earnings, and Liquidity) exam.

If problems are found to be serious after a few examinations, a bank will receive a "cease and desist" order that would force it to make the necessary changes.

The renewed faith brought about by the creation of a federal agency charged with insuring bank deposits resulted in a dramatic drop in the number of bank failures during the Depression. Between 1930 and 1933, before the FDIC was created, an average of more than 2200 banks were failing every year. Between 1934 and 1942, however, an average of only 54 banks failed every year. The annual number of failures continued to be minimal until the 1980s when deregulation, higher interest rates, regionally weak economies and bad loans to less developed countries put pressure on many banks, and especially S&Ls. Between 1983 and 1987, an average of 119 banks failed ever year, while in 1988, 228 banks went out business.

Federal deposit insurance now covers deposits up to $100,000, and must be obtained by all federally chartered commercial banks, savings banks, savings and loans, and credit unions from one of the federal insurance funds. Federal insurance is also provided to credit unions' depositors shares through the National Credit Union Share Insurance Fund (NCUSIF). The NCUSIF was established in 1970 and gives insurance of up to $100,000 for participating credit union members' shares. By contrast, state-sponsored insurance funds have fallen out favor, since so many failed in the 1980s. They are generally considered less secure than federal funds because state governments don't have the ability to print money, like federal governments do. In addition, state governments are usually very reluctant to raise state taxes to bail out banks if the state funds run out of money. Many state insurance funds encourage state chartered banks to get state insurance wherever possible, but state chartered institutions can also get federal insurance as long as they meet the standards set by the particular fund they are trying to get insurance from.

It's instructive to review the policies adopted by federal agencies to deal with bank failures during the 1980s, because it seems likely any bank failures resulting from Y2000 problems would be resolved in a manner more similar to that of the 1980s than of the 1930s. Two policies were implemented in the 80s by the federal insurance funds mentioned above. The first was called a "purchase and assumption" policy, under which the fund had two procedures it could follow when a bank was in danger of failing The first procedure was simple and straightforward: If a bank failed, the depositors would first be paid for their deposits up to $100,000. After the $100,000 ceiling was hit, depositors would either receive partial or zero settlement, when the assets of the bank were sold.[9] The second procedure consisted of allowing another bank to purchase an endangered institution and assume its liabilities, rather than letting it fail. The rationale for the second procedure is that if all the liabilities of the endangered bank are assumed, then no depositor loses any money; however, it's interesting to note that in some cases, the FDIC may decide to assist the acquiring bank in its purchase.

The second policy adopted by the insurance funds is known as a "too big to fail" (TBTF) policy. It had always been assumed that the FDIC was hesitant to close down large banks, and that the agency would try and organize purchases of ailing institutions. In 1984, the FDIC actually announced that one ailing bank, the Continental Illinois National Bank, was too big to fail. In addition, the FDIC said, the eleven biggest banks in the country, were also too big to fail. This policy was implemented in the case of Continental Illinois National Bank in 1984, and then again in 1988 for two large banks in Texas. In both cases, and for the "too big to fail" policy in general, federal regulators announced that 100% of deposits would be paid, regardless of the size of the deposits.

Historically, bank failures have usually occurred either because of a lack of liquidity, or from risky business and lending practices. In the 1980s, both problems occurred—especially in the case of S&Ls, which concentrate on acquiring funds from issuing checking accounts and different time deposits, as well as purchasing long-term mortgages. By contrast, the commercial banks use the funds acquired from various forms of savings accounts, time deposits, and checking accounts to create a diversity of loans to businesses, individuals, and state and local governments, as well as underwriting certain forms of securities. Throughout the 1970s, S&Ls did very poorly when interest rates were rising, because government-imposed interest rate ceilings at the time prohibited them from paying competitive rates. Because of the ceilings, funds would flow out of S&Ls, market interest rates rose, to institutions and accounts that would pay a higher interest rate. S&Ls were also prohibited from conducting any business besides accounts and deposits and guaranteeing home mortgage loans.

Deregulation legislation passed in the late 1960s and the 1970s, which helped S&Ls' profitability, but ultimately led to the demise of many. And in the early 1980s, more regulatory changes were made to help S&Ls increase profits (as opposed to the original focus of the S&Ls to promote housing and home ownership). In 1980, the Depository Institutions Deregulation and Monetary Control Act (DIDCMA) removed the ceiling on interest rates that had to be paid, and also increased the federal deposit insurance limit. These acts were relatively benign, but in the early 1980s, less benign legislation followed that allowed some dubious accounting standards, and that allowed serious dilution of the ownership of institutions. For example, in December 1982, the Nolan Bill was passed, which allowed California-chartered S&Ls to invest 100 percent of deposits in any kind of venture. Similar bills were passed in Texas and Florida.

Texas became one of the first regions where the consequences began to be visible when, because of excessively speedy deregulation, fraud, unsound methods of operation, and the plunge in the price of oil, several Texas banks collapsed. Many in Texas had become quite rich in the 70s and 80s when the price of oil skyrocketed; but when oil prices fell by over 65 percent in the mid-80s, many institutions failed. In 1982 and 1983, for example, Amarillo National Bank and First of Midland collapsed because they had expanded so rapidly that management control and oversight began to fail; it was later discovered that workers in both banks were getting kickbacks. Similarly, Texas Commerce was acquired by Chemical Bank when it ran into trouble from bad loans to individuals in the oil and real estate business. Then, the troubled Interfirst Bank merged with Republic Bank. The new bank, First Republic Bank, also failed when the real estate market took a plunge. With help from the FDIC, First Republic was sold to another bank and all depositors were repaid in full, in line with the "too big to fail" policy.

One of the banks that almost certainly would have failed in 1984 without help from a federal agency was the Continental Illinois National Bank. At the time, it was the seventh largest bank in the country, and it was in trouble because of bad loans it had made in the energy and agricultural sectors, which started performing very badly. In addition, a senior loan officer at the bank bought some bad loans from another bank after being approved on a large personal loan. As reports and rumors about the possible demise of the bank began to circle, the bank began quickly losing deposits. Within three days, the bank lost almost *$4 billion* in deposits. It is important to remember that this massive bank run occurred a mere 14 years ago, so this is not ancient history. Government action started almost immediately: The Fed provided loans at the discount window (where banks can borrow reserves from the Fed). Also, the FDIC proceeded to guarantee the full deposits of all the bank's depositors up to any amount, not just up to $100,000. This last action was undertaken because of the "too big to fail" approach outlined earlier. In this case, too, the "almost" bank failure came about because of both unsound practices and liquidity problems.

While failures of this nature may or may not occur at the turn of the millennium, it's interesting to see how relatively recent events in the 1980s have been influenced by the appearance or disappearance of government regulations. A more severe form of regulation, which many people assume has vanished since the 1930s, is the *bank holiday*, i.e., where the bank is closed for some period of time by order of the government. The obvious explanation for such an event in early 2000 would be that the programmers need more time to fix their Y2000 software problems, rather than the concomitant problem that the banks have no cash in their vaults. In any case, it's important to realize that bank holidays are *not* a forgotten relic of the Great Depression. In March of 1985, a bank holiday was called because of the anticipated failure of the Home Sate Savings Bank of Cincinnati, and the possible depletion of the state insurance fund. All state-chartered Ohio S&Ls were required to close, but eventually—after nearly a year—all those that could qualify for state insurance were allowed to reopen. In May of 1985, S&L failures caused a loss to state deposit insurance funds and Maryland taxpayers of $185 million. As a result of problems like these, there was only $4.6 billion left in the FSLIC insurance fund by August of 1985.

Aside from bank holidays, additional governmental regulations could involve currency regulations (e.g., prohibitions against importing or exporting foreign currencies), daily limits on cash withdrawals from banks, or restrictions on ownership of gold.[10] Unfortunately, the government doesn't always respond to bank failures in the most efficient manner. When the government takes steps to correct any problem, blame must inevitably be assigned to someone, and no one in government wants to be the blamee. If the government must take action to help banks suffering from Y2000 problems, the American people will undoubtedly ask, "Why weren't banks more prepared? Why wasn't more attention paid to the warnings from those members of Congress who were aware of Y2000?"

To illustrate the politics that we might look forward to in the event of Y2000-induced banking problems, consider this: Even into the late 1980s, S&L losses were allowed to grow because political pressure was put on the FSLIC to keep some unhealthy banks open. No member of Congress wanted S&Ls in *their* district to be declared insolvent. Not only did Congress put pressure on the FSLIC, but they wouldn't give the FSLIC sufficient funds to cover the losses it would incur by shutting down the insolvent savings and loan associations. Needless to say, Congress never admitted that it had contributed to and, yes, aggravated, the problem.

Finally, in January of 1987, the General Accounting Office (GAO) declared the FSLIC insolvent by almost $4 billion; as of December 1987, it had a negative net worth of almost $13 billion. It continued to operate because people continued to take FSLIC promissory notes and guarantees; FSLIC, in turn, continued to hope that Congress would make good on its pledge to make future payments. In 1989, under the Financial Institutions Reform Recovery and Enforcement Act (FIRREA), the FSLIC was abolished, and S&L regulation was shifted to the newly created Office of Thrift Supervision; meanwhile, the deposit insurance function was shifted to the FDIC. Also under this act, $50 billion in government-backed bonds were sold and transferred to the newly-created Resolution Trust Corporation, which took responsibility for all institutions that were shut down, merged, or aided by the FSLIC. When the government sells bonds, it is borrowing money, and increasing its debt. The revenues the government earns are principally from taxes, and principally from personal income taxes. Thus, when the government issues (sells) bonds to pay for bank failures, it is revenue from future income taxes that will be used to pay off the debt. *In other words, it is really the U.S. taxpayers who paid for the mismanagement of S&Ls and the poor handling of the situation by the U.S. Congress.* This was obviously not popular with taxpayers and has been a general embarrassment to the Congress. Perhaps to pacify the U.S. taxpayers (but probably to reduce current and future embarrassment to themselves!), Congress made penalties stricter on fraudulent directors of institutions, and strengthened laws and regulations of federally chartered and insured financial institutions.

Economic pessimists can then look beyond the possibility of bank closings to the possibility of a long-term deflation caused the reduction of money in circulation—i.e., monies that vanish because of bank failures. Conversely, we may find ourselves faced with massive inflation; for a plausible political response to massive runs on the major national banks could be an equally massive printing of new dollar bills, with massive loans from the Federal Reserve Banks to its member banks. The real question here is what the citizenry of the U.S. would do if it managed to successfully withdraw the funds currently sequestered in banks; a fearful population that observes its phones, its cars, its jobs, its banks, and its government reeling under the attack of Y2000 bugs might well decide to use its cash to purchase tangible goods such as food and clothing. The phenomenon of large quantities of cash chasing after a fixed amount of goods (indeed, potentially a shrinking supply of goods, since the nation's manufacturing facilities may also be affected by Y2000 bugs) could cause massive inflation. The possibility of bank failures is one that has been recognized by senior officials at the Federal Reserve, as reported by BusinessWeek on January 26, 1998:

> *Most major banks are well on their way to fixing their systems. But more than a fair number are lagging behind, especially midsize and small banks. Says George R. Juncker, vice president of the Federal Reserve Bank of New York: "I think definitely... some just won't be open for business on Jan. 3, 2000."*

By the way, there's one last irony to mention: In the past, whenever a country has faced a banking or currency crisis, those who are wealthy and/or nervous about their money have traditionally moved it to a safe haven in another country. The U.S. has traditionally benefited from this tendency, particularly within the past 200+ years of warfare in Europe and political instability in other parts of the world. Conversely, some Americans have found it prudent to store a portion of their wealth in Switzerland and other so-called tax havens. Thus, the potential banking problems discussed in this chapter might prompt the suggestion to remove one's money from Citibank or Chase or BankAmerica and move it... where?

And therein lies the irony: The problems faced by American banks are the same as those faced by British, Japanese, and yes, even the fabled Swiss banks. Indeed, U.S. banks may be better off than many of their international counterparts, simply because the awareness of Y2000 problems is higher, and the U.S. banks have gotten an earlier start. The problem is now getting global, coordinated attention. Bloomberg News reported on May 17, 1998 that leaders of the Group of Eight industrialized nations had met in England. Following is the Bloomberg story:

> *Leaders of the Group of Eight industrialized nations agreed to take "further urgent action" to tackle a computer glitch that could disrupt businesses and communications in the year 2000.*
>
> *Leaders of the U.S., U.K., France, Germany, Italy, Canada, Japan and Russia said in their final communique they'd work closely with business and international organizations such as the World Bank to alleviate disruption in telecommunications, capital markets, defense and central bank systems. The leaders said they would "share information, among ourselves, and with others."*
>
> *When the Year 2000 arrives, computer systems may fail because they're programmed to recognize "00" in the year field of a date as 1900, not 2000, throwing off data processing.*
>
> *"The conversion of computer programs for the year 2000 means enormous difficulties," saud German Chancellor Helmut Kohl in a press conference as the Group of Eight's weekend summit wrapped up....*

In spite of the above statement, much of the attention, as well as the scarce programming resources, of the European banks is being concentrated on the creation of a unified European currency called the "Euro." It is hard to imagine how there will be ample resources to do the computer work necessary for both the Euro and the new millennium, a fact we fear has not been sufficiently considered by the financial markets. As *Computerworld's* Allan E. Alter puts it:[11]

The last thing IS executives need is another big conversion project. But it's looming, right on the heels of the year 2000 problem: the arrival of the European Union's new currency, the Euro.

Already, information systems managers in the European Union (EU) are preparing for European Monetary Union (EMU) and the Euro, which is expected to gradually replace the national currencies of EU members between 1999 and 2002.

Banks will feel the impact first: In 1999, they will have the option of conducting electronic funds transfers in Euros. For other businesses, the crunch comes in 2002, when the Euro begins circulating and national currencies are phased out.

For now, many U.S. firms doing business in Europe are putting the Euro on the back burner. "I think the year 2000 is still the highest [priority]," says Lauris Nance, vice president and year 2000 project executive at Equifax, Inc., an Atlanta business information services firm. "People keep hoping [the Euro] will be delayed." Others question whether the adoption of the Euro will stick to its timetable or whether all EU countries will adopt the currency...

But European banks are planning for the Euro's impact on information technology. The initial goal for bankers is "multicurrency capability" adjusting applications so they can handle multiple currencies. The Federal Association of German Banks says automated teller machines, statement printers and system connections to customers and other banks will be affected.

By 2002, retailers will need point-of-sale systems and cash registers capable of handling two currencies as well as the century change. Companies will have to adjust their finance, accounting, payment and billing systems.

> *All told, converting to the Euro should cost about $100 billion worldwide, according to Bruce Hall, former research director at Gartner Group, Inc. in Stamford, Conn. That compares with $300 billion to $600 billion worldwide for the year 2000 problem.*

What's the Fed Doing About All of This?

One thing that politicians and government regulators cannot control with laws, acts, restrictions, levies, or taxes is the inexorable advancement of the calendar. Not since the days of Pope Gregory XIII (in the late 16th century) has someone tried to change the calendar, so it's unlikely that even the most ambitious president or proactive Congress could manage to pass legislation that would prevent the arrival of January 1, 2000 at the pre-ordained hour, minute, and second.

On the other hand, the potential for serious chaos within the financial community is beginning to provoke some action within the Federal Financial Institutions Examination Council (FFIEC), an agency within the Federal Reserve systems that appears to be in charge of imposing Y2000 policies and guidelines upon the member banks.

In a May 5, 1997 press release,[12] the FFIEC congratulated itself for having first alerted the banking industry to the Y2000 problem in June 1996, and for having recommended that institutions perform risk assessment and plan a strategy for repairing their Y2000-vulnerable systems. Since this vintage-1996 advice apparently had negligible impact upon the banking industry, the May 5, 1997 statement put things in somewhat stronger language. The FFIEC then made another statement in March of 1998, which we have excerpted below:

Key points addressed in this guidance include:

- *A financial institution can face increased credit, liquidity, or counterparty trading risk when its customers encounter Year 2000-related problems. These problems may result from the failure of a customer to properly remediate its own systems and from Year 2000 problems that are not addressed by the customer's suppliers and clients. By June 30, 1998, senior management should have implemented a due diligence process which identifies, assesses and establishes controls for the Year 2000 risk posed by customers. By September 30, 1998, the assessment of individual customers' Year 2000 preparedness and the impact on an institution should be substantially completed.*

- *The due diligence process outlined in this guidance focuses on assessing and evaluating the efforts of an institution's customers to remediate their Year 2000 problems. Year 2000 issues related to the institution exchanging data with its customers should be addressed as a part of the institution's internal Year 2000 project management program.*

- *The guidance recognizes that each institution must tailor its risk management process to its size, its culture and risk appetite, the complexity of its customers, and its overall Year 2000 risk exposure. The FFIEC understands that these differences will affect the risk management programs developed by financial institutions. However, financial institutions must evaluate, monitor, and control Year 2000-related risks posed by funds providers, funds takers, and capital market / asset management counterparties.*

- *The institution's due diligence process should identify all customers representing material Year 2000-related risk, evaluate their Year 2000 preparedness, assess the aggregate Year 2000 customer risk to the institution, and develop appropriate risk controls to manage and mitigate Year 2000 customer risk.*

- *Risk management procedures will differ based on a variety of factors, including the institution's size, risk appetite and culture, the complexity of customers' information and operating systems, and the level of its own Year 2000 risk exposure. The Year 2000 due diligence processes used by smaller institutions may not be as extensive or formal as those in larger institutions where customers may be more dependent upon information technology.*

The above statement makes it clearer than before that the risks to financial institutions are more pervasive than just within their own buildings, in their own computers. The statement clearly shows that the FFIEC understands that even if a bank is Y2K compliant, if its customers, counterparties, and suppliers aren't, the bank could be in serious trouble. We interpret the May 1997 statement made by the FFIEC as implying that the FFIEC will begin auditing its member banks, beginning in mid-1998, to determine whether they are Y2000-compliant. Considering that (a) there are more than 9000 FDIC-insured commercial banks in the United States, and (b) each of those banks has a software portfolio averaging 100+ million program instructions, and (c) both technical/IT and business managers within the bank may suffer the usual human tendency to minimize or even hide the extent of their problems, and (d) the regulators are unlikely to be computer experts, we find it quite difficult to believe that this nation-wide audit will be complete, comprehensive, and accurate. Nevertheless, the FFIEC auditors may be able to obtain a statistically credible estimate of the "degree" of Y2000-readiness for the nation's banking system as a whole; and that will leave 1999 for the inevitable political battles. Meanwhile, the clock will continue to tick.

The Federal Reserve plans on testing banks for Year 2000 compliance throughout 1998 and 1999. A spot inspection has already resulted in a "cease and desist" order against Putnam-Greene Financial Corp., a Georgia holding company.

Credit Cards

One of the authors is a computer consultant who makes regular business trips of one or two weeks' duration, not only across the U.S., but to clients and computer conferences in Europe, Asia, Africa, and South America. It's relatively easy to make such a trip, for which the overall travel expenses can amount to several thousand dollars, with no more than $10 or $20 in cash for the occasional tip to hotel porters, or for a magazine in the airport. The rest, including taxi fares, can be paid by credit card. Without the wallet full of plastic cards that most of us carry today, business trips and many of the other details of day-to-day life would be considerably more tedious.

We won't re-hash the basics of date-arithmetic problems here; suffice it to say that credit card transactions are essentially the same as banking transactions: Whether it's a purchase or a payment, or any other activity on your credit card, it's virtually certain to have a date attached to it. And as with our discussion about banking above, it's important to keep in mind that a typical credit-card transaction involves several parties: the customer, the merchant, the credit-card company itself (e.g., MasterCard, Visa, American Express), and a member bank with which the card is associated. In many cases, there are other organizations involved: It's common, for example, to have a credit card linked to one's airline frequent flyer account, so that each dollar of purchases produces a credit of one frequent-flyer mile.

There's at least one other item that distinguishes credit cards from bank accounts: Credit cards traditionally have expiration dates, while the typical bank account has no termination date. Since most credit cards have an expiration date two, three, or four years after the date of issue, it means that most of the credit card companies are already experiencing Y2000 problems. At the time the first edition of this book was being written, in the fall of 1997, all of the major credit card companies in the U.S. were restricting the expiration date of new cards to 1999 (or before), because of potential problems with merchants rejecting cards with an expiration date of "00".[13]

The other aspect of credit cards that differs substantially from one's checking or savings account involves the concept of liabilities versus assets. Our savings account is an asset: It's our money, and it belongs to us, and we have merely placed it in the bank's vault for temporary safekeeping. As noted above, if we suddenly get the impression that the bank has lost the money, or has closed its doors, it creates an emotional reaction of outrage; accusations of theft and embezzlement are hard to resist.

A credit card, on the other hand, involves a liability—i.e., a mechanism for incurring a debt. This is not true of the newer "debit cards," but these are not yet widespread in the U.S.; most of us use the familiar MasterCard or Visa plastic that allows us to accumulate a month-to-month debt. American

Express expects us to pay off that debt, in full, when each monthly statement is rendered; MasterCard and Visa are content to accept a minimal payment, in return for the privilege of levying interest charges that, in more conservative times, would have been labeled usurious.

The reason for reminding you of this difference is to suggest that the public reaction to a Y2000-induced failure of credit cards might be considerably different than a Y2000-induced failure of the banks themselves. If we can't withdraw the funds from our savings account, the reaction is immediate and visceral; lines will form at the bank's front door. But if the merchants and MasterCard and the associated bank somehow fail to send us our monthly credit-card statement, very few of us will rush to the bank in an effort to pay off the bill. Indeed, the Y2000 problem will only cause a visceral reaction for those who depend on credit cards for a ready supply of easy credit, and for those of us who prefer to travel, dine, and shop with a minimum of cash in our pockets. The latter group can learn to adjust; the former group may find it more difficult to do so.[14]

The Stock Market

Like banking and the credit card industry, Wall Street and the entire securities industry depends heavily on computers. Just before the Great Crash of 1929, Wall Street labored enormously to handle then-record volumes of 5 million shares per day; ticker tapes regularly ran an hour behind actual trading, and exhausted clerks worked nights and weekends to reconcile all of the paperwork. Today, stock market volumes frequently exceed 700 million shares per day, and the massive bookkeeping activities are all handled by computers. No computers means no trading. (The "no trading" phenomenon could also result from having no phones, and no banking system, but that has to do with the "ripple effect" phenomenon discussed in Appendix B.)

Since we wrote the first edition of this book, there has not been a significant increase in the attention or research devoted to the Year 2000. There is virtually nothing written in Wall Street research reports, and despite the growing number of Wall Street economists calling for a U.S. recession, very few of them mention the Year 2000. This, despite the fact that 29 major Wall Street firms undertook a week-long test simulating trading after the Year 2000. The firms involved make up half of Wall Street's trading. The test was said to have gone very smoothly, with errors in approximately 1 percent of the trades. Our concern with the validity of these results is that the other half of Wall Street's trading is made up of much more than 29 firms, and we don't know the status of the Year 2000 compliance of the other companies. Also, we don't know what type of trading was tested: Was it just straight buying and selling? Was it short-selling? Did it include swaps, swaptions, options, forwards, and foreign exchange? Did it include the unwinding of any complex derivatives? In other words, was it realistic?

Our concern seems valid: A survey taken in the summer of 1998 by the National Association of

Securities Dealers showed that 21 percent of the 5,160 securities firms surveyed had not yet prepared a plan for making sure their computer systems could function after the Year 2000. The survey also showed that 25 precent of the firms surveyed said they had completed 30 percent or less of the Year 2000 repairs. The survey included responses from 3,214 firms that initiate stock trades, 373 clearing firms, and 1,573 other securities firms.

We continue to believe that the Year 2000 issue will become important for Wall Street and equity analysts, and that the longer it takes to become a mainstream Wall Street issue, the more severe the reaction and possible panic will be. More stringent requirements by the SEC will force companies to disclose the costs of their Year 2000 repairs and testing as well as the approximate economic significance of the Year 2000 if it does not finish its repairs on time.

Again, the fundamental problem is that all of the stock-market transactions involve dates, which means that almost all of the computer systems within a securities firm is Y2000-vulnerable. And, like the banks, the problem is compounded by massive volumes of transactions, massive amounts of software to be converted, and a combination of scarce programming resources and limited time. Australia's *Financial Review* estimates the total Y2000 price-tag for the securities industry at $5 billion and the expenses of Merrill Lynch alone as $200 million.[15] Merrill Lynch, by the way, has expressed confidence that it will be finished with its

Y2000 conversions by the end of 1998;[16] if you ask most other Wall Street firms about their plans, the chances are that you'll hear the same year-end 1998 date, but without much detail to back it up. Recently, Merrill Lynch announced that was revising upwards its Y2K spending estimate to $375 million from its original estimate of $275 million.

One of the most sobering analyses of the state of Y2000 activity in both the securities industry and the rest of U.S. industry comes from the respected Wall Street firm of J.P. Morgan. In a May 15, 1997 report, Morgan's analysts summarize the state of Y2000 preparations in the U.S. private sector as "serious," with the following commentary:[17]

> *Project status varies quite a bit from industry to industry and company to company, although awareness is generally very high (even at senior management levels) and funding for projects is mostly under way. Overall, the insurance industry is a little ahead, while the financial services industry is coming on strong but has a long way to go. Telecommunications, caught in the cross-currents of deregulation and increased competition, also has a lot of work to catch up on. Although these three groups have often been cited as having difficult compliance issues, other industries, such as manufacturing and utilities, may also have big headaches in the form of embedded silicon chips, which may require complete hardware replacement.*

Assuming that Wall Street itself continues to function, there's a related question: What will investors think about the value of their stock holdings in companies whose earnings are already being affected by Y2000 expenses? What will they think when they begin to contemplate the possibility of massive post-Y2000 lawsuits against the companies they've invested in—lawsuits that could dwarf the tobacco, asbestos, and silicone-implant lawsuits of recent years?

We described in detail in Chapter 2 the impact on corporate earnings, and the subsequent impact on the share price, of Quaker Fabrics. This story was especially interesting to us as the company involved is not in an industry that is heavily dependent on computers, and because Quaker Fabrics was trying to update their systems in advance. The potential impact on corporate earnings was just beginning to emerge in 1997, when the first edition of this book was being written. As *Information Week* magazine points out,[18]

> *Year 2000 expenditures are reaching the bottom line. Several companies say they will cut corporate earnings to account for the cost of the millennium fix as they find they can't fund their entire year 2000 projects from existing IS budgets. Two research reports indicate that many more companies will have to go the same route.*
>
> *In its annual report, Equifax Inc., a $1.9 billion financial services company in Atlanta, deducted 1 cent per share from earnings to account for its 1996 year 2000 spending—and stated that additional year 2000 spending in 1997 and 1998 would trim four to five cents per share. Year 2000 costs ate up $1 million in the first quarter this year alone.*
>
> *Southern New England Telecommunication Corp. expects to spend $15 million to $20 million this year on its year 2000 fix, which means cutting its earnings for the year from $3.20 to as low*

as $2.90, estimates Scott Wright, a telecom analyst at Argus Research Corp. in New York. "That's not chicken feed," says Wright.

The summer and fall months of 1998 in the stock market have been very different than those of 1997. The U.S. stock market was technically on the brink of a bear market, being down a little over 19 percent from peak to trough (a bear market is technically defined as a 20-percent decline from peak to trough). Although there has been a recovery in the stock market in September and October of 1998, it has been a narrow recovery. Most small companies share prices are down over 50 percent from their high, and many large financial services companies (banks, insurance companies, investment banks, brokerage houses, and the like) are down a similar amount. Nonetheless, the drop in stock prices has occurred with little to no focus on the Year 2000 problem, and its potential economic impact. The troubles in emerging markets and problems with hedge funds have made all of the headlines in the fall of 1998, delaying further the day Wall Street wakes up to Y2K. Since *every* company is going to be hit with Y2000 costs, perhaps Wall Street will simply discount the entire Y2000 phenomenon as a one-time event, and maintain the current level of prices. On the other hand, the savvy investor will realize that some companies, within any given industry, will end up spending substantially more than others, because of a late start, incompetent managers, excessively complex software, and so forth. More important, some companies may come through the Y2000 crisis in a substantially weakened state, with future prospects dimmed by expensive lawsuits and continuing Y2000 malfunctions within its mission-critical computer systems. That kind of assessment would almost certainly drive down the price of a stock; and if such an assessment were made, collectively, about a majority of the companies comprising the Dow-Jones index, it would not be surprising to see a Y2000-induced slump that finally brings an end to the long bull market of the 1990s. The most likely outcome, in our opinion, is that the fear and uncertainty surrounding Y2K will have a very negative impact on financial markets. Wall Street and the analysts who recommend stocks, are able to discount *certain* negative news right away... what is far worse for Wall Street, and far more difficult for the analysts to deal with, is uncertainty.

Recap: Could Things Really Be This Bad?

Both authors, in their day-to-day lives, are cheerful optimists. We expect the sun to come up every day, and it never crosses our mind that the sky will fall, or that the earth will come to an end. But after reading the words we've written in this chapter, we worry that we might be labeled hysterical, gloom-and-doom pessimists. Hence a brief recap to put all of this in perspective.

First, it should be emphasized again that we desperately hope that the Y2000 problems can be overcome by dint of hard work throughout the financial community in the remaining years of the decade. As noted above, we too have savings accounts, and credit cards, and even a few stocks and bonds. It is no more in our interests than anyone else's (except, perhaps, a few aging hard-line Communists watching all of this from a remote corner of Russia) to see the American banking system collapse.

And we certainly don't expect a full-scale collapse. From the various commentaries cited above, it's obvious that the financial community *is* aware of the problem, and that substantial financial and human resources are now being committed to fix the problem. If the testimony at Senator Dodd's recent Senate hearing is to be believed, 10 percent of the banks are already Y2000 compliant, as of mid-1997. The question is: What will the percentage be at the close of business on Friday, December 31, 1999? Surely it will be higher than 10 percent, and as optimists ourselves, we would like to believe that it will be 80 percent or 90 percent or even 95 percent. But given the late start, and the massive size of the Y2000 problem, and the intrinsic complexity of modifying all of that computer software, we simply cannot believe that the figure will approach 100 percent.

The consequences of Y2000 failures in the remaining 5 percent, 10 percent, or 20 percent of the banks is unknown as we write this book, and will probably remain unknowable until the new millennium begins. However, if we could be absolutely certain that the Y2000 problem could be contained entirely *within* the offending banks, then perhaps it would be possible to take proactive measures. As noted above, the FFIEC has implied, with its statement in mid-May 1997, that it will begin auditing banks for Y2000 compliance in mid-1998. If this is true, and if the FFIEC has the authority to shut down non-compliant banks, then we might have adequate time during 1999 to effect an orderly transfer of funds and accounts to banks that have been certified as Y2000-compliant.

But this presumes that Y2000 compliance is a black-and-white, all-or-nothing proposition; it also presumes that the FFIEC auditors have a sufficient supply of time, resources, and competence to accurately determine a bank's compliance. As we noted above, even the most brilliant of computer programmers, equipped with the very best technology and procedures, have not been able to improve upon the record of one defect per million program instructions for large, complex computer systems. Alas, the software professionals working in the nation's banks and financial institutions cannot walk on water; the best that can be said is that they swim through water competently, and we regret to report that there are some who can barely pass water.

This point must be stressed: *Every piece of evidence that we have from 40 years of experience in the software industry tells us that an estimate of one defect per 10,000 instructions is the best we can hope for in a typical organization.* And it must also be stressed: *These are defects that <u>remain</u> in the computer programs <u>after</u> they have been officially tested and placed into an operational status.* Bottom line: Neither the bank's programmers, nor the FFIEC auditors, can be certain of finding all of the bugs in the Y2000-sensitive software they examine.

Thus, no matter how intelligent, resourceful, dedicated, earnest, and optimistic the banking community might be, the reality is that we will have an unknown number of defects in an unknown number of programs in an unknown number of banks. The situation in some banks and brokerage firms will be demonstrably better than others; but even in the best of the banks, there may be Y2000 bugs lurking in the programs, waiting to pop out at an inopportune moment. Finally, keep in mind that all financial institutions rely quite heavily on electricity, telephones, and the use of their computers. If even one of those are not working, Wall Street and most banks will literally be unable to function. So that, even if a financial institution is diligent about their Year 2000 repairs, and manage to test their systems and fix all of the bugs, if the lights can't be turned on, all of their work could be for naught.

If there is any certainty at all in this situation, it is that we will hear an optimistic assessment from business leaders, regulators, and most politicians. As John Kenneth Galbraith observed in the closing words of his history of the Great Crash of 1929:

> *But now, as throughout history, financial capacity and political perspicacity are inversely correlated. Long-run salvation by men of business has never been highly regarded if it means disturbance of orderly life and convenience in the present. So inaction will be advocated in the present even though it means deep trouble in the future. Here, at least equally with communism, lies the threat to capitalism.*

> *It is what causes men who know that things are going quite wrong to say that things are fundamentally sound.*[19]

Fallback Advice: The Two-Day Failure

Perhaps there are some who can read this assessment of the Y2000 threat to banking, and then continue on, without making any changes to their plans. If Galbraith's gloomy assessment is correct, that may be exactly what happens at the level of governmental leadership. But here's a metaphor to consider: If you were an average citizen in 1928, and if you had received a divine revelation that told you *precisely* when the Great Crash was going to occur, and if you thought that such a stock-market crash might well lead to the collapse and closure of half the nation's banks,[20] wouldn't you do something about it *before* the lines began forming in front of your bank?

Let's say you invested money in the stock market in January of 1928. (We think this is a good reference point, since it was almost two years before the famous stock market crash of 1929, and when we wrote the first edition of this book, we were approximately two years before potential stock market problems that could arise due to Year 2000 problems). The S&P 500 (a broader measure than the more-publicized Dow Jones Industrial Average) peaked in August 1929, and then fell *79 percent* to its trough in June of 1932. An investor would actually have lost a bit less money, because the above figures do not reflect the reinvestment of dividends, which most people elect to do in their mutual funds and stock holdings. But in any case, it took *another five years* for the S&P 500 to reach the levels it was at in January 1928.

So here we are, 70 years later. You may be reading this book in the winter or even the summer of 1999. You may be hearing encouraging words from the public relations departments of the Wall Street brokerage firms and the banking community. You may be hearing optimistic assessments from Senators and Congressmen, and even from the president.[21] Meanwhile, the clock is ticking, and you've seen no definitive proof that all the nation's banking computers have been fixed.

Why worry about stock market corrections, when everyone knows they peak and trough, and when everyone knows you will make your money back eventually? If you are saving for the very distant future, and if your tax-deferred savings are not too substantial, then you must cope with the reality that there will be blips, bleeps, and hiccups along the way in the stock market, no matter what. Hopefully, neither a Y2000 problem, nor a Great Depression, nor a crash of 1987 will have too material an impact on your retirement finances for 30 years from now. But it's very important for you to remember that the stock market returns of the past few years *are not* representative of the last 70 years, of history in general, or of common sense. As a young investor, you should not be fooled into thinking that 30 percent+ annual stock market returns will continue. Since 1928, the average 12-month return in the S&P 500 is roughly 7 percent (without dividends reinvested); since 1940, that return is a little over 8 percent; since 1950, roughly 9 percent; and since 1960 and 1970 a bit more than 8 percent. Since 1980 and 1990, the S&P 500 has risen an average 12 percent every 12 months. Since 1995, however, the S&P 500 has averaged over a 20-percent return for 12 month periods. This is a boom period, and boom periods do not last forever.

One proactive thing you can do with your 401K or IRA/Keogh nest egg is to make sure that the firm managing your retirement funds is Year-2000 compliant, or is definitely going to be so soon. No one can guarantee the survival of your small retirement nest egg if the portfolio management firm goes out of business—and since those funds are not federally insured, you can't be assured of getting your money back if the companies do indeed fail.

If you're extremely optimistic, perhaps your personal assessment will be something like this: "Well, things might be a little screwed up for the first couple days of the New Year. Maybe the ATM machine won't work right away; maybe there will be a few problems with my credit card; maybe there will be long lines at the bank when it opens on Monday, January 3rd." The simple solution is to ensure that you have a few days of spare cash in your wallet. That's not difficult, and it won't pose any problem for the banks: It's common for people to withdraw enough cash to last for a few days during the week, or for a weekend away from home.

This level of risk-management is, as we've repeatedly stressed throughout this book, the absolute minimum. Waking up on Saturday morning, January 1, 2000 with only a $5 bill in your wallet is the height of idiocy, unless you're one of the unfortunate members of American society who has only $5 left to his name.

Fallback Advice: The One-Month Failure

This, in our opinion, is a more realistic level of risk management, given the variety of problems that could occur. Perhaps your bank won't shut its doors for a full month (though it must be remembered that the Bank Holiday imposed by FDR in March 1933 lasted for 10 days); indeed, perhaps your bank will be capable of serving the rest of its customers with great success. It may turn out that only *your* account is the one that's frozen, because a Y2000 error deleted your database record, and no one can figure out how much money you have.

If you believe this is the scenario that has some likelihood of occurring, as we do, then there are two things we strongly suggest. The first is the most obvious, but also the most difficult and expensive: Accumulate a month's living expenses in cash, and sequester it away in a safe place *outside* your bank. As noted earlier, we see no benefit in opening a bank account in Switzerland or some other part of the world: *All* of the world's banks will face the same problem at the same time, and the U.S. banks appear to be in better shape than other international banks. We would also be *extremely* wary of a bank that begins aggressively advertising for new customers in 1999 on the basis that it is "certified" as being Y2000 compliant; even if the bank is managed by honest men and women, the "ripple effect" phenomenon can create difficulties when the Y2000 compliant bank attempts to interact with the rest of the banking system, and when it has to rely on outside utilities and telephone companies, as we well as vendors and suppliers.

Putting a pile of dollars under a mattress is not something that the last two or three generations of Americans are familiar with; perhaps more significantly, it can be quite difficult for the families that live from paycheck to paycheck, with only a few spare dollars in the bank. But if you begin preparing for this strategy in early 1998, it should not be an extreme hardship—especially if you focus on the expenses that absolutely *must* be paid in a timely fashion. If you're a month late paying the rent, and you've got the wonderful excuse that your bank is closed, it's unlikely you'll be evicted. It's equally unlikely that your phone will be disconnected and your lights turned off—unless, of course, you have a bad credit record and/or the phone and utility companies are plagued by severe Y2000 problems of the sort discussed in Chapter 3. But you will need cash for food, transportation, and other services and products whose providers demand instant compensation.

The second thing you must do to prepare for this scenario is ensure that you have a hard-copy record of your current bank statement, as well as financial statements from your credit card company, stock brokerage firm, and other similar financial institutions (including, perhaps, your insurance company and the firm that provides your home mortgage). If you've got $10,000 in your savings account, and your bank ruefully admits that a Y2000 bug has accidentally deleted the database record that describes your current balance, you need to have a piece of paper that can document your claim to your money. Indeed, this is a reasonable precaution even for the minor two-three day disruption discussed above.

One of the obvious problems banks could begin having in 1999, and after the Year 2000, is a bank run. Much like in the Continental Illinois National bank example we described above, even rumors of bank trouble can cause a *huge* drain on deposits. One big difference between the 80s and the coming years is that the Year 2000 problem will become more and more public. As Y2000 evolves from being a "techie" issue, to a Wall Street issue, and then finally becomes a Main Street issue, we believe the problems will begin with a "flow of funds" to banks that can prove (in writing, by an outside examiner, and so forth) that they are (as far as they know) Year-2000 compliant from those banks that cannot such make a statement. Indeed, we would recommend a similar course of action if you plan to leave some money in the bank: Demand some proof from your bank that they are Year 2000 compliant (of course, we think no one will be error-free, but getting an assurance from a bank means that *at least* they have performed some tests). After all, banks make handsome profits on your money... they don't deserve to have it if they are not acting prudently!!!

We believe this "flow of funds" we outlined above will generally be from small to large banks, with mid-size banks probably a wash. There is already the most pressure, protection, help, and focus from the Fed on large banks (which of course have the monstrous resources to do their best to fix the problem). And as we described earlier, the Fed considers the largest banks in the country "too big to fail." Along these lines, we also expect that the largest banks have some of the more modern computer programs. All of the largest banks are FDIC insured. Since almost 99 percent of bank deposits are FDIC insured, we don't expect there to be too much of an economic effect of people transferring money from insured banks to uninsured banks.

Of course, even if the large banks are what they consider to be Year-2000 compliant, some of them will likely experience problems lasting for some period of time. Because these banks will have had the most pressure on them, we think many of the most serious problems will have been worked out. When (not if) large banks do experience computer problems, we fully expect the Federal Reserve to publicly announce (as they already have said they will do) that they will provide the necessary liquidity (i.e., that they will loan money) to the banks until their problems are resolved. Nevertheless, we expect large banks to also experience a drain on deposits, though less than smaller banks, and to experience shutdowns or holidays of the duration we have explored throughout the book. We generally expect no outright failures in the large bank sector—if banks are in trouble, we expect them to be forced to merge with other banks. Outright failures of any of the largest banks in the country would have *severe* implications for the domestic economy—including a stock market *crash* (not a correction and not a dip), as well as a recession (if not depression), widespread consumer panic, and general gloom. In addition, the international financial market, and economic, ramifications, are unthinkable. This does not mean there won't be problems—indeed, we think the contrary holds true—but we do not think the Fed will allow even one of the largest banks to fail outright, so long as it has the power to provide liquidity. With the large banks sector, we expect most of the problems to be of the two-three day variety, with some at the one month variety.

In terms of the stock market, it is difficult for us to differentiate here between a one-month and one-year failure. The ramifications of a one-month shutdown in the stock market could be so severe that the effects are felt for over a year. Therefore, we lump the two together and we recommend a few different courses of action depending on what stage in life you are in, and what your financial responsibilities are. If you are like one of the authors—i.e., in your late 20s, with some savings, the small beginnings of a retirement nest egg, few financial commitments—put most of your savings into the money market deposit account (MMDA) of a *large* FDIC member bank (which has stated it will be Y2000 compliant), and then your money will be subject to the same risks as a checking or savings account. This money probably represents most of your liquid assets, and the funds you would need for a rainy day or for a few emergency months—and the Y2000 problem just may be that rainy day. The emergency that young people usually save for is unemployment, and that could be the result of a Y2000 problem as well as a sudden downturn in the economy and stock market. Putting your money in a large, federally insured bank account, which pays some minimal interest rate, is probably the most cautious step you can take (in addition to our earlier recommendation of having *at least* one month's worth of expenses in hard currency in your home). The small remainder that you leave in mutual funds (or whatever other investment you have) can be treated as a high-risk, diversification to your portfolio.

If you have already started contributing to a 401K/IRA retirement plan, you probably have several choices as to how you can allocate your money. If you are young, you probably have the bulk (60-75 percent) of your small retirement nest egg in equity funds, and you may be worried about these specific funds in the case of a downturn in the stock market. We think you should remember that this is *retirement* money, and that you should be treating it as such, without any intention of touching it for at least 30-35 years. Considering the penalties and taxes imposed on premature withdrawals, it is probably more financially advantageous to take out a loan from a bank than to withdraw your 401K/IRA money. If you follow that advice, we think you should leave your allocation alone. Yes, there might be a stock market correction, or maybe even a crash. Your retirement savings is meant for your retirement, and history teaches that during all market downturns, long-term investments will be successful. However, you probably have the option of changing your investment choices in your 401K program, and if you feel more comfortable moving money away from equities and into fixed income instruments, that could also be prudent.

On the other hand, what if your situation is more like the other author of this book: a generation older, with retirement looming only 10 years away, and with a substantial amount of savings accumulated over the years? In this case, you probably have a smaller proportion of your investments in equities, though probably a larger absolute dollar amount. We suggest that this group of investors add an extra risk premium to all asset classes. We recommend significantly increasing the percentage of your assets that are in FDIC-insured money market deposit accounts, and decreasing the percentage allocation to any of the riskier classes of assets. In this scenario, the results of past stock market corrections—especially the 1929 crash—suggest that you could lose half of your stock market investment from a serious Y2000 crisis, and might not be able to recoup the loss in time for a normal retirement.

One of the authors works in the alternative investment industry, which serves avid investors who want to make higher returns than what the money market account of a bank will offer. "Alternative investment" funds and investments are those that target acceptable financial returns in *all* market environments. These funds invest in many different securities; they sometimes employ leverage, go both long and short simultaneously, buy and sell emerging markets equity and debt and real estate, specialize in convertible arbitrage, risk arbitrage, commodities, and currencies... and the list goes on and on. These investments are constructed to perform regardless of the state of the U.S. stock market (though we must stress that if the investment managers can't buy and sell securities because of Year 2000 problems at the brokerage house they conduct business with, there will be a problem!). Another specialty in the alternative investment world is that of the short seller: If you think there will be a correction, crash, hiccup, downtrend, or other blip in what seems like the eternal rise in the Dow Jones Industrial Average, investigate some of the short-only funds. Some of these alternative investments have high minimums, and others have stringent criteria for investor suitability, but there are some that are more small investor oriented. The minimum investment requirements in hedge funds can be quite high (as much as $10 million for the very exclusive funds). After changes in investment regulations, mutual funds can also be "short" the stock market. There aren't many of these funds, but their minimums are more reasonable, usually $2,500 or so. Finally, many investors believe that traditional hedges like gold and silver are appropriate investments for the post-2000 era. Almost anyone can open a futures account with a broker, and invest in gold and silver through futures contracts. Alternatively, gold and silver can be purchased for physical delivery, along with the emergency cash that you put under your mattress. These alternative investments are subject to all of the same Year 2000 risks as other investments, except that they are designed to be "uncorrelated" with the stock market. If you have read any newspaper in late 1998, you probably have seen hedge funds mentioned quite frequently. Even hedge funds run by Nobel prize winners can get into trouble, and it should not be assumed that these investments are without risk.

With any investment choice you make, and with any bank you put money in, a high degree of "due diligence" is crucial during the next two years. If a financial institution cannot prove to you in writing that it will be Year-2000 compliant, think twice.[22] Also, it must be emphasized that neither of the authors are certified financial advisers or planners, and you should seek appropriate professional advice in order to understand the risks you take before investing in any new funds, or shifting the allocation of your own investments.

Fallback Advice: The One-Year Failure

A one-year disruption in access to your funds is clearly a serious crisis; how could such a crisis be allowed to occur? Again, we remind the reader that in the aftermath of the Great Crash of 1929, it took the Federal Government over three years to create the mechanisms that restored faith to the banking system; in the meantime, over 4,000 banks went under, taking the deposits and savings of millions of citizens with them.

Today, as we've noted, the FDIC exists as a form of insurance against such bank losses; and if it should fail (because of Y2000 problems, or because of the "fractional reserve" system upon which it, too, is based) one assumes that the Federal Reserve system and the printing presses of the U.S. Treasury could be called in as a lender of last resort, in the event of a severe emergency. Thus, if you're an optimist, and a firm believer in the competence and benevolence of government, you may wish to take the position that your funds are ultimately safe. *Even if my bank closes,* you might be thinking, *I'll get my money back, sooner or later.*

There are two problems with this line of thinking. First, it's likely to be "later" rather than "sooner" before your money is restored. If the Y2000 problem is serious enough to close one bank, it will probably be serious enough to close several banks; your refund application to the FDIC (for which you might want to get the appropriate paperwork and forms now, rather than later!) will be joined with several hundred thousand, if not millions, of others. Assuming that the FDIC doesn't have its own Y2000 problems to deal with, it's still likely to take 6-12 months before your funds reappear.

The second problem is that the *value* of those funds could deteriorate significantly in the interim. In the case of bank deposits, this would only be relevant in a period of severe inflation; as we noted above, hyperinflation is theoretically possible as a consequence of severe Y2000-induced banking/currency problems, though we have no way of evaluating the likelihood of such an event. However, most adults today can recall the early 1980s, when inflation reached nearly 20 percent; whatever combination of economic, fiscal, and monetary events caused that unhappy outcome, it was arguably far less severe and traumatic than the impending Y2000 situation. In any case, there is the risk that the $10,000 that's "frozen" in your defunct bank account might only be worth $8,000, in terms of present purchasing power, when you get it back from the FDIC. In the worst of all cases, if true hyperinflation sets in, it could be worth far, far less.

Indeed, that's what we're concerned about with investments in the stock market. If your stockbroker's computer system collapses because of a Y2000 problem, then you can't buy any new stocks from that broker, or—more importantly—sell the stocks held in "street name" by that broker on your behalf. Assuming that you can get through on the phone, you might ask for physical stock certificates; but if the broker's computers have crashed, it may be impossible for them to produce the certificates for several weeks or months.

In the worst case, the brokerage company collapses; happily, as you may be aware, your account is protected by an FDIC-like agency, up to a level of $500,000. But the question is: If you apply for a refund, will you get cash or stock certificates? If it takes 6-12 months to recoup your stock certificates, the price of the stock may have collapsed. The trivial, brute-force solution to this problem is to insist that your broker deliver old-fashioned, physical, paper stock certificates to you *now*, rather than in the post-2000 aftermath. Chances are that your broker will resist and delay, complain and argue about how foolish you are—but you have a legal right to obtain those certificates, as long as you own them free and clear (i.e., they haven't been purchased on a margin account).

The more extreme solution is to liquidate your stocks and bonds before January 1, 2000 (or perhaps even before January 1, 1999 if you're really worried!), and keep the proceeds in a money-market account, in which case they'll be subject to approximately the same risks as if they were in a savings account at your local bank. This means, of course, that you'll forego whatever profit-making opportunities might exist from further increases in the stock market averages and indices in the remaining months and years of the decade; that's a risk you'll have to evaluate on your own, and on which we deliberately avoid offering recommendations.

As for your bank account: If you were concerned about the possibility of a one-year shut-down of your bank, it's possible to withdraw all of your funds, and put *all* of it under your mattress. Or, slightly less drastic, perhaps you could withdraw sufficient cash to survive for a year without access to your bank account. Measures like these will almost certainly be seen as extreme and excessive, and we don't expect many will take them seriously. And indeed, it may not be necessary, if you can make the following four assumptions: (a) you've got enough cash to survive for a month, or at least until your next paycheck arrives from your employer, (b) your employer has not gone bankrupt, and your job is safe, (c) your regular salary is sufficient for your month-to-month living needs, without access to your savings, and (d) when you finally do recoup your money from the bank or from the FDIC, it hasn't been substantially devalued by hyperinflation. Of these four, assumption (b) is the most crucial; this involves the issues we discussed in Chapter 2.

Unfortunately, the existence of Year-2000 bugs in banks—of all sizes—could cause directors and bank officers to engage in unsound business practices. We do not direct this comment at anyone in particular; however, we worry that out of fear, some banking executives will say the banks they run are Year-2000 compliant when they are not. Or, out of fear, they will try to rush their process of fixing the Year-2000 problem, and make fatal errors and mistakes. Unsound business practices could also arise out of greed—banks who are Year-2000 compliant could attempt to profit from that through speculation, risky lending practices, and the like. Fear and greed can also give way to fraud, which took place in the last major banking crisis in the 1980s. We cannot assign any probabilities to what individuals will do because of fear and greed, nor can we say what kind of fraud will be committed. It is important to remember here that while the actual problem is technical, the manner in which it will be dealt with is determined by human beings. Human beings make decisions based on emotion, and despite all the economic theory, sometimes just do not act rationally. Because the future of this problem is based on humans, our book is *not* a science, and we cannot give expectations based on any kind of mathematical formula.

Fallback Advice: The Ten-Year Failure

An advanced nation of 260 million men and women would not tolerate the complete absence of a banking system for more than a few months, let alone a decade. We certainly don't foresee any possibility of a Y2000 crisis taking us back to the days when we relied upon gold coins, bushel-bags of wheat, or other forms of barter to conduct our economic affairs. Even if a nationwide wave of bank runs, and a total loss of investor confidence, effectively destroyed our existing banks and financial institutions and our currency, something new would emerge as a replacement within a few years. On the other hand, it could be argued that the nation's faith in its financial institutions was severely shaken, if not destroyed, during the decade between 1929 and 1939; if it happened once (and this was by no means the only such event in our history!), then arguably it could happen again.

If a Y2000 banking crisis turns out to be so severe that it requires a decade to restore faith and confidence in its stability, then it won't be something we can plan for on an individual basis. If all of the familiar banks collapse and are replaced by a new collection; if the Federal Reserve System collapses and is replaced by a new politically-created structure; if MasterCard, Visa, and American Express vanish and are replaced eventually by some new form of electronic credit; if our familiar greenback dollar-bills are recalled by the government and then replaced by a new kind of paper known as the Clinton; if all of these things, and possibly more, should happen, how on earth will we be able to protect whatever modest savings we've managed to accumulate in the years leading up to 2000? A few clever souls—those who are the most nimble, flexible, shrewd, and opportunistic—will find a way to profit from all of this; we see ample illustrations of this in modern-day, post-Communist Russia.

Most of us, though, are likely to suffer a fate similar to that of the average Russian. Our savings might well be wiped out; our corporate and Social Security pensions could prove to be worthless; and more fundamentally, the basic guidelines and rationale that we've traditionally used for making economic decisions could be destroyed, and replaced by something new. Those without any savings, without any pensions, and without any conscious economic strategy—which means, for the most part, the young adults entering the work force, and the poor—may find that they're no worse off than before, and that new opportunities are opening up. The middle-class, the middle-aged, the pensioners, and the numerous other members of society who have spent a life time "playing by the rules" are likely to find it *extremely* difficult to adjust to the utter elimination of those rules, followed by the creation of an entirely new set of rules. This is an extremely sobering scenario; again, look to post-Communist Russia to see vivid examples of how difficult it can be to adjust to a new economic order.

We repeat, once again, our fervent hope that things will not end up this way; it would be as painful for us, on an individual basis, as it would for any reader of this book. But painful or not, it's a possibility that we feel ought to be considered—even if only briefly, and even if the possibility is rejected after some thought. If you believe that a 10-year financial crisis is more than just a figment of our imagination, then our advice is: Simplify your life, pare down your debt and financial obligations, reevaluate the real importance of the material possessions in your life in comparison to family relationships and other fundamental values, and organize your affairs so that you can be as flexible and self-sufficient as possible, no matter what may come in the post-2000 years. There are some who will argue that this would not be such a bad piece of advice even without a Y2000 crisis!

Endnotes

1. One of our favorites is John Kenneth Galbraith's, *Money: Whence It Came, Where It Went*, revised edition (New York: Houghton Mifflin, 1995).
2. See *Investor's Business Daily*, Feb. 12, 1997 for a description of Citibank's efforts, and the March 1997 online version of *Software* magazine (located at http://www.sentrytech.com/sm037f1a.htm) for a discussion of Chase Manhattan's Y2000 efforts. In a routine filing, Chase Manhattan estimated that it would spend $250 million in Y2000 costs over the 1997-99 period.
3. To express this in a different way: it's a staff of approximately 300-500 computer professionals, working full-time over a period of two years. Most organizations have no excess software personnel sitting around in the back office, because they were eliminated during the downsizing, rightsizing, outsourcing, and reengineering period of the early 90s. For the software industry as a whole, there is a nationwide shortage estimated at 200,000 professionals as of mid-1997, and the figure is likely to get worse in the next few years.
4. This is not a casual bit of hyperbole; there have been numerous studies and analyses of software projects over the past 20 years that confirm this unpleasant aspect of computer software. See, for example, Capers Jones' *Patterns of Software Systems Failure and Success* (International Thomson Computer Press, 1997), which also points out that approximately 14 percent of all projects are late, and 24 percent are canceled before completion. The really bad news, which won't come as a surprise, is that the percentage of projects late or canceled is substantially higher for the very large computer projects.
5. Banks, being somber and conservative, are likely to do their best to provide a positive "spin" on the Y2000 PR notices they publish during 1998 and 1999; they would probably take issue with our description of "hastily-modified" software. But overall, the effort of the banking industry *is* hasty; as noted in the Associated Press report at the beginning of this chapter, only 10 percent of the banks had finished their Y2000 conversion effort at the time this book was written, even though articles in the computer trade press had been warning of Y2000 problems since as early as 1993 and the Federal Reserve system published its first advisory warning about Y2000 in June 1996. The fact that the end of the decade

is approaching is hardly a secret, and nobody forced the senior management of the banks (or any other company, for that matter) to dawdle and delay until panic set in during 1997.

6. John Kenneth Galbraith, *Money: Whence It Came, Where It Went*, *op cit.*, page 15.
7. John Kenneth Galbraith, *op cit.*, pp. 194 ff.
8. John Kenneth Galbraith, *op cit.*, pages 200-201.
9. Meanwhile, an account with a Savings & Loan institution is insured up to $100,000 by the Savings Association Insurance Fund (SAIF), which replaced the Federal Savings and Loan Insurance Corporation (FSLIC) in 1989, and which is under the jurisdiction of the FDIC.
10. The US has long since abandoned the gold standard, the last vestige of which was terminated by Richard Nixon in 1971. Thus, whatever else might happen, the government won't have to worry about demands from its citizens to replace paper money with gold.
11. Allan E. Alter, "Your other millennium problem," *Computerworld,* May 26, 1997.
12. "Federal Bank Regulators Outline Year 2000 Project Management Goals" available in full on the Internet at http://www.ffiec.gov/y2k/y2kpress.htm). The full text of the FFIEC Y2000 Task Force Statement is available on the Internet at http://www.FFIEC.gov/Y2000/ and can also be obtained by toll free telephone FAX BACK at 888-882-0982.
13. Of course, it's not the merchants themselves—these folks are inclined to accept *any* credit card, under even the most dubious of circumstances. But most merchants use a variety of credit-authorization terminals, which in term are connected to banks or other facilities. Depending on the way these authorization systems are programmed, the consumer's card may be rejected despite the most strenuous efforts on the part of the merchant. See "Credit cards offer a visible sign of the Year 2000 Problem," by Lon Wagner, *The Virginia-Pilot*, May 1, 1997 for more details.
14. This is the perspective of the individual citizen; the impact on mail-order businesses is far more severe. If we can't order an item by phone with a credit card, then we're forced to shop by mail (with a check), or in person in the local neighborhood.
15. "Merrill Lynch's $268m plan to kill 2000 bug," *Financial Review,* June 26, 1997. Note that the reference to $268 million, in the title of this article, refers to Australian dollars. The text of the article

quotes Merrill Lynch's Y2000 costs, as well as those of the overall securities industry, in U.S. dollars.

16. Howard Sorgen, "Merrill Lynch prepares for year 2000 conversion," *Computer Reseller News*, May 19, 1997. Note that Mr. Sorgen is a senior vice president and chief technology officer of Merrill Lynch.
17. William D. Rabin and Terrence P. Tierney, "The Year 2000 Problem: it's worse than we thought," accessible on the Internet at http://www.jpmorgan.com/MarketDataInd/Research/Y2Kupdate/Y2K.HTM. The Morgan analysts describe the state of Y2000 preparations in local, state, and Federal government agencies as "critical," and the European situation as largely unknown by "probably worse than critical."
18. Bruce Caldwell, "Year 2000 Hits The Bottom Line—Companies find they can't fund all projects from their existing IS budgets," *Information Week*, May 26, 1997.
19. John Kenneth Galbraith, *The Great Crash 1929,* revised edition (New York: Houghton-Mifflin, 1997), p. 194.
20. We hasten to add that historians and economists are still arguing about the degree to which the banking crisis of the Great Depression can be blamed directly on the stock market crash of October 29, 1929. But hardly anyone denies that there was some relationship between the two phenomena, and that it was probably a very strong relationship.
21. You can find some encouraging words from President Clinton in the opening quotation of Chapter 10, where we discuss the potentially serious Y2000 impact upon the government.
22. To emphasize the seriousness of this advice, we are not aware of *any* major bank or financial institution that could say it was fully Y2000 when the first edition of this book went to press in the fall of 1997. Indeed, it would have been virtually impossible to make such a statement, since the hardware, operating systems, and database-management packages that the banks rely on is not likely to be Y2000 compliant until sometime in 1998 or 1999. *Caveat emptor!*

Y2000 Impact on Food

Food probably has a very great influence on the condition of men. Wine exercises a more visible influence, food does it more slowly but perhaps just as surely. Who knows if a well-prepared soup was not responsible for the pneumatic pump or a poor one for a war?

G. C. Lichtenberg, Aphorisms, *"Notebook A," aphorism 14 (written 1765-99; translated by R. J. Hollingdale, 1990).*

If you're going to America, bring your own food.

Fran Lebowitz, Social Studies, *"Fran Lebowitz's Travel Hints" (1981).*

Introduction

We had not originally planned to devote a chapter to the subject of food, but then we were reminded of Samuel Johnson's astute comment that "he who does not mind his belly will hardly mind anything else."[1] Indeed, without a regular supply of food, we would hardly be in a position to worry at length about the state of our banks, our transportation systems, and the various other topics discussed in this book.

The vast majority of people in this country, as well as Western Europe and the various other "advanced" countries around the world, are in the happy position of having an ample supply of food, whenever and wherever they want it. Very few of us grow any of our own food these days, unless gardening is a hobby and we have a plot of land in the back yard. Even those who nurture a few tomatoes in the back yard, or who catch a few fish during their weekend visit to the lake, are likely to visit the local grocery store on a weekly basis to stock up on a dazzling array of meat, fish, fruits, vegetables, dairy products, pasta, bread and bakery items, desserts, beer, wine, and so forth.

Even more interesting is the fact that many of us have largely abandoned cooking during the past 20 years. In both the urban and suburban environments, breakfast often consists of a donut or bagel, or perhaps a bowl of cereal and a cup of coffee; lunch is a Whopper at Burger King or a slice of pizza at Pizza Hut; and dinner consists of whatever we can find at Kentucky Fried Chicken or Taco Bell, because it's too much trouble to throw a pre-packaged meal into the micro-wave oven. As Bill Bryson observes,[2]

> *Clearly, some time ago makers and consumers of American junk food passed jointly through some kind of sensibility barrier in the endless quest for new taste sensations. Now they are a little like those desperate junkies who have tried every known drug and are finally reduced to mainlining toilet bowl cleanser in an effort to get still higher.*

Without going any further into the culinary habits of Americans, suffice it to say that (a) it continues to be one of the fundamental human needs, and (b) we're highly dependent upon various parts of the social infrastructure to provide, cook, and deliver food to us in a convenient manner.

And that brings us back to the theme of this book: What happens if a Y2000 software problem interrupts this finely tuned aspect of our social infrastructure? We'll first discuss how this might happen, and then revert to our standard categories of advice for two-day, one-month, one-year, and ten-year failures.

Production of Food

As every school child knows, the combination of the Agricultural Revolution, the Industrial Revolution, and the Information Revolution means that a tiny percentage of the population produces all of the food that the rest of us consume. Gone are the days of the family farm; agriculture is now a big business, just as sophisticated in its own way as the mining and manufacturing industries.

Our purpose here is not to explain the details of the agriculture business, but simply to point out that computers are very heavily involved throughout the industry. At the highest level of abstraction, computers are used by agricultural conglomerates, and also by the farmers on huge ranches and farms, to schedule, plan, and organize their crops and herds. And at the lowest level of abstraction, microchips are embedded in tractors and a variety of other expensive, sophisticated equipment on the modern farm. In one way or another, many of these devices are vulnerable to Y2000-related failures.

On a more fundamental level, ranches and farms are just as dependent on the "iron triangle" infrastructure as everyone else. Without electricity, the modern farm comes to a screeching halt; and if electricity fails in the midst of a cold winter, chickens, hogs, and dairy cows may freeze to death. If the banks shut down, farmers and ranchers will have the same problems paying their bills that everyone else will; and if the telecommunication networks are disrupted, they'll have trouble communicating with family, workers, suppliers, and customers.

In some cases, Y2000 disruptions on the farm or ranch might not be visible right away in the grocery store; we may find, for example, disruptions in the spring planting season, or in the fall harvesting season. Rebecca Kutcher responded to the first edition of our book with an interesting email message:

> *What if Pioneer or one of the other biggies can't produce hybrid seed or can produce, but not be able to transport it?? There is no longer enough open-pollinated seed to go around. Many types of original seed have been allowed to die out, so some hybrids may be difficult to reproduce from scratch in the future.*

Disruptions in the production of hybrid seeds, which could occur during the early part of 2000, could thus disrupt the planting activities in the spring of 2001, thus propagating the consequences of the Y2000 problem even further into the future. And disruption in the transportation and distribution of vintage-1999 hybrid seeds could threaten the spring 2000 planting season.

Delivery of Food

Our primary concern involves *deliveries*, both to the neighborhood grocery store, and to the fast-food outlets that some citizens have come to depend upon.[3] Fresh food, by its very nature, has to be replenished and re-stocked on a frequent basis. Many other forms of food (including the hamburger patties at your favorite junk-food emporium) are frozen, and thus could presumably be stockpiled to provide ongoing supplies of food for months or years. But both the hamburger outlets and the grocery stores operate on razor-thin profit margins, which requires keeping low inventories and using a "just-in-time" (JIT) delivery mechanism to restock on a daily or weekly basis.

While you might not be able to determine the inventory levels at your local MacDonald's or Burger King, you can certainly investigate the situation at your grocery store. Chances are you'll observe daily restocking in many departments, especially in the fruit-and-vegetable area, as well as meat and dairy products. Most of the non-perishable items, including those packaged securely in cans, boxes, or plastic containers, are re-stocked once or twice a week.

Next, take a look at the inventory levels. As part of your normal shopping, you may have occasionally encountered the out-of-stock phenomenon, but it's fairly rare in American stores. It's far more common that you'll take one loaf of bread off a shelf filled with what might seem, to the casual observer, an infinite quantity of loaves. But it's more likely to be a few dozen loaves, or perhaps a hundred at most. The same is true for most of the other items in the store; most of the store's inventory is right in front of you, on the shelves.

Now ask yourself a simple question: What happens if you and a few dozen of your neighbors all decide to buy a loaf of bread on the same day? And what if you decided to buy a month's supply of cereal, instead of a one-week supply? The answer is pretty simple: The shelves would be bare, except for items like pickled kumquats and marinated pig's feet. However, in today's economy, *it doesn't matter*, because the shelves will be restocked tomorrow. And because everyone takes it for granted that that will be so, there's no need to get a month's supply of cereal; it's more convenient to buy enough to last for just a few days.

So, the bottom line is that precise inventory management, and a well-honed delivery infrastructure, are crucial for maintaining the well-stocked grocery store we take for granted. The same, by the way, is basically true for the fast-food outlets: Most of them operate as franchises, and are obliged to replenish their supplies from the franchise-owner. This allows the franchise-owner to achieve economies of scale (by purchasing millions of pounds of beef at a time), and also allows the franchise-owner to maintain control over the proprietary nature of the junk food (e.g., the secret formula for Kentucky Fried

Chicken, invented long ago by the fabled Colonel Sanders). Each franchise keeps careful track of the quantities of food sold, not only to maintain a reasonable reputation of providing hot, fresh junk food, but also to optimize the steady process of re-stocking by the franchise-owner.

The astute reader has probably anticipated where we are heading with this analysis: A Y2000 problem can easily disrupt the delivery and inventory-management process. Inventory management is still done without computers in some establishments—you may have noticed grocery clerks manually counting the number of boxes of cereal on the shelves—but more commonly today, it's computerized. The same grocery clerk is involved, but now he carries a hand-held scanner that reads bar-code labels; sometimes the clerk keys in a few entries to indicate the quantity of goods left on the shelf. In theory, this should not even be necessary, because the cash registers at the checkout counter are connected to a central computer, too, so that inventory-management reports can be printed out in the store-manager's office. However, the manual process is still important to keep track of spoilage, breakage, theft, and other forms of loss that might not be detected at the checkout counter.

Keeping track of how many boxes of cereal were sold, or how many Big Macs were consumed, is only the beginning of the inventory management process; what happens next is a *forecasting* computation to determine the likely number of days before the existing inventory will be completely exhausted, and whether the reorder-quantity should be larger or smaller than usual to account for fluctuating trends and patterns. Indeed, this process has become enormously more sophisticated in recent years, with massive computer computations involving something known as "data mining" to look for trends that might not have been obvious to the human eye. A computer analysis might indicate, for example, that on Saturday nights, there's a strong tendency for purchases of beer to be accompanied by purchases of potato chips; this information might motivate the store manager to make certain that the shelves of beer are located next to the shelves of potato chips—or, alternatively, to place the potato chips close to the checkout counter to accommodate the customer who visits the store on Saturday night for the primary purpose of buying beer, but who can then be persuaded to pick up an extra bag of potato chips if they happen to be easily visible at the checkout counter.

So there's a lot of computer intelligence behind the scenes, and—as you might have guessed—it's also Y2000-sensitive. Indeed, dates and date-calculations are essential to the whole process of inventory management; the U.K. establishment of Marks & Spencer has already run into Y2000 problems, because its computers are programmed to reject incoming deliveries of food items if the "expiration date" indicates that the food has spoiled. Many food items packaged in cans, boxes, or plastic containers could have an expiration date four years after the item was packaged; thus, an item delivered to the store in 1998 would have an expiration date of 2002. Unfortunately, if the inventory-management system has programmed its dates as two-year digits, it comes to the conclusion that the food-item expired in 1902, not 2002.

Thus, we worry that inventory management systems, delivery-scheduling systems, data-mining systems, and much of the "intelligence" that ensures the proper stockpiling of the proper items at the proper time may blow up on January 1st; indeed, a few of these systems are already blowing up. On the other hand, there's already an automatic fallback mechanism: If the shelves are empty, customers will complain vociferously, and the store-manager (or the Burger King manager) will pick up the phone and make a manual request for inventory replenishment. An astute manager will notice the problem before his customers inform him; if a manual inventory determines that stocks are falling low, the same unscheduled phone call can be made to the supplier.[4]

Nevertheless, we won't be surprised to see a moderate amount of chaos and confusion while all of this is being sorted out during the first few days, weeks, or months of the new millennium. The problem experienced by Marks & Spencer (and soon to be experienced by many other stores) is, in its own way, a blessing in disguise—for it will force the stores to fix their problems *before* January 1, 2000. But there will be many other computer systems in which the Y2000 bugs won't become evident until the stroke of midnight; and the result is that you find some empty shelves in your grocery store during the early days of the new millennium.

But this may not turn out to be the biggest problem. Assuming that the inventory-control computer systems are working, there is still the issue of transporting food items from the farm, the fishery, the bakery, or the slaughterhouse to the store. This requires a vast, intricate network of ships, planes, trains, and trucks—all synchronized to deliver the right amount of food items while they're still fresh. We discussed the potential vulnerability of the transportation system in Chapter 4; it simply bears repeating at this point that transportation problems could quickly "ripple" into food-delivery problems.

This is likely to be much more of a problem for the urban centers than for the suburban and rural areas for a simple reason: The rural areas are closer to food-producing areas, and are thus not as dependent on trucks, trains, and planes. During the writing of this book, one of us spent the summer in a small town in rural New Mexico, across a dirt road from a farm populated by a noisy collection of sheep, geese, chickens, and other animals. If a Y2000-induced food-delivery crisis were to occur, there would be some hope of obtaining fresh fish from nearby streams and lakes, fresh vegetables from the local farm-stands, and even fresh mutton and eggs from the next-door farm. The area also produces moderate quantities of corn, which could be used to supply the local bakery of tortillas and enchiladas. Obviously, this represents only a small part of the rich, varied diets that Americans have come to enjoy, but at least the basics could be locally obtained.[5]

Urban centers, on the other hand, may face a serious problem. Consider New York City, where one of the authors resides. While there might be the odd back-yard garden in Brooklyn or Staten Island, Manhattan is basically sidewalks and streets—unless one wishes to contemplate converting Central Park into a gigantic garden plot. Manhattan is an island, which means that no food will arrive unless transported by boat, plane, truck, or train from other parts of the country—and because a population of 8 million people enjoy eating as a daily activity, large quantities of food have to be delivered on a daily basis.

Some portion of this food is delivered by large companies (e.g., major dairy companies, or large companies like Dole and Heinz) to chains of stores throughout an urban region. Once the inventory-control problems and generic transportation problems have been worked out, we would expect these deliveries to resume in the normal fashion. But there are also numerous small food-suppliers who deliver their goods to small, independent merchants—e.g., the local delis that populate nearly every street corner in Manhattan. And even in the case of the large companies, the deliveries are often made by independent truckers; this latter category is especially important, for even if food is brought to the edge of Manhattan by boat or plane, the final portion of the delivery is almost always made by truck, directly to the store or merchant.

Now consider the following scenario: You're an independent trucker, based in New Jersey or Connecticut or Long Island; you spend your days filling your truck with rutabagas and onions at the railroad depot in Newark, and you deliver the fresh vegetables to a dozen small stores and delis in Manhattan. It's now January 10th, 2000 and you've been having a hell of a time finding gas for your truck and figuring out how to avoid all of the delays at the bridges and tunnels that lead into Manhattan. Not only that, the onions and rutabagas that were supposed to arrive in Newark last week were delayed by a snafu in the train system. But all of that has now been overcome, and you're ready to make your delivery, as long as one thing can be assured: Upon delivery, you'll be paid. Well, one other thing would be nice, too: Having been paid, you'll be able to drive back to your modest home in New Jersey without being shot, hijacked, or robbed.

Indeed, the very prospect of payment problems and crime problems will be enough to keep some of the small, independent truckers from making such deliveries. And this creates a ripple effect of its own: The residents of Manhattan want to eat regularly, just like the residents of Brooklyn, Queens, Staten Island, and the Bronx. Not only have the food deliveries diminished sharply, but the welfare checks and food coupons, which some members of the city rely on, have gotten fouled up in the computers in Washington. Oil deliveries have been delayed because of some other snafu, and with an early-January temperature hovering near zero, the heat has been turned off. This combination of events would be enough to put anyone—including the well-heeled residents of Park Avenue on the Upper East Side, as well as the less-affluent citizens in other parts of the city—into a foul mood. So, yes, perhaps there will be a few more shootings, hijackings, and robberies than normal.

The interesting question is whether the legitimate concerns of the independent truckers might keep them from making deliveries *anywhere* in Manhattan, not just the neighborhoods they might normally associate with higher levels of crime. And if a problem like this exists in Manhattan, one could make a good argument that it will also occur in Boston (beginning with Roxbury), Chicago (beginning with the South Side), and a dozen other cities. Even without the issue of crime, the smaller cities may have a problem—for they will be served, more often, by smaller trucking firms who will insist on cash, gold coins, wampum, or some other credible form of payment before they unload their trucks.

Fallback Advice: Two-Day Failures

Planning for the two-day disruption should be relatively easy; it simply requires stockpiling a couple days of food in the house. Keep in mind, though, that the food-related Y2000 problems may not occur promptly on January 1st; the kind of delivery problems we've outlined above could occur at any point during the calendar year 2000. Thus, it would be a good idea to ensure that, at all times, you've got a modest stockpile that could provide breakfast, lunch, and dinner if the stores shut down for a couple of days.

As we've noted throughout the book, residents of weather-sensitive areas of the country are quite familiar with this strategy. When they first hear of an impending hurricane or blizzard, many families drive to the local super-market to stock up on milk, bread, bottled water, and various other essentials; then they can ride out the storm without any major inconvenience. It's the city dwellers who will need to begin practicing this kind of stockpiling. There's not likely to be a problem of cost; except for the people at the bottom of the socio-economic ladder in the U.S., virtually everyone can afford to buy a few days' worth of food in advance. The biggest problem for the city dwellers will be laziness or procrastination.

Fallback Advice: One-Month Failures

Obviously, a one-month disruption in the food supply is far more serious than having to subsist on left-overs and peanut-butter sandwiches for a couple of days. Stockpiling a month's food is potentially expensive, and it's also inconvenient; since most Americans have *never* had the experience of being cut off from their food supply for a month, it will be difficult to convince them to plan for the eventuality.

Again, suburban and rural dwellers are at an advantage here, for they're more likely to have a freezer, a cool cellar, and various other storage sites in which they can stockpile food. Those who are near hunting and fishing areas, and those with a backyard garden plot, may already be in the habit of drying, smoking, canning, or freezing a supply of food—not for disaster prevention, but simply to take advantage of the fresh food or meat when it's available. The city dweller, crammed into a small apartment, barely has enough room in the refrigerator for a two-day supply of food; the notion of a freezer for additional food supplies is out of the question.

Nevertheless, it may be necessary—and if one plans for it now, the logistical problems *can* be overcome. In virtually every city, and in almost all suburban areas, there are now "mini-warehouse" facilities that can be rented at a modest cost; many families are already using these storage facilities to store left-over furniture and other items that would otherwise clutter up a small house or apartment. If you're determined to continue living in a large city, and if you believe (as we do) that a one-month disruption of food is indeed possible—*especially* in the big cities—then you should consider using such a mini-warehouse to stockpile a larger supply of food.

In this scenario, you probably won't have an opportunity to install a freezer; almost all of the mini-warehouses are unheated, empty spaces, with no electrical outlets or running water. Thus, you'll need to stockpile food that requires no refrigeration, but can also withstand cold (and possibly even freezing) temperatures. You won't stockpile a month's supply of fresh milk, but you might stockpile powdered milk, along with a supply of canned or freeze-dried foods. You may have sworn that you would never again eat the canned peas that you had to tolerate as a child; but canned vegetables do have the virtue of remaining edible for reasonable periods of time.

It's not really difficult to organize this level of stockpiling; it may require as much as a few hundred dollars, depending on your taste for food. It may require a commitment for the rental of a mini-warehouse. It will certainly require a few hours of effort to think carefully about the combination of food that you and your family will find nutritional and at least minimally pleasant to eat. It may require several hours, and multiple shopping trips, to accumulate the supplies and store them away. But you still have more than a year to do this; anyone who is serious—with the exception of those at the poverty level—can do it.

Meg Carter, who read an early draft of this book, offered the following valuable advice for those who are thinking of stockpiling food for the Y2000 problem:

> *You used the blizzard model, which is very familiar to people in the northern and mid-western states. I grew up in Ohio, so I can remember stocking up on staples and baking while we were snowed in for a week at a time. Although transportation was stopped, the utilities rarely were: we still had heat and electricity. I now live in Northern California where we're on constant earthquake preparedness, and I think the earthquake model is more like a Y2K scenario, where the possibility of being without electricity, heat, fresh water, and transportation for some period of time is likely.*

Here's what we're advised to do: stock up on canned and dried foods that do not need cooking and require a minimum amount of water to prepare. (Stock up on water, too, of course.) Pinto beans, for example, would not be a good choice because they require lots of water to clean, soak and cook and at least an hour of cooking time. But canned tuna would be good, as well as the sun-dried fruits and nuts that are available in health food and specialty stores in the fall and winter. A nationwide chain which specializes in dried fruits, nuts, trail mix, etc. is Trader Joe's.

Also, stores that specialize in recreation have prepackaged freeze-dried meals that need only a small amount of boiling water to prepare. This type of food is used by backpackers and mountaineers, who have to trek all of their food and cooking supplies into the wilderness and then trek them out, so it takes minimal space and is easy to prepare, while being high energy. A nationwide chain which specializes in this type of food is Recreational Equipment, Inc. (REI).

For people who live in urban areas, there are ways you can grow small amounts of fresh fruits and veggies year-round indoors, or in windowboxes or atriums (if you live in the Western or Southern states). Many apartment dwellers already have "gardens" devoted to flowers. It would be quite simple to convert them to lettuce, onions, tomatoes, carrots, etc. You could also can or dry (by sun or with a food dehydrator) fruits and veggies from the summer harvest, no matter where you live.

The biggest problem that we see in this area is psychological: No one will comment on a decision to keep two-three days of food in the house, but stockpiling a month's supply of food forces you to acknowledge that you *are* serious about Y2000 planning. Your family may disagree with you, and if you tell your friends and business colleagues, they may laugh at you. "What are you, some kind of end-of-the-world, gloom-and-doom nut?" they'll ask. No one wants to be branded a lunatic, and this level of stockpiling is likely to be the dividing line between normal caution and lunacy, in the eyes of your friends and family.[6]

It's also important to remember that "stockpiling" will be redefined as "hoarding" if there are food shortages in late 1999 or early 2000. Grocery stores are well stocked today, and nobody will notice or care whether you buy a can of tunafish, or an entire case. But if Y2000-related problems begin to surface by mid-1999 (e.g., as a result of computing problems that could occur when 46 U.S. states begin their 1999-2000 fiscal year on July 1, 1999), shortages may begin to develop; in such a scenario, there will be strong social pressure, and perhaps even legal restrictions, on the amount of food you'll be able to buy.

Ultimately, the decision here is a personal one, or one that is made by consensus within your family. Remember that a one-month supply of food is the best form of insurance: You can eat it if you don't need it. Indeed, that should be one of the major criteria for choosing emergency food in the first place: If it's so awful that you'll throw it away when the Y2000 emergency passes (or if it fails to materialize), then you shouldn't buy it anyway.

As we move into 1999, it's possible that food-stockpiling plans will move beyond the personal level, especially in small towns. Neighborhood groups, church groups, and others may decide to band together and pool their purchases; this is a particularly convenient way to acquire bulk supplies of basic foodstuffs. We may also see the emergency-preparedness groups in small towns organizing a stockpiling plan; but as of mid-1998, there is no public evidence of such planning at the state or federal level.

Fallback Advice: One-Year Failures

If a one-month stockpiling effort is difficult, then the notion of a one-year food stockpile is likely to be entirely beyond the ability of most. Indeed, most Americans would have no idea how to go about such a task; it's not something we were taught in school, nor have we ever seen anyone do it.

Does it make sense at all? Can anyone imagine the local food stores being closed for 365 consecutive days? If such a catastrophe were to occur, it would drastically change the landscape of most urban centers; there would be food riots in the street for some period of time, and then everyone would leave—for while there might be a few ultra-conservatives with a one-year food supply, the overwhelming majority would have no such reserves. And assuming that the farms, fisheries, and ranches are still producing edible food (we haven't bothered exploring the possibility of Y2000 problems so severe that this part of society breaks down, too!), then sooner or later food *will* show up in the cities, for whoever happens to be left. The same would presumably be true for the small towns, suburban, and rural areas; the primary difference is that the people in these areas would have been somewhat more self-sufficient in the interim.

The point here is that we're not trying to suggest that a Y2000-induced food-distribution problem will completely eliminate the supply of food for a full, solid year. But there's also no guarantee that the confusion and chaos will magically end on December 31, 2000; indeed, if food-distribution problems are combined with transportation problems, electrical problems, and problems in the various other areas discussed in this book, it's not at all unreasonable to imagine recurrent, unpredictable problems with the food supply over a period of three-five years, each one lasting for a day, or a week, or a month. Thus, the notion of a one-year food stockpile would most likely be meaningful for those concerned about these long-term difficulties.

Building a one-year food stockpile is something that will be difficult for most Americans to accomplish without professional assistance. While some canned or bottled goods might last for a year, many of the items one would normally buy in a grocery store were simply not intended for long-term storage. Most food items are packaged in plastic, cellophane, boxes, or other containers that contain a certain amount of air; the air contains oxygen, and the oxygen contributes to a slow but steady spoilage of the food. There are some items in the store that are vacuum-packed (including junk-food snacks like Pringle's potato chips, for example) or freeze-dried (including many varieties of coffee), but this accounts for only a small part of the overall diet that a normal family would require.

Thus, if you're going to pursue this level of protection against Y2000 failures, you're probably going to need the products from one or more food-supply or food-packaging companies. You'll need to do some research in the library or on the Internet to find such companies, because many of them are relatively small; when we searched the World Wide Web to find a list of such suppliers, we discovered that fully a third of the ones listed had gone bankrupt or disappeared. However, here are two that you can contact for information: [7]

- Walton Feed, 135 North 10th, P.O. Box 307, Montpelier, ID 83254; phone (800) 269-8563, Internet/Web address: http://www.waltonfeed.com
- Millennium Gourmet Food Reserves, accessible via email at food@itsnet.com or by phone in Provo, Utah at 800-500-9893.

In a message posted on the authors' Y2000 Internet discussion forum, Skipper Clark added the following additional food suppliers. We have not had an opportunity to investigate any of them; be sure to ask for prices, references, and delivery schedules before you make a commitment:

> *Here are a few other companies—Alpineair, Ready Reserve Foods (phone 800-453-2202), Maple Leaf Industries (phone 800-671-5323), Nitropak phone (800-866-4876—most of their food comes from Walton but they carry the entire line of Oregon Freeze Dry—expensive but if you can afford it you can eat like a king—relatively speaking), Perma Pac (phone 801-268-3913), Best Prices Storable Foods (Bruce sells Walton but see food line #2), Life sprouts (phone 800-241-1516—sprouting seeds and supplies), Emergency Essentials (Walton [though they won't admit it] and others), Shield's Date Garden—phone 760-347-0996—date crystals-excellent sweetener will last practically forever—I've stored them for 15 years and they were still good!), School of Natural Healing (phone 800-372-8255—Herbalism home study course, in case you run out learn to identify and use wild stuff), Millenium Foods. Send email address for more info to skipper@cncnet.com*

Most of the emergency-food suppliers assume that a one-year supply will include a substantial amount of corn, wheat, rice, and pinto beans; thus, it's likely that to use these supplies, you'll need to be willing to bake your own bread, as well as cooking meals that are probably much simpler than the meals you now enjoy.

As noted above, planning for this kind of Y2000 contingency is not easy, particularly because it's likely to create scorn, ridicule, and merciless teasing on the part of your friends and neighbors. It's also more expensive—a one-year food package for an individual adult is likely to cost $700-$1,000, depending on the supplier—and it obviously takes much more storage than the two-day or one-month options listed above. But it *can* be done; the question is simply whether you feel the risk warrants such action.

Fallback Advice: Ten-Year Failures

A ten-year disruption in the food supply only makes sense if you're willing to assume that almost all of the other problems areas discussed in this book have occurred in their most serious form. If the phone system, transportation system, governmental systems, electrical utilities, and all other aspects of our socio-economic system were to utterly collapse because of computer failures, then we would be reduced to an agricultural society reminiscent of America in the mid-19th century. There might be a few pockets of "advanced" civilization, but in this scenario, everyone else would be back on the farm. Unfortunately, the last few generations of Americans have never seen a farm, let alone lived on one or worked on one. A few hardy survivors might be able to make such a transition in life-style, but most of us would not; the 10-year scenario would entail a great deal of starvation in this country, and several others around the world.

We're concerned, and occasionally pessimistic, about the outcome of the Y2000 problem, but not *that* pessimistic; but it's up to you to make your own assessment. However, it does occur to us, from time to time, that this scenario describes the current state of China fairly accurately. Wouldn't it be ironic if China escaped most of the Y2000 problems because of its agrarian society, and the U.S.—because of its extreme dependence on computers—was reduced to the level of China's economy?

On the other hand, the notion of a billion cheerful Chinese farmers planting and harvesting their crops by hand is a bit naïve. As John Yellig points out, the Y2000-induced agricultural disruptions might be serious in the U.S., but it could be far, far worse in other parts of the world:[8]

> *The U.S. would be able to recover from a shortage much quicker than the Third World. In this hypothetical situation, the U.S. would have to "circle the wagons" and reserve what little resources it had for itself in order to make it through the crisis while Third World countries such as Afghanistan, Somalia, Angola, and Haiti, which depend on food subsidies and other humanitarian aid from the West would suffer unfathomable consequences from a disruption in the food chain. Their already shaky governments could easily be toppled if the citizens faced mass starvation. Mass exoduses from the starving countries could resort thereby spreading the instability to their neighbors.*
>
> *Other more independent countries in the Third World which do not rely on food aid from the West could nevertheless also face famine and civil unrest. Because of the Green Revolution introduced by Western countries in the second half of the Twentieth Century, which used products such as petrochemical pesticides and fertilizers to maximize crop yield, these "independent" Third World countries would be at the mercy of the ability of Western suppliers to deliver their necessary chemicals. Since the production of these chemicals could be interrupted by breakdowns in their factories due to embedded chip*

malfunctions, there exists a strong danger that Third World agricultural production would be severely limited.

To use another metaphor, Y2000 is like an onion: Every time you peel off one layer, there's another layer beneath it. Our discussion began with the possible impact of Y2000 on food production and distribution—but by the end of the chapter, we have seen that serious disruptions in food production and distribution could have geopolitical consequences, particularly in Third World countries.

Endnotes

1. Samuel Johnson, quoted in James Boswell, *Life of Samuel Johnson*, August 5, 1763 (published in 1791).
2. Bill Bryson, *The Lost Continent: Travels in Small Town America*, Chapter 3 (1989).
3. We should also note that the "ripple effect" might cause problems beyond those of food delivery. The August 8, 1997 issue of *Computerworld* reported that "a Michigan produce store has filed what is believed to be the first year 2000-related lawsuit because its cash registers freeze when customers use credit cards with year 2000 expiration dates. Produce Palace International in Warren, Mich. recently sued Tec-America Corp in Atlanta and local service vendor All American Cash Register Inc.... claiming the companies sold a defective computer system they knew they couldn't fix."
4. However, it's becoming increasingly common to see EDI (Electronic Data Interchange) as the mechanism for communicating an order to a supplier. This is especially true for the chains of stores, in which the items to be re-stocked are transmitted (by computer) from each store to a central headquaters; the aggregate order is then transmitted by computer to the supplier. Thus, there are additional opportunities for Y2000-related disruptions.
5. Although New Mexico is not usually known for its wine or beer, it turns out that there are numerous vineyards throughout the state, a few of which of which produce a decent Cabernet and Chardonnay; and there are numerous local micro-breweries. Fortified with

enough alcohol, perhaps one would not even miss the food delicacies from other parts of the country!

6. On the other hand, some religious groups, including the Mormon Church, have long advocated stockpiling food for unforeseen emergencies. Thus, at least a portion of the U.S. population may be well-prepared, even though they would never have guessed it was a Y2000 computer problem that would be the source of the problem.
7. As the second edition of this book was being prepared in the summer and fall of 1998, at least one of these food suppliers had a backlog of six-nine *months*, depending on the items being ordered. Thus, if you do decide to order food, be sure to obtain a guarantee of timely delivery—or be prepared to visit the supplier and take delivery yourself.
8. John Yellig, "Y2K and Agriculture: Potential Effects and Consequences," posted on the Westergaard web site at http://www.y2ktimebomb.com on April 15, 1998.

Y2000 Impact on Your Home PC

... it's worth remembering that the typical family home today has more computer power in it than the entire MIT campus had 20 years ago.

President Bill Clinton, speech at the National Academy of Sciences, *July 14, 1998*

Electronic aids, particularly domestic computers, will help the inner migration, the opting out of reality. Reality is no longer going to be the stuff out there, but the stuff inside your head. It's going to be commercial and nasty at the same time.

J. G. Ballard, Interview in Heavy Metal *(April 1971; reprinted in Re/Search, no. 8/9, San Francisco, 1984)*

Introduction

In preparing this book, we have been intrigued by the number of non-technical friends and colleagues, not to mention reporters and other members of the media, whose first question about the Y2000 problem is, "What about our home PCs?" We were puzzled by the frequency of the question, because only half of U.S. households have a PC at all, and in most cases, the PC is used for games, or children's homework, or for writing an occasional letter. While these are pleasant, and often even useful activities, they hardly seem as fundamental and important as most of the other topics discussed in this book. To put it bluntly: If the lights are out, the phones are dead, and the banks are closed, it's unlikely that you'll spend much time worrying about the status of your home PC.

Nevertheless, people *are* interested in the potential impact of Y2000 problems on their home PC; perhaps it's just because the PC represents a significant investment. Most people are vaguely aware that they really haven't learned how to exploit all of the power and potential of their PC, and perhaps they worry that it's their own lack of technical skills that will render their PC inoperable on January 1, 2000.

However, there are a few people—particularly those who use computers all day long in their office—for whom the home PC is just as important as the automobile. One of the authors uses his Macintosh to organize most of his life, and often jokes that if the computer was stolen, he would have to commit suicide. Such people often have a backup PC in case of serious hardware problems, and are diligent about making daily backups of important data, and monthly archival backups that are stored in the local bank's safety deposit box, along with birth certificates and other important documents.[1]

We'll assume that most readers of this book are not quite *that* fanatical about their computers, but we'll also assume that for more and more individuals and families, the home PC is becoming an important "appliance." Perhaps it's not quite as important as the family car, but its absence could create a moderate degree of discomfort. That being the case, let's turn to the fundamental question: Are home PCs vulnerable to the Y2000 problem?

The answer is: "It depends." For those using relatively new computers (i.e., purchased within the last year or two) and who carry out relatively simple, mundane functions (e.g., writing school reports with a simple word processor), there should be little or no problem. But for those using older computers, and also for those using very elaborate, sophisticated software applications on their PC, there's a much higher likelihood of Y2000-related problems.

It's important to realize that the situation is *not* entirely black-and-white, even though many spokesmen for the PC industry have made unilateral statements to the effect that *nothing* about PCs is vulnerable to the Y2000 problem. Articles in the popular magazines and newspapers have contributed to the confusion by strongly implying that Y2000 problems *only* exist in mainframe COBOL programs written 25 years ago by Neanderthal programmers. The reality is that the problems can occur anywhere, any time on any machine; indeed, while the first edition of this book was being written in the summer of 1997, a Y2000 problem was reported in one of the very newest of PC-style programming languages: Javascript.[2]

In case you don't find this sufficiently convincing, consider the following commentary from Karl Fielder,[3] whose company, Greenwich Mean Time, specializes in Y2000 work:

> *Greenwich Mean Time has now checked more than 4,000 microcomputer programs (including some on the shelves today) and has found some alarming figures:*
>
> • *28 percent of the programs with Year/2000 date failures were claimed by their manufacturers to be Year/2000 compliant.*
>
> • *21 percent of development tools were capable, in their normally installed configuration, of creating non-compliant programs.*
>
> • *20 percent of the programs use a date windowing technique to expand YY to YYYY, and these date windows are mostly different and are not changeable by the end user. [See Appendix A for a discussion of the "window" approach fixing Y2000 problems.]*
>
> • *4 percent don't know 2000 is a leap year.*
>
> • *4 percent will only run during the 20th century*

To fully understand the range of Y2000 problems that might affect your PC at home, we need to talk about the hardware, the operating system, and the application programs. The same areas of vulnerability exist on the older mainframe computers, by the way, but we've concentrated our mainframe discussions throughout this book only on the application programs, since the hardware and operating system are largely "invisible" to the external user or customer. This is not the case for PCs: You're responsible for your own hardware; and you may have a choice about which operating system you use; and you definitely have a choice about which application programs to use.

There are hundreds of different makes, models, and manufacturers of PCs in the marketplace, but the overwhelming majority fall into two categories: Intel-based computers with DOS or Windows operating systems, and Apple Macintosh computers with the MacOS operating system. If you're still using an Apple II, or an Atari 400, or a TRS-80 Radio Shack machine, you'll have to investigate the situation based on the guidelines and discussion below; but there's a good chance that you're in trouble, simply because those machines are so old that they probably have not incorporated Y2000-compliant features.

Hardware Vulnerability

The first area of Y2000 vulnerability has to do with the hardware and "firmware" on your computer, especially the part that keeps track of the time. Almost all home PCs have an internal hardware time-of-day clock that "ticks" at the rate of once a second, or perhaps as frequently as 60 times per second. The clock can be accessed and/or updated by a low-level part of the computer called the BIOS (for "Basic Input-Output System"), and can then be used in whatever date calculations or displays are required by the operating system or other parts of the computer.

The problem is that the hardware clock and/or the BIOS logic in some of the older computers is *not* Y2000 compliant. On January 1, 2000 the hardware clock (sometimes referred to as a "Real Time Clock," or RTC) will roll over, or "wrap around" to either January 1, 2000 or January 1, 1900, depending on the make and model of the computer. This may not be immediately apparent to you, because the calendar display on your computer screen may show 01-01-00; but internally, the date may be incorrect, and the problem will eventually manifest itself in the operating system or the various application programs on your computer.

As noted earlier, the hardware clock is accessed by the computer's BIOS. Karl Fielder, whose comments about microcomputer programs were cited above, has this to say about BIOS problems:[4]

> *GMT also checked some 500 different BIOSs and found:*
>
> • *BIOS test results vary from PC to PC, even between BIOS versions which seem to be identical in name and date.*
>
> • *Pre-1997 BIOSs failed in 93 percent of those machines tested.*
>
> • *1997 BIOSs failed in 47 percent of those machines tested.*

As mentioned earlier, this problem exists most commonly in the older computers, especially the Intel-based machines built prior to 1996. None of the Macintosh computers have this kind of rollover problem at the hardware level (which does *not* necessarily mean that Mac applications are safe). As for the various other kinds of computers, you'll have to test them yourself. A common way of doing this (after you have safely backed up whatever files are important to you!) is to manually reset the system clock on your computer to 11:59 PM on December 31, 1999 and then wait to see what happens a minute later. If it appears that the Y2000 rollover has worked correctly, then repeat the experiment—but turn your computer off after you've set the clock to 11:59 PM on December 31, 1999; wait a few minutes, and power the machine back on again.[5] If things work properly, carry out a similar test to ensure that your computer recognizes February 29, 2000 as a legitimate date.

It's also a good idea to check with your computer manufacturer to see what they have to say about the Y2000 problem. In most cases, you can visit the vendor's Internet Web site and find their Y2000 section fairly easily; here is a list of the Web addresses for some of the more popular PC vendors:

- IBM—http://www.ibm.com/IBM/year2000/
- Apple—http://www.apple.com/macos/info/2000.html
- Compaq—http://www.compaq.com/year2000/index.html
- Dell—http://www.dell.com/year2000/index.htm
- Gateway—http://www.gateway.com/corp/y2k/y2k/default.html

- Packard Bell—When the second edition of this book was being prepared in the summer and fall of 1998, it appeared that Packard Bell had no public statement about Y2000; we found no results when searching the site for terms "Y2K", "Y2000", or "Year-2000."

- Microsoft—http://www.microsoft.com/y2k/

If it turns out that your computer does have a hardware and/or BIOS problem, you may be able to get a replacement at little or no cost. BIOS upgrades are often available free from the vendor, and a replacement clock is likely to cost only a few dollars. The biggest problem will be that the hardware vendors are not very interested in servicing and repairing vintage 1983 PCs any more, nor are the local computer stores. You may have to shop around, read through the back pages of various computer magazines, and talk to your friends. For obvious reasons, it's strongly recommended that you do this *now*, rather than waiting until December 29, 1999.

Operating System Vulnerability

As noted above, the hardware and associated BIOS logic in a PC can be interrogated to read the current time of day, and/or updated to change the date/time information stored by the computer. In most cases, this is accomplished by the operating system on the computer—e.g., MS-DOS, Windows 3.1, Windows 95, Windows 98, or OS/2 on an Intel-based PC; or MacOS on the various Macintosh computers. Thus, even if the hardware and BIOS are Y2000-compliant, the operating system may inject its own Y2000 errors. As a corollary: Since the end-user (i.e., people like you and us) primarily interacts with the operating system to accomplish the time/calendar functions, it's not always clear where the fault lies when a Y2000 problem emerges. All you know is that the wrong date is showing on the display screen; you don't know (and probably don't care) where the problem originated.

That being said, here's the bad news: Most of the older versions of Microsoft's MS-DOS and MS Windows 3.1 operating systems will perform a Y2000 rollover to January 4, 1980. The good news is that Microsoft Windows 95 and Windows NT are almost completely compliant, Windows 98 is reputed to be fully compliant, and Apple's MacOS operating system is fully Y2000-compliant. Thus, if your home-PC environment involves relatively new hardware (e.g., a Pentium-based computer or a Mac PowerPC) and an up-to-date operating system, you're probably safe. But if you're still running on an old 286- or 386-class Intel computer, and if you're still running DOS or Windows 3.1, you may be in trouble.

What kind of trouble? Well, most of the problems will be manifested in the application programs that you run *on top* of the operating system—e.g., the word processor, spreadsheet, home accounting programs, and so forth. But it's possible that you could run into some problems at the operating system level, particularly with file-manipulation commands. For example, suppose that on the morning of January 1st, you fire up the word-processor on your PC, and dash off a few letters to your friends and relatives. Each of the letters would typically be stored on your computer as a separate file, and the operating system automatically records the date and time that the file was created, as well as the date and time of last modification.

Perhaps you've decided to keep all of these word-processing files in a directory (or "folder," depending on the vocabulary of your computer and operating system) called LETTERS. From time to time, perhaps you ask the operating system to display a list of all the documents (e.g., with the MS-DOS operating system, you would type a DIR command), so that you can clean up the contents of the directory/folder by deleting all of the old documents. In fact, if you're a bit more clever than the typical home-PC user, you might even have constructed a "script" or a "batch file" to accomplish this clean-up operation automatically, each time you turn on the computer. The problem, of course, is that the Y2000 problem causes a file whose *actual* creation date was January 1, 2000 to have an *apparent* creation date of January 4, 1980. Thus, your newly-created files will appear older than the ones created in 1999—and they may thus be inadvertently deleted.[6]

If you do experience problems of this kind, don't expect a lot of sympathy from Microsoft, or from the company from whom you bought the computer.

Their attitude is that you shouldn't be using an old computer and/or an old operating system. As far as they're concerned, they've solved the Y2000 problem (and thus absolved themselves of any responsibility) by providing newer computers and newer operating systems. The fact that you can't afford to upgrade your computer, or that you don't want to upgrade your computer, is considered *your* problem, not *their* problem. *Caveat emptor!*

This may sound more critical of the manufacturers and computer stores than is appropriate, and we don't mean to imply that any of these organizations are malicious or dishonest. It's important to remember that the overwhelming majority of PC computers are sold to business organizations, not homes; and business organizations are far more likely to replace their computers every two or three years, thus creating the impression in the minds of the vendors that *everyone* does so. The individuals who work at Intel, Microsoft, IBM, Apple, and other computer organizations are generally well-paid technocrats; they replace their own home computers every couple of years (assuming their employer doesn't give them a new machine for free!), and they tend to assume that even a household with a modest income will do the same. While this might be the case if home computers cost only a hundred dollars, most middle-income families feel that a $2,000 investment in a home computer is *not* something they intend to do on an annual basis!

Remember also that we're talking about a problem that will manifest itself on January 1, 2000.

While there might be a good argument for continuing to operate a DOS or Windows 3.1 system in 1998, the argument becomes less and less persuasive as time goes on. An old Intel 386 computer purchased in 1992, with 640K bytes of memory and an ancient version of DOS, will be quite antiquated by late 1999. Technically, such a computer *should* continue to work after the beginning of the new millennium; but the practical reality is that you won't get any sympathy from the companies who built that computer. It would be like complaining to Ford Motor Company that you're very upset that they don't stock replacement parts for their Model-T cars any more.

Application Vulnerability

Though Y2000 problems can certainly occur at the hardware, BIOS, or operating system level, a home computer purchased in the latter half of the 1990s probably won't experience these problems. But the newer computers *are* still vulnerable, because most of the computational processing is done at the "application level" above the operating system and hardware. That is, most end-users spend less and less time interacting with the operating system on their computer, and progressively more time interacting with their word processor, spreadsheet program, home-banking system, or Internet Web browser.

Depending on the programs, and the underlying nature of the application itself, these applications may or may not be date-sensitive. Any application program that wants to deal with a date will typically do so by sending a request to the operating system (which interrogates the BIOS logic that reads the hardware clock); the application program might then display the date on your computer screen, or print it in a report, or store it in a database record. At this level, the variety of operations is as vast as in the mainframe world; it's hard to know whether you're vulnerable to a Y2000 problem unless you investigate the various applications that you use on your computer. One of the authors, while working on this chapter, took a quick look at the contents of his PC, and found some 75 distinct application programs; any one of those programs might turn out to be non-Y2000 compliant.

How could this happen? Quite simply: Even if the operating system provides a legitimate date, with a four-digit year-field, there's no guarantee that an application program will use it. For reasons of efficiency, sloppiness, or downright ignorance, the programmers who created some of your favorite applications may have decided to truncate the high-order two digits of the year, and to carry out all subsequent processing with a two-digit year-field—thus creating the famous Y2000 problem.

In a recent article, consultants Joe Celko and Jackie Celko describe the Y2000 problems with the popular home-accounting system Quicken—specifically Quicken version 3 (which is *not* the latest version) running on MS-DOS version 6.[7] They also list a few other culprits:

Other PC applications known to exhibit the year 2000 difficulties includes Microsoft Access, Fox-Pro, and Visual Basic; CA Clipper; Borland Delphi; Gupta SQLbase; and Oracle. Fixes or workarounds for many of them are widely available as freeware.

As with most things, the 80-20 rule applies here: Chances are that 80 percent of the activity on your computer involves only 20 percent of the application programs. It's likely to be your word processor, your home-finance system, the email program, and a few popular games. Those are the ones you should check first for Y2000 compliance; and depending on the outcome, you can then determine how much disruption would be caused by Y2000-related problems in those programs. This is a simplistic version of the "triage" strategy now being employed by large businesses: There are a few applications that may be absolutely essential to one's survival, though that is less likely for a home-PC than for a business computer; there may be some applications that are "important," in the sense that we depend heavily on them, and would find it very expensive and difficult to do without. And then there are the non-essential programs, like the PC games; while one's children might suffer temporary withdrawal symptoms from being deprived of their alien-invader games, it's not likely to have any lasting consequences.

The one nice thing about this aspect of Y2000 planning is that it probably won't cost you any money at all: As the Celkos note in their *Byte* article, fixes or workarounds can usually be obtained at no cost. The easiest way to get these is from the vendor's Internet site (e.g., Microsoft's Y2000 site at http://www.microsoft.com/y2k/), but you should also be able to call the vendor's customer service department for assistance. However, there are two situations where you won't be able to get away with a free update: If you have a very old version of the vendor's product, you may be instructed to upgrade to the latest (Y2000-compliant) version; this is likely to cost $30-50, and it might even require additional memory or disk storage on your computer.

Things are worse, of course, if you call the vendor and find that the phone has been disconnected—i.e., they've gone bankrupt. This is particularly common with some of the older computer games, but there are many other "standard" applications—word processors, spreadsheets, database packages, calendar programs, and the like—that were built by innovative little startup companies in the mid-80s who finally had to concede that they couldn't compete against the software giants. If this happens to you, you'll be in a position to empathize more closely with the large corporate IT departments: This is exactly the problem they face, but on a larger scale. In your case, you have no option but to find a newer software package, produced by a company that will hopefully still be in business in the post-2000 years. The sooner you begin this process, the easier it will be.

We Have Met the Enemy, and He Is Us

It's far less likely that we'll see a lot of problems of this sort for the home PC—except in the case of the

PC being used to support a serious hobby, or a part-time business. If you're a stamp collector, you may have created a database of all your stamps, using Microsoft Access or some other popular database package. If you're a freelance writer, you may have constructed a simple spreadsheet to keep track of your proposals, queries, payments, royalties, and related expenses, using Microsoft Access or Lotus 1-2-3. And even if those vendor-supplied application packages are fully Y2000 compliant, you may have innocently created your own Y2000 problems by storing date-related information with a two-digit year.

This point needs to be emphasized: Not all of the dates in an application program are time-of-day information read from the computer's hardware clock; many of them are manually entered dates. Your database of rare stamps, for example, may include the date when you acquired the stamp, and the date when you sold or traded it for some other stamp; chances are that those pieces of information will have been manually entered, rather than entered automatically. You may have informed the database program that a certain "field" of data was intended to contain date-related information (in order to prevent yourself from accidentally typing a telephone number into that field), and it's possible that the database program will then use that knowledge to force you to type in a date in YYYY-MM-DD format; but it's just as likely that you were sloppy and provided no such clue to the database program at all (in which case, the field would have been defined as a "text" or "alphanumeric" field, which does provide the convenience of allowing you to express a date as "the day before Christmas, on the year before I got married").

Obviously, if you have this category of Y2000 problem, nobody is going to be sympathetic; it is, in the final analysis, *your* problem. And the situation you face is similar to that being faced today by business organizations: You need to begin by investigating your own home-grown applications to see if they *are* Y2000 compliant, and you need to fix them in the remaining months before the decade comes to an end. Most people have few, if any, such applications—and as a result, they may decide to wait until late 1999 to tackle the job. A few are beginning to realize that it's a big job, and that they'd better start now.

Fallback Suggestions: the Two-Day Failure

All of the advice above is proactive in exactly the same nature being carried out by business organizations facing their own Y2000 problem: Analyze your hardware and software to see if the problem exists, and then take appropriate steps to upgrade defective components, or replace defunct software with entirely new software.

But the whole premise of this book is that businesses won't be 100-percent successful, no matter how hard they try, because there are too many complexities and uncertainties. We could take a more optimistic stance towards home computers—simply because they're much less complex, and because you're likely to be much less dependent on them.

However, for the sake of discussion, let's assume the "downside" scenario: Suppose that even with the precautions described above, things go slightly haywire when you turn on your PC on January 1, 2000.

If it's a minor problem that prevents you from using the computer for two or three days, you probably won't be too concerned. The problem, though, is that if your computer begins spewing out gibberish on January 1, 2000, you may not be able to tell whether it's a minor problem that will require a day or two to fix, or a more serious problem of the kind discussed below.

Thus, the first piece of advice is: Make sure that *before January 1, 2000* you have created a backup of all your important data on a floppy disk, or a magnetic tape cartridge, or some other reliable storage medium. Second, make a hard-copy printout of any information that you might need from your computer—e.g., copies of your resume, your favorite recipes, your stock-market portfolio, the mailing list of your family and friends, and so forth.

By the way, note that a problem of this magnitude could occur for a reason that's not the fault of the computer: As discussed in Chapter 3, electrical power might be out for a day or two. Thus, if you really *must* use a computer 8 hours a day, 7 days a week (which is definitely the case for one of the authors), then you should also ensure that you have backup power, typically in the form of batteries, and that the batteries are fully charged. This may prove awkward for standard desktop computers, for which the readily available equipment provides protection against power surges and spikes, but not long-term power outage. Owners of laptop computers, though, may find their batteries to be especially useful during a brief Y2000-induced power failure.

Fallback Suggestions: the One-Month Failure

Suppose the problem is more serious: An important program on your PC turns out *not* to be Y2000-compliant, and because of the backlog and confusion, the vendor tells you that it will be a month before an updated version can be shipped to you. Or it turns out that the BIOS in your computer is defective, and it will take a month to have it replaced with a new BIOS. What then?

If it's a software problem, and if you're dependent on that particular piece of software, you have no alternative but to wait. But you might also have the option of switching to an equivalent software package that *is* Y2000-compliant. You should have checked out all of these details *before* December 31, 1999, of course, but that advice will no longer be particularly useful as of January 1, 2000. Thus, some people may find, perhaps to their enormous surprise, that their favorite word processor no longer works;[8] whether they like it or not (and people *do* become quite attached to version-N of word-processor X), they may have to switch. In almost all cases, this is nothing more than an inconvenience, because any competent word-processing package can import documents produced by any other word processor. But if you're using a specialized program that creates its own database (e.g., a name-and-address mailing-list database of your friends and business contacts), it might be more difficult to export that data to another program.

In any case, the biggest problem here is similar to that mentioned in the "minor" category above: If your computer is down for a month, you may not know whether it really *will* be up and running a month later, or whether things will deteriorate further into the one-year category. Maybe the software vendor will be so overwhelmed by its Y2000 problems that it goes bankrupt; maybe the local computer store that promised to help you obtain and install a new BIOS will renege on their promise—and in the worst case, they too might go bankrupt, with your defective computer locked in their office.

So, if you think this level of difficulty could occur, our strong advice is to ensure that you have a *complete* backup of *everything* on your computer. You probably have a backup of all the programs—i.e., the original "master" copy of the programs, on CD-ROM or floppy disk, when you first purchased it. (If you've lost the floppies or CD-ROM, get a replacement now, while things are still relatively calm!) And you'll need to make a copy of *all* the documents, files, and data you care about, because you may need to "port" your entire computing environment to a brand-new machine, if things can't be fixed and restored within a month.

Fallback Suggestions: the One-Year Failure

The family that purchased a home computer as an amusing curiosity may not be particularly concerned about the prospect of a one-year disruption. The authors have friends who are already saying, "We bought that stupid computer for our kids to do their homework, but after they played a few space-invader games, they said it was more boring than the video games down at the local candy store. And we were planning to put our budget on the computer, but it turned out to be too much work, and the computer is too hard to use. So the damn thing is just sitting there, gathering dust." If that's the situation, then who cares if the mothballed computer has a serious Y2000 problem?

But if you're using the computer actively—for school homework, or household budgeting, or for daily email to family and friends, or for writing the Great American Novel—then a year is an unacceptable amount of time to wait for a repair. If you have followed our advice and backed up all of your programs and data before January 1, 2000, and if your computer has such serious problems that a one-year delay seems likely, then the most sensible thing to do is acquire a new computer that *is* Y2000 compliant, and donate the old one to charity, assuming it ever works again.

We realize, of course, that this will be an economically unattractive option for middle-income families with tight budgets; for some families, the stark reality is that they'll have to retreat back to their precomputing days, when people used typewriters, paper, and pencils. It's simply a question of priorities: For some families, the home computer has become almost as important and indispensable as the family car. If it breaks and can't be repaired in a reasonable time, then there's not much choice but to replace it.

Fallback Suggestions: the Ten-Year Failure

This last scenario is entirely irrelevant for most people in the U.S., and we've included it here primarily so that we can follow the same pattern you've seen in other chapters. However, in the computer field, it's common to hear technical people speaking of "dog years": things change and improve so quickly that one year of calendar-time in the computer field is almost like seven years in any other field.

The point to remember is that the newest home computers *do* have Y2000-compliant hardware and BIOSs, and the latest versions of operating systems are Y2000 compliant.[9] The application programs will eventually be updated to become Y2000 compliant, even if a few companies go bankrupt in the process; and things will eventually get back to normal. Assuming that the manufacturing capabilities of the major computer companies hasn't been destroyed by their own Y2000 problems, the computer industry will be happily producing Y2000-compliant systems for all of us to buy. Even if we had to throw away all of our pre-2000 computers and start all over again, it would only take a few years—indeed, most businesses are already prepared to throw their computers away every few years, because the technology changes so quickly.

There's only one area where this argument makes no sense: the Third World and "emerging" countries that, in many cases, are using hand-me-down computers they've acquired from Western countries. The 10-year-old computer that most Americans would sneer at is still quite useful in much of Africa and other poverty-stricken regions of the world. It's sobering to realize that a university-educated computer programmer in India is likely to be making only U.S. $4,000 per year; thus, a typical, well-equipped home computer is likely to represent a substantial portion of a year's salary. Meanwhile, the school in a rural Indian village may have only installed electricity a few years ago, and barely has the budget to spend $100 for an old vintage-1986 computer that Americans would have thrown in their trash heap. In *that* kind of environment, if it turns out that the majority of "legacy" home computers are Y2000-impaired, it's conceivable that a decade could go by before replacement computers could be afforded.

On the other hand, it's precisely *because* of this situation that many of these societies are perfectly capable of operating without computers at all—in the home or in the business. The abacus is still a widely used computing device; and it doesn't require electricity! So the ultimate irony would be to find that the Third World countries actually survive better than we do, because they have no home computers to worry about!

Endnotes

1. It's also clear that PCs are extremely important within the business community, where they are often used for mission-critical applications; small businesses, for example, tend to run *all* of their business applications on one or more PCs. Large organizations frequently have tens of thousands of PCs connected to one or more mainframe computers; the IRS, for example, is reported to have 130,000 PCs. For the large organizations, the problem is one of logistics: finding, inspecting, repairing, and testing 130,000 PCs is a monumental job, and then ensuring that the environment remains stable (without having new Y2000 problems introduced) is also a difficult job.
2. "Javascript Hits Snag—Developers Face Year-2000 Headaches," *Infoworld*, July 10, 1997. The problem affects both Netscape's Java Script 1.1 and Microsoft's Jscript. According to the article, "The InfoWorld Test Center tested date objects in JavaScript in Netscape's and Microsoft's [Web] browsers and found inconsistencies in the documentation and implementation of the scripting language."
3. Karl Fielder, "PCs Not a Problem—Think Again!" *Year/2000 Journal*, Vol. 1, No. 3, page 6.
4. There is ongoing debate among Y2000 technical experts about the consistency and credibility of some of the BIOS-checking programs. In addition to Mr. Fielder's organization, you can find additional information on BIOS-checkers on the Internet at http://www.rightime.com and http://www.solace.co.uk.
5. Before you do this, make sure that you have performed a backup of any important files and documents on your computer.
6. Les Holmes <designer@wsnet.com>, who was understandably annoyed when he found several glaring technical inaccuracies in the first draft of our book, responded to our concerns about the display of files in a computer directory: "If you bothered to try experimenting with the situation in Windows 3, you would find that (assuming you went to the terrible trouble of setting the RTC using the DOS DATE command [8 seconds or so]), while the file date display may leave something to be desired, newly created files sort properly." We concede the point, but we're not convinced that

many laymen computer-users will remember (or will know how) to use the DOS DATE command.

7. Joe Celko and Jackie Celko, "Double Zero," *Byte*, July 1997, page 90.
8. Microsoft, for example, has acknowledged that MS Word 5.1 has Y2000-compliance problems that could turn out to be quite serious, leading to (among other things) possible corruption of word-processing documents. But it's quite possible that many home-PC users are unaware of this, and have never bothered upgrading to Word 6.0, Word 95, Word 97, or Word 98. It's possible that they will continue using Word 5.1 after January 1, 2000—and it could take days, weeks, or months for them to discover that they have been damaging their documents.
9. However, if you're using the UNIX operating system, then you have another problem to worry about: the Year-2038 problem. UNIX keeps track of time with an internal memory register that is Y2000 compliant, but it will roll over to zero sometime in the year 2038. We haven't bothered talking about it in this book, because it's not relevant to most readers. However, it's just that kind of attitude—i.e., the problem is so far in the future that we don't have to worry about it—that caused the Y2000 problem in the first place!

Y2000 Impact on News Information

The greatest felony in the news business today is to be behind, or to miss a big story. So speed and quantity substitute for thoroughness and quality, for accuracy and context. The pressure to compete, the fear somebody else will make the splash first, creates a frenzied environment in which a blizzard of information is presented and serious questions may not be raised.

Carl Bernstein, Guardian
(London, June 3, 1992)

Introduction

During the writing of this book, one of the authors spent the summer in a small town in New Mexico, where "getting the news" meant watching the first seven minutes of the *Today* show on television, and reading the weekly town newspaper. The former consisted of brief sound-bites about events so far away they seemed irrelevant; and the latter consisted of front-page reports of donations to the local library.

Meanwhile, the other author spent the summer working in New York City, where news is considered as stale as yesterday's oatmeal when it's only a few seconds old. Not only does everyone in Manhattan seem to be both aware and concerned about the latest scandals, fashions, and sports events, but the Wall Street community experiences financial paroxysms within seconds after the announcement of a change in the unemployment rate of Germany or the Japanese Prime Minister's pronouncements about the strength of the yen.

In New Mexico, it's not clear that a Y2000-induced disruption in the delivery of news would even be noticed, or that it would have a great deal of impact on the day-to-day lives of its citizens. By contrast, news is the lubricant that greases the machinery of Manhattan; if the news stops, many of its citizens would have great difficulty carrying out their day-to-day jobs. And since the news is carried on the same media as the primary entertainment media—TV and radio—many of its citizens would have no idea what to do with their time when they got home from work in the evening.

Thus, it's hard to tell how much emphasis to put on Y2000 failures in this area of society; it matters a lot to some, but only a little to others. The notion that there could actually be a Y2000-induced disruption in the delivery of news should not be a large surprise at this point. We'll discuss briefly how this could happen in the realm of TV and radio, as well as the substantially different medium of newspapers and magazines.[1] Then we'll provide our usual list of guidelines for dealing with two-day, one-month, one-year, and ten-year disruptions.

Television and Radio

At first glance, television and radio would seem to be immune to the problems of many other utilities and services: It's free, and it's delivered over the airwaves to anyone who wants to tune in. Thus, it doesn't have to be addressed to a specific person, and we don't have to worry about Y2000-vulnerable computers getting into trouble when they carry out their billing operations.

There is one major exception to this optimistic view: cable TV. Whether it's associated with a satellite dish or a cable brought to the door, roughly 60 million Americans are dependent on the likes of TCI and other cable giants to bring a clear, sharp TV channel into the house.[2] We pay $20-50 per month, on average, for the privilege of having a set-top box and a remote-control unit that allows us to surf through hundreds of channels, so that we can watch Dan Rather *and* Tom Brokaw *and* Peter Jennings each night. If we don't pay the bill, the cable TV company shuts off our service; thus, the Y2000 problems in this area will be similar to the ones discussed in Chapters 3 and 14.

For the remainder of this chapter, though, we'll assume that people are receiving their news broadcasts over "free" channels. Here are the other major areas where Y2000 bugs could disrupt TV/radio news:

- *Broadcasting and distribution of the material:* The news is typically recorded by microphone or TV camera, mixed and edited in a control room, transmitted via satellite or telephone line to local stations, and then broadcast over a transmitter. Some of these operations are manual (after all, there were news broadcasts in the pre-1950 days when only the Defense Department had computers!), but much of it is heavily computerized. Much of the equipment contains embedded computers (which we'll discuss in more detail in Chapter 11), and much of the news content is "time-stamped" for archiving and retrieval purposes, and also so that it can be transmitted properly to areas of the country with different time zones. Thus, dates are very much involved in all of this, and Y2000 bugs can certainly exist.

- *Bringing the news broadcasters into the studios:* We noted in Chapter 4 that airplanes can't fly without their crew; the same situation applies here. Entertainment shows can be "canned" and re-broadcast, as we all know; but most of the news that we watch or listen to is delivered by a live human. No human, no news.

- *Getting the news content from the "field" to the studio:* The authors sometimes wonder whether news broadcasters spend their entire lives in insulated broadcasting booths, inventing whatever news they feel like broadcasting—it certainly seems that way with weather reporters, who will tell you that it's sunny when a casual glance outside would confirm that it's pouring. In any case, aside from the occasional editorial commentary created in the studio by the news team, most of the "real" news occurs "in the field"—e.g., in Bosnia, Washington, or even Truth or Consequences, New Mexico. This has to be captured by on-the-scene correspondents, who transmit the appropriate information by telephone, satellite, telex, fax, or some other form to the studio. Many American citizens were awed by the live coverage provided by on-the-scene reporters in Baghdad during the Persian Gulf War in the early 90s, but it would have been impossible without the sophisticated satellite-supported transmission system. Recall the Chapter 4 discussion about the upcoming problems with the GPS navigation system; we can only hope these problems are fixed before the rest of the Y2000 chaos engulfs us. In any case, the conclusion is simple and obvious: With no telephone or satellite connections, "live" news reports from the field become nearly impossible.

- *Managing the commercials that pay for the broadcasts:* It's no secret that what pays for almost all TV and radio broadcasting, including the news, is commercial messages from sponsors. It's true that most cities have a "public" TV station supported by contributions and government grants; and it's true that National Public Radio (NPR) provides a superb news-reporting service without the usual commercial entanglements. But these are not the primary sources of news information, and we wonder how long they would continue receiving contributions and grants in a post-2000 world. In any case, the main sources of news are subsidized by commercial messages, which are marketed by the broadcasting organizations, and carefully scheduled and synchronized to fit appropriately into the rest of the broadcasting schedule. This entire activity, as you might have guessed, is also heavily computerized—and the software that manages it depends heavily on date calculations. The immediate consequence of a Y2000 failure in this area might be commercial-free broadcasting, which most of us would consider a blessing; but with no commercials, there is no revenue. And if there is no revenue, then the TV and radio stations can't afford to continue operations. A two-day disruption would be annoying, but not fatal; if

> the problems escalate to the one-month or one-year level, it probably *will* be fatal, especially for the smaller broadcasting stations.[3]

Newspapers and Magazines

Newspapers and magazines form the other major source of news for many of us; and while these "hard-copy" publications may seem rather low-tech, and thus impervious to Y2000 failures, the reality is quite different.

Many of us receive such publications on a subscription basis; we pay in advance, and the publication arrives in our mailbox on a regular schedule. Thus, the Y2000-related invoicing and billing problems that we've mentioned throughout the book could be relevant here. However, if *Newsweek* and the *New York Times* refuse to deliver their publication to us for alleged lack of payment, we always have the option of going to the local news stand or magazine store to purchase a copy.

This assumes, of course, that the publishers can keep their distribution network functioning. As with the discussion of food distribution in Chapter 6, magazines and newspapers are delivered to the retail outlets through a complex network of planes, trains, and trucks; if something goes wrong with this mechanism, the publications won't arrive. The situation is compounded by the fact that many publications—especially the larger newspapers like *USA Today* and the *Wall Street Journal*—are created in one location, and then broadcast electronically to various locations around the country (and around the world) for local printing and distribution. Thus, the newspapers (and in a few rare instances, magazines too) are dependent upon the satellite and telecommunications network for distributing their product.

Magazines and newspapers are also dependent upon the telecommunications network for receiving news reports from the field. In this case, we're not dealing with quite the same degree of real-time immediacy that the television stations achieve—but if the satellites or telephone systems are down for a day, there may not be *any* news that the *New York Times* considers fit to print.

Similarly, magazines and newspapers depend upon advertisements for the bulk of their revenues, just like television stations depend on commercials. The advertising material is delivered in a variety of forms to the publishers, and much of this is also computer-dependent. As noted above, the issue of "immediacy" is a little different than it is for TV commercials; a newspaper might be able to hold its printing run for an hour or two until its biggest advertiser manages to deliver the copy and graphic layout for an expensive full-page advertisement. But whether it's a daily, weekly, or monthly publication, the degree to which the advertising "system" depends on computers determines the degree of vulnerability to Y2000 problems.

Finally, there's the question of how newspapers and magazines will be affected in their production and printing operations. The era of manual typesetting has long since disappeared; today's publications are partially, if not wholly, dependent upon computers for phototypesetting, page composition, graphic design, and a host of other production details. For the larger publications, this often involves very expensive, specialized computer equipment; it would require a case-by-case analysis to determine whether these machines are Y2000-compliant. On the other hand, it's intriguing to see how many magazines and smaller newspapers are composed and printed with the same desktop PCs and laser printers that many of us use in our office or at home. They may be somewhat bigger, and they may have more RAM, a bigger display screen, and a higher-resolution printer—but they still use the same operating systems and page-layout systems (e.g., Quark Xpress, PageMaker, Ventura, and so forth) that we use for the church newsletter that we produce on our home computer. As we saw in Chapter 7, these computers are indeed quite vulnerable to Y2000 problems.

Finally, newspapers and magazines require large quantities of paper, ink, dyes, glue, and other materials. Some of this can be stockpiled, but in many cases (particularly paper), it's so bulky and expensive that the publishers acquire it on a "just-in-time" basis. This leads to another potential Y2000 problem: If the paper companies and ink manufacturers can't get their raw materials to the publisher in time, then there will be no publication.

Fallback Advice: Two-Day, One-Month, One-Year, and Ten-Year Failures

As noted above, a two-day disruption in news delivery wouldn't even be noticed by some Americans, nor would it cause any serious inconvenience. Ironically, there might be an exception in the early days of the new millennium: If as many things begin breaking down as we've suggested in this book, it might become *very* important to get the latest news about disruptions in transportation, banking, government services, and so forth.

In any case, if the prospect of a two-day news blackout worries you, what should you do? Our advice is based on an optimistic premise that we can't prove: Not all sources of news delivery will be knocked out at the same time, or for the same period of time. If NBC is down for two days, perhaps ABC will still be running; if all the TV stations in your town are knocked out, hopefully radio will still be available, and so forth. In the worst case, we may need to depend on news broadcasts from Canada, Europe, or other parts of the world; conversely, their news broadcasts could be affected by the same Y2000 problems, so they may be tuning in to our broadcasts.

Thus, the basic strategy for coping with short-term news disruptions is to ensure that you have "redundant" sources. Most people have that already, but since they often depend on just one source (e.g., the TV news on CNN), they often let the others atrophy. There was a time when everyone listened to the radio in the household; now, many of us listen only to the car radio. In preparation for the Y2000 problem, make sure that you *do* have a working radio in the home (and perhaps one that will operate on batteries); make sure that your newspaper and magazine subscriptions are up to date; and so forth. If you're really feeling paranoid, get a shortwave radio that can pick up overseas broadcasts.

If you're concerned about a month-long disruption in the basic infrastructure—e.g., blackouts, telecommunication failures, bank closures, lack of food distribution, and so forth—then it will be important to have some means of receiving news. A battery-operated portable radio might last for a week, and you might be able to keep things going a bit longer if you have spare batteries; but for longer periods of time, it may be worth investing a modest amount of money to purchase a hand-crank radio, such as the Baygen Freeplay Radio. Sixty cranks on the spring-driven internal generator will provide enough power to operate the radio for 30 minutes; such radios are available from suppliers such as Walton Feed (http://www.waltonfeed.com) for approximately a hundred dollars.

Much the same advice applies for longer-term disruptions of a year, or a decade. Conceivably, your local TV station could be out of operation for a month; your local newspaper could shut for a month, or even a year; and perhaps some forms of news delivery will disappear for a decade. But because they all involve different technologies, different transmission and distribution mechanisms, and different companies, the chances that there will be *no* news from *any* source for long periods of time is pretty close to zero. However, if your career, or your peace of mind, depends on timely, uninterrupted delivery of news, then the more redundancy you can provide for yourself, the better.

Endnotes

1. We've left the Internet out of this discussion, even though it's beginning to represent a major source of news for the "digerati," as *Wired* magazine calls the technically elite computer-savvy part of the population. Access to the Internet and the World Wide Web depends, for almost all of us, on access to the telephone network; we'll discuss that in Chapter 13.
2. We are greatly indebted to Phil Govert (pgovert@aol.com) who read through the first draft of our book and then tracked down a December 11, 1995 FCC report entitled "Annual Assessment of the Status of Competition in the Market for the Delivery of Video Programming" (CS Docket No. 95-61), which states, in part, "The number of homes passed by cable grew from approximately 90.6 million at the end of 1993 to approximately 91.6 million at the end of 1994, which is 96% of all television households in the United States. The number of subscribers increased from 57.2 million to 59.7 million between the end of 1993 and the end of 1994. Penetration (i.e., the number of subscribers as a percent of homes passed) rose 3.3% from the end of 1993 to a penetration of 65.2% at the end of 1994." We think it's a conservative estimate indeed to prognosticate that by mid-1998, the number of subscribers will have reached 60 million or more.
3. The absence of commercials will presumably cause a decrease in sales on the part of the advertisers, which will create a different set of problems; on the other hand, it's possible that some companies would find that their sales are unchanged, which might help eliminate the mystique and glamour of TV and radio advertising. In any case, this is all an example of the "ripple effect" situation discussed in Appendix B.

Y2000 Impact on Health/Medicine

[Y2000] is a complex test that requires us all to work together—every government agency, every university, every hospital, every business, large and small... The government's Health Care Financing Administration, known affectionately by the governors and others as HCFA, which runs Medicare, processes almost 1 billion transactions a year. It's computer vendors must painstakingly renovate 42 million lines of computer code.

President Bill Clinton, Speech at the National Academy of Sciences, *July 14, 1998*[1]

I have troubling news today. Clearly, the health care industry is not yet ready for the Year 2000. If tonight when the clock struck midnight the calendar flipped to December 31, 1999, large portions of the health care system would fail. There are some six thousand American hospitals, 800,000 doctors, and 50,000 nursing homes, as well as hundreds of biomedical equipment manufacturers and suppliers of blood, pharmaceuticals, linens, bandages, etc., insurance payers, and others that are not yet prepared.

Senator Robert Bennett, opening remarks at the Special Senate Committee on the Year 2000 Technology Problem Hearing: "Will the Health Care Industry Be Prepared for the Year 2000?" *July 23, 1998*[2]

Introduction

Some of the topics covered in this book may be regarded as "necessities" for modern life, but if questioned closely, we would have to agree that we can survive without television and telephone for days at a time. If we lost our job and our bank account, we could start over; if the utilities failed and our car didn't work, life would somehow go on. But then there are the *real* necessities, like food, water, and air—and, as we will discuss in this chapter, medicine.

Today's health and medical industry is supported by a vast array of high-tech instruments and devices, in the laboratory and the hospital and the doctor's office. And the industry is surrounded and controlled by a vast bureaucracy, which many feel is on the verge of collapse even without an external perturbation like the Y2000 crisis. In any case, a moment's thought will convince you that all of it—medical instruments and paperwork bureaucracy alike—is heavily dependent on computers. We'll explore several specific aspects of Y2000 vulnerability in this chapter; one reason for doing this is the industry surveys throughout 1997 and 1998 indicating that health-care providers are far behind banks, insurance companies, and most manufacturing companies in their Y2000 efforts.[3] Indeed, one recent survey from Gordon & Glickson, an IT law firm in Chicago, found that 30 percent of the 1,600 hospitals surveyed hadn't even begun to develop a Year 2000 strategy.[4] However, it does appear that the industry is beginning to recognize the urgent need for action; one source of information on the Internet about current Y2000-related activities in the medical/health-care is the Rx2000 Institute Web site at http://www.rx2000.org.[5]

Interestingly, this may be one of several areas where the Y2000 problem has generational overtones. Overall, Americans are a reasonably healthy lot, and the healthiest age group tends to be those in their teens through middle adulthood. Aside from an annual visit to the dentist, many young adults will tell you they've never been inside a hospital, and don't even have a "family doctor" they visit regularly. For this group, a Y2000-induced disruption in the health/medicine industry would have no immediate impact—unless, of course, they sustained a sudden injury or illness.

Meanwhile, another segment of American society needs regular, constant medical attention. In addition to those of all ages who have acute illnesses, a significant part of the elder generation—typically those in their 60s, 70s, and 80s—are heavily dependent on Medicare, Medicaid, and various insurance programs to provide a regular supply of prescription medicines, as well as regular visits to their doctor or hospital. It has been one of the blessings of the late 20th century that we have had the technology and the economic prosperity to provide a longer and healthier life to so many Americans—but if the computers stop and the bureaucracy collapses, it will cause a significant crisis indeed. And while it may not get much immediate attention from those in their 20s and 30s, there is likely to be enormous and immediate political pressure from those most dependent on medical supplies and services.

Y2000 problems may also exacerbate the tensions between rich and poor, particularly in today's era of HMOs and managed health-care plans. Just as disruptions in the food supply may be visible in the poorer neighborhoods first, disruptions in the complex network of hospitals, doctors, and prescription medicines are likely to be felt in those same neighborhoods. Those in the affluent neighborhoods, and the middle-class suburbs, are more likely to have private practitioners they can turn to for help—at least in the short term.

Medical Devices and Hospital Systems

Let's begin with the computer-augmented medical devices that one sees in a well-equipped doctor's office, as well as most hospitals across the country. The familiar example, which most of us have seen on popular TV programs like *General Hospital* or *E.R.*, is the monitoring device that's attached to a patient who has just completed an operation. Complete with flashing lights, display screens, digital read-outs, and audible "beeps," these bedside monitors record and display a patient's heartbeat, blood pressure, temperature, and various other vital signs. More importantly, they *monitor* these vital signs, constantly watching to see that they remain within acceptable limits. If an indicator goes above or below a threshold, medication can be automatically administered through an IV; if the indicator goes significantly beyond its acceptable range, an audible alarm can be generated in the nurse's station.

Beyond the patient-monitoring systems popularized by TV dramas, there are dozens of additional devices that doctors, nurses, and medical technicians depend upon for both routine and emergency medical practices. Whether it's a CAT scan or an MRI or a heart-checkup or the dazzling devices in the operating room, they're all computer-controlled, or computer-augmented. In most cases, they simply wouldn't operate if the computer shuts down.

And that brings us to the obvious question: *Could* they break down on January 1, 2000? The sobering answer is: We don't know, and in many cases, the hospitals don't know either. We received an email message from Dr. Paul R. Lindeman, an Emergency Medicine physician, who reviewed the first draft of our book and commented:

> *In a general sense, most routine bedside medical monitoring devices tend to be ignorant of the year and are as such probably (there's that word again!) immune from y2k. These devices include the ubiquitous "IV pumps" which deliver fluid and medication at precise rates, as well as the heart rate monitors which display waveform and rhythm / rate and perhaps a BP (and generally nothing else). Some of the more exotic devices found within the ICU may not be similarly classified.*

You can interpret that as "good news" if you have the luxury of standing outside the hospital on New Year's Eve, with all of your friends and loved ones standing around you. However, it's not very reassuring news if you happen to be on the operating table at that moment, with cathodes and IV tubes connected to a device whose failure could kill you by commission (e.g., giving you an overdose of medication) or omission (e.g., failing to sound an alarm). Or they could simply shut down, as is likely to be the case with medical devices whose internal computer-controlled clocks mistakenly decide that they've operated too long without being serviced or re-calibrated.[6] While we were researching the material for the first edition of this book, we came upon an e-mail exchange between members of a Y2000 health-care "user group," in which one individual offered the following assessment for his organization's medical systems:

> *I am the Y2K Project Manager for the ____ Medical System. We too are in the assessment phase, however, we are approaching this as a potential disaster because we don't know where the problems lie. We have 29 mission critical off the shelf clinical applications, over 15,000 medical devices from approximately 2000 vendors, another 2 to 3000 suppliers of goods and services, 5000+ PCs, plus the complete hospital infrastructure (elevators, security, chillers, heating & cooling, etc.). All of the above has to be verified and tested for Y2K compliance. Testing alone could take 6 months to 1 year. We have already had failures and know that at least 1 of our systems is two versions behind the Y2K compliant version. So I believe it is wrong to assume that this is a small problem.*[7]

This problem has not dissipated very much in the ensuing year between the first edition and second edition of this book. While preparing the second edition, we came across an interview with John

Grimm, vice president of information services for the Hospital Council of Western Pennsylvania. "There are potentially 10,000 to 15,000 medical devices that could be affected," Mr. Grimm said. "The problem is you don't know which ones will be affected and which ones won't. It's imperative to work closely" with the manufacturers.[8]

The potential Y2000 vulnerability of all these devices is associated with both a very simple, and a very complex, aspect of computers. The simple part has to do with the nature of most "real time data acquisition" or "process control" computer systems: They "sample," or read, a sensor at frequent intervals of time. In the case of an automobile computer, the sensor may be the internal temperature of the carburetor; in the case of a patient monitoring system, it may be the body temperature of the patient. The automobile computer might have to monitor the temperature 1,000 times a second in order to ensure a smooth combustion mixture of fuel and oxygen; the patient monitoring system might only have to sense the patient's temperature once a second. But in any case, it's accomplished with a hardware chip that measures the passage of time in appropriate units. *If* that hardware chip was acquired from a computer manufacturer that incorporated day, month, and year into the chip, and *if* the associated hardware and software logic is Y2000 sensitive, then there is a definite risk that the chip will exhibit aberrant behavior on January 1, 2000.

In the case of the hospital system, it's highly likely that the time-sensing chip is part of a much larger system that includes some date-sensitive logic. Thus, the patient-monitoring system that administers medication via an IV tube has probably been programmed not to administer the medication for more than 24 hours without a manual approval (and perhaps a "reset" of the device) by the nurse or doctor. Or it may have been programmed to administer a lower dosage at night, when the patient is sleeping; or it may have been programmed to store all of the sensor-readings in a database, in order to compare this patient's prognosis with other patients.

For example, in a recent Congressional hearing, Ms. Ann Coffou testified that:

> *...every time a heart pacemaker detects an irregular heartbeat it sends a shock to the system and then records the time the event occurred. This information is regularly downloaded to a computer system so it can be analyzed by medical personnel. Whenever the information is downloaded, the pacemaker resets itself. The downloaded information is used by cardiologists to detect patterns and irregularities in the patient's heart rhythms. If the software in the receiving system starts recording faulty times for the shock deliveries, the cardiologist could misinterpret the results and administer improper medical care.*
>
> *The U.S. Veteran's Administration funded a project to interview the top five pacemaker manufacturers to see if they were aware of this potential problem. One company was aware of the problem and said they would have it corrected by the end of 1997. Two companies said that the problem would be fixed before the Year 2000, one before 1998. Finally, one company flatly refused to acknowledge the problem and when pushed declined to discuss the topic any further.*

> *A physician in a heart clinic in Spartanburg, South Carolina, related that a new shipment of heart defribulators the clinic received recently were recalled by the manufacturer. The defribulators use an embedded device that calculates the time since last maintenance similar to elevators. Like the elevator, if the time since the last maintenance check surpasses a certain time frame, the defribulator will not operate, thereby reducing the possibility of malfunctioning on a patient. The manufacturer voluntarily recalled their products when they discovered they were not designed to handle the change in century.*
>
> *The legal ramifications for these and other medical system malfunctions have the ability to become enormous, precedent-setting lawsuits, not to mention the backlash effect on physician malpractice insurance.*[9]

Most of this programmed computer logic will have been written by the medical equipment companies that provide the patient-monitoring systems and the various other kinds of medical devices. As with the software for electrical generators and nuclear reactors, this software tends to be written much more carefully, and tested much more thoroughly, than the business applications developed in a typical corporate IT department; indeed, the software (and the rest of the equipment) has to be approved by the Food and Drug Administration and/or other governmental regulatory bodies before it can be used at all. But this does *not* mean that the software is bug-free; completely independently of the Y2000 problem, there have been several documented cases over the past decade where software bugs have caused serious medical problems—including a few cases where patients have been killed.

The FDA and government regulators now include Y2000-compliance in their checklist of tests and audits required to approve a *new* hospital/medical device, but that won't eliminate the problem for the *existing* equipment—not unless every one of them is tested for Y2000 compliance. Again, it's important to recognize that the Y2000 problems can occur at several "levels": within the hardware and its associated BIOS logic for recording the time, within the operating system, within the programming language, within the database system, or within the application programs.

The problem is likely to be compounded by additional application programs written by the hospitals themselves. Almost all hospitals, except the very smallest, have a computer staff that deals with all the "business" programs for billing and insurance paperwork; they also install, maintain, and fix minor problems in the patient-oriented systems described above. But in addition to that, the larger hospitals have research departments developing their own computer systems; and they have doctors who often feel the urge to write their own computer programs for various medical activities they're involved with.

Colleagues of ours like to joke that doctors are lousy pilots, and should never be allowed to handle small airplanes; their power in the operating room makes them feel God-like, and they act as if they're omnipotent when coping with bad weather and other airplane hazards. Whether or not this is true, we can report from personal experience that doctors are lousy programmers (as are nuclear physicists, and members of various other highly skilled professions). They have brilliant ideas, and they have the best of intentions when it comes to translating those ideas into computer programs; but they're very impatient, and very unwilling to deal with the minute, niggling details of computer programming. Their testing is spotty, their documentation is nonexistent, and their willingness to explain the details of their program to anyone else is roughly the same as their willingness to explain brain surgery to a kindergarten child.

Like all generalities, this characterization is flawed, and we realize that there are numerous exceptions. Nevertheless, we predict that a hospital whose medical devices and computer systems include a substantial amount of "amateur" programming by doctors, is going to be even more susceptible to Y2000 failures.

Doctors

Doctors, as we've discussed above, are an active participant in the hospitals that we visit for operations and serious illnesses. But many of them also maintain a practice *outside* the hospital; indeed, that's the most common form of doctor-patient interactions that most of us experience.

A doctor's office is a small business unto itself; there may be two or three physicians, a few nurses and medical assistants, and a few secretaries, receptionists, and administrative assistants. As we've already discussed, a typical doctor's office will also contain computer-controlled medical devices; there won't be as many as there are in hospitals, and they may not be quite as sophisticated, but they're still computer controlled, and they're still vulnerable to Y2000 problems.

However, our main concern here is the vast amount of paperwork that the doctors have to cope with these days. Some of this is still maintained in file folders, stored away in massive file cabinets; you've probably noticed this whenever you visit your doctor, for there's bound to be a manila file folder with all kinds of details about your medical history and your previous interactions with the doctor. Some of the information in the file folder consists of printouts from the medical devices (e.g., EKG readouts when you had your last cardiac checkup), and some of it consists of reports and printouts from various computer systems in the doctor's office, or from your hospital, or from other doctors you've visited, or from a medical lab that reported on your cholesterol level. But at least it's all on paper, and in a well-managed doctor's office, it's been filed someplace where people can find it; if a Y2000 failure knocks out all the computers, a permanent record of your medical situation still exists.

But the ability of the doctor's office to function as a "business" is more and more dependent on computers. This is largely because of the billing and reporting bureaucracy associated with insurance companies, Medicare/Medicaid agencies, and various state and federal regulatory bodies that monitor the kind of medication and medical practices administered by doctors. Much of this, of course, involves money: If the doctor charges $100 for your annual checkup, the bill might be paid by a combination of your employer's insurance plan, your personal insurance policy, Medicare, and your own personal finances (in the form of a check, cash, or credit card). Keeping track of all of this is a massive job, and during the past ten years—as desktop computers became cheap enough that doctors could afford them—most of the details have become computerized.

In the early days of such computerization, it was often the doctors themselves who wrote the computer programs; a few of these legacy systems may still be in operation. For the most part, though, today's doctor's office is supported by a software "package" that can be purchased from professional software companies who specialize in this kind of application. But while some of this software comes from large, reputable companies like IBM, much of it comes from much smaller companies—some of whom are no longer in business, even though their software is still running in the doctor's office.

Thus, from a Y2000 perspective, doctors are in the same position as many other small businesses who carry out their invoicing, receivables, payables, inventory control, payroll, and other business activities on a computer. Most of this software runs on standard, general-purpose, desktop computers; in some cases, an ambitious doctor has augmented this by connecting several of his office computers in a network, and/or connecting the computer(s) to the nearby hospital via modem and the Internet. As we saw in Chapter 7, these computers are highly susceptible to Y2000 problems, especially if they're more than a year or two old; to compound the problem, many doctors (who behave in the omnipotent/amateur fashion discussed above) are incredibly sloppy when it comes to backups and archives of their databases. Thus, it will be of little surprise to the authors if doctors begin reporting massive failures, disruptions, and data loss after January 1, 2000.

This may be of little immediate concern to you, if you're the typical healthy American who only sees his or her doctor for an annual checkup. But if you depend on a regular prescription medicine, and if the prescription has to be authorized by the doctor before the pharmacy will refill it, then you'll be *extremely* annoyed if the doctor tells you that he's lost all of your records.

Medicare, Insurance, and Hospital/Doctor Paperwork

We've already noted that doctors and hospitals are inundated with paperwork associated with medical practices and services. Twenty years ago, we would have pointed the finger of blame (to the extent that "blame" should be attached to something that virtually everyone regards as an onerous task) at the insurance companies; the patient, the doctor, and/or the hospital would file a claim for payment, in the hope that the insurance company would cover most, if not all, of the cost of the medical service.

Today, there's another entity whose paperwork requirements dwarf that of the insurance companies within the private sector: Medicare. Gary North, a prolific and outspoken observer of the Y2000 problem, has recently drawn attention to a May 16, 1997 report to Congress from the General Accounting Office entitled *Medicare Transaction Systems: Success Depends Upon Correcting Critical Managerial and Technical Weaknesses*, authored by Joel M. Willemssen. North's conclusion: The anticipated volume of one *billion* insurance claims and payouts of $288 billion in the year 2000 are highly imperiled by a combination of administrative and managerial fiascoes that the likelihood of Medicare being Y2000-compliant is extremely low. Actually, his words are: "My conclusion: Medicare will not make the year 2000 deadline."[10,11] The staggering volume of Medicare paperwork was documented again in mid-July 1998 at the Senate Committee on the Year 2000 Technology Problem, in which it was reported that the daily output of the medical industry is nearly 4 million Medicare claims and approximately 27 million pages of medical records.[12]

In his July 10, 1997 testimony before the GAO's Technology Subcommittee,[13] Mr. Willemssen detailed a number of problems, including those associated with a massive effort currently underway to replace 70 private firms that currently administer Medicare's day-to-day operations with a single government-run system. As Mr. Willemssen points out:

We also reported and testified this past May that the Health Care Financing Administration (HC-FA)—a major component agency within the Department of Health and Human Services (HHS)—had not completed numerous critical assessment activities for the systems run by its contractors to process approximately $200 billion annually in Medicare claims. Specifically, HCFA had not required systems contractors to submit year 2000 plans for approval, and lacked contracts or other legal agreements detailing how or when the year 2000 problem would be corrected, or indeed whether contractors would even certify that they would correct the problem. We made several recommendations to HCFA to address its shortcomings in this area, including regular reporting to HHS on its progress. HHS reported in May that it expected to complete the assessment phase last month."

There's another aspect of the problem that consumers and citizens might not think about: Without regular payments from HFCA, many hospitals and medical practices would suffer severe cash flow problems almost immediately. In her May 7, 1998 testimony to the Subcommittee on Oversight of the House Committee on Ways and Means Hearing on the Year 2000 Computer Problem, Jennifer Jackson, General Counsel and Vice President of Clinical Services for the Connecticut Hospital Association, said:

On average, America's hospitals and health systems receive roughly half of their revenues from government programs like Medicare and Medicaid. If that much revenue were to be suddenly cut off, hospitals could not survive, and patient care could be jeopardized. Hospitals would not be able to pay vendors. They would not be able to purchase food, supplies, laundry services, maintain medical equipment—in short, they would

> *not be able to do the job their communities expect of them. All this would occur even as hospitals and health systems faced the substantial costs of addressing their own Year 2000 system needs.*[14]

If you're a gambler, and a believer in miracles within government, perhaps you can find a way to read reports and statements like this and still believe that everything will work properly on January 1, 2000. If you're a cynic, or a hard-nosed manager, your attitude might be, "Those jerks will run around in circles and get nothing done until the last possible minute, until someone cracks the whip over their heads and tells them to get to work. The result is that it will be *much* more expensive, and it will waste millions of the taxpayer's money." Ah, if only it were that simple! As we discuss in detail in Appendix A, software problems are not the sort of thing that can be solved by throwing massive quantities of money and people at them. Even professional software managers fall victim to this illusion from time to time, and we expect that professional politicians will march bravely forward with a strategy roughly equivalent to asking nine women to somehow produce a baby in one month.

If you don't believe in miracles, but you do enjoy gambling, then it would be nice to know what your odds are with Y2K; unfortunately, one of the serious problems plaguing hospitals and the medical industry is that a large percentage of the vendors and suppliers are "stonewalling" requests for Y2000 compliance information. At a mid-July 1998 hearing conducted by the Special Senate Committee on the Year 2000 Technology Problem, the undersecretary of for veteran's health at the VA, Kenneth Kizer, pointed out that 233 of the 1,600 manufacturers that have supplied medical devices to the VA have not responded to the agency's "multiple inquiries" in the past year as to whether their devices are Year 2000-compliant.[15]

But hospitals and government agencies are gradually accumulating lists of both compliant and non-compliant products. The British medical journal *Health Informatics Journal*, for example, posted a list of non-compliant hospital and medical products on the Internet at http://www.shef.ac.uk/uni/projects/hij/y2kdef2.htm; it's instructive to read this list to get a sense of the range and severity of problems that the hospitals are beginning to anticipate. Meanwhile, the U.S. Food & Drug Administration (FDA), published a database of Y2000 compliance information for medical manufacturers on the Internet at http://www.fda.gov:80/cdrh/yr2000/y2krp298.html; but it prefixed the following caveat to that database:

> *Data is posted to this database as it is received from the manufacturer. Submission of data is voluntary. There is no assurance of the compliance status of any manufacturer who does not respond. For manufacturers whose assessments are incomplete, the data will be updated when additional information is received from the manufacturer. The Food and Drug Administration, however, cannot and does not make any independent assurances or guarantees as to the accuracy or completeness of this data.*

Unfortunately, the stonewalling problem affects the FDA, too; in a July 23, 1998 presentation to the

Special Senate Committee on the Year 2000 Technology Problem, Acting FDA Commissioner Michael A. Friedman, M.D., reported that:

> *In a letter dated January 21, 1998, Department of Health and Human Services (DHHS) Deputy Secretary Kevin Thurm, asked approximately 16,000 biomedical equipment manufacturers to voluntarily provide information on the Year 2000 compliance status of their products. Included in the mailing were all registered manufacturers irrespective of the specific kind of device produced, even though only about 2,700 manufacturers are believed to produce computerized products which might be sensitive to Year 2000 problems. Approximately 3,000 of the manufacturers included in the mailing are not regulated by FDA; for example, scientific instrument manufacturers... .*[16]

But 90 percent of the vendors did not respond to the Y2K compliance letter; under normal circumstances, one would assume that a manufacturer *would* respond if they were confident that their product was indeed Y2000 compliant.

Prescription Medicines

Prescription medicines, by their very nature, are regulated. They're not like tomatoes or peaches, which you can buy from a neighborhood farm-stand if the local supermarket shuts down. In addition to being regulated by the FDA and/or other government agencies, many of them are protected by patents—i.e., they represent highly profitable *proprietary* products invented by a drug or pharmaceutical company. The more highly regulated, and the more proprietary the product is, the more vulnerable it becomes to Y2000 disruptions. We're not so concerned about a disruption in the supply of Anacin or cough syrup, but we are concerned about specialized medicines for treatment of heart disease, cancer, AIDS, diabetes, and various other illnesses.

The first problem we worry about, of course, is a bankruptcy, shut-down, or serious disruption within the pharmaceutical company itself. These are companies with highly specialized manufacturing processes (not to mention the R&D processes, which are busily at work on the next generation of medicines), which are—no surprise—highly dependent on computers. And like any other business, the pharmaceutical companies have elaborate business applications to manage their finances, their inventories, their payroll, and so forth. If the Acme Sausage company breaks down because of a Y2000 bug in its mainframe computer, both employees and customers of the sausage company will be affected; but if the very same mainframe bug disrupts the computers of the Acme Miracle-Drug Company, it could have far more serious consequences.

Another interesting comparison: A shut-down of the Acme Sausage company probably won't cause many lawsuits, if any. Indeed, it would have to be a fairly serious flaw in the production process—e.g., mixing ground glass with the bratwurst—before we would expect to see any lawsuits at all. By contrast, the potential litigation associated with pharmaceutical failures could be massive indeed. We've already seen examples of multi-million dollar, if not multi-*billion* dollar, lawsuits against pharmaceutical companies in recent years. We have no way of knowing whether such lawsuits will emerge in the post-2000 days and months, but given the litigious nature of American society, it would be no surprise. And the point of this discussion is simple: It doesn't take very many mega-dollar lawsuits to shut a company down.

Finally, we note that drugs and medicines, whether "prescription" or "over the counter," have to be delivered from the pharmaceutical manufacturing facility to doctors, hospitals, pharmacies, and retail outlets. In this regard, medicine is like food; and the potential disruptions fall into the same category as the ones we discussed in Chapter 6.

Fallback Advice: Two-Day Failures

If you're an optimist, then perhaps you'll believe that all of the problems described in this chapter will be identified in advance by the appropriate authorities, and that almost all of the problems will have been remedied *before* January 1, 2000. In this optimistic scenario, only a few problems will slip by the programmers and the testers and the government regulators, and the disruptions will require only a few days to fix.

Though some problems of this minor nature could occur all during the first year of the new millennium, the most likely period of difficulties will be the first few days of January. Thus, no matter how optimistic you're feeling, prudence suggests that you should avoid elective surgery until at least mid-

January. For expectant mothers whose due-date is January 1st or January 2nd, especially those with fetal complications, there is a real life-and-death decision to be faced: Should one hope that the medical equipment will continue functioning, or should one opt for a slightly premature Cesarean-section birth on December 30th? We are in no position to offer advice to an unknown reader in this area; all we can do is ask you to think carefully about the tradeoffs if the situation applies to you.[17]

What if your doctor is unavailable for a few days because of a Y2000-induced disruption? If it's an emergency, you may not be able to wait that long; thus, you should take steps to provide a backup mechanism to contact your doctor, and perhaps even find some backup doctors that you can visit if you or your family have a medical history that includes occasional emergency situations. For those who find themselves dealing with HMOs or other managed-care forms of treatment, this will be difficult—for the relationship between doctor and patient is becoming more and more impersonal, which makes it more difficult to the attention one needs in an emergency. As recommended in our discussion of utilities in Chapter 3, it makes sense to cultivate a personal relationship with a competent doctor, in order to improve the chances of getting the necessary attention if a post-2000 problem develops.

The issue likely to be of concern for a much larger number of people is prescription medicine. Common sense suggests that you maintain a *minimum* inventory of two or three days of whatever medication you depend upon—and never let the inventory fall below that level. Indeed, given the reasonable cost and ample availability of most medicines, it probably makes far more sense to ensure that you have a two-three month supply, unless your physician or pharmacist specifically recommends against it.

Fallback Advice: One-Month Failures

While two or three days of Y2000-induced disruptions in medicine is likely to be only a minor nuisance for most, a one-month disruption could be a serious problem for even those who consider themselves reasonably healthy. Again, it will be difficult to impress young, healthy adults or teenagers of this problem, for they typically go several months between visits to a doctor or dentist. But parents of young children should be more concerned, as should older citizens and anyone else with serious medical needs.

Most of us don't expect to develop serious, life-threatening illnesses over the course of a month; whether it's a toothache or a bout of the flu, the reaction of most people to going without medical attention for a month would be a shrug—take some Vitamin C, go to bed for a couple days, and just muddle through it. But it's not always that easy; parents, for example, realize that their young children can develop serious illnesses almost overnight. Thus, if you're worried about the possibility of a one-month

Y2000-induced medical/health disruption, it would be a good idea to have some medical reference books on hand. Many parents already have such books, for they sometimes need rapid access to medical advice in the middle of the night, when the doctor isn't available to tell them how best to cope with a fever or a rash or some other sudden problem. For more serious advice on how to cope with medical problems if the doctor isn't available in the morning, here are two reference books:

- *Where There Is No Doctor: A Village Health Care Handbook* (Revised English Edition), Werner, David with Carol Thuman and Jane Maxwell (The Hesperian Foundation, 1992).
- *Where There Is No Dentist*, Dickson, Murray (The Hesperian Foundation, 1983).

There is one particular form of medical problem that could affect everyone in the event of a one-month Y2000 disruption: contaminated water. If the water purification systems and sewage systems are disrupted, there is a significant danger of dysentery, cholera, and other diseases. Particularly in crowded urban areas, one would hope that health officials would provide adequate warning, as well as emergency supplies of potable water; still, it suggests that the prudent family ensure that it has an emergency supply of drinking water, and/or a stockpile of water purification tablets (available from camping stores, "survival" stores, and emergency-food suppliers such as Walton Feed).

If your primary concern is access to prescription medicine, then the stockpiling suggestion mentioned earlier may still be applicable. It may be more expensive to maintain a one-month supply of blood pressure pills or insulin, but it shouldn't be a serious strain on the budget for most people; in any case, if you begin preparations now, you can spread the cost over a year or more. A more serious problem is likely to be that of the doctor and the pharmacist, who typically regulate the supply of prescription medicines to minimize the chances of misuse on your part; in addition, some prescription medicine is tightly controlled in order to prevent patients from misusing it or giving it away to others. Such practices are particularly common if the medicine is expensive and if its cost is subsidized or covered by an insurance program; the insurance companies are legitimately interested in keeping their costs under control, and thus do their best to prevent you from building up a stockpile.

What if you're concerned about the possibility that a Y2000 problem will prevent you from seeing your doctor, or will make it impossible to get appropriate medical care in a hospital? If you're dealing with elective surgery, or non-critical illness, then the advice is simple and obvious: Wait for a month, until the Y2000 problem is overcome. But for those with acute illnesses or injuries, that option may not be available—and the only advice we can offer is to make the proactive decision to move to a less-populated area, where you're more likely to find doctors and nurses who have not been overwhelmed by the urban problems of Medicare and Medicaid.

Of course, Y2000 software problems could occur in medical equipment regardless of the size of the city in which they exist. One could argue that the urban centers are likely to have the latest, and most sophisticated, medical equipment—but as of mid-1998, when the second edition of this book was being written, there was no indication that "current" medical equipment was any more likely to be Y2000-compliant than devices built 5 or 10 years ago. So the patient-monitoring systems, the life-support systems, the EKG machines, and CAT-scan devices, could just as easily fail in Truth or Consequences, New Mexico as in New York City. But we believe that you're more likely to get direct, personal, humane attention from a doctor in a smaller city than in a larger one; this isn't guaranteed to happen automatically, but it should be easier to *create* a personal relationship with a doctor, in advance, within a smaller community.

Paul Lindeman, whose observations were noted earlier, added:

> *Two types of patient bear specific mention, the diabetic and the patient on dialysis (all too often the same individual). Glucometers are handy little devices which diabetics use to monitor their blood sugar levels. Oftentimes they rely on this information to determine how much insulin to give themselves. Many of these newer devices are capable of storing results and so contain date information. Most units display the date in mm / dd / yy format, and thus must be considered y2k vulnerable.*

Diabetics who must self-administer insulin have an additional concern, and that is refrigeration. All insulin must be refrigerated.

In summary, then, diabetics ought to ensure a 3 month (minimum) supply of insulin, syringes, needles, and testing strips. They must also have a back-up plan for refrigeration of their insulin in the event of power disruption. They would also be well advised to contact the manufacturer of their glucometer and inquire about compliance.

Dialysis patients rely on this technology for their very life. Many dialysis machines are rather old (some would say too old) and do not store date information. Newer machines however do store date information, primarily for use in reports, and are to some extent y2k vulnerable.

Independent of the age and type of dialysis machine; each and every dialysis session requires a filter, be it disposable or reusable. Because this entails a pre-requisite flow of supplies in order to support the dialysis (replacement filters, solutions for washing reusables, etc.), this brings to bear issues of supply, distribution, transportation, ripple effect, etc., as discussed elsewhere in this work.

Fallback Advice: One-Year Failures

Is it possible that hospitals will shut down, doctors will be inaccessible, and prescription medicines unavailable for a period as long as a year? Phrased in this way, it hardly seems likely; after all, the Red Cross manages to provide emergency medical services in situations far more extreme than the "serious" Y2000 scenarios we've envisaged. In any case, we don't think it's a likely scenario for the more common aspects of medical equipment and services. However, it *is* a possibility for the more expensive, esoteric kinds of equipment and services.

If, for example, your hospital has a million-dollar medical machine used to diagnose and/or treat rare illnesses, and if that machine has a Y2000-vulnerable computer system in it (which is not so difficult to imagine), then it could easily take a year for the hospital to get a replacement. In the best of all cases, the manufacturer of that medical device will ship some new software to the hospital, and the machine will be fixed within a matter of days. But in some cases, the offending computer chip will have to be physically removed and replaced; and the waiting list for such replacement parts could be several months or longer. Indeed, in the worst case, the manufacturer will have suffered such traumatic Y2000 problems of its own that it goes bankrupt; in that case, there will be no replacements until a new company pops up in the marketplace.

In any case, there's a point beyond which stockpiling of medicines, and development of personal relationships with neighborhood doctors, can protect us from such a calamity. If you envision this kind of serious Y2000 scenario, then take whatever proactive steps you can: Stockpile a supply of medicine and practical medical reference texts, take care of any optional/elective medical procedures before January 1, 2000, move to a more hospitable community, and engage in appropriate preventive practices to improve your health as much as possible. And then hope for the best.

Remember our discussion in Chapter 1 about the need for *qualitatively* different strategies for coping with disruptions of vastly different durations. In the case of a one-month disruption, it's conceivable that one could stockpile enough water purification tables and/or bottled water to avoid any serious health problems from contaminated water. But it seems highly unlikely that one could extend that strategy for a year; if Y2000 disruptions should prove to be so catastrophic that drinking water cannot be supplied to a city for a year, then for all practical purposes, the city is dead. Aside from a few hard-core fanatics, virtually everyone would be forced to move to a different location where potable water could be obtained.

Fallback Advice: Ten-Year Failures

There's only one scenario that we feel worth mentioning, in terms of a ten-year failure: the possibility of a collapse in the governmental agencies that subsidize and support medical care. While it may seem an exaggeration, the reality is that a substantial number of American citizens—not only the elderly, but also those in low-income brackets—are alive today *only* because of the financial support of Medicaid, Medicare, and similar systems.

We've already discussed the possible breakdown in the massive computer systems developed by the federal Medicare agencies; this could easily be exacerbated by Y2000 problems in the insurance companies, the hospitals, and the doctors' offices. The entire system barely works in today's environment, and many experts argue that it's already on the verge of collapse; a series of systemic Y2000 failures could push the entire thing over the cliff.

And then what? Obviously, new government agencies could be created; new legislation could be passed; new forms and paperwork procedures could be designed and implemented. All of this would take more than a year, but it's difficult to imagine that it would take a decade—except for one thing: *politics*. President Clinton's first-term attempt to introduce a national health-care policy is a good example, and one can find continuing examples in the ongoing debate about "reforming" the medical system at the local, state, and federal level. Powerful lobbies and special-interest groups are involved, billions of dollars are at stake, and intense emotions are ignited whenever political debates about health and medical insurance are raised.

We're not so pessimistic that we would predict the debates going on for a decade—though a cynic might argue that they *have* been going on for a decade, without any satisfactory resolution of today's problems. However, if a serious Y2000-induced problem caused the utter collapse of the Medicare/Medicaid bureaucracy and much of the nation's medical facilities, we assume that there would be enough sense of urgency to force some kind of political action with a matter of months... or perhaps a year.

The question is: What kind of policies and bureaucracies would emerge as a replacement for the current medical-insurance system? Our crystal ball is no better than yours when it comes to predicting this aspect of a possible post-2000 future. However, it occurs to us that if Y2000-related medical problems are combined with the various other Y2000 problems discussed in this book, the political mood of the country *could* turn sharply to the right, in which subsidized medicine could be sharply reduced, if not eliminated. Of course, one could argue the opposite, as well: A newly-elected Class of 2000 in the House and Senate, together with a newly-elected President, could respond to the Y2000 crisis in a fashion reminiscent of FDR's New Deal program. But even in that scenario, it's likely that jobs, banking, national defense, Social Security, and other issues might well take precedence over Medicare and Medicaid—at least for the first few years of post-2000 recovery.

Thus, if you're a pessimist, it's not at all difficult to imagine a Y2000 scenario that marks the end of government-supported health-care, as we currently know it. It's a grim prospect indeed.

Endnotes

1. Available on the Internet at http://www.whitehouse.gov/WH/New/html/19980714-5571.html.
2. Available on the Internet at http://www.senate.gov/~bennett/pr072398.html.
3. For example, a 1997 Gartner Group report which can be retrieved from the Internet at http://cwlive.cw.com:8080/home/online9697.nsf/All/970924gartner184E2, observed that "Vertical industries that are leading the remediation effort include financial services companies—including banks, brokerages and insurers—and most types of manufacturers. At the bottom of the heap are

health care providers—88% of all health care providers surveyed are at Level 1."

4. See http://year2000.dci.com/articles/1998/06/17medic.htm for details.
5. Also, consult the May 1996 white paper "U.S. Government Year 2000 Issue, Implications for public health Information and Surveillance" from the Centers for Disease Control (CDC), which argues that "It is vital that the public health community begin aggressively addressing this issue to avoid serious negative programmatic effects across public health." CDC's perspective on the Y2000 problem can be found at their Web site at http://www.cdc.gov/y2k/
6. You can find the full text of Mr. Wilemssen's testimony on the Internet at http://www.house.gov/science/willemssen_7-10.html.
7. In a followup message to one of the authors, this Y2000 project manager provided these additional details:

   We have 33 hosts represent a variety of the following:

   - IBM ES-9000
   - IBM RS/6000
   - HP-9000
   - DEC Vax

   The platforms support seven different operation system architectures and employ over 300 gigabytes of mass storage.

   We use twenty-six mission critical applications which are Commercial Off-the-shelf with few or no modifications. The data comm network is comprised of approximately 6,000 desktop computers, 125 file servers and the normal number of routers and other equipment for a network of this size. The network architecture is a mixture of Novell V3.11 and V4.11, Windows NT V3.51 and V4.0 and varieties of UNIX. Desktop software is primarily Windows 95 or Windows 3.11 with Microsoft Office V4.3. Although there is a standard suite of software, users augment their systems by providing their own additional software. Some of this software could turn out to be mission critical.

   The numbers on the medical devices remained approximately the same with the Clinical Engineering Dept. have responsibility for approximately 14,000 pieces of equipment representing approximately 2,000 vendors. The Radiology Department is responsible for approximately 200 pieces of computerized equipment from approximately twelve vendors.

One of the areas everyone overlooks is the Physical plant. Systems within the physical plant are all commercially supplied and fall into the following thirteen general categories:

- Bulk storage of medical gasses/Surgical air pump system
- Energy Management and Thermostatic Controls
- Chilled H2O, Chillers and Controls
- Heating, ventilation and Air Conditioning, Distribution and Controls
- Electrical Distribution—High Voltage, House, Emergency and Un-interruptible Power
- Electronics—Fire Protection Sensors and Annunciators, Paging and Nurse Call Systems
- Beds and Bassinets—These are electronically controlled
- Security Systems
- Steam and Plumbing
- Heliport Operations and Fire Quenching
- Wireless Communications—VHF, UHF, Repeaters
- Vertical Transportation—Elevators, Pneumatic Tubes
- Telecommunications

We have approximately 3,000 suppliers of goods and services and have not yet determined the number of payers.

8. See "Is your pacemaker ready for 2000? Your hospital hopes answer is 'Yes'," by Jane-Ellen Robinet, *Pittsburgh Business Times*, April 27, 1998; available on the Internet at http://www.amcity.com/pittsburgh/stories/042798/focus3.html.
9. Ann K. Coffou, Managing Director, Giga Year 2000 Relevance Service, to the Subcommittee on Technology and Subcommittee on Government Management, Information and Technology, March 20, 1997, "Year 2000 Risks: What Are the Consequences of Technology Failure?" posted at http://www.house.gov/science/couffou_3-20.html.
10. Gary North, "You Bet Your Life," *Remnant Review*, Vol. 24, No. 7, page 2. North, who covers a variety of conservative economic issues in his newsletter, first began reporting on Y2000 in late 1996; all of the monthly issues in 1997 and 1998 have focused on specific aspects of the Y2000 problem. His newsletter is published by Agora Inc., 1217 St. Paul Street, Baltimore, MD 21202, phone 410-234-0691. He also has what we regard as the most comprehen-

sive Y2000 Web site for the average citizen (as opposed to sites like http://www.year2000.com, which is populated primarily by computer professionals and Y2000 vendors); we encourage you to visit it at http://www.garynorth.com.

11. You can find the full text of Mr. Willemssen's testimony on the Internet at http://www.house.gov/science/willemssen_7-10.html.

12. See "How will Y2K hit hospitals?" by Erich Luening, *CNET News.Com,* July 23, 1998, available on the Internet at http://www.news.com/News/Item/0,4,24479,00.html?owv.

13. You can find the full text of Mr. Willemssen's testimony on the Internet at http://www.house.gov/science/willemssen_7-10.html.

14. See http://www.house.gov/ways_means/oversite/testmony/5-7-98/5-7jack.htm for the text of Ms. Jackson's statement.

15. See "Y2K bug may infect VA health: Manufacturers not responding to queries of medical devices' Y2K compliance," by Orlando Bruce, *Federal Computer Week*, July 27, 1998; also available on the Internet at http://www.fcw.com/pubs/fcw/1998/0727/fcw-newsva-7-27-98.html.

16. See http://www.hhs.gov/progorg/asl/testify/t980723b.txt.

17. Colleagues have pointed out to us that some parents may want the notoriety of giving birth to the "first baby of the Millennium," and may thus carefully schedule conception and pregnancy commencing in late March 1999. The level of public awareness and concern may not be high enough at that point for the prospective parents to fully appreciate the risk that they are taking.

Y2000 Impact on Government

We know first we have to put our own house in order, to make certain that government will be able to continue to guard our borders, guide air traffic, send out Social Security and Medicare checks, and fulfill our other duties. We've worked hard to be ready. I set a government-wide goal of full compliance by March of 1999... I've met with the Cabinet and charged them personally to produce results and report quarterly to OMB on progress. We're working with state and local governments to do the same thing.

We have made progress... the Social Security Administration has more than 90 percent of its critical systems ready. Other agencies, like EPA, FEMA, and the VA, are well on their way to meeting our goal. But not every agency is as far along as it should be. I have made it clear to every member of my Cabinet that the American people have a right to expect uninterrupted service from government and I expect them to deliver.

President Bill Clinton, speech at the National Academy of Sciences, *July 14, 1998*[1]

Introduction

We could easily fill this book with an account of the actions of federal, state, and local governments on the Y2000 problem; as you'll see in this lengthy chapter, there is much to discuss. But for those who are impatient, we'll follow the advice of Hollywood directors and "cut to the chase":

- The U.S. federal government is working on the repair, replacement, or retirement of approximately 7,336 "mission-critical" computer systems,[2] as well as 66,000 "non-critical" systems. The president has ordered his Cabinet secretaries to achieve full compliance by March 31, 1999; recent reports from his Y2000 "czar," John Koskinen, have expressed confidence that this goal will be largely fulfilled.[3] But numerous reports by House and Senate committees, as well as the OMB and GAO,[4] raise serious questions about the ability of several major federal agencies to be compliant by December 31, 1999; indeed, Congressman Stephen Horn's committee estimates that some agencies may not finish their work until 2004, 2012, or even 2019.[5] Meanwhile, the federal government's 1999-2000 fiscal year begins on October 1, 1999. In the best of all worlds, all of the federal agencies will at least finish repairing their mission-critical systems; but it seems to us, from a statistical perspective, that the chances of all 24 agencies succeeding (especially considering their track record in the past!) is fairly small.

- State governments are generally considered substantially behind the federal government, with less awareness, less funding, and less of a sense of urgency about achieving Y2000 compliance. A handful of states—including Nebraska, Washington, Michigan, Massachusetts, and Ohio[6]—are regarded as leaders, but many others are reporting problems acquiring sufficient resources and achieving sufficient progress.[7] New York State begins its 1999-2000 fiscal year on April 1, 1999;[8] another 46 states begin their 1999-2000 fiscal year on July 1, 1999; and the remaining states have a fiscal year beginning August 1, September 1, or October 1. In the best of all worlds, all 50 states will have finished repairing their mission-critical systems in time; but since they have *less* time to complete their tasks than the federal government, we think it's statistically unlikely that they will all succeed.[9]

- Local governments (city, county, and so forth) are even further behind, and generally have a very low level of awareness. Indeed, a spring 1998 survey indicated that approximately 55 percent of municipal governments feel their computers will not be impacted by Y2000, and thus need not make any preparations.[10] The reality, though, is likely to be quite different: A city of 100,000 people may not have any mainframe computers, but it's likely to have hundreds of PCs, dozens of networks, and thousands of embedded systems in its buildings, fire trucks, traffic lights, and water treatment systems. The lack of funding compounds the problem of achieving Y2000 compliance within the smaller cities, as does the relative lack of personnel and expertise. According to population predictions,[11] there will be 9 American cities in 2000 with a population of 1 million or more, 100 cities with a population of 185,000 or more, and thousands of small towns and villages throughout the country. The statistical odds of all these cities, large and small, being prepared for Y2000 is, in our opinion, extremely small.

- Foreign governments are, in general, further behind than their U.S. counterparts. We'll discuss the international situation in more detail in Chapter 14; suffice it to say that, as of spring 1998, more than half of the 200 members countries of the United Nations did not have a national Y2000 initiative. Considering the number of national, provincial, state, county, and city governments around the world, it seems reasonable to expect that at least some will experience some moderate-to-serious Y2000 difficulties.

How Did All of This Begin?

Whatever your opinion of government, here is an important point to keep in mind: It was government that funded and acquired the first modern American and British computers in the 1940s, and it is government that continues to own and operate the largest amount of computer software today. Much of this has a military overtone: Not only the early World-War II computers, but even the technology that now forms the Internet, was funded by various branches of the U.S. Department of Defense (DOD). And according to the Y2000 metrics collected by Capers Jones, the military has more software than any other government agency or corporation within the private sector—with 6 million separate applications, 1,000 software sites, 200,000 software professionals, and 300 million function points of software[12] (approximately equal to 30 *billion* COBOL statements, though COBOL makes up only a portion of the DOD inventory).

Governments have been working with computers, accumulating vast stores of legacy programs, and building up enormous databases, far longer than most industries. Though punched cards have largely disappeared from computer installations today, the so-called "Hollerith card" was invented by Herman Hollerith in 1880 as a means of recording and retrieving information for the decennary U.S. census.[13] Since then, billions of dollars have been spent to acquire computers that can count, tabulate, compute taxes, and perform the myriad collection of bureaucratic activities that government is so often associated with. Combining the Federal and State government agencies (but not including DOD), Capers Jones estimates an aggregate of 1,688,891 applications, 650 software sites, 95,000 programmers, and 96 million function points of software.[14]

We tell you this not to brag on behalf of government; indeed, quite the opposite. The point is that just as most large companies are bedeviled by ancient mainframe legacy programs that nobody understands any more, so is government. But in the case of government, the software applications are likely to be much older. And there are more of them, written in a wider variety of programming languages. Many of these programming languages, especially within DOD, are so obscure that they're not used anywhere else (with the possible exception of Defense Departments in a few other unlucky countries); thus, it will be difficult to find and/or train programmers to examine these programs for Y2000 problems. Similarly, the phenomenon of tight budgets means that many of the government computer systems are running on ancient hardware, with operating systems the rest of the civilized world considers dead. It's not only difficult to find computer professionals who can work with these old computers (especially because most of the younger computer professionals vastly prefer working with the very latest and most powerful computers, and because almost any programmer can make 50-100 percent more money in the private sector), but it's also difficult to get the computer vendors to provide support for products they've abandoned years, if not decades, ago.

Then there is the procurement problem. The standard procedure for many government computer projects (as well as a wide variety of other engineering projects, construction projects, and so forth) is to document the requirements in a massive tome known as an RFQ (Request for Quote) or RFP (Request for Proposal), and make it available to vendors in the private sector who want the dubious honor of winning the contract for the project. The process of writing the RFP can take months; the bidding, evaluation, and award process can take several more months; and to further complicate things, the losing vendors sometimes sue, complaining that they were evaluated unfairly. Somewhere in the midst of all this, the budget has to be estimated, documented, justified, and then sent up the political hierarchy for approval. A common joke among the "Beltway Bandits"—the mini-industry of defense contractors, engineering firms, and computer software organizations whose offices are located near the Interstate "Beltway" surrounding Washington, DC—is that most government agencies won't even be finished with the procurement process for their Y2000 projects until 2001. It's not quite as bad as that, in reality... but it's close enough to the truth that the joke receives loud gales of laughter from the Y2000 software organizations.

There is one last problem to point out: In general, the competence, organizational ability, and level of motivation of software project teams in the various branches of government is at the opposite end of the spectrum from what you would expect at Microsoft, IBM, Hewlett-Packard, and other familiar companies in the private sector. No doubt this is an unfair criticism of some programmers, some managers, and some government project teams; and the reason we make the observation is not to offer a gratuitous insult, but to add an additional item for consideration when estimating the likelihood that a government-oriented Y2000 project will finish on time.

Part of the problem is that government attracts both the best *and* the worst of the computer programmers, software engineers, database designers, and related computer specialists. We suspect that this is true for other professions, too, but our own personal, substantial experience in the computer field confirms it for software development. It's important to emphasize that there are men and women of extraordinary talent, energy, dedication, and enthusiasm who are attracted to various branches of the government because (a) they want to work on projects far larger than would ever be attempted in the private sector, (b) they want to work on leading-edge projects, such as Star Wars or NASA, (c) they have a sincere desire to contribute their efforts to the betterment of mankind and society, or (d) they want the career stability supposedly associated with a Civil Service grade. These people occasionally accomplish miracles, either because of their individual efforts, or because they inspire the others on their team to levels of performance that would otherwise not have occurred. To these men and women, we offer our gratitude, respect, and admiration.

Unfortunately, even the most dazzling superstar can be buried in the bureaucracy and political intrigue so often associated with government organizations; the same thing happens in the private sector, to some extent, but it's positively Byzantine in government. And to compound the problem, the relatively small number of government-employed superstars are out-numbered by people who are average, as well as an even larger number whose lack of talent and skill, and whose utter lack of energy and enthusiasm, would certainly prevent them from being hired in the private sector.

Even in the best case, many of the Y2000 projects are going to require long stretches of 7-day work-weeks, and 16-hour work-days, during the next two years. This is "business as usual" in companies like Microsoft, during the final stages of developing a new product; and though it's not what most banks, insurance companies, and other private-sector organizations normally expect of their programmers, it's also not an alien experience. Again, it's not our intention to needlessly insult government workers, and we're sure that some will be working just as hard as their private-sector counterparts; but on the whole, we expect to see the typical Y2000 government programmer working an eight hour day. As one such programmer confided to one of the authors, "Listen, *every* computer project in this organization is late, and *every* project is screwed up. Always has been, always will be. I don't care what kind of official statements they make, this Y2000 stuff is *not* going to finish on time. No project we've ever done in this organization, in the 20 years I've been here, has *ever* finished on time. So if that's the way it's going to be, why should I get ulcers and ruin my life? I'm going home in the 4:42 carpool, and that's that."[15] Time will tell—in only a very few months from now—whether this programmer's cynical assessment is accurate or not.

But on the assumption that it *might* be accurate, we think it's a good idea to look at some of the government agencies whose Y2000 failures could affect our lives. Arguably, *every* government agency can have some impact on us, but some are more visible, and have a more immediate impact on us, so we'll focus on only a few. Then we'll proceed with our standard categories of advice for minor, moderate, serious, and catastrophic forms of Y2000-related problems.

Social Security

Let's begin with one of the largest and most visible government agencies, and one that is generally regarded as being farther ahead than any other Federal agency in its Y2000 conversion efforts: the Social Security Program (SSA). SSA was signed into law on August 14, 1935 as part of FDR's New Deal program, and until recent years, it was almost universally accepted by American society as the agency that guaranteed a modest, but viable, retirement income to all Americans, regardless of background or social class.

In recent years, there has been increasing emphasis on the financial plight of SSA, with dire predictions of bankruptcy when a generation of Baby-Boomers reach retirement age in the early part of the 21st century. This has been accompanied by massive amounts of political rhetoric from both political parties, together with proposals and campaign pledges to "save" SSA, "re-finance" SSA, and so forth. Analyzing and discussing the economic viability of SSA is a complex and controversial task, and is entirely outside the charter of this book. However, if SSA experiences severe difficulties, or a partial collapse, because of Y2000 problems (or any other technical problems, for that matter), it could well be used as political ammunition by leaders in power in 2000 to justify whatever political changes they felt appropriate.

Meanwhile, ordinary men and women of retirement age are receiving monthly checks, and are depending on them just as heavily as were the retirees of the 70s, 60s, 50s, and 40s before them. And the ordinary men and woman of *less* than retirement age are continuing to find that larger and larger portions of their paycheck are disappearing into a tax category called FICA; if nothing else, they need to be reassured that their FICA contributions have indeed been credited to their account, and that if Social Security does still exist 10 years from now, then they'll get their fair due.

All of this is imperiled by the Y2000 problem, of course. It's hard to imagine an application more date-sensitive than the various programs within SSA. When were you born? When did you begin working? How much of a FICA contribution did you make in each of your income-generating years? When did you stop working? When did you begin drawing Social Security payments? On and on... all of this information involves dates, and much of the computational logic within SSA involves date arithmetic. Dates and date-arithmetic are embedded in a portfolio estimated at 30 million lines of code, which SSA began working on in 1989.[16]

Stop for a moment and take a look at that date: *1989*. That's more than five years before most private-industry organizations began focusing on the Y2000 problem, and light-years ahead of the other government agencies. It's also before most of the automated computer tools had appeared from Y2000 software vendors to help mechanize the process of scanning, analyzing, and converting the programs; thus, much of the work in the early years of the SSA effort was carried out manually, or with home-grown tools. That probably explains why, as of June 30, 1996, 400 SSA programmers assigned to the Y2000 project had only converted 6 million of the 30 million program instructions in its overall portfolio. If one extrapolated those figures forward, it would be easy to conclude that SSA wouldn't be able finish the job on time; however, far more sophisticated tools are now available, and many additional programmers have been assigned to the Y2000 effort. As a result, the agency has been publicly proclaiming that it *will* be finished in time, albeit just barely; and the quarterly "report card" issued by Congressman Stephen Horn (R-Ca), Chairman of the House Subcommittee on Government Management, Information, and Technology, has consistently given SSA an "A" grade.

But this optimistic assessment almost certainly ignores the "systemic" Y2000 problems discuss in Appendix B. The payments calculated by SSA are actually transmitted to a group within the Treasury Department known as the Financial Management Service (FMS) to be printed as checks; thus, if FMS is non-compliant, or if the interface with SSA doesn't work, the checks won't go out.[17] In addition, payments by SSA and other government agencies are frequently deposited directly into the recipient's bank, rather than being printed out and mailed through the postal system. This means that there are at least two computer systems within SSA (one that was developed originally for computing and printing retirement checks, and a newer one to siphon off a subset of those payments and transmit them to the bank, via magnetic tape or telecommunications link), plus at least one computer system within the banks to process the incoming payments and funnel them into the proper account, plus one or more computer systems that support the "interbank" financial transfers between all manner of financial institutions. Thus, even if SSA does its job correctly, there's no guarantee that a retired widow will find that her monthly check has landed in the right account at the right time.

Welfare, Food Stamps, Medicare, and the Like

In Chapter 9, we noted the possibility that the vast Medicare system could encounter serious difficulties because of Y2000-related computer problems; the likelihood of this occurring increased, in our opinion, when the government decided in September 1997 to cancel a computer-modernization project that had been outsourced to an external contractor.[18] A similar situation exists for food stamps, welfare, unemployment payments, Veteran's benefits, farm-assistance subsidies, education grants, low-income housing assistance, and myriad other programs that provide payments to specific industries, companies, or individuals. The few that we've listed here are among the more obvious ones, but our basic advice is: If you get a check (or any other form of payment) from any government agency, you're vulnerable. The details will vary, but all of these computer applications are date-sensitive, if for no other reason than they are scheduled to be made on a periodic basis (weekly, monthly, quarterly, or annually).

If you're *not* a recipient of any government subsidy, payment, or assistance program, then your natural instinct is to ignore the issue. But remember the ripple effect: The fact that large numbers of *other* people are experiencing problems can eventually bounce back to you. An interesting example of this popped up in the newspapers while we were writing the first edition of this book during the summer of 1997: An article discussing the impact of welfare and food-stamp reductions in New York City made the interesting point that as much as 80 percent of a store's business can be conducted with food stamps in the Southside section of Williamsburg, Brooklyn.[19] If the distribution of food stamps is disrupted for a month because of a Y2000 problem, a number of grocery stores in low-income areas around the country will find it difficult to survive. But that could turn out to be a small problem compared to the consequences of having a lot of hungry people in these same neighborhoods.

Internal Revenue Service

You know who these folks are, and it won't come as a surprise to learn that their computer systems are date-sensitive, and thus vulnerable to Y2000 failures. Here's how the IRS describes the size and scope of its computer operation:

> *The Information Systems (IS) organization of the Internal Revenue Service (IRS) is a huge enterprise—employing in excess of 7,500 personnel across the United States, budgeted in excess of $1 billion annually and responsible for the design development and ongoing support of a highly complex and vast array of technologies which, taken together, comprise the technology-based engine that powers the IRS. A $1.4 trillion Financial Services Program, IRS business enterprises are unprecedented in size and scope—a Fortune One company—with service centers, district office and*

> *regional office operations, staffed by more than 100,000 employees, largely dependent on highly automated processes as well as the currency, comprehensiveness and availability of vast storehouses of computerized data.*[20]

And here are a few things that you might not know about the IRS:

- The portfolio of computer applications within the IRS consists of approximately 50,000 computer programs, comprising roughly 100 million program instructions. Thus, the software inventory is about three times larger than that of SSA, but about four times smaller than the largest banks.[21]

- The IRS has had ongoing difficulties for several years with its aging and overtaxed (no pun intended) computer system. In early 1997, it essentially abandoned a troubled $4 billion modernization program, and began developing new plans, for review by the GAO and various Congressional oversight committees. Whatever the reason for its past difficulties, the track record of the IRS in working on large, complex computer projects has been mediocre-to-abysmal. That obviously raises serious questions about the likelihood of it successfully completing what will almost certainly be a far more difficult effort to accomplish Y2000 projects with a fixed deadline. But even more important, the IRS is now proposing to outsource its modernization project to an external vendor, *and that modernization project includes some of the Y2000 conversion work*. That might be good news if the external vendor had been hard at work for the past few years, but the IRS schedule calls for reviewing proposals and carrying on negotiations from October 1997 to the end of September, 1998; the contract is scheduled to be awarded in October, 1998. That's incredibly late in the game to begin doing any Y2000 conversion work on such a large, complex system.

- In April, 1997, the Chief Information Officer (CIO) of the IRS told Congress that he planned to move 300 IRS programmers away from other work, in order to focus on Y2000 projects. An observation: This is fewer people, and a later starting date, than SSA.[22] Of more interest, perhaps, is the fact that the CIO, Arthur Gross, resigned from the IRS in early 1998; as the second edition of this book went to press in the fall of 1998, he had not yet been replaced.

- The IRS has approximately 130,000 PCs[23] that need to be examined for possible Y2K repairs or upgrades; as of early 1998, that process was awaiting the de-

> livery of new, compliant software products. The logistics of inspecting, repairing, and testing 130,000 machines (desktop PCs, print servers, file servers, laptop machines, and so forth) are daunting; keeping them Y2000-compliant after they've been inspected is also a logistical nightmare.

You can draw your own conclusions from this. From our perspective, it's difficult to draw any other conclusion than the obvious one: The chances that IRS personnel will be celebrating New Year's Eve, 1999 with smiles on their faces is close to zero.[24] Indeed, it's interesting that the IRS reported to Congress in mid-June 1997 that it would need an additional $258 million in 1998 in order to become Y2000-compliant, a figure that was increased to approximately $600 million in September 1997,[25] and then $850 million by early 1998[26] and finally to approximately $1 billion. Considering that the IRS apparently underestimated the scope and cost of its Y2000 effort by approximately a factor of five, it seems difficult for us to imagine that the IRS will actually finish its work in time. Yet, to our astonishment, IRS Charles Rossotti announced in an October 23, 1998 speech that the IRS will be finished remediating its "key systems" by January 1, 1999.[27]

And there's an interesting point to keep in mind about the IRS's Y2000 problems—problems that are not yet widely known, but almost certainly will be as the deadline approaches. While most people sincerely hope that the banks, insurance companies, telephone companies, and other components of society will find a way to solve their Y2000 problems, they're much less likely to feel so kindly about the IRS. Indeed, it's hardly an exaggeration to suggest that a substantial percentage of the tax-paying public would be delighted if the IRS sank beneath the weight of its computer problems and was never heard from again.

Whether or not that's a rational way to view the situation is a topic for a separate discussion, one likely to be colored by one's political opinions about taxes, government bureaucracy, and so forth. But the point we want to emphasize here is that the anticipation of severe Year-2000 problems in the IRS could lead to additional problems. Obviously, it would be inappropriate (if not illegal) for us to suggest that anyone avoid paying their taxes, and we have no intention of doing so. However, that won't eliminate the almost certain tendency of some taxpayers to engage in wishful thinking along the following lines: "Hmmm, if I liquidate my stocks and engage in various other highly profitable activities in 1999, it won't have to be reported, and the taxes won't have to be paid to the IRS, until April 15, 2000. But by then, there won't *be* an IRS. For that matter, if I don't file my estimated taxes and withholding taxes in the fourth quarter of 1999, there won't be an IRS to come after me in calendar year 2000."

We have no idea whether such a daydream is at all realistic; for all we know, the government has contingency plans for mobilizing the National Guard to collect taxes (that's intended to be a joke, by the way). What we *do* know is that the current tax system, as implemented by the Internal Revenue Service, depends heavily on voluntary compliance. If that compliance disappears, because of real and/or perceived Y2000 computer problems, the political consequences would be enormous. And perhaps that explains why IRS Commissioner Rossotti's speech, mentioned above, was made to an audience of several hundred CPAs.

The Defense Department

As noted earlier, the U.S. Department of Defense (DOD) has at least two unique problems compared to other government agencies. First, it has far more software than any other Federal or State organization—more, even, than entire industries in the private sector; current estimates of the aggregate military software portfolio are in the range of 30 billion program instructions.[28] Second, its software has been written in dozens of arcane programming languages that are no longer in current use—including high-level languages like Jovial, and low-level assembly languages for computer hardware that's no longer being manufactured.

And there's a third obvious problem. Some, though not all, of the DOD software is embedded in weapons, for which the consequences of a Y2000 software bug could be catastrophic. Planes, missiles, bombs, tanks, satellites, ships, air-defense systems, and devices whose existence DOD has never admitted in public—all of these and more are controlled by, scheduled by, or interact with, date-sensitive computers.[29]

Aside from the weapons, DOD is a massive human organization, employing (in a manner of speaking) millions of men and women in the United States and dozens of countries abroad. Thus, there are massive computer systems dealing with payroll, housing, insurance, retirement benefits, scheduling and logistics of people and equipment, and so forth. These systems are similar to the business applications in private-sector organizations, and they are vulnerable to the same kind of Y2000 problems.

To further complicate matters, DOD is not a single organization, with a simple hierarchical management structure. The Army, Navy, Air Force, and Marines all have their own separate computer systems, in addition to some that they share on an inter-agency basis; the Army alone has acknowledged, as of mid-1998, that it has slightly over 200,000 non-compliant computers, systems, and devices.[30] Then, too, there are the computer systems of the CIA and NSA, as well as other defense-related organizations. And most of the weapons and equipment used by the military agencies—along with the associated computer systems—are built by aerospace companies and defense contractors. Thus, it's not entirely unreasonable to say that the military is Y2000 compliant only if the Boeings and Lockheeds and TRWs and several hundred other private-sector companies are Y2000-compliant, too.

Notwithstanding these problems, DOD now appears to be addressing the Y2000 problems with considerable energy and financial resources. But progress is slow, and on August 7, 1998 Defense Secretary William Cohen issued a memo to the Joint Chiefs of Staff and several other high-ranking officers and officials complaining that DOD was making "insufficient progress" in its Y2K efforts.[31] Unfortunately, DOD is famous within the computer industry for projects that are years behind schedule, millions of dollars over budget, and ultimately useless when delivered. While this may sound like a blanket criticism of everything DOD does, we should also point out that the requirements and constraints of DOD software and DOD computer projects make banking systems and other corporate business applications look like child's play by comparison: Not many systems are involved with saving lives, defending lives, and destroying enemy lives on the scale that DOD attempts.

But while we sympathize with the difficulty and complexity of DOD's work, the fact remains: The Y2000 work that DOD faces will, by far, be the largest and most difficult project it has ever undertaken. Frankly, we think the odds of it finishing *all* of its work on time are virtually zero; the only hopeful note is that DOD, far more than any other organization we've discussed in this book (with the possible exception of the medical industry), *truly* understands the meaning of triage. We assume that DOD is concentrating its resources on the weapons systems and appropriate support systems that are truly crucial.

On the other hand, reports like the one excerpted below from the GAO certainly don't improve one's confidence in the DOD Y2000 effort:[32]

> *If CCSS cannot correctly process dates on and after January 1, 2000, military equipment, such as tanks, artillery, aircraft, missiles, munitions, trucks, electronics, and other supporting materials for the soldier, in all likelihood, will not be ordered, stored, transported, issued, paid for, or maintained. Mobilization plans and contingencies would be significantly impaired if materiel is delayed. However, LSSC has yet to resolve several critical problems associated with the assessment phase to ensure that (1) systems are adequately tested, (2) contingency plans are developed, and (3) interface partners are fully aware of LSSC's Year 2000 plans. Furthermore, during the same time that LSSC is addressing the Year 2000 issue, the agency is also working to implement considerably more software projects than it has in the past. This unprecedented workload is compounded by a reduced staff level and LSSC's basic lack of a mature software development and maintenance process. Together, these factors raise the risk level of the Year 2000 project beyond what is normally expected of a software modification effort of this magnitude. Until these problems are resolved, LSSC is not well-positioned to move forward into the more time-consuming phases of renovation, validation, and implementation. As a result, we believe LSSC will find it increasingly difficult to prepare CCSS in time for the arrival of the year 2000.*

Other Federal Agencies

Of course, the government consists of more than the IRS, SSA, and military services. There are dozens of other agencies, and it would require an entire book to discuss them one by one. The "scorecard" published by Congressman Stephen Horn's Y2000 Congressional subcommittee in September 1998,[33] is an interesting summary of the overall state of affairs:

Agency	Grade	Expected year of completion
Social Security Administration	A	1999
National Science Foundation	A	1999
Small Business Administration	A	1999
Government Services Administration	B+	1999
Department of Commerce	B	1999
Environmental Protection Agency	B	1999
Department of Veteran Affairs	B-	1999
Federal Emergency Mgmt Agency	B-	1999
NASA	C+	2000
Department of Agriculture	C	1999
Housing & Urban Development	C	2000
Department of Treasury	D+	2000
Dept. of Transportation	D	1999
Office of Personnel Management	D	2000
Department of Defense	D	2001
Department of Labor	D	2001
Department of Interior	D	2005
Nuclear Regulatory Agency	D	2001
Dept. of Health & Human Services	F	2002
Department of Energy	F	2002
Department of State	F	2027
Department of Justice	F	2030+
Department of Education	F	2030+
Agency for International Development	F	2023

The grades shown above were intended to mimic a student's report card; but in the context of Y2000, a "D" means "behind schedule," and an "F" means "dangerously unprepared."

State and Local Agencies

While state governments are obviously much, much smaller than the Federal government, their Y2000 tasks are also daunting—especially in such large states as New York, California, Illinois, and Texas. Even the city governments can be critical: Consider the consequences of a severe disruption in utilities, public transportation, medical care, welfare, police, and other services in cities like Chicago, Los Angeles, or New York.

There are, of course, 50 states; and within those states, there are several hundred medium- and large-sized cities, plus thousands of smaller towns and villages. The states are all working on Y2000 projects independently; at the time this book was being written, it appeared that California and Florida were making good progress in their Y2000 efforts, and another eight states have made some progress.[34] But most have not—either because of lack of awareness, or lack of budget authority. As Bob Violino reported in March 1997

> *Many states are off to a slow start. Only 13 of 44 CIOs said their states were in the implementation or testing stage of year-2000 fixes, according to a survey conducted by the NASIRE year-2000 working group. Twenty respondents didn't know how many lines of code they needed to convert; 11*

hadn't set a target completion date for conversion; and 20 didn't have an estimate of how much year-2000 fixes would cost.[35]

One of the problems with budgeting for Y2000 repairs in state government organizations is (a) budgets are limited in the best of cases, and (b) the estimates for Y2000 work are often hysterically optimistic to begin with, and then escalated dramatically shortly thereafter. A good example is North Carolina: The state legislature had allocated approximately $7 million dollars for Y2000 repairs as of the spring of 1997, but the State Controller reported, at about the same time, that the current estimate for repairs was $300 million.[36] In a report compiled by Steve Davis, the Budget Manager of Montgomery County, Maryland (see http://www.erols.com/steve451/impact.htm), the estimated aggregate *salary* cost for fixing the Y2000 problem at the state level is $75 billion. For states that are already squeezed for budget appropriations, this is going to be difficult; if nothing else, we can be reasonably sure that it will provoke prolonged (i.e., time-consuming) debates before the funds are allocated. Meanwhile, the clock is ticking.

Bottom line: We expect that a few states will come through the Y2000 problem in reasonably good shape; perhaps as many as a dozen others will do a moderate-to-mediocre job. But that leaves quite a number of states (and their associated county and local governments). According to a report compiled by the U.S. Department of Health and Human Services in April 1997,[37] two thirds of the states had not even completed the "assessment" stage of their Y2000 projects; we doubt very much that they will be finished.

What Is Government Doing About the Y2000 Problem?

In a nutshell: lots of testimony before House and Senate committees,[38] lots of urgent activity within the federal government agencies, less activity in the state agencies—and relatively little from the President and Vice President. President Clinton issued a Y2000 speech at the National Academy of Sciences on July 14, 1998, but it was not covered by any of the major TV channels; similarly, he avoided any public mention of Y2000 in his highly publicized State of the Union message in early February 1998, but then issued an Executive Order[39] two days later that created the Y2000 Conversion Council headed by John Koskinen.

Reports from the GAO and OMB, and presentations to various technology-related Congressional committees and subcommittees, have at least served the useful purpose of creating some public exposure, and providing some credibility to what otherwise might have been dismissed as paranoia on the part of a few computer freaks. The first major hearing of this kind occurred in September 1996, and there have been a number throughout 1997 and 1998, as the first and second editions of book were being written. We expect that things will probably build to a fever pitch as we move into 1999; but it's important to remember that nothing *happens* in these committee hearings; experts are invited to present a speech, government officials wring their hands and agree with one another that the situation is dangerous, or they give optimistic reports on the progress they're making. And then the hearing is over, and everyone goes home.

In terms of national leadership—i.e., in the House, Senate, and Executive branch of government—we believe that there has been far too little active leadership. A few Congressmen and Senators have expressed concern (it should be remembered there are a few technically literate members of the House and Senate, including former executives in computer companies); among the more outspoken are Senator Robert Bennett (R-UT) and Congressman Stephen Horn (R-CA). Though it may appear that Republicans are leading the Y2000 awareness effort, it should be acknowledged that the first serious call for action came from a Democrat: Senator Daniel Patrick Moynihan of New York. Moynihan introduced a bill (S.22) into the Senate on January 21, 1997 "to establish a bipartisan national commission to address the year 2000 computer problem"; the bill was read twice (we can't help wondering if that was necessary because some of the attending members were hard of hearing, or perhaps sound asleep) and then referred to the Committee on Governmental Affairs. The bill has remained in a state of limbo, though one could argue that the president's creation of a Y2K Conversion Council, and the Senate's creation of a Y2K Committee was a direct result of the bill. In any case, Senator Moynihan continues to be one of the most outspoken advocates for serious attention to the Y2000 problem.

Neither of the authors have the kind of first-hand political reporting experience that P.J. O'Rourke exhibited so eloquently:[40]

> *The government is huge, stupid, greedy and makes nosy, officious and dangerous intrusions into the smallest corners of life—this much we can stand. But the real problem is that government is boring. We could cure or mitigate the other ills Washington visits on us if we could only bring ourselves to pay attention to Washington itself. But we cannot.*

But we can make some reasonable guesses about the likely actions from government both before and after New Year's Eve, 1999. We can also offer some thoughts about what government leaders *should* be doing, though we doubt that much of this advice will be followed. *Before* the Y2000 deadline occurs, we expect to see a steadily rising level of rhetoric and activity in Washington—and, to a lesser extent, in the various state capitols. Here's what it's likely to consist of:

- *Exhortations, edicts, and regulations*—Congressional committees will continue to proclaim, in ever-louder terms, just how serious the situation is, and how important it is to do something. Agencies that have any power to enact regulations and restrictions on products, services, and activity in the private sector will begin doing so; indeed, the FDA *has* already begun doing so. Perhaps more interesting was the February 1998 statement from the OMB, which publicly threatened to restrict future IT expenditures in four of the agencies (Agriculture, Transportation—which includes the FAA), Education, and Aid for International Development—because "they missed completion dates for assessing systems, did not show measurable improvement since the May report, did not keep to their schedule for completion of the phases for best practices and failed to update their information, because they had not met their own published schedule, and were not demonstrating adequate progress in their Y2000 plans."[41]

- *Committees, commissions, and task forces*—Senator Moynihan's bill calling for the creation of a national commission was a noble gesture—and there are now Y2000 committees in both the House and the Senate, as well as the Y2K Conversion Council in the Executive Branch. Technical committees that establish computer interfaces for exchanging post-Y2000 data will be helpful,[42] but committees that provide yet another opportunity for the Democrats to yell at the Republicans (or vice versa) won't delay the Y2000 deadline by even a second.

- *Massive last-minute funding*—During the early- to mid-1990s, when money could have been productively used to pay for Y2000 programmers or Y2000 computer tools, budgets have been tight; in February 1997, when there was arguably some chance of finishing all of the government computer repairs, the Office of Management & Budget (OMB) warned Congress that it could not count on the government to come up with extra money for Y2000 projects. By mid-1998, the official budget figure for the federal government's Y2000 repairs was up to $4.9 billion, but in July, 1998 a House Committee vetoed the president's request for an additional $2.25 billion "emergency" funding for Y2000 projects.[43] We expect this to change in 1999, as the deadline looms ever closer; political leaders, being even more oblivious than senior corporate managers about the realities of software development, are likely to announce last-minute emergency appropriations to solve the Y2000 problem. They'll expect applause from citizens, and a sigh of relief from beleaguered agency officials. But computer programmers across the land will look at one another and whisper *Brooks' Law: Adding more programmers to a late software project just makes it later.*

Notice the fundamental, unspoken premise that underlies all of this: Political leaders assume that this is "merely" a technical problem, and that by definition, technical problems can be solved. It's just a matter of exerting the appropriate level of authority, finding the appropriate amount of money in the budget, and *commanding* that the problem will, by God, be solved. With that perspective, one could argue that gravity is a "technical" problem. But no amount of money or authority or eloquent speeches is going to change the law of gravity; and while the Y2000 problem doesn't involve something quite as absolute as gravity, it does share the common property that it cannot be coerced by political persuasion. As a result, most of the pre-2000 political activity concerning Y2000 is likely to be about as effective as rearranging deck chairs on the *Titanic*.

What happens *after* January 1, 2000? That depends, obviously, on the severity of the Y2000 failures that emerge. If it turns out that *all* of the consequences are nothing more than a few sporadic, unrelated, two-day disruptions, political leaders will proudly announce that it was their brilliant foresight that saved the day (2000 is an election year, after all!), and no further activity will be required. It's instructive to note, for example, that Senator Moynihan's S.22 bill calls for the dissolution of the national Y2000 commission on December 31, 1999.

But suppose the problem is worse; suppose the problems are systemic, interrelated, and long-term in duration. Suppose the stock market goes into a free fall reminiscent of October 1929, and a thousand banks fail during the first six months of 2000. Suppose the lights go out for a month in a dozen major cities, and armed warfare breaks out in the streets because of the failure of food, food-stamp, and welfare-check distribution. Suppose the airports shut down for six months because the FAA has far worse Y2000 problems than anyone has imagined. Obviously, it would be far better for everyone if none of these things happened—but suppose God is in a bad mood after December 31, 1999, and several of these things *do* happen. What should we expect the federal government (and in a similar vein, the various state governments) to do?

Obviously, we don't know—nor does anyone else. And if you could get a competent politician to talk about it today (off the record, of course!), whatever he told you would be a "best guess," depending on the specific nature of the crisis, and also depending on the political mood of the moment. Nevertheless, the history of political reactions to previous crises leads us to make what we feel are some plausible predictions:

- *Finger-pointing, and cover-your-ass speeches*—The first instinct of a politician will be to ensure that he or she cannot be blamed for having caused the Y2000 problem, either through omission or commission. Corporate leaders are worried about this, too, and they have the additional concern about stockholder lawsuits, class-action lawsuits, and even criminal liability because they are in a position of fiduciary responsibility. Political leaders will probably be able to wiggle out of this; it's unlikely we're going to see a Y2000 version of the Nuremberg trials. But political leaders have their own form of Judgment Day—usually called Election Day. As noted earlier, 2000 is an election year, and politicians with a survival instinct will be trying to show everyone that they did their best to warn Congress of impending doom. Though we believe that Senator Moynihan is sincerely concerned about taking steps now to prevent the Y2000 problem, it must have occurred to his aides, if not to himself, that his proposed S.22 legislation could help ensure his reelection in the post-2000 years.[44]

- *Enormous amounts of debate and wrangling over the steps to be taken, with a high risk the wrong steps being taken* — This is a reasonably safe prediction, for momentous decisions about difficult problems have always caused massive debate. Keep in mind that the Y2000 problem, if it turns out to be serious, is not going to be a situation like Pearl Harbor. There won't be a reasonable excuse for Bill Clinton (who, in the normal course of events, will still be president when the clock chimes midnight at the end of 1999) to convene a joint session of

Congress, as FDR did after the December 7th "day of infamy," and declare war on a tyrannical enemy. How can you declare war on a bunch of invisible software bugs in computer programs? Perhaps that won't stop Mr. Clinton; perhaps he'll declare war on the Y2000 problem, just as recent national leaders have declared war on inflation, drugs, apathy, and racial tension. It could make for a stirring speech, but before any decisions can be made, Congress and the Senate will argue about it until they're blue in the face. If there's one thing that almost all historians and economists agree about the situation immediately after the Great Crash of 1929, it's that government took far too long to do anything, and then generally did the wrong thing for quite a while before taking some significant action. We see little reason to be more optimistic about government's reaction to a Y2000 disaster.

- *Public statements of optimism, and earnest appeals for calm*—We have a picture, in our mind's eye, of a Fireside Chat, televised from whatever room of the White House still has fireplaces, in which Mr. Clinton tells us that we have nothing to fear but fear itself. Business leaders will tell us the same thing in the early days of a serious post-2000 crisis, because they don't want their banks to close, their businesses to fail, and their stock holdings to evaporate. It is a tribute to FDR's leadership qualities that a significant percentage of Americans apparently *did* believe that there was nothing to fear; it remains to be seen whether Mr. Clinton will be able to evoke such confidence and support in a serious Y2000 crisis, especially considering the sex scandals that have plagued him throughout most of 1998. Since the Y2000 problems are likely to be *worse* in government agencies than in the private sector, it's hard for us to imagine why any rational citizen would believe anything that a political leader said during the post-Y2000 aftermath—but in any case, the barrage of optimistic statements, and appeals for calm, is a virtual certainty in the post-2000 years.

- *Frantic efforts to apply a "quick-fix" to Y2000 mistakes, and to complete any unfinished Y2000 conversions*—If food stamps, unemployment checks, Medicare payments, and/or Social Security checks can't be generated by computers in the aftermath of a Y2000 problem, the idea may well occur to politicians that they can be written by hand. The volume of transactions will probably make such a desperate attempt totally unworkable, but it will look good politically; we can envision televised reports showing thousands of government bureaucrats frantically writing checks with quill pens and bottles of ink. Meanwhile, the efforts to fix and finish the Y2000 projects that should have been finished long before December 31, 1999 will be doubled, and redoubled, and redoubled again. Programmers will collapse from exhaustion (if they haven't had the good sense to quit long before things reach this stage), but new ones will be drafted.

- *Emergency legislation will be enacted*—When a truly *serious* crisis occurs, political leaders either become paralyzed, or they invoke emergency powers to restrict and curtail the policies and procedures that operate under normal circumstances. The details depend on the severity of the crisis and the political climate, but the most likely actions we would see in a severe Y2000 crisis would include currency restrictions (e.g., you can only withdraw $100 a day from your bank account); rationing of critical resources; price freezes, massive intervention by the Treasury Department to prop up the stock market and major banks; and perhaps even martial law. We say this not to be alarmist; we simply observe that in the past, severe crises have led to severe actions.

What *Should* the Government Be Doing About Y2000?

We are not political leaders, elected representatives, or appointed officials of any government agency; thus, we offer the suggestions below with the greatest humility. But we do feel very strongly that there is a fundamental question that must be addressed before any intelligent discussion about preferred government actions can take place. The question is: *Do you believe that serious Y2000 problems and consequences can be completely avoided through concerted efforts on the part of business and government?*

If you believe the answer to this question is "yes," then the logical advice about governmental action (as well as advice to corporate leaders in the private sector) will be *preventive* in nature. Spend more, work harder, plan better, and so forth. The premise of the Y2000 optimist is that, with enough work and money and people and dedication, the problem *can* be solved. And, for whatever it's worth, that was still the prevailing tone of the articles that laymen and professionals found in the newspaper and magazine articles being written in mid-1998, though the tone has become decidedly less optimistic than when we wrote the first edition of our book in 1997.

If *we* believed that the answer to our question was "yes," we would not have written this book—for in that case, what would be the point of imagining scenarios in which critical services were disrupted for a month or a year? So our advice about appropriate governmental action is predicated on the assumption that *Y2000 efforts will fail*, despite the best efforts of hundreds of thousands of dedicated, hard-working people. Yes, of course, most of the computer systems will be converted; but if you've understood the arguments we've presented in this book, you'll know why we think that some Y2000 problems will slip through the cracks. Not just one or two, and not just the minor ones—but a sufficient number of major problems that we will see will be serious, systemic disruptions in the economy and the nation's infrastructure.

So our first piece of advice to the government is: Take this book, and any other information you can find, as a starting point for your own scenario planning. Develop your own predictive models to determine the possibility of major disruptions of the kind described in this book. If you feel there's a non-trivial chance of such disruptions occurring, then *invest money in post-Y2000 disaster planning*. That could include such things as:

- *Creating emergency contingency plans, to be implemented with Army or National Guard troops*. We've already suggested that riots could break out in the aftermath of a Y2000 problem. Why not prepare emergency food and shelter in advance, just as authorities would do for an approaching hurricane?

- *Provide detailed disaster-planning advice and guidelines for citizens.* The ideas in this book could be a starting point, but more detailed checklists and guidelines will be important. How should city dwellers plan on heating their apartments if they lose their oil heat and electricity, especially during winter periods? What steps should be taken in the event of disruptions in the food supply? How should people plan to communicate in the absence of a telephone system or Internet connection? (In the absence of any such plans from the government, we recommend that you start with the very useful and common-sense ideas from the Cassandra Project's web site at http://www.millennia-bcs.com/casframe.html.)

- *Plan damage control before January 1, 2000.* We will probably be accused of being isolationist in nature, but it seems to us that American troops would be much better utilized protecting American cities than Bosnian cities in the days following January 1, 2000. And if a scenario-planning exercise confirms that things could be as bad as the worst-case scenarios we've outlined in this book, then various systems and organizations should be shut down *before* New Year's Eve, 1999. Bring the troops home, shut down the

Y2000-sensitive military systems, and shut down whatever part of Washington is virtually guaranteed to fail after January 1, 2000. In the context of a Y2000 disaster, *no* action from government may be better than *wrong* action.

- *Provide a realistic assessment to citizens of how bad the Y2000 situation is, and how long it's likely to last.* This assumes that government leaders can exhibit characteristics of honesty and forthright, direct communication; it also assumes they will treat the public as mature, intelligent adults. These assumptions may be somewhat naïve, but it seems to us that most intelligent citizens would prefer to hear an accurate assessment of the situation, and an honest estimate of how long the crisis is likely to last. Faced with this information—unpleasant as it might be—we could then make whatever plans we felt appropriate. The counter-argument is that the population might panic if they knew how bad the situation was; but as a colleague of ours pointed out in a recent Y2000 computer conference, we have no hesitation teaching young children how to carry out fire-drills. If the procedures are explained properly, children don't have nightmares about burning to death in a fire; and we believe that if Y2000 is explained properly to mature, responsible adults, they'll be able to cope with it.

We could elaborate on these points, for there's obviously a great deal of detail that would be required in order to implement them effectively. But we won't do so, for a very simple reason: Everything we've suggested in this section of the chapter contradicts common behavior and practice in the political environment of the United States and every other country we're familiar with. In the ideal world, a government planning department would have written this book; we could have devoted our energies instead to solving the Y2000 problem, rather than warning people about it.

Fallback Advice: Two-Day Failures

If the various government agencies we've discussed in this chapter should go into a tailspin for no more than a couple of days, we would consider it a miracle. In many cases, no one would notice: It's relatively uncommon to find anyone who requires day-to-day access to, and interactions with, SSA or the welfare, unemployment, and food stamp agencies.

However, there *is* the possibility that the day or two of disruption could turn out to be the day your monthly retirement check was supposed to be mailed, or the day you were supposed to pick up your unemployment check from the state unemployment agency. Many of the computer systems run in monthly cycles—e.g., everyone whose surname begins with an "A" has their check generated on the first day of the month, everyone with a "B" has his or her check generated on the second day of the month, and so forth. Given the nature of the first two days of January, 2000, the "A" and "B" folks would run the risk of being told by a frazzled clerk that their checks didn't get generated. In the best of all cases, the check would be generated a few days later, when the government agency corrected whatever minor blip caused the problem; but given the volume of processing involved, it's also possible that the "fallback" strategy within the agency will be to wait until the first day of the *next* month, at which point two months' worth of payments can be made. Thus, even a minor problem, which affects only a small percentage of the constituency served by the agency, could have month-long consequences.

There are other aspects of government service for which even a short-term breakdown could be serious; in particular, we're concerned about the services provided by police, fire departments, Coast Guard units, and the like. Obviously, there's not much the average citizen can do to influence this, and the only reasonable advice we can think of is to maintain a low profile during the first few days of calendar year 2000.

Fallback Advice: One-Month Failures

If the Y2000 problem turns out to be significant enough to shut down one or more government agencies for a month, there are likely to be serious social and political consequences—both of a direct nature, and of a secondary, ripple-effect nature.

To the extent that you depend on government for financial support, it means that you'd better have a "buffer" of a month's emergency funds. The unfortunate paradox, of course, is that the people who would be most seriously affected by a month-long disruption in food stamps, welfare checks, and the like, are precisely the same people who lack the means to set aside a month's living expenses. But there are others whose financial situation is less extreme—e.g., many middle-class Social Security retirees—for whom the advice of stockpiling a month's financial resources might not be so absurd. We have no "instant cure" solution for this problem, and the only optimistic observation we can make is that it's better to be aware of the prospect of a serious problem a year in advance than it is to be taken entirely by surprise. If a problem of this magnitude develops sometime in the first few months of 2000, there are bound to be a lot of angry people—both middle-class retirees, as well as low-income welfare recipients, who sputter indignantly, "Why didn't someone warn us about this in advance?" If nothing else, you should consider this book to be your warning.

A more serious concern is that of a major social collapse in various urban centers, if government services are disrupted for a month. It could take two or three months of non-delivery of Social Security checks before people begin marching on Washington; but it could take much less time for riots and looting to break out in urban ghettos if the food stamps, welfare checks, and other forms of financial assistance are disrupted. The situation could be compounded by Y2000 problems in the police, fire department, and other civil services; New Yorkers, for example, could look forward to the possibility of a shutdown in garbage-collection services, as well as the subways and the city-financed schools.

America's cities, alas, have some experience with riots, looting, and various other forms of urban unrest. They've often been triggered by individual events—e.g., the Rodney King incident in Los Angeles in 1994, or the electrical blackout in New York City in 1977—and they have often required substantial police force to bring under control. In this case, the "trigger" could be the disruption in welfare checks or food stamps, but there is likely to be much more of a "systemic" nature to the problems that motivate hungry, unemployed, and generally disgruntled people to take matters into their own hands. If the Y2000 disruptions go on for a month, there's no reason to believe that the riots will last only a week; indeed, we could well find a situation where government authorities have no alternative but to impose martial law.

All of which leads to a basic question: Do you want to continue living in an urban center under circumstances like these? Even if you have a one-month supply of TV dinners in your refrigerator (and a generator to power the refrigerator in the event of electrical failures), it may not be safe on the streets for weeks at a time. The prospect of this kind of Y2000-induced social breakdown might not be enough to persuade you to sell your home and move out of the city *now*, but it should be enough for you to make "fallback" plans to leave your urban residence for a month-long sabbatical if things get bad.

Our assumption is that the situation would not be as bad in the suburban and rural areas, but this could turn out to be a dangerous assumption indeed. For example, both the federal and state government agencies sometimes turn out to be a major employer in smaller towns and suburban areas; whether it's a regional processing center for the IRS, or an administrative center for the state unemployment agency, it could well turn out that a significant number of people are furloughed by a Y2000 shutdown that lasts more than a few days. We don't expect that furloughed IRS workers are going to indulge in looting and rioting, but the point is that if these agencies represent a major part of the economy in a small town, then the effect of the disruption could be significant.

Fallback Advice: One-Year Failures

What if the Y2000 problem is sufficiently serious that food stamps, unemployment benefits, Society Security checks, and other government services are disrupted for a year? If you're financially dependent on any of these organizations, the unavoidable reality is that you're going to have to change your life style. The likelihood of the average citizen taking this seriously, and making some proactive decisions now, is fairly small; it's such an unpleasant prospect that most people would prefer to simply cross their fingers and hope that the Y2000 problem will somehow be solved at the last moment, just as we've come to expect in most "disaster" movies. And as we've already noted, the low-income, unemployed, and welfare-class part of the population has little, if any, ability to make proactive decisions about their economic future.

So this part of the discussion has to be aimed at the reader who has some degree of flexibility for proactive Y2000 planning, even if the potential choices all seem unpleasant. If you're a retirement-age person in reasonable health, you should consider a "backup" form of employment—even if it's flipping hamburgers at McDonald's. If you're a farmer or small business owner who has been able to take advantage of government subsidies and benefits, you've got one last year to restructure your business so that it can survive, if not prosper, on its own. And if you're concerned about the dangers of living in an urban center whose low-income residents have been cut off from food stamps and welfare for a year, then you should move to a safe area now—while you can. And while you're thinking about this, keep the ripple-effect problem in mind: In addition to disruption in government services, we've already discussed the possibility of disruptions in utilities, transportation, banking, communications, news, and your own job.

The alternative is to cross your fingers and hope for the best—which is what we expect 90-95 percent of the population to do. But in that case, events are out of your hands, and you're no longer in control. The low-income, unemployed, and welfare-class citizens might shrug their shoulders and remind you that they've never had much control over their situation; but the middle- and upper-class elite in most urban centers have traditionally had the luxury (or perhaps the illusion) that they *are* in control. Thus, the consequences of a systemic Y2000 disruption could be quite a psychological shock, in addition to everything else.

Fallback Advice: Ten-Year Failures

Will government vanish from our lives for a decade? Will the police and fire departments vanish from cities for 10 years? Will we have to wait for a decade for a new Thomas Paine to write a *Post-2000 Common Sense* that will galvanize a new generation of leaders to create a new Constitution? Or could things even be as bad as they were in Kevin Costner's recent movie, *The Postman*?

Such an apocalyptic future is far beyond anything we can imagine, despite the rather gloomy nature of everything else we've written in this book. Presumably, some form of current government will survive; presumably there will still be a Congress and a Senate, and presumably our political leaders will still find a way to raise taxes to pay for the army and the bureaucracy.

But the devil is in the details. While our three-branch, representative form of government will presumably survive, the balance of power between the states and federal government could shift substantially. Even if there's a Congress and a Senate, there might not be a Social Security Administration, or an IRS, or a Medicare. Changes like these would be revolutionary in nature, at least from the perspective of the segment of society whose entire lives have been influenced or controlled by these government agencies. As John Kenneth Galbraith observed about revolutions:

> *All successful revolutions are the kicking in of a rotten door. The violence of revolutions is the violence of men who charge into a vacuum.*[45]

The important thing to remember here is that while faulty technology may be responsible for creating a serious Y2000 crisis in various government services, technology won't be responsible for the long-term disappearance of those same services. If, for example, all of the computer systems and all of the computer programmers of the Social Security Administration implode into a black hole, along with every other employee and every piece of furniture, the whole thing could be reconstructed within a few years—*if* government and society felt strongly motivated to do so. The problem (or the opportunity, depending on your perspective) is that leaders in government, as well as various lobbying groups, and ultimately the voting public itself, will be saying, "Since we have a chance to start with a clean slate, we should organize Social Security in an entirely different way... let's do it *this* way..." The debate would continue for months, if not years, and the ultimate decision would be a *political* decision, not a technological decision, to re-build Social Security exactly as it was before, or in a radically different way—or not to build it at all.

If someone predicted that the sun was not going to come up on January 1st, it would be a terrific shock. Assuming you could get past the "denial" stage and sincerely believe the prediction, it would still be a difficult concept to cope with; after all, a great deal of your life is predicated on a regular, predictable separation between night and day. While it may seem a bit of an exaggeration, a substantial number of citizens have a similar reaction to the prospect of their favorite government service disappearing.

This would not have been the case a century ago, because the average citizen was far less influenced by and/or dependent upon government services; indeed, this entire chapter would have been reduced to a paragraph or two. It's also intriguing to note that the two generations represented by the authors of this book are relatively blasé about the prospect of Social Security collapsing at some future date, and *not* being a reliable source of post-retirement income—simply because we've been warned of this possibility on a regular basis for the past 20 years. The problem is that warnings of a Y2000-induced collapse of Social Security or any of the other government services discussed in this chapter have only begun this year—and for the most part, the average citizen has not heard the warning, or has decided not to believe what he hears.

If you've read this far, then consider yourself warned again. Social Security could disappear. Food stamps could disappear. Farm subsidies could disappear. Unemployment and welfare assistance could disappear. Student loans and low-income housing assistance could disappear. All of these things, and more, could disappear for a decade or for the rest of our lives, beginning in January 2000—not because it's technologically impossible to build entirely new computer systems, but because the political reaction to a Y2000 crash might banish them from the landscape forever.

How do you plan or prepare for such a contingency? The words are easy, but the actions will be difficult. The words are: Become self-sufficient, remain flexible, and don't assume that the government services you depend upon are as eternal and as reliable as the daily rising of the sun.

Endnotes

1. The entire speech by President Clinton was posted on the Internet at http://www.whitehouse.gov/WH/New/html/19980714-5571.html.
2. It's interesting to note that in an OMB report issued July 10, 1997 (when the first edition of this book was being prepared), the various government agencies listed 7,649 mission-critical systems; a year later, the number has dropped by 318 systems. One of the minor debates in the Y2000 community is how to determine, in a consistent fashion, exactly what is "mission-critical" and what's not.
3. See http://www.govexec.com/dailyfed/0798/072898t4.htm for a July 28, 1998 article from *Government Executive*, which reports that, " 'Virtually all' of the federal government's mission critical computer systems will be ready for the Year 2000 by President Clinton's due date of March 31, 1999, administration Y2K czar John Koskinen said Tuesday."
4. The most recent GAO report we could find while writing the second edition "Year 2000 Computing Crisis: Strong Leadership and

Partnerships Needed to Mitigate Risk of Major Disruptions," presented as testimony before the House Subcommittee on Government Management, Information and Technology, by Joel C. Willemssen, Director of the GAO Civil Agencies Information Systems, on August 13, 1998. See http://www.gao.gov/new.items/ai98262t.pdf for a PDF version of this report.

5. See http://www.house.gov/reform/gmit/y2k/980602.htm for a June 2, 1998 summary of the committee's assessment of the Federal government's Y2000 status as of May 15, 1998.
6. This is based on the assessment of Larry A. Olson, deputy secretary for information technology in the state of Pennsylvania. See http://www.ncsl.org/programs/lis/LRL/yr2.htm#update for a more complete discussion of the state-level situation from the summer-1998 National Conference of State Legislatures.
7. A mid-1998 survey of a state-level IT association called NASIRE, indicated that 23 states were still in the planning stages for their Y2000 projects, while 19 states were in the midst of implementing and testing their conversions. Four states reported being in both the planning and implementation stages. For more details on the current situation, visit NASIRE's web site at http://www.nasire.org/year2000/index.html.
8. In that context, you may find it interesting that despite the estimate from N.Y. Governor Pataki and the State's Y2K directors that they'll need $250 million to repair their systems, the state legislature decided to cut finding to $40 million. For more details, see "Budget cuts may hurt solving of 'Year 2000' computer woes," *Boston Globe*, April 29, 1998, also available on the Internet at http://www.boston.com/dailynews/wirehtml/119/Budgetcutsmay-hurtsolvingofY.htm. Similarly, California's Department of Information Technology has estimated that it will cost $240 million to fix its Y2K problems; but an independent organization, the Legislative Analyst's Office (LAO) disputes the figure, arguing that it's too low; see http://www.lao.ca.gov/generalgovtcrosscuttinganl98.html. But it hardly matters: the California state legislature appropriated only $55 million for 1998, with another $19 million for 1999. Smaller states, of course, have smaller problems: an article in the May 22, 1998 issue of the Caspar, WY *Tribune* reports that the state of Wyoming estimates that it may have to spend $13 million to fix its Y2000 problems, but the state legislature has rejected the Governor's request for $6 million, failed to approve a separate budget allocation of $3 million, and has thus

far only allocated $1 million. See http://www.trib.com/NEWS/HEAD/statey2k26.html for more details.

9. At least one governor seems to be worried, too. Wisconsin's Governor Tommy Thompson was quoted in the July 28, 1998 issue of *Milwaukee Journal Sentinel On-Line* (available at http://www.jsonline.com/archive/july98/news/state/980728thompson headingoffcom.stm) as saying at a news conference, "I am very fearful. Experts predict that only half (of all organizations) will be ready. I think that's overly optimistic."

10. See http://www.govtech.net/services/news/Mar698news.shtm for more details on the survey conducted by the International City/County Management Association and Public Technology Inc., to which 3,600 cities responded.

11. You might want to visit the Web sites of the top 50 cities in the country, organized alphabetically at http://www.wplwloo.lib.ia.us/50cities.html to see whether they provide any information about their Y2000 projects. You can also find a list of the top 100 cities, in terms of estimated population in 2000, at http://cgi.amcity.com/journals/demographics/report57/57-1.html.

12. Capers Jones, *The Year 2000 Software Problem: Quantifying the Costs and Assessing the Consequences*, Addison-Wesley, 1998, page 80.

13. Later, Mr. Hollerith founded the company that became IBM. This, too, is a common pattern: government often provides the funding and/or the justification for a computer project; it then moves in various ways into the private sector.

14. Capers Jones, *op cit.*, page 80.

15. Similar comments can be heard from first-level and second-level managers, whose frustration with the bureaucracy has embittered them over the years. The interesting thing is that even if a mid-level manager made such a statement in public, and even if one could somehow prove that the Y2000 project failed because of the manager's lack of enthusiasm, there would probably be no legal recourse. Y2000 projects are being spurred on in the private sector partially because of fears of massive litigation from angry customers; but with rare exceptions, citizens are not allowed to sue their Government. Indeed, nearly a dozen states have passed legislation in the past 12 months to ensure that that does not happen!

16. However, in early 1998, an additional 30 million lines of code were discovered, which deals with the reporting of disability benefits from the various states to SSA.

17. An August 3, 1998 article from the *Washington Post* provides the optimistic assessment that "The Treasury's Financial Management Service, which prints benefit and tax refund checks, has started testing its computers to ensure they can receive orders from Social Security and other agencies, as well as mass produce the checks and clear them through the Federal Reserve." See http://www.washingtonpost.com/wp-srv/WPlate/1998-08/03/134l-080398-idx.html for more details. But see also http://www.house.gov/ways_means/oversite/testmony/5-7-98/5-7crai.htm for the May 7, 1998 testimony from Constance Craig, Assistant Commissioner of Information Resources, to the House Ways & Means subcommittee about the current status of FMS. And while you're at it, take a look at the June 16, 1998 issue of *Federal Computer Week* (available at http://www.fcw.com/pubs/fcw/1998/0615/web-ssa-6-16-1998.html), which reports that Rep. Pete Sessions (R-Texas), vice chairman of the House Subcommittee on Government Management, Information and Technology, is sufficiently worried that the Y2000 problem could disrupt the delivery of about 50 million Social Security retirement and disability payments, that he plans to study whether to transfer the responsibility of the payments from the Treasury Department to the Social Security Administration.

18. We have no way of knowing whether the contractor was doing a good job or a bad job, or whether they deserved to be fired from the project. The point is that such abrupt changes in the middle of any large, complex software project almost always create delays and disruptions, even in the best of cases; in the worst of cases, such a change is the straw that breaks the camel's back. It remains to be seen what happens with the Medicare project.

19. Joe Sexton, "Merchants with Stubborn Hopes," *New York Times*, July 19, 1997, p. 1, 20.

20. This can be found surfing to http://www.ustreas.gov/treasury/bureaus/irs/prime/primerfc.htm on the Internet, and then selecting "Request For Comment No. TIRNO-97-H-0010." It's a 116-page Adobe Acrobat document describing the new IRS modernization program. It describes a complex system on the verge of collapse, and a staggeringly complex plan for modernizing it.

21. An email message from an IRS programmer sent to members of a Y2000 Internet mailing list claimed that the figure was closer to 62 million lines of code. But other IRS documents have strongly implied that nobody is quite sure what the number is—for there are an unknown number of computer programs, spreadsheets, and databases that have been developed on personal computers spread throughout the vast IRS organization.
22. Bob Violino and Bruce Caldwell, "And Now For The Bad News," *Techweb*, April 21, 1997. You can retrieve this article from the Internet at http://techweb.cmp.com/iw/627/27iuyr4.htm.
23. This figure was cited by IRS Commissioner Charles Rossotti in testimony to the U.S. House Ways and Means Committee on May 7, 1998; see http://www.house.gov/ways_means/oversite/testmony/5-7-98/5-7ross.htm for details.
24. Normally, an organization that faces the risk of not finishing its Y2000 activities would create contingency plans—e.g., "workarounds" or a backup form of manual processing in case the computers aren't ready. It's not clear that the IRS is doing so; in testimony to Congress, IRS Commissioner Charles Rossotti is quoted as saying, "To do viable contingency planning, we would have to divert our resources from year 2000 work, and we are trying not to do that." See "Industry rep voices doubt over federal 2000-readiness," by Peyman Pejman, *Government Computing News*, June 15, 1998; also available at http://www.gcn.com/gcn/1998/June15/industry_rep_voices_doubt_over_f.htm . Similarly, IRS Y2000 project coordinator John Yost is quoted as saying "As long as we stay on target, we're not going to create a specific contingency plan." See "IRS Unlikely To Meet Y2K Deadline," by Mary Mosquera, *TechWeb*, also available at http://www.techweb.com/wire/story/y2k/TWB19980227S0017 .
25. See the September 15, 1997 issue of *Computerworld*, available at http://cwlive.cw.com:8080/home/print9497.nsf/All/SL37irs15ABE for details.
26. See the April 3, 1998 issue of the *Washington Post*, available at http://www.washingtonpost.com/wp-srv/WPlate/1998-04/03/118l-040398-idx.html for details.
27. "IRS will be Y2K ready by 1999," Reuters/CNET News.com, October 23, 1998. See http://www.news.com/News/Item/0,4,27886,00.html?st.ne.ni.lh for text of the article.
28. Another estimate of the extent of DOD computers and equipment was provided in "The Pentagon's Nightmare Scenario," by James

Kitfield, *Government Executive*, June 22, 1998; also available on the Internet at http://www.govexec.com/dailyfed/0698/062298t2.htm. The article reports that "DOD operates more than 1.5 million computers, 10,000 data networks and 28,000 automated information systems. In a February survey, various defense agencies reported that more than half of the 730,000 personal computers they had examined had, to one degree or another, a Year 2000 problem."

29. So are the planes, missiles, and bombs of other advanced computers. To minimize the possibility of Y2000-related failures being misinterpreted as some kind of "cyber-attack," it appears that DOD is offering to share appropriate information with Russia. An article in the July 15, 1998 issue of *Most New York* quotes Pentagon spokesman Kenneth Bacon as saying, "We have offered to share or engage in joint early warning projects with Russia, and maybe with other countries as well."
30. In addition, the GAO reported at the end of May, 1998 that 120 of the Army's 376 mission-critical automated information and embedded weapons systems still need Y2000 repairs. And as of February 1998, 12,120 of the Army's 19,731 nonmission-critical systems still required Y2000 repairs. See "GAO targets Army's Year 2000 effort," by Bob Brewin, in the June 1, 1998 issue of *Federal Computer Week*, also available on the Internet at http://www.fcw.com/pubs/fcw/1998/0601/web-ary2k-6-1-1998.html.
31. This memo is a publicly available document, available at http://www.dtic.mil/c3i/y2k/secdefmemo.html . The first paragraph of the memo says, "The Department of Defense (DoD) is making insufficient progress in its efforts to solve its Y2K computer problem. To improve the accountability for correction actions, I am directing the following activities in addition to those already underway."
32. "Defense Computers: LSSC Needs to Confront Significant Year 2000 Issues." GAO report AIMD-97-149. 21 pp. plus 2 appendices (6 pp.) September 26, 1997. Available on the Internet at http://www.gao.gov/new.items/ai97149.pdf.
33. See http://www.house.gov/reform/gmit/y2k/980909.htm for the full report produced by Congressman Horn's office.
34. In "Two More States Claim Year 2000 Compliance," (*Information Week*, July 7, 1997), reporter Bruce Caldwell reports that Illinois, Wyoming, Arkansas, California, Georgia, Missouri, Oklahoma,

Michigan, and Oregon claim that their financial-management systems are now Y2000-compliant. That leaves *lots* of other systems to worry about, and lots of other states.

35. Bob Violino, "50 States of Alert," *Information Week*, March 24, 1997. You can retrieve this from the Internet at http://www.techweb.com/se/directlink.cgi?IWK19970324S0054.
36. See Patrick Thibodeau, "Squabbling agencies endanger year 2000 work," *Computerworld*, April 21, 1997.
37. See Patrick Thibodeau, "Squabbling agencies endanger year 2000 work," *Computerworld*, April 21, 1997.
38. An excellent Internet source for all of these hearings is Heath's site at http://home.swbell.net/adheath/testimony.htm.
39. See http://www.itpolicy.gsa.gov/mks/yr2000/exord.htm for the text of the Executive Order.
40. P. J. O'Rourke, *Parliament of Whores,* "The Mystery of Government" (1991).
41. Nicole Lewis, "Feds signal deepening Y2K crisis," *Federal Computer Weekly*, Sep 22, 1997.
42. For example, the computers at IRS and SSA exchange tax-related information; both agencies are busily trying to convert their respective systems, and it's highly likely that a "windowing" approach will be used for at least some of these systems. Thus, the computer programs will be modified so that any two-digit year will be assumed to exist within a century-wide "window." But if IRS decides that its newly-defined window runs from 1940 to 2039, while SSA uses a window stretching from 1910 to 2009, then any date-sensitive data passed between the two agencies would be interpreted in an inconsistent fashion. Agreeing on a common windowing convention between all of the government agencies would be a massive job, and could best be accomplished by keeping the politicians away from these committees.
43. See "Appropriations bill: Sex, pay and Y2K," by Brian Friel, in the July 20, 1998 edition of *Government Executive*, available on the Internet at http://www.govexec.com/dailyfed/0798/072098b1.htm.
44. It's also interesting that Republicans have already begun to take aim at Al Gore, the presumed high-tech Democratic candidate for President in 2000. Even though the Republicans could be faulted for not launching a major Y2000 initiative under George Bush's presidency (which would have been early enough to have finished most of the repair work without the last-minute frantic activity we see now), it's the Democrats who have been at the helm since

the 1992 elections. But a Democratic President Clinton could also point out that the Republicans have held control of the House and Senate since the 1994 elections; so nobody is blameless.

45. John Kenneth Galbraith, *The Age of Uncertainty,* chapter 3 (1977).

Y2000 Impact on Embedded Systems

Now, no one will ever find every imbedded microchip, every line of code that needs to be rewritten. But if companies, agencies, and organizations are ready, if they understand the threat and have backup plans, then we will meet this challenge.

President Bill Clinton, speech at the National Academy of Sciences, *July 14, 1998*

The world is divided into two categories: failures and unknowns.

Francis Picabia "L'Humour Poetique," in La Nef, *no. 71-72 (Paris, Dec. 1950—Jan. 1951; reprinted in* Yes No: Poems and Sayings, *"Sayings," edited by Rémy Remy Hall, 1990).*

Introduction

In several of the earlier chapters of this book, we've mentioned the possibility of Y2000-related failures in "embedded systems." Because there are so many different kinds of embedded systems, and because they affect so many other parts of the social infrastructure, we'll discuss them in a more general fashion in this chapter.

First, what do we mean by an "embedded system"? Historically, the term was used within the computer industry to describe a small "micro-computer" that was literally *embedded* within some larger piece of engineering equipment or industrial product. The embedded system provided the intelligence associated with "process control" systems (e.g., the control of mixing machines and heating vats in a chemical refinery) or "data acquisition" systems (e.g., a smart radar unit that can perform on-the-fly analysis of both friendly and enemy aircraft).

As an example of the kind of problem that computer software professionals are worrying about within plants, refineries, and manufacturing organizations, consider the following excerpt from the January 8, 1997 issue of *The Dominion*, a Wellington, New Zealand newspaper that reported on the consequences of a non-Y2000 date-calculation problem:[1]

> *A computer glitch at the Tiwai Pt [in South Island of New Zealand] aluminium smelter at midnight on New Year's Eve has left a repair bill of more than $1 million [New Zealand Dollars]. Production in all the smelting potlines ground to a halt at the stroke of midnight when the computers shut down simultaneously and without warning. New Zealand Aluminium Smelters general manager David Brewer said the failure was traced to a faulty computer software programme, which failed to account for 1996 being a leap year.*
>
> *The computer was not programmed to handle the 366th day of the year, he said. "Each of the 660 process control computers hung up simultaneously at midnight," Mr Brewer said. The same problem occurred two hours later at Comalco's Bell Bay smelter, in Tasmania [Australia]. New*

Zealand is two hours ahead of Tasmania. Both smelters use the same programme, which was written by Comalco computer staff. Mr Brewer said the cause was difficult to trace and it was not till a telephone call in the morning from Bell Bay that the leap year link was made. "It was a complicated problem and it took quite some time to find out just what caused it."

Tiwai staff rallied through the night to operate the potlines manually and try to find the cause. The glitch was fixed and normal production restored by midafternoon. However, by then, the damage has been done. Without the computers to regulate temperatures inside the pot cells, five cells over-heated and were damaged beyond repair. Mr Brewer said they would have to be replaced at a cost of more than $1 million.

Twenty years ago, these specialized computer systems were very expensive, and were thus used in a relatively small number of sophisticated factories and engineering installations. But in the past decade, computer chips have become dramatically smaller, cheaper, and more sophisticated—so that the term "embedded system" now encompasses almost any device that has "built-in" computer logic. Thus, the sophisticated oil refineries and radar systems still have embedded systems (for which the consequences of a Y2000 failure could be disastrous, as illustrated in the above example), but we now have a similar kind of technology embedded in consumer appliances ranging from microwave ovens to VCRs to digital wristwatches to automobiles. A more dramatic example of "embedding" is the modern pacemaker that's literally embedded into a patient's body to help monitor and regulate the heartbeat of a patient with cardiac problems.

A total of 3.5 *billion* microprocessors (the "chip" that constitutes the embedded system) were sold in 1995, and 7 *billion* were sold in 1997.[2] It's reasonable to expect that equally large numbers will be sold in 1998 and 1999; thus, we're likely to have an aggregate of 25+ billion of these little machines floating around the planet on New Year's Eve, 1999; indeed, one industry expert, David Hall, estimates the figure at 40 billion.[3] As we'll discuss below, only a small percentage of these chips are likely to be "year-sensitive," and only a small percentage could be described as "mission-critical" (in the sense that a failure could cause severe economic consequences and/or loss of life)—but even a small percentage of a small percentage can be a large number when we start with a population of 25-40 billion chips.

The vast quantity of these embedded systems is one of the key issues that you need to keep in mind. There are simply not enough programmers, not enough repair technicians, and not enough time to inspect, repair, and/or replace them all; even if only one-tenth of one percent of the 25 billion chips are Y2000-defective, that still leaves us with 25 million repair jobs. And according to a mid-1998 report from the Gartner Group, only 11 percent of companies have begun testing their embedded systems;[4] similarly, a survey conducted by Cap Gemini in the spring of 1998 indicated that only one-sixth of large firms had progressed past the initial stages of inventory and assessment to actually begin repairing their embedded systems.[5]

The problem is compounded by the nature of the embedded system: The "logic" carried out by the system is "burned into" the computer chip and, in most cases, cannot be changed. This is fundamentally different than the situation with your home PC and with the typical business computer system, where a Y2000-defective software program can be modified and re-installed on the same computer. Thus, if it turns out that the word-processor on your home PC is Y2000-defective, you can ask Microsoft or Corel (makers of the two most popular word-processing programs) to send you an updated/corrected version of their word processor, and you would never dream of throwing the entire PC in the garbage can. On the other hand, if your digital wristwatch turns out to be Y2000-defective, chances are that you'll have to throw it away and buy a new one.

In some cases, the manufacturer can extract the microprocessor chip from the device in which it's embedded, and insert a replacement chip. That might be a viable option for an expensive household appliance like a VCR or a fancy phone/fax/answering-machine device. But in many cases, the manufacturer never planned for such replacements, and has no replacement chips available; this is particularly likely if the device is more than a few years old; to compound the problem, the manufacturer may have gone bankrupt in the interim. The cost of such a replacement is going to be staggering, because it's labor-intensive work and because large volumes are involved; thus, it will often turn out that the most practical solution is one of replacing the entire device, rather than attempting to replace the defective chip within it. Indeed, even this option may not be convenient, as in the case of the following apocryphal story quoted by *The Times of India*:[6]

> *Robin Guenier, the man charged with solving the "single most expensive problem in history", tells a story.*
>
> *"The micro-chip controls when the bank vault can be opened and closed. It allows the jackpot vault to be opened during the working week, but keeps it closed at weekends. For security reasons, it has been buried inside the 20-ton-door of the vault, and can only be inspected by removing the whole door."*
>
> *"The big problem arises because the bank building has been built around the vault, again for security reasons. So to inspect or change the micro-chip requires half the building to be demolished and the door removed. The people who built the chip, the vault and the bank never imagined that the chip would have to be removed in the lifetime of the building," he added.*
>
> *"But at midnight on December 31, 1999, something they never foresaw will happen. The chip has been programmed to read only the last two digits of the year, and assumes the 19 prefix. So it believes that it is back in 1900. That would make no difference, except that January 1, 2000 falls on a Saturday, while the same date in 1900 was a Monday. The vault will open on Saturday and Sunday, but not on later working days. So, to ensure depositors have access to their deposits, the bank building has to be demolished. That sums up the millennium problem."*

This hints at another problem common to the industrial-variety of embedded systems: It's often very difficult to locate, identify, and manipulate the embedded systems. The embedded systems in satellites are an obvious example; indeed, that's the essence of the problem with the Navy's GPS satellite system discussed in Chapter 4.

Similarly, embedded systems submerged underwater in oil-drilling platforms won't be easy to retrieve and fix. Researchers in the oil and gas industry put it more bluntly in an April 1998 article:[7]

> *"It is estimated that the average oil and gas firm, starting today, can expect to remediate less than 30% of the overall potential failure points in the production environment."*

Obviously, none of this is relevant unless the embedded systems are vulnerable to Y2000 failures. In some cases, it's fairly easy to tell, but in many cases, it's almost impossible for even a trained computer professional to predict the Y2000-related behavior of an embedded system, and this has led to enormous debate within the computer industry. A relevant example: Is a typical automobile vulnerable to Y2000 problems—and if so, how would we know in advance? As we noted in Chapter 4, the obvious solution would be to get a definitive statement (complete with a legal warranty) from the automobile manufacturer about the Y2000-compliant status of its products; the fact that so very few of the auto manufacturers have made such a statement, as of the time this edition of the book was being written, is sobering.

Several computer professionals have suggested a common-sense way of analyzing the situation: If an embedded system does not provide a human operator, or end-user, with a means of setting the "current year" information, or changing that information, then it's unlikely that the embedded system is aware of, or dependent on, the year. In other words, it won't know that the year has "rolled over" from 99 to 00, and it won't care; it's not Y2000-vulnerable. One can imagine a scenario where the chip *is* year-aware, even though the year can't be set by the end-user; the manufacturer may have "burned" a starting date into the chip corresponding to the year in which the chip was created. It's possible, but unlikely—so, for most people, the simple guideline will be: The newer the device (and thus the more sophisticated its internal micro-chip is likely to be) and the fancier its operating characteristics are, the more likely it is to be year-aware, and thus Y2000-vulnerable.

For example, one of the authors spent the summer of 1997 writing the first edition of this book with the assistance of coffee produced by a newly-purchased Mr. Coffee automated coffee-maker. The device allows the end-user to set the time of day, and can distinguish between AM and PM; but it won't allow the user to set the day, month, or year. Ergo, it probably doesn't keep this information internally, and won't care about the Y2000 rollover. The typical newly purchased VCR, on the other hand, *does* allow the end-user to program year-sensitive dates into the device, in order to specify when a specific TV show should be recorded in the future. Hence it *is* highly likely to be Y2000-vulnerable, and there's no obvious way of knowing whether the device is indeed Y2000-compliant.[8]

In some cases, the situation may be a little more subtle. For example, the owner of today's modern automobile will probably discover that while he can set the time-of-day on his auto dashboard-clock, he cannot set the day or year. But when he takes his car into the highly computerized service station for the annual tune-up, the auto mechanic can attach a diagnostic computer to the car; this enables the mechanic to read and/or update various "parameters" with the car's embedded systems (including, for example, a mileage counter that tells the auto owner how many miles remain before the car is due for its next servicing—an item that the mechanic forgot to reset when one of the authors last brought his Jeep into the shop for a tune-up!). The interesting point here is that there are embedded systems within the car that the owner may not even be aware of; for example, Jim Rivera made the following observation on a recent Y2000 Internet discussion group:[9]

> *There is a federal (U.S. gov) standard for a car's emissions control systems logging any failure conditions of the components, for example a fuel injector being open longer than it is supposed to due to some dirt in the fuel. The name for the logging system is OBD2 (On Board Diagnostics 2).*
>
> *This next is informed speculation. Suppose there is date-time logging for the failure. Suppose that the date routine for some of the software is (surprise) not Y2K compliant. Suppose the failure mode is either to lockup or refuse to run the car (unlikely but not impossible). I have seen state-*

> *ments in both directions—that some automotive engine control processors will or will not fail after The Day. It seems to me that it is likely that those who know (because they wrote the software) are probably contractually bound to keep quiet. The rest of us are just guessing.*

Of course, the fact that an embedded system is year-aware and Y2000-vulnerable does not necessarily mean that it will fail on January 1, 2000; it simply means that we should take steps to find out *in advance* if it will fail, and what the consequences of a failure might be. The sense of urgency associated with this advance investigation depends on the nature of the system itself; we might not bother checking the Y2000-compliant status of a $19.95 digital wristwatch, but we probably should check the status of our car. To put it another way: suppose the public-relations office at General Motors, Ford, or Chrysler (or for that matter, Toyota, Honda, and BMW) responds to your inquiry with the comforting assurance, "don't worry about your car's computer being Y2000 compliant; the engine will run just fine after January 1, 2000." But if you're hurtling down the highway at 80 mph on New Year's Eve, 1999 and your engine suddenly dies at the stroke of midnight, it won't be very easy to track that PR representative down and ask for a refund.

The natural assumption is that automotive engineers would design hardware-oriented failsafe mechanisms, *independent of the onboard computer*, that would prevent an abrupt shutdown in the event of a computer failure. And it's easy to imagine that the worst consequence of a Y2000-related computer failure would be an annoying red alarm light on the auto dashboard that says, "This car needs to be serviced *now!*" But the question is: *Are you willing to bet your life that it won't be any more serious than that?* Unless you have a legally binding warranty from the auto manufacturer, it seems to us that the best way of testing the Y2000-compliance of your car is to park it in your garage or driveway on New Year's Eve 1999, and wait until the morning of January 1st before turning on the ignition to see what happens.

Here's a summary of the situation we'll all be facing with regard to embedded systems that are "year-aware"—and both business organizations and government agencies will have a similar situation. A good example of a high-risk embedded system for a business organization is its PBX telephone system; if it fails, then there's no telephone service even if AT&T continues functioning smoothly. As discussed in Chapter 9, medical electronic systems are "high risk" for both the patient and the hospital. So are the elevators in high-rise office buildings.

	Non-Y2000 compliant	Y2000 compliant
High-risk embedded system	Dangerous	Safe
Low-risk embedded system	Nuisance, but not dangerous	Nice, but somewhat irrelevant

Other systems—including many household appliances—fall into the category of low-risk embedded systems. As we've mentioned, many household appliances are not even aware of the year, and are thus not vulnerable to Y2000 failures; it's the fancier and more sophisticated devices that may be vulnerable. If it turns out that your VCR fails, then you're unable to tape reruns of the *Seinfeld* show; chances that you'll find a way to survive. But if you have an office at home, and your integrated phone/fax/copier/answering machine stops working, it could have more serious consequences.

To prepare for the Y2000 rollover, you need to begin by making a list of the embedded systems that you depend on and/or interact with during your normal day-to-day life. For many people, this will require some careful attention, and even some detective work—for it simply doesn't occur to us that computers are embedded in almost every device that we use. If your household appliance, office machine, or apartment-building elevator has an LCD display (e.g., a bright green, or bright red, display that tells you the temperature of your oven, or the phone number being dialed on your office phone, or the floor number of your elevator), then it probably has an embedded system. If the LCD display shows the calendar date, it's a dead giveaway that it's year-sensitive, and thus Y2000-vulnerable. And even if it doesn't display the date, it may still be Y2000-vulnerable. To help illustrate the variety of devices and systems that may be impacted—and whose failure could impact *your* day-to-day life—here's a list compiled by New York State's Y2000 project office:[10]

FACILITIES:

Lighting systems (incl. backup lighting)
Backup generators
Heating, air conditioning & ventilating systems
Climate monitoring systems (incl. thermostats)
Elevators, escalators, and lifts
Building management systems
Lighting systems
Refrigeration systems
Sprinkler/fountain systems
Switching systems
Water and sewage systems
Water pumps
Vending machines

MEDICAL EQUIPMENT:

Monitoring devices
Automatic medication dispensing equipment
Pacemakers

SECURITY/FIRE:

Security systems (incl. Burglar alarms)
Safes and vaults
Door locks
Fire control systems (incl. alarms, sprinkler systems)

TRANSPORTATION/PARKING:

Vehicle preventative maintenance chips
Gate systems
Variable message signs
Traffic lights
Traffic monitoring devices

ADMINISTRATION:

Fax machines
Phone systems (PBX, voicemail, switching)

Mailroom equipment (Incl. Postage meters)
VCRs Timeclocks

MANUFACTURING/PROCESS CONTROL:

Energy control systems
Power grid systems
Power plants/stations
Switching systems

A good question to ask yourself is: *Does the device exhibit intelligent behavior?* By "intelligent," we don't necessarily mean the full-blown artificial-intelligence kind of behavior exhibited by IBM's Deep Blue chess-playing computer or HAL in the classic movie *2001*. What you need to look for is a device that responds in different ways to different environmental conditions—and, in particular, to different time-oriented schedules. The reason we're concerned about elevators in high-rise office buildings, for example, is that many of them are programmed to behave differently on weekends than they do on weekends. As in the case of the Y2000-defective bank vault mentioned previously, a Y2000-defective elevator could erroneously conclude that January 1, 2000 was actually January 1, 1900—which was a Monday. In that case, it might revert to its weekend behavior on Thursday, January 5, 2000—which could leave office workers stranded on the top floor of the building while the elevator stubbornly parked on the ground floor.

Many of us have come to accept "intelligent devices" as commonplace, and we don't even stop to think about it any more. Thus, the prospect of a Y2000 failure requires us to pay much closer attention to the engines, appliances, and devices that are so much a part of our life. Indeed, sometimes the intelligent behavior is truly hidden from the end-user, as in the case of the fuel ignition and braking systems of a sophisticated modern automobile. Fortunately, the manufacturers of these devices and appliances are prone to brag about such features—for the next two years, it's worth paying attention to the TV commercials and newspaper ads to see whether the manufacturer is indirectly warning us of potential Y2000 problems.

If you identify a date-sensitive embedded system, the next question to ask is, "What *kind* of failure might this system exhibit if it's non-compliant?" In some cases, the failure might not affect you at all—e.g., your digital watch may display the wrong date, but if you use it *only* for displaying time-of-day, you might be able to live with the non-compliant behavior forever. Other problems may be annoying, but less onerous than a full-scale replacement of an expensive system. For example, it's conceivable that your automobile might display a red warning light on the dashboard, warning you that it's been 98 years since you last had it serviced; while annoying, it's probably something you can live with for a few weeks or months. On the other hand, a failure that causes a complete malfunction, or dangerous operating behavior, needs to be identified in advance. In some cases, you may be able to determine this yourself, but with the more sophisticated systems (e.g., your automobile, or the elevator system in your apartment building), it will require discussions with the manufacturer or vendor.

Fallback Advice: Two-Day Failures

From the perspective of an embedded system, there is no such thing as a Y2000-related two-day failure—the device either works, or it doesn't work. As we've already pointed out, defective Y2000 logic in an embedded device is essentially part of the hardware, not part of the changeable, modifiable software; thus, we don't have the option of calling in a programmer to make a few changes and thereby remedy the problem.

Thus, for household appliances, and other devices that are under your direct control and ownership, there is a simple reality: Once the device has failed, it has failed for good. In a few rare cases, you might be able to order a replacement micro-chip from the manufacturer, and replace the defective chip within the appliance unit; but in the majority of cases, you'll have to replace the entire device. If you're willing to pay for the replacement yourself (and if the stores are open, the lights are working, your credit card is operational, and so on), then you might be able to find a replacement within a day or two. But if you send the device back to the manufacturer for an upgrade/repair, it's likely to be months before you get it back.

The only scenario where the concept of a two-day disruption is relevant is the embedded device that's *not* under your direct control, but is instead controlled by a business or government agency that might have the resources to achieve a relatively quick replacement or repair. Thus, you might ask yourself: *What happens if the elevator in my apartment building has a Y2000 failure, and it takes the elevator company two-three days to replace the defective computer? What happens if the security system in my office building is defective, and nobody can get into the office for two-three days?* In most cases, the consequences won't be immediately life-threatening; the important thing is to plan for such contingencies in advance, so that you won't be taken by surprise.

Fallback Advice: One-Month Failures

Because a Y2000 failure in embedded systems requires replacement of a computer chip, we believe that most failures will indeed take much longer than two-three days to repair. Household appliances can be replaced in two-three days, even if it requires the expensive option of buying a new appliance at the local store. But that's not a viable option when we're dealing with elevators, office-security systems, and other expensive, sophisticated industrial-oriented embedded systems.

There are several areas where bottlenecks and delays are likely to occur. First, a "field" technician must be available—after all, we can't pull the elevator out of the office building and ship it back to the manufacturer, so a repair technician has to visit the office site to make the repairs. Ironically, the reason that many of these embedded systems will fail on January 1, 2000 is that even though the manufacturers already know that there products are defective, there aren't enough repair technicians available to fix them in advance. The problem won't get any better in the days immediately after January 1, 2000.

Second, the embedded system has to be located and "acquired," so that the repair work can be done. There's no problem locating the elevator in an office building, though there might be some minor problems "acquiring" it if it's stuck mid-way between two floors. But the situation described earlier with the Y2000-defective bank vault is a good example of the problem some companies will face; similar problems exist with embedded systems on the ocean floor, or in a satellite, or submerged in a mine shaft.

Third, a Y2000-compliant replacement chip has to be available. In the case of elevators and other sophisticated high-risk embedded systems, there's a very good chance that such chips will have been manufactured and stockpiled in advance. But this is less likely to be the case for the lower-risk, less-expensive devices, especially office machines and household appliances. Because the micro-chip industry is extremely competitive, and because the technology has been changing very rapidly, new chips are introduced on an annual basis, and sometimes even more frequently. Thus, if you have a vintage-1992 VCR device that turns out to be Y2000-defective, there's a very good chance that the manufacturer will politely explain that (a) it's no longer under warranty, (b) it's obsolete, (c) the chip manufacturer, from whom they acquired the chip to provide the VCR with its programmable intelligence, has discontinued that chip because it has a newer one that's 10 times faster and 3 times cheaper, (d) the new chip is installed in all of the current-vintage VCRs, but (e) the new chip won't work in the old VCR. Bottom line: You're screwed.

Thus, there is the distinct possibility that some of the embedded systems that you depend on will be out of service for a month or longer—until they can be replaced or upgraded with a Y2000-compliant micro-chip. If it's an embedded system that belongs to you, you'll have to decide whether it's worth replacing with a brand-new unit, which will probably be done at your own expense. Perhaps you can tolerate the absence of your phone/fax/copier/answering machine for a couple of days, but you simply can't operate your home-business for a month without such a device. The proactive strategy, of course, is to find out *now* whether the device is Y2000-compliant, so that you can remedy the problem (ideally at the manufacturer's expense, rather than your own) *before* January 1, 2000. But if that turns out to be impractical, then the post-2000 strategy for one-month disruptions of personally owned embedded systems is likely to be simple, straightforward, and expensive: Be prepared to spend money for replacements.

A one-month disruption in a corporate- or government-owned embedded system is obviously a different matter; as a private citizen, you don't have the option of replacing a Y2000-defective elevator in your apartment building. If embedded system failures occur within the office environment, it could lead to a month-long shutdown of your employer's business; thus, you may be faced with the unemployment scenarios that we discussed in Chapter 2. A month-long embedded system failure in hospitals could render some medical devices inoperable; this could lead to the scenarios we discussed in Chapter 9. And embedded system failures in the security, heating, air-conditioning, elevator, plumbing, and other environmental systems could render modern apartment buildings unsafe or unlivable for a month at a time; as we've discussed in previous chapters, you may need to plan for a vacation to a tropical island where you can live in a grass hut for a month.

Fallback Advice: One-Year Failures

Severe backlogs, delays, and associated problems could conceivably cause year-long disruptions for some of the embedded systems we've discussed. Again, this is not likely to be the case for simple household appliances: If the manufacturer of your VCR is unable or unwilling to provide a replacement, you can always buy one from a competitor. Household appliances, digital watches, and many other examples of embedded systems are *commodities* today, and while there might be a temporary shortage created by Y2000 problems, we don't expect that it will last for a year.

But the expensive, sophisticated, industrial-strength embedded systems are *not* commodities, and it's conceivable that the delays could last well beyond a month or two. In addition to the bottlenecks and delays already discussed above, the ability of, say, an elevator manufacturer to cope with all of the required upgrades and repairs of elevators that it has installed all over the country could be further impaired by the various "ripple effect" problems we've discussed throughout this book. Indeed, Brand-X elevator company could go bankrupt six months after the onset of Y2000 problems; the remaining elevator manufacturers could easily take the position that they're unable and unwilling to repair the products of their former competitor; they might insist that the elevator be completely replaced with one of their own products. Given the other problems and delays associated with the overall Y2000 phenomenon, it could well take a year before the Brand-X elevator has been replaced by a Brand-Y elevator.

Unfortunately, it's simply impossible to predict in advance where, when, and how such year-long Y2000 problems might occur. The only thing that we can be sure about is that if it *does* occur, it will necessitate an entirely different response, on your part, than a month-long failure requires. Thus, your fallback plan should be of a similar nature to the one-year disruption plans that you have for your job, your bank account, and other important aspects of your life.

Fallback Advice: Ten-Year Failures

As with the other aspects of Y2000 problems, it's hard to imagine anything having such a devastating impact that a full decade would be required to get things back to normal. The technology required to produce Y2000-compliant micro-chips already exists, and some vendors are already producing Y2000-compliant embedded systems with them. Even if some go bankrupt, and even if a substantial number of non-Y2000-compliant "legacy" chips had to be replaced, it wouldn't take more than a couple of years. So what's the problem?

Clearly, we're not concerned about long-term problems with household appliances; and when it comes to decade-long consequences, we're not even concerned about elevators in high-rise office buildings. What we *are* concerned about is the embedded systems in underwater oil-drilling rigs; or embedded systems in nuclear reactors; or embedded flight-control and guidance systems in military satellites and guided missiles; or embedded process control systems in a natural-gas refinery located at the edge of a city. There are a few such scenarios where a Y2000-related failure could involve radiation leaks, massive oil spills, or significant loss of life.

Obviously, these systems are beyond the control of ordinary citizens. You might want to write letters to your local community leaders and your Congressional representatives; if you're really concerned, you might want to participate in some lobbying efforts. But for the most part, we all have to hope that our business leaders and government officials are focusing their efforts on the high-risk problem areas of this kind, rather than wasting precious time and energy to ensure that everyone's $19.95 digital watch remains Y2000 compliant.

Endnotes

1. The important thing to remember about this is example is that there are additional opportunities for leap-year miscalculations on January 1, 2000. If a year is divisible by four, it's a leap year, unless the year is evenly divisible by 100 (e.g., the year 1900), in which case it's not But there's an exception to the exception: if the year is evenly divisible by 400, then it *is* a leap year.
2. See "Embedded systems: Analyst's take," *PC Week*, July 6, 1998; also available on the Internet at http://www.zdnet.com/pcweek/y2k/0798/06case1.html. In addition to documenting the 7 billion figure, the article also quotes Martha Daniel, president and CEO of Information Management Resources Inc. as saying that 10 percent of the chips are *not* Y2K-compliant.
3. See the May 18, 1998 report from the National Radio Astronomy Observatory at http://www.cv.nrao.edu/y2k/sighting.htm. Mr. Hall estimates that between 1 and 10 percent of the chips are date-sensitive.
4. See "Corporations Still Behind In Race Against Millennium Bug," Tim Wilson, *Internet Week*, August 17, 1998; also available on the Internet at http://www.techweb.com/se/directlink.cgi?INW19980817S0017.
5. See "Users Demand Y2K Lemon Aid," Joe Feeley, *Control Magazine*, March 1998; also available on the Internet at http://www.controlmagazine.com/0398/c0200398.html#1.
6. Frank Kane, "Moving to Millennium Meltdown," *The Times of India*, May 18, 1997.
7. See "Will the millennium bug give your operations the flu?" by Scott M. Shemwell, Jerry Dake and Bruce Friedman, *World Oil*, April 1998; also available on the Internet at http://www.gulfpub.com/wo/archive/archive_98-04/bug-shemwell.html.
8. Here's a more subtle variation, involving the older VCR's that do not allow the end-user to specify the year when programming the

device for recording sessions. The machine might still require the user to specify the year during the initial "set-up" configuration; equipped with this information, the device can calculate the day-of-the-week from the Julian date—e.g., it will be able to figure out that September 7, 1998 is a Monday. This is important for those occasions when you want to program the VCR to record your favorite show at 9:00 PM every Monday. But it's also a problem if the calculations are carried out in a non-compliant fashion; as we've discussed elsewhere in this book, January 1, 2000 is a Saturday, but January 1, 1900 was a Monday.

9. Jim Rivera, "Re: cars an Y2K?" comp.software.year-2000 USENET newsgroup, Tue, 29 Jul 1997 23:32:48 -0700.
10. See http://www.irm.state.ny.us/yr2000/embedlst.htm for a tabular layout of this list of items.

Y2000 Impact on Education

Because the [Y2K] difficulty is as far flung as the billions of microchips that run everything from farm equipment to VCRs, this is not a challenge that is susceptible to a single government program or an easy fix. It is a complex test that requires us all to work together—every government agency, every university, every hospital, every business, large and small.

President Bill Clinton, speech at the National Academy of Sciences, *July 14, 1998*

It is an axiom in political science that unless a people are educated and enlightened it is idle to expect the continuance of civil liberty or the capacity for self-government.

Texas Declaration of Independence, March 2, 1836

People commonly educate their children as they build their houses, according to some plan they think beautiful, without considering whether it is suited to the purposes for which they are designed.

Lady Mary Wortley Montagu Letter, 19 Feb. 1750, to her daughter Lady Bute (published in Selected Letters, edited by Robert Halsband, 1970)

Introduction

In earlier chapters, we drew the analogy between Y2000 disruptions and blizzards that can shut down a city for a few days. If you mention this to a school child, he or she will leap to the obvious inference: "A blizzard means no school. Do Y2000 problems mean no school, too?" To extend the analogy further, our answer might be: It's a question of degree. Just as a one-inch snowfall rarely closes a school, we can imagine a variety of minor Y2000 problems that would not interrupt the educational system. A twelve-inch snowfall probably would close most schools for a day or two, except in those regions of the country that experience heavy snow on a regular basis. And a three-foot blizzard, accompanied by gale winds and sub-zero temperatures, might keep schools closed for a week. We can easily imagine the equivalent degrees of serious Y2000 problems; the most serious Y2000 scenarios could close schools for a month, a year, or even longer.

The nature of a Y2000 impact on schools is similar to much of what we've discussed in earlier chapters. If electric power and/or other utilities (gas, oil, water, sewage, etc.) are disrupted, the schools have no alternative but to shut down. If there's no telephone service for a few days, it's questionable whether schools will continue operating. The same is likely to be true if food supplies (for school lunches) are disrupted, if the teachers can't travel to the schools because of breakdowns in the transportation systems, or if the school buses are unavailable to bring the children to the schools. School is a "job" for a number of adults, and thus it's vulnerable to the kinds of problems we discussed in Chapter 2; but the point we want to emphasize in this chapter is that school is a "job" for children, too. If schools shut down, then the children are out of "work" just like their parents.

Large school districts and universities often have computer systems as complex and widespread as the medium-sized business; school lessons, homework assignments, student-teacher communications, research, and scheduling of administrative activities, and payroll are all driven by computer programs. Of course, not every school is computerized, and not every school depends heavily on its computers; in some cases, the computers sit quietly in a "lab," to be used for the once-a-week "computer appreciation" courses. But it's quite different in most universities, and in some of the leading high schools; these schools are so thoroughly "wired" for computers that if the computers are shut off, the administration might as well turn off the lights, too. If the computers stop, the school comes very close to shutting down.

Another example of a heavily computerized school application is that of assigning students to classes, and assigning teachers to classes. The computer programs that carry out the scheduling assignments—which can be enormously complicated for high-school and college students—are definitely date-sensitive, and possibly Y2000-sensitive. In the simple case, the scheduling program might ask the school administrator to type in the day, month, and year of the beginning of a school semester; if the year is recorded as two digits, then the scheduling program might decide that its computations should be carried out for the year 1900, rather than 2000. As we noted in Chapter 11, the problem is that January 1, 2000 is a Saturday, while January 1, 1900 was a Monday. Thus, the Y2000-defective scheduling program might erroneously schedule children for Saturday and Sunday classes, which would obviously cause some confusion.[1]

While businesses have to worry about the Y2000 impact on their customers and their revenues, schools have a somewhat different perspective. Their "revenues" come from a local school district, which is augmented by monies received from state and local governments. Ultimately, all of this is derived from taxes: property taxes at the local level, and income taxes at the state and federal level. In addition, there are numerous forms of grants and subsidies—for school lunches, student loans and scholarships, grants to teachers, etc. None of this is likely to be affected in the first instant of January 1, 2000—but as we discussed in Chapter 10, government agencies at all levels are extremely vulnerable to Y2000 problems, which means that their ability to continue providing the stream of payments (by whatever name they're called) to schools, students, and teachers could be impaired within a matter of weeks or months. Thus, while schools might have sufficient funds in the bank (assuming the banks are still operating normally!) to last through the first half of 2000, a serious Y2000 problem in the government arena could keep the schools from opening in the fall of 2000. [2]

It's important to note that there are some differences between school-as-work and jobs-as-work. For one thing, we wouldn't want to expose our children to the kind of physical discomforts and dangers that an adult might have to tolerate in the event of a Y2000 disruption. In order to remain employed, adults might be willing to put up with a lack of heat in the office, or a lack of public transportation to travel to and from the office; it's far less practical to envision such a scenario for an eight-year-old child.

Another point to remember is that school serves as a surrogate baby-sitter for most parents. While children look forward with eager anticipation to "snow days" when they can stay home, parents find the experience doubly annoying: not only do they have more trouble getting to work, but they have to find a backup mechanism to take care of the children while they're home playing in the snow. High school and college students can look after themselves, of course, but one of the serious side-effects of a moderate, month-long Y2000 disruption is that parents will have to cope with the equivalent of a second summer vacation.

Finally, remember that a month or a year in a child's life has a different meaning than a month in an adult's life. A one-month Y2000 disruption would obviously be unpleasant for an adult, but it would probably be treated as "putting your life on hold" for a month. But a month-long disruption in the school schedule means that the required curriculum might not be fully covered; as a result, the school year might have to be extended. A more serious disruption of 6-12 months would mean that many students would have to repeat a year of school; among other things, this raises some interesting questions about tuition payments for colleges and private schools. University and private-school tuition payments for the first half of 2000 will be due and payable in December 1999, if not earlier. Thus, if a serious Y2000 disruption forces the school/college to shut down for an entire semester, a lot of grumpy parents will want their money back; and the *anticipation* of such a scenario might well prevent some parents from sending their tuition checks to the universities in December 1999.

Thus, the impact of Y2000 computer problems on the field of education may not be as fundamental and serious as the impact on other parts of the economy or social infrastructure—but it's serious enough that it ought not to be ignored. In particular, it *can't* be ignored by parents of young children, since a shutdown of the schools would eliminate the surrogate baby-sitter service upon which they rely.

Fallback Advice: Two-Day Disruptions

As with most of the previous chapters, there isn't a strong argument for planning for two-day disruptions in the educational infrastructure. While such disruptions could theoretically occur at any point during 2000, it's most likely that they will occur during the first few days of January. College students are likely to be enjoying their Christmas break at that point, since most colleges and universities don't resume classes until mid-January or later. But it's possible that high-school and elementary school students will be scheduled to return to school on Monday, January 3rd. Be prepared to keep the kids home for a couple of days.

Fallback Advice: One-Month Disruptions

If Y2000 problems turn out to be somewhat more severe, students may be faced with a one-month sabbatical. As noted earlier, this can cause problems in households where both parents work; if you anticipate this level of Y2000 disruption, it would be a good idea to plan for backup babysitting or child-care services in advance. Don't depend on government-sponsored day-care centers; they're likely to have problems of their own. Instead, make arrangements to have older siblings, grandparents, or neighbors look after your children. Just as many adults have found it beneficial to car-pool, they may find it useful to pool their babysitting and child-care services. The details will obviously vary from family to family, but the key point is to create a network of sympathetic and like-minded parents or family members *before* January 1, 2000.

As noted above, a one-month disruption in the educational schedule may cause problems with the school's requirement to cover a minimum educational curriculum (a requirement often imposed at the state level, in return for certification and eligibility for funding). If schools are shut down for the month of January, 2000 then it's possible that the school year will be extended an extra month into the summertime; but it's also possible that school districts will expect children to catch up on homework, reading assignments, and written reports on their own. Thus, if you're concerned about the possibility of your child falling behind, you should meet with the child's teachers in late 1999 to get as much information as possible about upcoming educational topics and work assignments. Since month-long Y2000 disruptions could occur at any point in 2000 (e.g., if the school budget is exhausted in the spring of 2000, and the state and Federal agencies are unable to provide their normal funding), you may need to continue meeting periodically with the teachers to ensure that you're always a month ahead of your child's current assignment.

Keep in mind that you'll probably be coping with your own Y2000 disruptions during this period. If your office shuts down and you have to stay home for a month, then you'll have plenty of time to deal with your child's school problems. But it's also possible that you'll be spending longer-than-normal hours traveling to and from work, as well as dealing with the extraordinary problems of providing food, shelter, and clothing for your family in the post-2000 days. Thus, advance planning to cope with your child's problem will be all the more important.

Fallback Advice: One-Year Disruptions

A one-year disruption sounds almost unbelievable—after all, how difficult can it be to get the lights back on, and the children back in school? But remember that many of the schools in crowded urban areas are already facing disruptions—budget problems, union problems with custodians and teachers, overcrowding, asbestos and other health problems, violence and crime in the classroom, and so forth. There is very little in the way of a "reserve buffer" to deal with extraordinary problems, and Y2000 could well turn out to be just such a problem. If the school district's payroll computers break down, for example, or if the banks experience severe problems, then the teachers, custodians, and administrators won't get paid; and in a school district where there's already a lot of union-management strife, it won't take long for the affected workers to go on strike. Combined with the various other problems that the schools may be facing, it won't take more than a month or two of disruptions before some schools will simply declare that they're closed for the semester—or until the beginning of the following year's school term.

Obviously, no one wants this to happen, and we think the chances are relatively small; if it does happen, it's likely to be on a community-by-community basis. But it *could* happen—and if it does, the situation will be qualitatively different than a one-month vacation or a two-day holiday. College students and high school students might spend the year working (assuming the economy hasn't collapsed a la the Great Depression), or finding ways to help their parents cope with the strain of a severe Y2000 disruption—but what can you do if your elementary school child has no school to attend for the entire year of 2000?

The straightforward strategy is to extend the backup-babysitting mechanism discussed above, so that a relative or trusted neighbor continues to look after your children. But this is a lot to ask, unless there are grandparents available on almost a full-time basis to take on the burden of child care. Perhaps more important, the typical American parent would be deeply concerned about "wasting" a year that could be, and should be, spent educating the child in the traditional reading-writing-arithmetic skills. We can imagine some lively debates among educators and parents about a child's mind will stagnate after a year away from the traditional classroom—but it's a safe bet that many parents will consider it unacceptable.

The possible solution, if you're truly concerned about this, is home-schooling. Approximately 1.1 million students are already acquiring their elementary and/or secondary-school education in this fashion[3]—either for religious or political reasons, or because they (or their parents) feel that the locally available schools are inadequate. Accredited home-schooling institutions already exist, and appropriate educational materials can be acquired at a moderate cost; if you're interested in pursuing this option, a good starting point is The Home School

Resource Center on the Internet at http://www.rsts.net/home/home.html or the National Home School Association at http://www.alumni. caltech.edu/~casner/nha.html.

Fallback Advice: Ten-Year Disruptions

If you've been following the line of thinking that we've documented in previous chapters, you can probably anticipate the nature of our ten-year concern for education. We're not concerned that the "physical plant" of the schools will collapse if they're shut down for a few months, or even a year. We're not concerned that teachers are going to commit mass hara-kiri and vanish from the face of the earth; and we're not concerned that books will be burned, or that the supply of pens and paper will disappear. Schools that are highly dependent on computers today—especially the ones that depend on computer-based training, as well as networked interactions between students and teachers—might have an adjustment period if a severe Y2000 problem rendered all of the existing computers unusable. But the adjustment wouldn't take more than a year or two—and we suspect that a large number of teachers would be secretly overjoyed to get rid of computers, and return to the "old-fashioned" approach to teaching.

So what's the problem? Simple: As noted above, most schools survive because of funding provided by three levels of government bureaucracy. And that's only the direct funding; some schools survive only because of the proliferation of grants, scholarships, and funding sent to students and parents in order to enable the child to attend the school. We've already noted in previous chapters that the current form of Social Security, unemployment benefits, food stamps, Medicare, and welfare benefits could disappear in the event of a severe Y2000 crisis—and by the same argument, the same could happen to the current mechanisms for funding schools, and subsidizing students.

This is not as radical and far-fetched as it may seem. After all, there are ongoing debates about the ineffectiveness of the education-oriented spending and initiatives at the federal level, with periodic proposals that the Department of Education be eliminated entirely. At the state level, many states—including, for example, California—have been faced with steadily shrinking budgets, which in turn have forced cutbacks throughout many of the state universities whose attractiveness is at least partly due to the low tuition costs enjoyed by state residents. Even at the local level, there continue to be battles over funding, with scattered incidents of budget cutbacks.

Even with a severe, long-term Y2000 crisis, we don't think for a moment that American parents would decide to stop educating their children. But they might well find that the government bureaucracy has been paralyzed, and that Senate/House leaders voted into office in November 2000 want to focus their emergency-aid activities on more pressing issues of providing food and jobs. As a result, control *and* funding of the nation's school system could revert entirely to the local level, at least in the short- to medium-term. And while that might be a welcome change for some neighborhoods—especially the affluent neighborhoods that could acquire funding directly from the parents and local property owners—it could be a disaster for the urban ghettos and rural areas whose school systems are heavily dependent on government funding.[4]

In the long run, a severe Y2000 crisis could be the catalyst that causes the nation's educational system to be completely re-examined and overhauled. Perhaps the year 2010 will see a nation-wide school system with a uniform curriculum, and testing standards for both students and teachers, administered by a newly chartered federal agency. Or perhaps we will see the opposite end of the spectrum in 2010: Perhaps a national consensus will conclude that the federal government should play no role at all in deciding how our children should be educated, and that even the states should play a minimal role, with far less funding authority than they have now. In the long run, perhaps the educational system will be transformed into something far better... or something far worse.

In the long run, of course, we'll all be dead. And in the "long run" of 10 years, a child of 8 will have become a young adult of 18, at which point any discussion of reforming the elementary and high schools is moot—at least for that child, and for the generation of his or her peers. Thus, if you're not planning to have any children until 2005, you can afford to wait and see how things turn out, assuming that we're halfway through a severe Y2000 crisis at that point. But if you have young children now, you don't have the luxury of waiting a decade—children can't be put into a cryogenic freezer, to be thawed when the crisis passes.

As with the other "severe crisis" scenarios we've postulated, there's nothing specific that we can recommend at this point. The likelihood of a crisis so severe that it essentially paralyzes the current educational system for a decade is sufficiently small that 95 percent of the parents in this country would probably reject any serious proposal to remove their children from the public school system in 1999, with the intention of providing the remainder of their education at home.[5]

But it's important to note that parents won't be forced to make such an extreme decision in the early days of January, 2000. If the Y2000 crisis does turn out to be severe, it might be a matter of months, if not more, before the reality becomes widely accepted. Indeed, one of the paradoxes of the ripple-effect that we've discussed throughout this book is that there might be *no* Y2000 crises within the schools themselves; but apparently unrelated Y2000 crises in business or government could eventually trigger the kind of economic crisis that could lead to severe budget cutbacks and policy changes. Thus, in this worst-case scenario, it might not be until 2001 or 2002 that the trends became unmistakably clear; but at that point, it might be too late to begin making plans for alternative education schemes.

We've deliberately avoided offering our personal opinions about the state of the current educational system, or what the best possible outcome might be. From the perspective of the Y2000 phenomenon, our personal opinions and your personal opinions don't matter much at all. If a catastrophic Y2000 disruption occurs, it will create an entirely new, unique—

and unmistakably alien and frightening—environment, in which old political opinions will be radically altered, and new ones created overnight. As we've suggested throughout this book, when discussing the possibility of severe Y2000 disruptions, flexibility and self-sufficiency will be extremely important for weathering the storm. It's difficult enough for adults to do this; it's all the more difficult when trying to plan for the education of one's child.

And perhaps this is a good way to wrap up the message of this chapter: Even if you don't feel like making Y2000 contingency plans for your own sake, do it for the sake of your children. No matter what happens, and no matter how bad the Y2000 crisis may be, it will be today's children that will carry our culture and civilization into the decades of 2010 and 2020. We need to protect them and prepare them as best we can, even if our own lives are exhausted in the process of doing so.

Endnotes

1. This may turn out to be one of the examples where a technique known as the "28 year rollback" might work. It turns out that 1972 has the same cycle of days-of-the-week and leap year as 2000 (and 1971 has the same characteristics as 1999, etc.). Thus, if the scheduling program is told to prepare a schedule of student assignments for 1972, it should produce the same results as if the program had been Y2000 compliant in the first place. This strategy doesn't always work (for reasons that are too obscure and technical to describe in detail here), and most computer professionals regard it as a temporary strategy, at best.
2. One university professor responded to this paragraph in the first edition of our book with the comment, "At some universities like mine, Federal Assistance is important for enrollment. No Federal Assistance for our students and no enrollment. Will the Depart-

ment of Education be ready? Who knows—but students may not get student aid and not be able to attend." Unfortunately, the prognosis as of June 1998 was not very encouraging: as we pointed out in Chapter 10, the Education Department was given a "D" rating by the Congressional committee overseeing Y2000 preparation efforts, with an estimate that it would not finish its Y2000 remediation work until 2002.

3. See Karl M. Bunday, "Homeschooling Has Been Growing Rapidly in Recent Years," available on the Internet at http://www.concentric.net/~kmbunday/homeschool_growth.html.

4. An example will help illustrate this point. One of the authors has a friend whose role as a single parent is more difficult than most of us experience: his children are physically handicapped, and without personalized, expensive assistance from specialists within the school system, their education would suffer enormously. After months of investigation and analysis, and several more months of difficult personal changes (changing jobs, selling his house, etc.), our friend moved his family from California to Nevada. The reason: California's budget cutbacks have severely curtailed the availability and quality of special assistance his children need, while the lucrative gambling profits of Nevada's casinos have helped to create a generous state educational system in Nevada, which *does* provide a superior level of educational assistance. Fortunately, our friend's children will have finished their schooling before January 1, 2000; the planning and decision-making process would have been enormously complicated if it had been necessary to take Y2000 into account. Our friend is a computer expert, so he is fully aware of the Y2000 problem; the point is that such decisions need to be made carefully, and in advance, for once having been made, they are extremely difficult to change at a moment's notice.

5. The study by Karl Bunday, cited earlier, indicates that approximately 1.1 million students, out of a total of 46 million students nationwide, are already receiving their education through various forms of home-schooling. That's slightly more than 2 percent of the student population already, so it's not entirely unreasonable to suggest that advance warning of a Y2000 crisis in 1999 might cause a lot more parents to pull their kids out of the public school system.

Y2000 Impact on Telephone and Mail Services

The consequences of the millennium bug, if not addressed, could simply be a rash of annoyances, like being unable to use a credit card at the supermarket... It could affect electric power, phone service, air travel, major governmental service.

President Bill Clinton, Speech at the National Academy of Sciences, *July 14, 1998*

Transport of the mails, transport of the human voice, transport of flickering pictures—in this century as in others our highest accomplishments still have the single aim of bringing men together.

Antoine de Saint-Exupéry Wind, Sand, and Stars, Chapter 3 (published in Terre des Hommes, *1939)*

Introduction

In the midst of writing the first edition of this book in the summer of 1997, United Parcel Service (UPS) experienced a 16-day nationwide strike. Though memories of that strike have now faded, it was sobering to learn that approximately 5-7 percent of the nation's Gross Domestic Product (GDP) moves through UPS. Thus, the strike had an immediate and pervasive effect on the nation's economy; the nightly TV news reports during that period showed numerous small businesses and individuals whose lives were already being affected.

Of course, we would have preferred that the strike had not occurred—but it did have one unexpected positive result: It demonstrated quite vividly how dependent society is on the smooth functioning of a complex, interconnected infrastructure. It may be difficult to accept the possibility of banking failures or power-grid failures we've discussed in this book, and the comparison between a Y2000-related computer failure and a blizzard may seem too academic for some readers. But the UPS strike was very real and relatively recent, and since UPS moves 12 million packages a day, it didn't take long before everyone was affected.

UPS and its competitors—Federal Express, DHL, and so forth—provide one form of communication. And while the recent strikes illustrated the importance of these service-providers, an even more critical form of communications is also threatened by the Y2000 problem: telecommunications. The importance of telecommunications was underscored by a more recent event that occurred while we were preparing the second edition of this book: The failure of a single computer in the Galaxy IV satellite (and the subsequent failure of the on-board backup computer to operate) on May 19, 1998 caused widespread problems across the country. As Joel Willemsen, of the General Accounting Office, observed in testimony to the Oversight Subcommittee of the House Ways and Means Committee on June 16, 1998:

> *Another failure occurred on May 19, 1998, when a communications satellite went into an uncontrolled spin after failure of a control system. The satellite's failure disrupted the operations of credit card authorization services, paging services for 80 to 90 percent of all pagers in the United States, and the distribution of television programs. While these failures were not caused by a Year 2000 problem, they illustrate the degree to which we depend upon reliable, available, interoperable telecommunications.*[1]

We'll begin this chapter by discussing the impact of Y2000 problems on the telephone, fax, electronic mail, and Internet services; then we'll discuss the mail services. This will lead to our now-familiar set of guidelines for coping with minor, moderate, serious, and devastating Y2000-induced disruptions.

Telephone, Fax, and E-mail

Along with banking and the electric power grid, the nation's telecommunications network is part of what a colleague, Steve Heller, refers to as the "iron triangle." If any component of the iron triangle fails in a Y2000 collapse, the other two are likely to fail quickly, too. And if the iron triangle goes down, most of what we refer to as "modern society" goes down with it.

Obviously, we could survive for a while without the social use of telephones—e.g., the phenomenon of teenagers spending hours on the phone each evening with their friends. And obviously, some businesses can get along without phones: The corner newspaper stand, and many other mom-and-pop businesses might still expect their customers to show up in person to transact business. But Wall Street and the nation's banks cannot function without telephones; nor can the vast majority of large businesses carry on their day-to-day operations with customers, suppliers, partners, and vendors. Indeed, it even turns out that the electric utilities and railroads are highly dependent on reliable telecommunications.

Similarly, a shut-down of the telephone system means, for all practical purposes, that the Internet and the World-Wide Web, and the pervasive phenomenon of electronic mail, grinds to a halt. After we had posted the draft versions of the first edition of our manuscript on the Internet in 1997, we received an email message from the Network Operations manager of a small Internet Service Provider (ISP):

> *...Y2K is almost certainly the death of the Internet.*
>
> *It's a problem on multiple levels: many OSs that act as Internet routers are not Y2K compliant. Many older hardware platforms aren't Y2K compliant. Worse, even state-of-the-art routers aren't Y2K compliant on the embedded systems and OS level.*
>
> *Example: we run two [vendor name] routers. [Vendor name] isn't Y2K-compliant, though it's at a more esoteric level than other OSs.*
>
> *Most shockingly, however, are our brand new [vendor name] routers. I'm uncertain about the chip-level, but I know for a certainty that the*

> *firmware isn't Y2K-compliant—[vendor name] admits as much. The Internet is filled with [vendor name] routers...*
>
> *I've got a spare router for testing that I plan to put on a test network filled with non-Y2K-compliant machines and "roll them over" to see what happens. I'll advise you when this is done and inform you of the results.*
>
> *I'm advising my employer to be sure our contract language specifies we'll provide Internet connectivity only on hardware and software actually owned by my company. We'll not guarantee service over any other hardware / software—which includes Ameritech, WorldCom MFS, Nap.net, and anyone else in ours or other routing tables.*
>
> *One thing I'm certain of: I'm out of a job on 1-1-2000.*[2]

This sounds alarmist in nature, and it's important to realize that we are *not* trying to construct an end-of-the-world scenario. We're not trying to suggest that all phones, everywhere in the world, will fail permanently on January 1, 2000. But we *are* suggesting that some phone companies could stop providing service to their customers for a few days, or perhaps a month... or possibly longer. Again, we remind you that a few days of a UPS strike caused significant discomfort across the country—what would be the impact of a three-day outage on the part of AT&T, MCI, or Sprint? What happens if a combination of network switching problems, billing problems, and bureaucratic snafus shuts down the phone system in your company for a month?

We're not the only ones with such concerns. On April 28, 1998, the chairman of the Federal Communications Commission (FCC), William Kennard, made the following comments in testimony before the Senate Committee on Commerce, Science, and Transportation:[3]

> *At the FCC, we are very concerned that the Year 2000 problem has the potential of disrupting communications services worldwide. The communications infrastructure is absolutely critical, not only to the economy, including the general commerce, transportation and banking sectors represented on this panel today, but also to national preparedness, military, public safety, emergency and personal communications.*
>
> *Every sector of the communications industry—broadcast, cable, radio, satellite, and wireline and wireless telephony—could be affected: the United States Emergency Alert System relies on television and radio broadcasts, the transmission of which may be affected by the Year 2000 problem; in some areas of the country, radio, cable and satellite systems are the only sources of up-to-date news and information; and police, fire departments and other emergency personnel rely on radio systems to communicate. We must ensure that all of these forms of communications continue uninterrupted.*
>
> *All sectors of the global economy, including financial markets, depend upon reliable telecommunications networks to conduct transactions. It therefore is critical that telecommunications networks continue to be able to handle national and international financial transactions. Every night, billions of dollars in financial transactions move across the country and around the world over telecommunications circuits. Any failure to handle that special traffic correctly could cause a major economic disruption. Because global telecommunications rely upon the*

seamless interconnection of networks, the international dimensions of the Year 2000 problem are especially significant.

Satellite systems also present a significant concern to us. Satellite systems interface with virtually every aspect of the global economy, including banks, air traffic systems, cable systems, and government systems. Failure to make satellite systems Year 2000 compliant could cause disruptions in a range of day-to-day activities. . . .

Because we cannot know how many of the Year 2000 problems will be fixed by January 1, 2000, it is impossible to make an accurate prediction about what will happen on that date. That will depend entirely upon how well industry deals with the problem—how much time, attention, money, and staff they devote to fixing their computer and communications systems. . . .

For the record, the large telecommunication vendors *do* plan to finish repairing their internal systems and hardware by the end of 1998, with most of 1999 spent on testing. AT&T network operations center spokesman Dave Johnson commented to the *Oklahoman Online* journal on June 25, 1998:

In 1997, the company spent $113 million for 2000 compliance, Johnson said. "This year we have budgeted $350 million. We want to be 95 percent or more compliant at the end of this year. Then we will wrap up whatever loose ends there are next year. But we are basically going on record that by the end of June of next year, we will be 100 percent on line, and we will have tested, double-tested and triple-tested everything to make sure it does work right."

But it's a huge effort, not only for AT&T, but for all the other major telecommunication vendors. GTE has budgeted $350 million for its Y2000 efforts, and has assigned 1,200 people to work on the project.[4] MCI is spending $400 million;[5] Sprint plans to spend $200 million through the end of 1999; Bell Atlantic expects to spend $200-$300 million; SBC Communications has budgeted just under $250 million for its modifications and has "300+" programmers working on the project;[6] and BellSouth set its cost at $100-$200 million through the turn of century.[7] AT&T has budgeted $500 million, has "thousands" of people working on the problem, and has described the overall effort as "possibly the most critical problem" it has ever faced.[8]

These are massive amounts of money, which obviously implies massive projects (i.e., with hundreds, or even thousands, of software professionals); as we've noted throughout this book, the software industry has a notorious track record of missing deadlines and budgets for such projects. But let's assume for the moment that all of the individual telephone companies (including even the 1,400 smaller firms) finish repairing their own systems in late 1998 or early 1999. That still leaves the problem of system-wide testing—and as FCC Commissioner Michael K. Powell testified[9] before the Senate Special Committee on the Year 2000 Technology Problem on July 31, 1998, it's a difficult problem indeed:

> *Without a doubt, the telecommunications network is a tremendously complex and interdependent thing, and consists of millions of*

interconnected parts. The public switched telephone network processes millions of calls per minute. To transit each and every call, automated and intelligent machines and systems (in the possession of the thousands of telecommunications carriers and users described above) make calculations for the most efficient multi-path, real-time interaction of all points along the established circuit between the call's origination and destination.

For example, in milli-seconds, a phone call from Washington, D.C. to New York travels from your telephone, to the Private Branch Exchange (i.e., switchboard) in your building, to the local exchange carrier's central office switch, through the carrier's network components and systems that route your call to an inter-exchange carrier (or carriers), through long-distance trunk lines (or other telecommunications facilities like microwave, satellite, fiber optic), to another local exchange carrier's central switch, and ultimately to the telephone on the other end. Make the same call two minutes later and the call may be routed in a completely different manner as calculated by the network.

The foregoing description points to the mathematical impossibility (i.e., the infinite number of permutations and combinations of routing possibilities and service events to transit a voice or data call) of testing the entire public telephone network for Year 2000-readiness or of expressing a high degree of confidence about the readiness of the network. If any one of those components/ systems (e.g., central office switch), network elements (e.g., advance intelligent network, Signaling System 7), or network interconnectors (e.g., local exchange carrier, interexchange carrier,

Internet Service Provider, private telecommunications network user) is affected by the Year 2000 Problem, a call might be disrupted.

There are three aspects of telephone service that concern us: the network switches, the "private branch exchange" (PBX) systems that control the internal telecommunications in most large offices throughout the country, and the financial/administrative systems within the "carrier" companies.

Network switches are the devices that establish the connection between your phone and another phone whenever you make or receive a call; indeed, several switches are likely to be involved in a telephone conversation, unless both parties live in the same local neighborhood. The switches are manufactured by companies such as Lucent Technologies, Inc. (formerly Bell Telephone Laboratories), Nortel, Inc., and Siemens AG. Until the mid-1960s, the switches consisted mostly of massive electromechanical relays, with relatively little software-based intelligence; but starting with products known as ESS-1 ("Electronic Switching System 1"), Bell Labs began introducing computerized switches that were faster, cheaper, smaller, more energy-efficient, and far more sophisticated. Combined with the computer systems provided by the carriers (AT&T, Sprint, MCI, GTE, and so forth), the switches support call-forwarding, call-waiting, call-blocking, caller-ID, and a variety of services that simply didn't exist 25 years ago.

Although the switching systems are not responsible for billing or any of the other accounting and finance applications within the phone company, they play one vital role, vis-à-vis Y2000 problems: They record the starting time and ending time of a telephone call. And because a phone call can cross the "boundary" between one day and the next, or one month and the next, or one year and the next (e.g., a 10-minute call originating at 11:55 PM on New Year's Eve), the switch has to record the year, date, hour, minute, and second of the beginning and ending of the phone call.

What makes the situation particularly difficult is that long-distance calls and overseas calls almost inevitably involve multiple network switches, which may have been manufactured by several different vendors. Thus, if some switches are Y2000-compliant and others are not, the phone call may not get through.

Since all of the switch manufacturers are aware of the Y2000 problem, and most (if not all) have already produced Y2000-compliant versions of their products, our optimistic assumption is that all of the major carriers will have upgraded or replaced any faulty switches by the end of the decade. But as the British telecommunication authorities have warned, we also need to worry about the Y2000-compliance status of international telephone companies; while most of the concern centers on telephone companies in Africa and various developing nations,[10] it turns out that many countries in the Asia-Pacific region are also behind schedule on their Y2000 projects.[11]

Joel Willemsen's June 16, 1998 testimony to Oversight Subcommittee of the House Ways and Means Committee, cited above, included the following sobering commentary on the international situation:

> *FCC has also noted that Year 2000 issues have not received the same level of attention abroad as in the United States, with the exception of the United Kingdom. This was confirmed by the results of the State Department's initiative to assess the Year 2000 readiness of foreign carriers. As shown in table 2, the department received information from 113 countries, updated through March 1998. Of those, 25 countries (22 percent) expected to be compliant by this December; 26 countries (23 percent) expected to be compliant by December 1999; 33 countries (29 percent) stated that they were addressing the Year 2000 issue but were having problems; and 29 countries (26 percent) were unaware of or had not begun to address the problem. The State Department is continuing its activities to determine the Year 2000 readiness of its foreign posts, and is developing contingency plans to ensure continuity of diplomatic telecommunications services. . . .*

Much of the international telephone traffic today uses satellites; thus, it's also important to ensure that the satellites themselves, as well the ground-based systems that communicate with the satellites, are Y2000-compliant. In July 31, 1998 testimony before the U.S. Senate Special Committee on the Year 2000 Technology Problem, Ramu Potarazu, Vice President and Chief Information Officer of INTELSAT, made the following comments:[12]

Our satellite manufacturers have advised us that there are no known Year 2000 problems on our satellites. Typically, a communications satellite does not use a time and a date. It uses a satellite reference, what we commonly refer to as "satellite local time." This is a reference to the sun. When there is a reference to the sun, there usually is no reference to a specific year. INTELSAT's own analysis and testing will seek to confirm this information. Thus, at this time, we do not believe that our INTELSAT satellites have any Year 2000 issues. Satellites are only one piece of the INTELSAT system...

Now, let me turn to your next question: "What are INTELSAT's concerns about international communications?" This, quite frankly, is INTELSAT's biggest concern and is one that is mostly out of our control. The customer satellite dishes and the local phone companies, broadcasters, business networks, and other end users, are the biggest challenge in addressing the Year 2000 issue. Because these entities are out of our control, our emphasis has been on education.

Many of the customer earth stations throughout the world have several hundred pieces of computer equipment from various manufacturers that control their ability to receive telecommunications information. For example, if the antenna control units fail at the customer location, this failure could cause complete loss of pointing to the satellite by the antenna. And no information could be sent or received even though the INTELSAT portion is compliant.

Perhaps I can use an illustration to demonstrate INTELSAT's concerns about Year 2000 issues affecting international satellite communica-

> *tions. A significant part of INTELSAT's international system is a two-way communication that uses an INTELSAT satellite between country A and country B. Suppose country A's ground network is Year 2000 compliant. INTELSAT, being the supply chain in the middle, is also compliant. And suppose, further, that country B's ground network is not Year 2000 compliant. The result: you will have a failure of the complete chain. This is why INTELSAT has some concerns about the Year 2000 compliance of all international communications.*

And closer to home, we need to worry about the status of the *thousands* of smaller telephone companies[13] that have sprung up in the current environment of deregulation. One of the authors, for example, spent the summer of 1997 working on the first edition of this book in a small town in northwestern Montana; telephone service in the region was provided by such tiny companies as the Blackfoot Telephone Cooperative, the Ronan Telephone Company, and PTI Communications—but *not* the major regional "Baby Bell" companies. If these tiny telephone companies turn out to be non-Y2000 compliant, the local residents won't get much solace from the fact that AT&T, Sprint, and MCI have upgraded their computers. Indeed, the problem could be worse: Non-compliant data generated by the small telecom vendors could corrupt the systems of the large companies.

The problem faced by many of the telephone companies is that in addition to updating their own computer systems, and their own connections to standard network switches, they're also faced with the need to establish more and more links with new telecommunication vendors spawned by the current environment of deregulation. Connections to cellular vendors, "personal communication service" (PCS) vendors, Internet vendors, and startup telecommunication vendors has created a small degree of chaos within the telecommunications industry, which further complicates the Y2000 problem.

One of the most important kinds of telecommunications switches is the PBX system installed in many medium- and large-sized companies, as well as government agencies. The Y2000 problem is particularly significant for "call centers" that handles tens of thousands of calls each day for reservations, telephone mail-order centers, customer service and inquiry hot-lines, etc. A recent article in a computer trade magazine estimated that "as much as 25% of installed call-center equipment may need to be replaced to handle the year 2000."[14] One of the reasons for this is that approximately half of the companies with PBX systems don't upgrade their technology regularly, and "most of the installed base [of customers] is at least two software releases behind [the current version].

And this raises the obvious question: Are the network switching computers Y2000-compliant? The answer is that most, if not all, of the major switch vendors have been offering Y2000-compliant switch products since the mid-90s. But even the most reputable manufacturers will acknowledge that their older products had problems:[15]

The R2 Call Management System, provided by Lucent and based on AT&T's old 3B2 computer, will not function because the 3B2 does not recognize the year 2000 as a valid date. "It really breaks, and we recognized that up front," admits Tom Nash, call-center offer manager for Lucent, the former AT&T unit that now supports the R2. Lucent recommends that R2 customers upgrade to newer equipment. The customers will get a 20% discount from the normal upgrade price of $40,000 to $75,000. Lucent guarantees that any of its products introduced after Sept. 30, 1996, will be year 2000-compliant—or Lucent will pick up the tab for making the products compliant.

While all of this is being discussed openly and candidly in the computer trade magazines, it's quite likely that many smaller companies are completely unaware that their PBX phone system is vulnerable. Others have heard of it, but are procrastinating because of the cost of an upgrade. And if these companies suddenly decide to upgrade their systems in late 1998 or 1999, they may find it's too late—because, as we discussed in Chapter 11, the PBX systems, like most embedded systems, require a field-service technician to visit the office and install the upgrade. One of the authors has a colleague who is a nationally recognized Y2000 expert; during an email dialogue, the expert offered the following observation:

My problems with the electrical and telephone companies is that without them, nothing else works. Clearly, banking and finance is next. My guess is that finance is in better shape than the other two, especially because of this wall of silence. I don't have a lot of information on the subject, except for a friend of mine who used to be the head of the GTE Y2K project. His estimates are that it will take about 1/2 day to fix each of their switches and they have 500,000 switches! The problem is numbers here and everywhere else.

If this estimate is correct, it would require an army of approximately 1,000 people, working full-time for a full year, to fix all of the switches. Lucent, Mitel, Nortel, and the other vendors are dealing with similar numbers; all of these vendors are likely to face increasing backlogs of upgrade and repair work as the calendar moves into 1999.

Finally, we need to mention the "business applications" in all of the telephone companies—including not only the vendors of switching systems, but also the major carriers like AT&T and MCI, as well as the regional operating companies (Bell Atlantic, Southwestern Bell, and the like), and the smaller local telephone companies. These computer systems handle the billing, record-keeping, scheduling of phone installations and repairs, as well as the internal marketing, administrative, and financial operations of the company. Industry experts estimate that AT&T has 500 million lines of code to analyze, and Sprint has 100 million lines; MCI has not publicly disclosed the scope of its Y2000-related software portfolio.[16]

As we've discussed in previous chapters, Y2000 problems in this software could lead to billing problems, erroneous decisions to block calls or shut off service, and various other customer-related difficulties. Thus, in the worst case, your phone could be shut off even though the switching network is operating perfectly.

Mail and Parcel Post: FedEx, UPS, DHL, and the U.S. Postal Service

The 1997 UPS strike demonstrated that disruptions can come from human causes, in addition to the Y2000-related problems we've discussed in this book. The strike also provided some interesting statistics about the size and importance of the shipping industry. In 1996, the combination of domestic air shipments, domestic ground shipments, parcel and air exports amounted to 4.7 billion shipments and $65.3 billion in revenue. UPS currently holds approximately 63 percent of the market share (and 80 percent of ground shipment of packages), while Federal Express has 13 percent, and the U.S. Postal Service comes in third with 4 percent. [17]

Another interesting tidbit from the strike was the size of the air fleet that UPS uses to move its packages: The company has 200 of its own aircraft, plus approximately 300 chartered airplanes, which serve 400 airports in the U.S., and 200 airports in other countries. The strike by 185,000 UPS workers was further exacerbated by 2,000 pilots who are members of the Independent Pilots Association, and who refused to fly during the strike.[18]

One last item: Because of early threats and predictions of the UPS strike, some companies made contingency plans in advance—just as some companies will be doing if there is a Y2000-induced disruption in the shipping industry. As the *New York Times* reported:

> *Some of America's biggest businesses, especially those that do a heavy mail-order trade, had seen the strike coming and made contingency plans, arranging for their products to be shipped by Federal Express and other air express companies or through the United States Postal Service. But the extra load on those services was a burden as well as a boon. U.P.S. normally handles 80 percent of packages shipped by ground nationwide, and transportation experts say FedEx and the postal system cannot take up all the slack.*[19]

While the UPS strike focused attention on parcel-post packages and overnight courier mail, we mustn't forget "ordinary" mail, which is transported primarily by the U.S. Postal Service (USPS) as first-class, second-class, bulk-rate mail, and various other categories. USPS interacts with 7 million customers daily, in 40,000 post offices, and processes an average of more than 600 *million* mail pieces daily, of which approximately 14 percent is carried by air.[20] Because it deals with stamps, money orders, and various other financial functions, as well as an enormously complex mail-sorting and logistics operation, its computer systems are as complex as most of those in the major Federal government agencies we discussed in Chapter 10.

What does this tell us about the Y2000 situation? Simply that if a disruption similar to the 1997 UPS strike should occur, it will have a noticeable impact almost immediately. If the disruption lasts more than a few days, or if it hits more than one carrier, then businesses across the country will find it increasingly difficult to ship products, contracts, and other packages.

It's easy to understand how a union strike can bring a major shipping carrier to a halt. But what kind of problems would a Y2000 software bug cause? Here are a few:

- A substantial number of cross-country and international shipments; all of the major carriers have their own air fleet, though not as large as the UPS fleet. We've already seen in Chapter 4 how Y2000 problems could ground the country's air traffic; this could affect not only the passenger airlines, but also the cargo and package transport flights.

- UPS, FedEx, and the other shippers (including USPS) have sophisticated computer systems to schedule, route, and control the movement of packages from pickup to delivery. Along the way to its destination, a package will typically spend part of its time in a pickup truck, a delivery truck, local offices in the city of origin and the city of destination, one or more airplanes, and one or more dispatching centers. The computer systems that schedule and coordinate all of this are extremely complex; if they suffer Y2000 disruptions, packages can be lost, misrouted, or left stranded en route.[21]

- Like other businesses, the shipping carriers have elaborate billing, marketing, and other business applications. Individual packages shipped by "retail" customers are generally invoiced and paid for (by the person making the shipment) before the package is accepted; but corporate customers are more likely to maintain an ongoing account with Fed Ex or UPS, with monthly invoices that cover all shipments made during that period. A Y2000 problem in these systems probably wouldn't cause the shipper to shut down right away, but it could cause billing problems and other administrative problems.

Fallback Advice: Two-Day Disruptions

As we've pointed out several times in this book, Y2000 disruptions won't necessarily occur *en masse* on January 1, 2000; depending on the nature of the computer problems and the associated bureaucratic snafus caused by those problems, we might see the equivalent of the UPS strike in August 2000. But if you're a gambler, the "safe bet" is that January 1, 2000 is the most likely time that disruptions will start to be noticed; and just as some business organizations were able to make plans in advance of the August 1997 UPS strike, so it will be possible to make plans in advance of a possible January 2000 disruption.

The main thing, of course, is to ensure that any important business packages are shipped substantially before January 1st. The Christmas season is busy enough under normal circumstances, and there may be a number of cautious people trying to avoid potential problems as the New Year approaches; thus, you should make sure that you've allowed a few extra days. If you wait until Monday, January 3, 2000 to ship a critical package to a client or a customer, you have nobody to blame but yourself if you find that the shippers have been grounded.

Beyond that, there is no obvious "silver bullet" strategy. Given the nature of Y2000 problems, it's quite possible that FedEx might be grounded while UPS is operating—or vice versa. It's quite possible that the disruptions will be localized and sporadic; we may simply have to accept that the claims by shipping vendors that a package will "absolutely, positively" arrive overnight are no longer quite as dependable.

As for two-day disruptions in the telephone system: The same kind of preparations are appropriate. If you live in a suburban area, you may already have experienced occasional telephone outages—e.g., during the aftermath of an ice storm, tornado, or blizzard; it may require more conscious effort for city dwellers to imagine such a scenario, but it's likely to be an easy problem to deal with. If you have friends or relatives whom you would normally expect to call to offer a Happy New Year's greeting, be aware that either your phone or their phone might not be working.[22] If your office hasn't bothered upgrading its PBX system, be aware that you may be *sans* telephones on Monday, January 3rd. If you have a cellular phone whose service is provided by a different vendor than your land-based phone, you may find that it comes in very handy during these brief outages; in case there are also intermittent electrical outages, you should ensure that you have spare batteries, and that they're fully charged before you become too giddy from champagne on New Year's Eve.

Fallback Advice: One-Month Disruptions

At this point, things become fairly serious: A month without telephone service or mail service is enough to shut down most of today's business operations. Indeed, smaller companies with minimal cash reserves could find themselves bankrupted because they couldn't receive orders by phone, or payments by normal first-class mail. Larger organizations might be able to limp along, but there's a good chance that workers would be furloughed until the problem could be fixed. As for the ripple effect: A month-long telephone outage in the Wall Street area of New York, or the downtown centers of Chicago or Washington, would have devastating results.

As noted above, the major carriers and regional telephone operating companies are in the process of upgrading their technology now. While their business systems may not be completely Y2000-compliant in time, we're reasonably confident that any problems in the network switches will be fixed in a matter of days. But the smaller telephone companies might have more difficulty—simply because of limited resources and technical expertise. The real problem, we believe, will be in the PBX systems. The June 1997 *Information Week* assessment of the PBX situation gave an interesting example that illustrates the point:

> *Siemens Business Communications Systems Inc. in Santa Clara, Calif., says systems and upgrades it delivered after Aug. 1, 1996, are compliant, and it estimates that through routine upgrades 90% of the company's installed base will be compliant by January 2000.*[23]

From the vendor's perspective, 90 percent probably sounds like an acceptable percentage. But simple arithmetic tells us that Siemens expects that 10 percent of its customers will *not* have Y2000-compliant PBX systems on January 1, 2000. If the same is true of the other PBX vendors, then 10 percent of the country's office telephone systems won't be working in early January—and that might include the telephone system in *your* company. It might also include the offices of your bank, or the electric power company, or the fire department.

The reason we're discussing the PBX problem again in this section of Chapter 13 is that the sudden discovery on Monday, January 3rd that the phones don't work will lead to a panicked call (whoops! From whose phone?) to the company that installed the equipment. That company might be a local telecommunications service company, rather than the manufacturer of the PBX hardware/software unit; and since the PBX may have been installed several years earlier, the service company may be unresponsive or even out of business. In any case, there are likely to be a flurry of such calls in the early days of January, 2000—and the backlog could easily lead to one-month delays before the PBX can be upgraded, replaced, or repaired.

What kind of planning should you do if you believe that one-month outages of your phone service or, in a similar fashion, your FedEx/UPS/USPS service? To whatever extent is practical, make sure that you've got backup services available—e.g., a cellular phone if your normal house phone doesn't work, or an alternative carrier for your important business documents. Encourage your friends, relatives, and business associates to do the same; and be prepared to use the more primitive fallback mechanisms of ordinary first-class mail, if necessary.

Of course, this isn't going to help you if your office phone system is down for a month, or if you work for a mail-order shopping company (e.g., Land's End or the Sharper Image); the most likely consequence a month-long corporate disruption in telecommunications is temporary unemployment, or a permanent loss of one's job. This involves the job-related issues we discussed in Chapter 2; so our primary advice in this chapter to is to take stock of your situation now, while you still have the flexibility of changing jobs, to see if you're more dependent than you really want to be on the telecommunications and mail-delivery services.

Fallback Advice: One-Year Disruptions

We fully expect to see a rash of two-day failures across the country, mostly associated with PBX problems and minor glitches in other parts of the telecommunications infrastructure. For reasons discussed above, we wouldn't be surprised to see a few month-long failures—not on a nationwide basis, and probably not even affecting an entire city, but nevertheless painful and disruptive for the individual neighborhoods or companies so affected.

Is it even possible to contemplate a one-year telecommunications failure? The only plausible example we can imagine is a possible breakdown in international communications between the U.S. and certain other countries. England, Western Europe, and most of the advanced countries will be grappling with virtually identical problems, and it wouldn't be surprising if there were some minor-to-moderate glitches in the overseas links. But we expect that these would be fixed in a matter of weeks or months, if not sooner. The real problems are likely to occur in eastern Europe, Africa, parts of Asia, and parts of South America (parts of which, as noted in Joel Willemssen's testimony above, had not even begun to consider the Y2000 problem at the beginning of 1998). In several of these countries, bureaucratic government monopolies are still in charge of both the telecommunications and mail-delivery services; the equipment is old, and service is miserable. It wouldn't surprise us, for example, to see a one-year telecommunications collapse in a country like Brazil (which privatized its telephone company in mid-1998) or in some of the former Soviet republics.

Should such a scenario come to pass, it could mean that all modern forms of communication with these countries is cut off. After all, the overall focus of business and government in the U.S. is likely to be on fixing its own problems and re-establishing contact with other advanced countries. Fixing the telecommunication problems with Venezuela and Uzbekhstan will probably not be a high priority. Of course, it *might* be a high priority for you, if a major part of your job or business activity involves these stranded countries—and it might also be an urgent matter if you have close friends or relatives in those countries.

We have no easy answers for a problem of this magnitude; all we can do is ask you to think about the problem carefully now, while you still have time to make some alternative plans.

Fallback Advice: Ten-Year Disruptions

Especially within the United States, the telecommunications industry is highly competitive—and has been so for well over a decade, ever since the U.S. government made the landmark decision to break up the AT&T monopoly and to foster a more deregulated environment. Thus, even if a Y2000 problem completely destroyed an MCI or a Sprint or an AT&T, we're highly confident that the remaining vendors would take up the slack, and rebuild any part of the telecommunications infrastructure that required it. This might take a couple years, but certainly not a decade.

Similarly, the competition between UPS, Federal Express, Airborne Express, DHL, and other carriers is intense; if one of those carriers should be bankrupted in a Y2000 crisis, we're confident that the others would carry on, at least in the field of parcel-post and overnight mail delivery. The UPS strike that took place while this chapter was being written did provide some convincing evidence that neither the U.S. Postal Service nor the smaller carriers could take over all of UPS's business instantaneously—but given a year or two, we assume they would be able to expand their resources and fill the vacuum left by even the largest of carriers.

The only component of the telecom/mail infrastructure for which a 10-year "disruption scenario" is plausible is the U.S. Postal Service. Our reasoning here is similar to what we've discussed in previous chapters: Though quasi-private in nature, the Post Office is still largely dependent on the federal government for its existence. Though it has improved substantially in recent years, the USPS is still large, inefficient, bureaucratic, and floundering under its own weight—even in today's pre-2000 "normal" times. Millions of Americans cheerfully spend $10-15 to send a package via Federal Express, DHL, Airborne, or UPS, rather than spending 32 cents for what the Post Office euphemistically refers to as "first-class" mail. In the aftermath of a serious Y2000 failure, it's conceivable that the nation's leaders might decide to let the private sector deal with *all* mail delivery, and simply abandon the Post Office, to see if it can survive on their.

Obviously, a $15 FedEx package is too expensive for most middle-income and lower-income people who merely want to send a letter across town; but UPS has demonstrated that it can move large quantities of packages and documents across the country for a modest price, so it's not inconceivable that the private sector *could* take over mail delivery at an acceptable price.

However, it's important to remember that the Post Office delivers much more than just first-class letters and Express Mail packages. It also delivers second-class magazines and newspapers, as well as staggering quantities of third-class and fourth-class materials that the public generally refers to as "junk mail." While many citizens would be deliriously happy if junk mail disappeared, the elimination of a subsidized bulk-rate mail delivery service could be devastating to many American businesses that depend on it for their marketing activities. Catalogs, brochures, and other forms of direct-mail solicitations would be prohibitively expensive if they had to be sent at the first-class postage rates currently charged by the Post Office, not to mention the even higher rates that might be charged by private mail delivery firms. The ripple-effect consequences of such a change would be far-reaching indeed.

The notion of eliminating the USPS sounds so radical that most people probably won't give it serious consideration. Indeed, it really *is* unthinkable in countries where both the telephone system and the mail system are operated by government monopolies. But in the U.S., there has been a steady movement toward deregulation and privatization (of which FedEx is a notable example); and there is an increasing awareness that there are many alternatives to "snail mail" in today's high-tech world. Thus, if a severe Y2000 crisis provides the opportunity or the necessity (depending on whether you're an optimist or a pessimist) to start over with a clean slate, it's inevitable that serious, thoughtful, sincere people will ask, "Do we really *need* a Post Office any more?"

Endnotes

1. Available on the Internet at http://www.house.gov/ways_means/oversite/testmony/6-16-98/6-16will.html.
2. There are actually four separate areas of vulnerability for the Internet. First are the phone lines that most of us use to connect to the Internet; if you don't get a dial tone, you don't get on the Internet. Second is the collection of potentially old, non-compliant routers, switchers, multiplexers, DNS and email servers, hubs, gateways, and other arcane components mentioned by the Network Operations manager who contacted us. Third is the growing amount of Java and Javascript code that interacts with the end-user via his Web browser; just because Java is new and sexy does *not* guarantee that programmers will write Y2000-compliant code. And fourth is the "back-end" mainframe legacy applications to which the "front-end" Internet and Web browsers are connected. Aside from mundane functions like e-mail, one of the most important aspects of the Internet for business organizations is the ability to provide product information, take orders, and carry out all of the aspects of "e-business." But this typically requires access to pre-existing databases and application programs that were written 10-20 years ago, and which still run on big mainframe computers.
3. See http://www.fcc.gov/Speeches/Kennard/Statements/stwek824.html for the full text of Mr. Kennard's testimony.

4. See "Businesses work to put price on repairing computer problem to circumvent," by Mark P. Couch, in the April 25, 1998 Fort Worth *Star Telegram*; also available on the Internet at http://www.star-telegram.com/news/doc/1047/1:BIZ71/1:BIZ71042598.html.
5. See "MCI Gets Serious With SNA," by Kate Gerwig, *Information Week*, July 6, 1998; available on the Internet at http://www.techweb.com/se/directlink.cgi?INW19980706S0017.
6. See SBC's Web site at http://www.sbc.com/News/y2k.html.
7. See "Bell Companies Expect To Spend $1.2 Billion On Y2K Compliance" in the August 14, 1998 issue of *Communications Daily*;also available on the Internet at http://web.lexis-nexis.com/more/cahners/11368/3662685/10.
8. See the testimony of John Pasqua, Program Management Vice President of AT&T'sYear 2000 initiative, before the Oversight Subcommittee of the House Ways & Means Committee on June 16, 1998; available on the Internet at http://www.house.gov/ways_means/oversite/testmony/6-16-98/6-16pasq.htm
9. See http://www.fcc.gov/Speeches/Powell/Statements/stmkp819.html for the full text of Mr. Powell's testimony.
10. According to a survey conducted by British Telecom (as reported in the January 8, 1998 edition of *Computerweekly News*) only 11 percent of its "interconnect partners" in Africa and the Middle East had begun a Y2000 project as of the beginning of 1998.
11. See, for example, "Out of the telecoms cacophony, an order of sorts takes shape," by Margaret Banaghan, *Business Review Weekly* (Australia), June 22, 1998; also available on the Internet at http://www.brw.com.au/content/220698/brw21.htm.
12. See http://www.intelsat.com/cmc/policy/98-44tes.htm for the full text of Mr. Potarazu's testimony.
13. In the first edition of this book, we referred to "hundreds" of small phone companies. But like many other aspects of Y2000, we're now able to quantify the scope and extent of the problem in more detail. According to "Are Telcos Ready For Year 2000?" by Mary E. Thyfault And Bruce Caldwell, *Information Week*, June 22, 1998 (also available on the Internet at http://www.techweb.com/se/directlink.cgi?IWK19980622S0100), there are 1,400 telephone companies that collectively account for 2% of the nation's phone traffic. Even if all of them failed, it would only inconvenience a small number of people—but it would almost certainly be people

in rural areas that are even more dependent on telephones than most urban residents.

14. Mary E. Thyfault, "Call Center Crisis?—Outdated PBXs called vulnerable to date-field problems," *Information Week*, June 2, 1997. See also "Feds tackle telcom date problems," in the September 29, 1997 issue of *Federal Computing* Weekly (accessible at http://www.fcw.com/pubs/ fcw/1997/0929/fcw-newdate-9-29-1997.html), which says that approximately 25% of all government telecom switches need to be fixed because of Y2000 problems.
15. Mary E. Thyfault, *op cit.*
16. Kim Girard and Robert L. Scheier, "Telcos lag on year 2000, analysts warn," *Computerworld*, November 11, 1996.
17. David Stout, "Shippers Scramble as Strike Hits U.P.S.," *The New York Times*, Aug 5, 1997, page A12.
18. David Stout, *op cit.*
19. David Stout, *op cit.*
20. See http://www.usps.gov/news/press/97/97071new.html and http://www.usps.gov/news/press/97/97019new.html for USPS press releases containing these figures.
21. Embedded systems, which we discussed in Chapter 11, are also involved here. It's now customary to attach to each package a shipping label with a "bar code" that can be scanned by delivery personnel and by workers in the offices and dispatch stations; in addition, UPS delivery personnel carry hand-held computers to log the pickup and delivery of packages. All of this greatly improves the operating efficiency of the shipping companies, and helps ensure that packages are not lost in transit; but if the embedded computers turn out to be Y2000-sensitive, the faulty chips will be to be manually replaced or upgraded.
22. Remember that if your phone system isn't working, you will also have trouble connecting to the Internet. Many families have discovered in recent years that the Internet has made it possible for far-flung relatives and family members to stay in touch, communicating far more frequently and easily than was possible with telephone and "snail-mail." All of this could be seriously disrupted by a Y2000 failure that brings down the Internet.
23. Mary E. Thyfault, *op cit.*

Y2000 Impact on the Rest of the World

I think it is important that the United States recognize that the more we can do to help other countries meet this challenge in a timely fashion, the better off our own economy is going to be and the more smoothly our own businesses will be able to function as we pass over into the new millennium. The United States, to try to help, will provide $12 million to support the World Bank Year 2000 fund for developing countries.

President Bill Clinton, Speech at the National Academy of Sciences, *July 14, 1998*

It was the best of times, it was the worst of times, it was the age of wisdom, it was the age of foolishness, it was the epoch of belief, it was the epoch of incredulity, it was the season of Light, it was the season of Darkness, it was the spring of hope, it was the winter of despair, we had everything before us, we had nothing before us, we were all going direct to Heaven, we were all going direct the other way—in short the period was so far like the present period, that some of its noisiest authorities insisted on its being received, for good or for evil, in the superlative degree of comparison only.

Charles Dickens,
A Tale of Two Cities, *Chapter 1*

Introduction

If America's Y2K progress seems frustratingly late and disorganized, here's the bad news: Europe is roughly a year behind us, Asia is so preoccupied with its immediate financial crises that it's even further behind—and Africa and South America are sound asleep. We think the international aspect of this problem deserves its own chapter, especially given events in the financial markets and economies over the past year. We'll begin by discussing the relative state of international economies, and where we all stack up as we head into the year 2000. Then we'll describe the Y2K efforts of our international trading partners (as well as the countries we don't do as much trading with), and where we think foreign countries are more or less vulnerable than the United States.

Why devote an entire chapter to international countries and economies? First, Y2K is a global problem that will happen at the same time to everyone, all around the world. Our relative vulnerabilities lie in how much we depend on computers, and how healthy our economies are going into the year 2000. Second, as cliché as it may sound, we truly live in a global economy—an economy where for the most part, trade is free and international competition brings better, cheaper, more innovative, and more efficient products to the global marketplace. Even if you do not have any direct exchanges of goods or services with a foreign person or company, it is very likely that you depend on foreign countries, companies, or people, without really thinking about it. Perhaps you live in a town, state, or region that's dependent on tourism for its revenues and for the business that provides jobs to many of its residents. Maybe it is Colorado, where thousands of people (both foreign and domestic) enjoy skiing in the winter, and hiking in the summer. Maybe it's New York City, where people of all nationalities come to see the Empire State Building, the Metropolitan Museum, or Yankee Stadium. Maybe it's California, and its beautiful beaches and vineyards... you get the point. Perhaps your town or state doesn't attract too many tourists, but it's quite possible that the largest employers in your town depend heavily on business in foreign countries. Perhaps this employer is a plant or factory whose products are generally sent overseas for consumption. If the overseas economy slows, there is less demand for the goods produced by that company, and falloff in demand could lead to layoffs, which could then have a secondary "ripple effect" on the rest of your town's economy. Perhaps you own a small business and the bank where you do your company banking has loans to companies in emerging markets... if there are problems with those loans, overall perceived credit risk could go up, and you could have to pay higher interest rates on your next loan, despite your continued good credit status. In the worst case, your bank could go out of business because of its bad loans, even though its computer systems (as well as the computer systems in your own company) were 100-percent Y2000-compliant.

We were pleased to have many international readers of the first edition of our book, and many people from different countries who sent us emails and letters. We are also pleased to note that the first edition of *Time Bomb 2000* was translated into other languages. Our international readers cannot escape the Y2K problem both because of what takes place in their own countries and also because of what happens in the United States. The impact of the U.S. economy on other countries is obvious: The United States is a big importer. In June 1998, for example, the U.S. imported $6 billion of goods and services from China, $10 billion from Japan, and $16 billion from Western Europe.[1] If the United States falls into recession because of Y2K, we will import fewer goods and services from international economies, and those economies will suffer. Similarly, the United States also relies on the economic strength of other countries for its exports (though the U.S. has run a trade deficit for the past several years, where imports are greater than exports).

We don't want to belabor this issue, but what we do want to make clear is that if there are major shocks in international economies (whether they are developing countries or advanced economies), we are sure to feel the effects in the United States, whether or not we as individuals have direct or indirect exchanges with international people. Similarly, if there are shocks to the U.S. economy, people around the world are certain to feel the effects.

The State of International Economies and Financial Markets

Until the late summer of 1998 in the United States, it was the "best of times", as Charles Dickens said in *A Tale of Two Cities*. The U.S. had low inflation, a budget surplus, a roaring stock market, low unemployment, low interest rates—all in all, things could not have seemed better, despite the Asian crisis that began in the fall of 1997. The dramatic declines in Asian currencies and financial markets led to a steep one-day decline in the U.S. stock market in October 1997, but things gradually picked up; and by the end of 1997, many people were coming to the conclusion that problems in Asia would not dramatically affect corporate profits. Unfortunately, things seem to be falling apart as we prepare the second edition of this book in the summer/fall of 1998: credibility issues with the U.S. President, international terrorism and U.S. retaliation, the Russian devaluation and financial default, the Asian crisis and the correction (soon to be bear market??) in the U.S. stock market.

Japan, though not in the news these days as much as other Asian countries, is in one of the worst bear markets in its history. For the past eight years—indeed, virtually the entire decade of the 1990s—Japan has been in recession; during this time, its stock market has declined from almost 40,000 to a meager 14,000 in August 1998. This leaves the Nikkei-225 index at its lowest level since 1986. In addition, Japan's unemployment rate has risen to over 4.0 percent, down only slightly from a post-World War II high. Although that number doesn't appear high on the surface, most economists agree that Japan's real unemployment rate is far higher, as Japan counts as employed anyone who has worked even one hour in the previous month. Furthermore, Japan's largest banks (which are, by the way, the world's largest banks) are in quite dire straits: The three banks with the most assets have bad loans exceeding100 percent of their respective equity.[2] By contrast, the 22 largest banks in the U.S. had bad loans representing an average of 58 percent of equity[3] at the height of the U.S. banking crisis in 1991. Another new Prime Minister in Japan in 1998 has done little to raise hopes that credible banking reforms will be put in place. We will devote a large part of this chapter to a discussion of Japan, as we think Y2K could potentially push Japan into a deep depression, and severely harm its status as a global superpower.

Aside from Japan, the economic situation in the rest of Asia is also quite dire. Korea, Malaysia, Indonesia, the Philippines, Hong Kong, and Thailand have all suffered monstrous collapses in their equity markets. Most of these stock markets fell more than 50 percent from the beginning of 1997 to mid-1998, as illustrated on the chart at the top of the next page.[4]

The IMF has come to the aid of a few of these countries, though it will take years for the region to work its way out of the economic mess that it is in. Most countries in Asia reached this situation by overleveraging; i.e., by borrowing too much. In Korea and

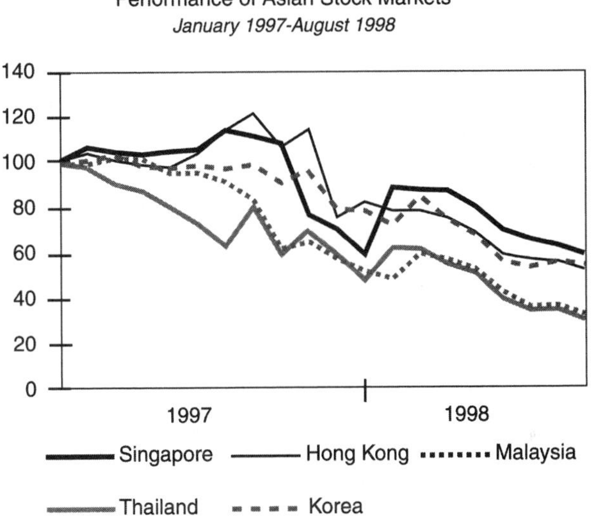

Indonesia specifically, most of the excessive borrowing was done by companies, where the loans were made in dollars. As companies found themselves unable to pay back loans, foreign confidence in those companies and countries declined, and capital was withdrawn from their capital markets. As this happened, their respective currencies declined, and companies found that they had to pay back loans in dollars that were suddenly much more expensive. Most of the currencies of these countries have been devalued, bringing on the most-unfortunate prospect of massive inflation. Rising unemployment rates in all of these countries are causing social unrest as we write the second edition of this book.

The economies of many of these countries are expected to continue contracting over the next several years: The Thai government, for example, expects a contraction of 7 percent in its economy in 1998 (a downgrade of an earlier forecast of a decline of 4-5 percent). China had not devalued the Hong Kong dollar while we were preparing this second edition, but a devaluation is a very serious possibility, the actuality of which would quite likely cause even more havoc in the rest of Asia. The Hong Kong government reached the very drastic stage, in the summer of 1998, of intervening in its own stock market to stem further declines. When a government is forced to support its own stock market, it is often a sign of sheer desperation.

In the late summer of 1998, Western Europe was enjoying moderately good times; most European countries had fairly strong economies, big equity market gains for 1998 and falling unemployment rates. The first wave of the single European currency, the Euro, is due to begin on January 1, 1999. Because of the stringent economic and financial criteria attached to this participation, most European countries have been working hard at reducing their budget deficits, bringing down inflation, and reducing the level of outstanding government debt. As a direct result of this politically imposed priority, these same countries have devoted far less money and programming resources to the Y2000 problem. Ironically, the programming effort required to support the Euro currency is actually more complex than that required for the Y2000 problem; but in any case, the consensus of most American Y2000 experts is that Europe might have been able to complete its Euro-related computer work, or its Y2000-related computer work, in time for the deadline—*but not both efforts simultaneously.*

In the UK, which is not participating in the first wave of the Euro, the jobless rate had fallen to 4.7 percent by July 1998, and the stock market had posted gains of 14 percent through the end of July (though much of the gains were erased in August). In Germany and France, which are participating in the first wave of the Euro, the economies were growing but both countries had relatively high unemployment rates (10.9 percent in Germany and 11.8 percent in France), a problem that continues to leave both of those countries on the edge of social malaise. In the late summer of 1998, things were looking quite wobbly throughout Europe—German banks, for example, are the largest creditors to Russia, and as Russia defaulted on its debt, devalued its currency, and watched its stock market fall 80 percent, German equities and banks suffered as well.

In Eastern Europe, the overwhelming story is Russia, which is unequivocally in the "worst of times". The country is in absolute turmoil as we write this second edition: President Yeltsin has fired his government (once again), the country has defaulted on its debt, devalued its currency, and has been unable to pay many of its workers for several months. Social unrest has begun, as people line up outside of banks, desperate to change their rubles (which are declining in value by the hour) into "hard" currency with the currency of choice being the U.S. dollar. Footage on television has shown fights erupting as people push each other out of the way to get into these banks. Banks are routinely closing their doors early in Moscow, putting signs on their front doors reading, "No Hard Currency." The official devaluation was one of 33 percent, though as the currency was allowed to float in late August and early September, it fell by more than 60 percent. A severe devaluation, or weakening of a currency, almost always has severe inflationary effects, especially on those countries that are heavily reliant on imported goods. This puts Russians in another unfortunate spot, as their biggest imports are truly necessary items like grains, so the average man on the street will pay much more for food, without earning any more money. It also puts the Russian computer industry in an unfortunate spot, as very few companies or government agencies have the money or the "sense of urgency" to focus on Y2000 as their most important problem to solve.

As shown on the following chart, the ruble fell from 6.0/US$ to 10.0/US$ at the end of August, 1998. In the first few days of September, the ruble fell to approximately 17.0/US$. Finally, the last kick in the stomach for Russia has been the steep decline in the price of oil, the production of which is one of Russia's biggest and most profitable industries. The lower the price of oil has gone, the less profitable this industry has become for Russia. As we write in the summer/fall of 1998, the price of oil is near its low at $13.50 per barrel. As a nuclear superpower, the collapse of this economy has truly spooked the rest of the world, for while the economic effect of its

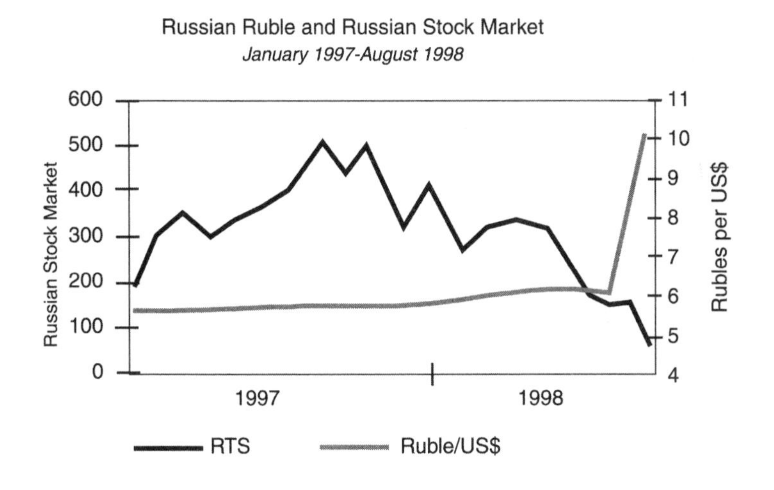

collapse is not monumental, the possibility of Communists regaining power, and being in possession of nuclear weapons, is quite monumental indeed. We also devote time to discuss Russia to emphasize that even in modern times, financial collapse can cause social upheaval.

In South and Latin America, the troubles in emerging markets in Asia and Eastern Europe are starting to impact our southern trading partners. In August of 1998, we have seen substantial pressure on currencies and equity markets of the larger South American and Latin American countries, including Mexico, Brazil, Argentina, and Venezuela. All of those countries have dealt with devaluations of their currencies and the ensuing inflationary periods. Most of these countries have implemented successful currency programs, either currency pegs or currency boards, which have allowed them to tame inflation and reduce the social upheaval that inevitably comes with soaring prices. The reduction in inflation, and stability in their currencies, has encouraged foreign capital and investment. The problems in Asia and Russia have cast a pall over all emerging markets, so that there is a massive capital flight out of the markets and economies of our southern neighbors despite the relatively benign economic fundamentals. In short, we are seeing what is known as a "flight to quality", where funds are removed from assets considered risky, like emerging markets, and put into safer assets, like U.S. Treasury bonds.

Canada, Australia, and New Zealand (the other "dollar" economies) are in relatively good economic shape; however, the steep decline in commodity prices has hurt all three of these countries, as they are both big exporters of natural resources. As commodities prices have declined, their currencies have followed suit with the Canadian, Australian, and New Zealand dollars down 14 percent, 29 percent and 30 percent, as of early September 1998, respectively against the U.S. dollar since December 1996. The economies of Australia and New Zealand specifically have been hurt by the crises in Asia, as they tend to be major trading partners. As the emerging markets crisis has spread in the summer of 1998, the continued weakness in the Canadian dollar has forced the central bank of Canada to raise short-term interest rates to defend its currency.

Aside from the few dozen "advanced" countries we've discussed, there are well over a hundred underdeveloped and "developing" nations, particularly those in Africa and the Middle East. As we learned in the early 1970s and again in the early 1990s, the Middle East has an enormous influence on the economies and politics of the advanced countries because of its oil resources. And while the other underdeveloped countries may not have a significant impact on the import-export statistics for the U.S., they often supply critical raw materials ranging from coffee and bananas to such exotic metals as chromium, platinum, and gold. As we'll discuss later, the developing nations have far fewer computers than the advanced countries; but those computers are generally older, "hand-me-down" machines that are far more likely to suffer Y2000 problems.

In summary, in isolation, the United States and Europe are in relatively good economic shape, with the U.S. better off than European countries. The rest of the world, though, is really in turmoil, with Russia, most of Asia, and Latin America, leading the way. What does this mean? The fragile economic state of most of these countries means that resources are currently being devoted to problems at hand (social unrest, bank collapses, company defaults, IMF packages, debt restructurings, dismissals of governments, currency devaluations,and the like) and not the Y2000 problems that are 12 to 16 months away. Those countries who are not paying sufficient attention to Y2K—i.e., those whose economies are in trouble—will suffer more severe Y2K-induced problems because there will not have been sufficient work and planning done on the Year

2000. In addition, any depressing economic effects of Y2K will be all that much worse because their economies are already in such a fragile state. As we commented in the beginning of this chapter, we in the United States do not live in isolation, and our economy will feel the effects of weaker economies around the world.

Finally, many economists and journalists have noted that recessions are rarely caused by anticipated events. It is our opinion that while the Year 2000 is obviously an anticipated event, the outcome is uncertain, and the effects and disruptions are completely unknown. In addition, we stress that a Y2K-induced recession will happen not because of the absolute number of dollars that will be spent on the problem, but because of the disruptions in economic activity that will take place because of Year 2000-induced problems.

What is the International Progress on Year 2000?

Where are international countries in terms of their Y2K efforts? One of the greatest areas of worry is Japan, as its economy is in the worst shape of the world "superpowers." Furthermore, it has been in very bad economic shape for the past eight years.

The Gartner Group has commented that some Western companies are beginning to show concern about the lack of awareness in Japan about Y2K. While the fundamental nature of the Y2000 problem is the same all over the world, there are some subtle differences; for example, in the United

States, the bulk of software applications are "packaged" products sold by such vendors as IBM, Oracle, or Microsoft; in Japan, by contrast, approximately 70 percent of applications are still customized. Thus, Japanese companies are more likely to find themselves responsible for fixing their own Y2000 problems in their own customized software applications; in the U.S., it's more likely that companies will be at the mercy of package-suppliers to provide appropriate updates or new versions of their software packages.

What exactly is the progress on Y2K in Japan? The *Nihon Keizai* newspaper recently reported that the Bank of Japan (the Japanese central bank) has taken a survey of Y2000 activities within Japan's 19 major banks. The survey found that 42.1 percent plan to fix their "internal and network" computer systems by March 1999, with a further 42.1 percent by June 1999, and then 100 percent plan to do so by September 1999. The descriptions of these plans, of course, are inadequate and discouraging. As we have stressed repeatedly in this book, over 40 years of data in the software industry suggest that almost 15 percent of *all* software projects are late, by an average of approximately 7 months. The above data suggests that the majority of Japan's biggest banks are giving themselves the minimum amount of breathing room. More depressing is a Bank of Japan survey saying that second-tier regional banks plan to be working on the Year 2000 problem until December 31, 1999.[5] We consider this a veiled admission that they won't be ready, because no business, bank, or government agency has publicly stated (yet) that they won't be compliant until after January 1, 2000.

BoJ Net, the country's largest clearance and settlement networks system, handles 428 domestic financial institutions, 264 foreign exchange accounts, 450 government-bond settlement accounts, with 533 participating institutions, all of which are connected with other international settlement systems.[6] A Bank of Japan official has reported testing of this system will begin on December 20, 1998. The official added that it has "recommended" that institutions participating in the network be compliant by the end of 1998, noting that the BoJ does not have the authority to require companies to meet any standards.

Christopher Wells, the Chairman of the Banking and Securities Subcommittee of the American Chamber of Commerce in Japan, was quoted as saying that international institutions will soon have to determine whether Japanese institutions are "sufficiently" compliant "to be permitted to participate in the international financial system."[7] This same chamber recently issued a report commenting that there is a lack of central authority and coordination, and that there may be a gap between American and Japanese testing and compliance standards.

We hesitate to spend so much time on Japanese banking; however, the Japanese financial system is so frail, and the economy so weak, that we fear severe disruptions in Japanese banking could push the massive economy into a deep depression, from which it might not emerge for several years. Also, as we discussed in our comments about Russia, financial collapse, currency devaluation, and inflation can cause extreme social upheaval. As a final note of worry, Bloomberg reported that Japan's 19 nationwide banks are spending an estimated 164 billion yen ($1.2 billion) on Year 2000, according to a survey by the Financial Supervisory Agency (FSA). For comparison purposes, Citicorp alone has reported in SEC disclosure statements that it plans to spend $ 650 million on its Y2K effort, so we seriously doubt the credibility of these reported spending plans of the major Japanese banks. The FSA survey also went on to say that the 38 life insurers that completed the survey are planning on spending 18 billion yen ($112 million). Finally, FSA reported that 29 percent of Japan's 223 brokerages and 37.42 percent of the nations 318 credit cooperatives have finished estimating how much it will cost them to fix their Y2K problems.

Other depressing news out of Japan include a survey done by the Small and Medium Enterprise Agency, which shows that 10 percent of small companies "don't understand" the problem.[8] The Ministry of International Trade and Industry (MITI), in conjunction with the Ministry of Posts and Telecommunications, plans to ask the government for increased funding for small companies to deal with their Y2K problems, out of the JY 150 billion (approximately US$ 1 billion) allocated for information-related projects through fiscal 1999. The Nihon *Keizai Shimbun* also reported that many Japanese companies are postponing their Y2K fixes, claiming financial hardship as the reason for the delay. According to the paper, Fujitsu Ltd. reported that an "increasing" number of clients have delayed Y2K work, and that it expects Y2K work involving 2000 engineers to be delayed.

Meanwhile, most European countries have been focusing their programming efforts on converting to the Euro. The Euro is the single European currency that must be implemented January 1, 1999 by those countries that were chosen to participate, which include France, Germany, Italy, Ireland, and Belgium, among others. We offer a brief comment on specific areas of their respective Y2K preparedness.

In January of 1998, the Italian Bankers Association (ABI) warned that Italian banks are poorly prepared for both the Year 2000 and for the Euro. According to an Italian newspaper, the ABI said that the largest 50 banks are making a "sufficient" effort to adapt their systems, but that 100 other banks were much further behind.

In Sweden, the government is contemplating shutting down its nuclear power plants if it can't guarantee that they will operate safely in the Year 2000. Some tests in Sweden have already led to a malfunction in the water-feed system to a reactor. The water-feed system is necessary to keep reactors operating at full power.

The UK is not participating in the first "wave" of the Euro, and is one of the countries furthest ahead in its Y2K efforts. UK Prime Minister Tony Blairs has said that it will cost the government approximately BP 3 billion to fix the problem, and has established a special cabinet to handle the problem.

Another country not participating in the first wave of the Euro is Norway, whose Trade and Industry Ministry said through a local paper that many Norwegian companies have started their Y2K efforts too late.

In other parts of Asia, specifically in China, an expert with the Chinese Academy of Sciences' Computer Technology Institute said that there is not enough time to convert all of China's systems and that the project will take several years to complete.

In Australia, the Deputy Governor of the Reserve Bank of Australia offered the not-so-comforting comment that "in relation to all critical systems, the ones that really have to function, the banks will be well placed to have those remediated by the end of the year."

As a group, the international community seems to be doing a fair job in banding together, and trying to work together to present some unity. The G8, which includes the US, UK, France, Germany, Italy, Canada, Japan, and Russia, issued a communique in May saying they would "share information, among ourselves and with others." In addition, a committee within the Bank for International Settlements (BIS), which coordinates payments across borders, has encouraged system operators to share their progress on Year 2000. Exactly nine countries have filled out the form and returned it to the BIS.

More broadly, the Gartner Group estimates that at least one-third of all nations won't be ready for

Year 2000. A study by the World Bank estimates that only 10 percent of 120 nations classified as "developing" have a government-wide Year 2000 program.

To summarize, the head of the CIA office that is studying the issue, Sherry Burns, was quoted by CNN (as reported on cnn.com on May 5, 1998 in an article titled "CIA says many unprepared for Millennium glitch") as saying that Canada, Great Britain, and Australia are approximately six months behind the U.S. in their Y2K efforts, and that the rest of Europe (including Germany!!) were 9-12 months behind. Ms. Burns added that most Asian countries were also 9-12 months behind. The United Nations director of information technology, Joyce Amenta, was quoted as saying that the "likely" failure of developing countries to fix their Y2K problems on time could lead to civil unrest and bank panics. She added, "We face economic instability, factories shutting down... foreign banks are at risk. Civil stability, which we don't normally think about here, is at risk."

Conclusion

This is not a chapter where we can give our usual advice of problems lasting a varying degree of time. It is fair to assume, though, that since most countries are further behind the United States, disruptions are likely to be more serious elsewhere than in the United States. This is especially true in those countries that are in economic and financial turmoil, and that do not have the resources to devote to

Y2K. Severe disruptions in other countries mean more severe disruptions for the United States. This chapter was written for the most part as a reminder that Y2K is a global problem that every country must deal with and finish at the same time.

Endnotes

1. As reported by the U.S. Census Bureau.
2. As reported by the *New York Times* on June 27, 1998, using Fitch IBCA as a source. For reference, the three largest banks listed are Tokyo-Mitsubishi, Sumitomo and Dai-Ichi Kangyo.
3. Also as reported in the *New York Times* June 27, 1998.
4. These equity indices were all reindexed to begin at 100 in December 1996.
5. *The Nihon Keizai Shimbun,* August 20, 1998.
6. *The Nihon Keizai Shimbun*, May 25, 1998.
7. *The Nihon Keizai Shimbun*, May 25, 1998.
8. *The Nihon Keizai Shimbun*, August 20, 1998.

Conclusion

... if we act properly, we won't look back on this [Millennium bug] as a headache, sort of the last failed challenge of the 20th century. It will be the first challenge of the 21st century successfully met. That is the American way, and together we can do it.

President Bill Clinton, Speech at the National Academy of Sciences, *July 14, 1998*

We are close to dead. There are faces and bodies like gorged maggots on the dance floor, on the highway, in the city, in the stadium; they are a host of chemical machines who swallow the product of chemical factories, aspirin, preservatives, stimulant, relaxant, and breathe out their chemical wastes into a polluted air. The sense of a long last night over civilization is back again.

Norman Mailer, Cannibals and Christians, *"Introducing Our Argument" (1966).*

Introduction

As we wrote both the first and second editions of this book, we posted chapters on our Web site in order to solicit feedback and commentary from both technical and non-technical readers around the world. Among the many hundreds of comments and messages we received, this one (from a 50-year-old man who asked us to withhold his name) eloquently expresses the uncertainty, hesitation, and concern that all of us face after thinking carefully about the potential consequences of Y2000:

> *As I plan my own fallback based on a one to ten year scenario, I am still searching for any hard evidence that those in denial will ultimately be correct. I am not anxious to go through all the changes. Instead, the more I look, the worse it gets.*
>
> *I programmed for two years in the early 70's as I installed the first system for my parent's business on a DEC PDP-8. I also presided over a doomed attempt in 1979 to totally re-write the system and install it without running parallel. Yes, I know, very dumb! We pulled the plug after three disastrous days and threw away all that work and recovered to the old system. My promotion to president was permanently put on hold. Needless to say, I am wary of optimistic forecasts to replace 40 years of programming world-wide, most of it in less than three years.*
>
> *Please tell me where you see the optimism, if you do... The problem is that no one in authority will tell the truth if they are not going to be ready, and they probably won't until after 2000. In the meantime, we all have to address continually the risks as we work on our own fallback plans.*

We too would like to find some hard evidence that the Y2000 problem has been solved, or that its impact on society will be minimal. We'd like to find a major electric utility, bank, airline, automobile company, or government agency that can say it's fully Y2000 compliant, and that all of its software professionals have been reassigned to normal maintenance work. However, we have to admit that we would be slightly skeptical if and when such assurances are made by major corporations, as we expect they might be in 1999. What we *really* would like to see is the kind of independent testing that we've come to expect from *Consumer Reports* magazine and the *Underwriters Laboratory* for commercial products—i.e., an unbiased statement that says, "Yes, we've tested this product thoroughly, and it really *is* Y2000-compliant."

As the second edition of this book goes to press, we still have not seen any such assurances; the more deeply we've delved into the Y2000 situation over the past three years, the worse it looks. Meanwhile, the clock is ticking; if we're going to make fallback plans, especially those that involve time, money, and significant effort, we need to get started sooner rather than later.[1]

And like our anonymous correspondent, we're not anxious to go through the kinds of changes that will be required if we take all of this seriously. We suspect that you feel the same way; and we suspect that there's an element of doubt in your mind, which says, "Does it really make sense to trust all of the gloom-and-doom conclusions in this book? Should I really begin making some unpleasant changes in my life, when nobody around me seems to be concerned about the Y2000 problem?"

Ultimately, this is a decision you'll have to make, either alone, or in concert with your family, friends, and loved ones. You may find this to be a difficult, lonely decision—as did one woman who emailed us after reading the first draft of our book on the Internet:

> *Y2K has been on my mind for some time now. My 72 year old father opened my eyes to it and directed me to these websites. I took him to buy his first computer two years ago. Today I drove to Wal-Mart and started preparing for Y2K. Lanterns, flashlights, bottled water. On my way there I thought that I must be out of my mind and almost turned around and went home. It was a hard step to take. I know that I have a lot of work ahead of me yet, but I am going to be ready for at least 6 months of trouble. Something that I find to be hilarious as I write this. The TV is on in the background blathering about Marv Albert and his sex life. Almost makes a 2000 crash something to look forward to.*

To help come to a decision—whether to accept or reject the possibility of serious Y2000 problems—we suggest that you do your own "reality test" to follow up on what we've already discussed in this book. We also suggest that you carry out your own personal assessment of the impact of a Y2000 disruption. And most of all, we strongly suggest that you spend the remaining months until the new millenium paring down and simplifying your life, so that you can face it with as much flexibility as possible.

Do Your Own "Reality Test"

This book may have been your first exposure to the Y2000 problem, but it certainly is not the only source of information. We've referred to several magazine articles and sources of information that were available to us during the writing process; there will undoubtedly be much more during 1998 and 1999, and you should be able to find them in your library, newstand, or bookstore.

If you have access to the Internet and the World Wide Web, you will find a wealth of up-to-date information about Y2000; indeed, a Web search on the keyword "Y2K" is likely to produce a list of nearly 10,000 relevant pages. And if you have concerns about the Y2000 status of specific companies, industries, or government agencies, a modest amount of investigation with Web search engines is likely to produce some relevant information. If you don't have access to the Internet, this is a good time to start; new information is being made available on almost a daily basis now, and we expect it to intensify in the coming months. While the Y2000 information is readily accessible on the 'Net, you may not find it in your local newspaper or general-interest magazines.[2] This is particularly true when it comes to Congressional hearings and status reports from various government agencies; they may or may not get a superficial "sound-bite" mention on the evening TV news program, but you can find detailed coverage, if not the verbatim transcripts of testimony and presentations, on the Internet. We've listed several relevant Y2000 Web sites in Appendix C.

While we were writing the first draft of this book, Norman Kurland sent us an email message with some excellent advice:

In this and other chapters, you do not say much about assessing the readiness status during 1999 in order to decide which level of fallback planning may be most reasonable.

By early to mid 1999 we should have a good idea of what the impact of Y2K in various sectors is likely to be. That means that individuals and organizations should have a more solid basis for making their fallback plans. For example, if it is clear that there is likely to be serious disruptions in services during January, schools might plan to close for a month and to give study assignments so that students (and teachers) might be able to use the time productively.

I anticipate that by early 1999 someone is going to give regular updates on Y2K readiness in various sectors. That should help reduce panic (assuming that the readiness reports are mostly positive) and help people prepare more intelligently for the BIG DAY.

We also recommend that you talk to knowledgeable people about the technical and business ramifications of Y2000. However, keep in mind that spokesmen, business leaders, and even computer professionals who have not had a direct involvement in Y2000 efforts are likely to shrug it off. The email message that we received from Brian Oates during the writing of the first edition of this book is a good example:

Being a programmer myself I considered the y2000 compliance issue and basically blew it off. I use Windows 95 and 75% of our computers have been purchased in the last year. However since reading several chapters of yours I get the feeling I'm living in a Michael Crichton novel. I've asked two of my computer friends about it.

> *One said he's stayed out of it, the other hasn't given it a passing thought. "They'll fix it", he said. "It's just changing their databases to hold a four digit year instead of two." (He's been programming for over five years, he should know it's never that easy...)*
>
> *If programmers who should know better aren't alarmed, how can we hope to lessen the ripple to anything less than a year?*

As you've seen from the discussions in this book, there *are* Senators, Congressmen, banking officials, and other business leaders who are grappling with the consequences of Y2000; track down some of these people and ask them whether they're currently feeling optimistic or pessimistic about the outcome. There are also thousands of computer programmers and software managers working full-time on Y2000 projects; it shouldn't be too much trouble to track down one of these people through your network of friends and acquaintances. In short, ask someone who is *involved* in Y2000 what they think of the situation; it's conceivable that things will have improved by the time this book reaches the bookstores, but we don't think so.

Also, try out the Y2000 phenomenon on your own computer.[3] If you have a home PC, try setting the date to January 1, 2000 and see if everything works correctly; then try setting the date to 11:55 PM on December 31, 1999 and watch to see if it "rolls over" correctly after 5 minutes. If so, then power down the computer, power it back up again, and see if everything still works correctly. Try your favorite application programs to ensure that they handle four-digit dates correctly.

Finally, carry out your own Y2000-compliance tests when you interact with computers in your day-to-day life. Whether it's an ATM machine, or a programmable VCR, or any other form of date-sensitive computerized equipment, see what happens if you enter a date beyond December 31, 1999. Ask your banker, ask the utility company, ask the manager in your favorite super-market; ask anyone whose ability to provide goods and services to you is dependent on computers. In the summer of 1997, when the first edition of this book was being written, our own experience was that the most common response from such people was a blank stare, and a question: "What's Y2000?" This was understandable, and perhaps forgivable at the time; by 1998, it was a dangerous answer, for it implied that the organization had not yet begun repairing its computers.

If everyone you talk to can give you concrete, tangible evidence that the Y2000 problem has been solved, then you're welcome to disregard everything you've read in this book. If the majority of people you talk to say, "Don't worry, they'll have it fixed in time," then you should start asking some specific questions. Who is "they"? How many of them are there, and when did they start working on the problem? What kind of budget have they established for their Y2000 effort? What's their schedule for finishing the Y2000 conversion efforts, and what evidence can they provide that will make you confident of their ability to finish on time?[4]

The acid test—and one that we strongly urge you to use whenever you have any doubts about what you're hearing—is the ability to provide a written guarantee of Y2000 compliance. Here, for example, is what the Federal Reserve said to its member banks about the revisions that it is currently making to the PC versions of its "Fedline" software:

> *Testing Fedline for year 2000 certification will span all business applications and many of the various hardware and software platforms that we support (e.g., 286 and up, and DOS 3.3 and higher). While it will be impossible to test with every make and model of PC used by our customers, we will identify all platforms on which testing has been successful. You also will want to take action to ensure that the equipment you have, or may be planning to purchase, will function correctly in the year 2000.*
>
> *Although we will rigorously test the Fedline software with date simulation tools, this software is furnished strictly on an "as-is" basis. We do not warrant that our software will meet the needs of a customer's applications or that it will be compatible with customer-owned equipment or that all software defects can be corrected. We will, however, provide reasonable assistance in resolving software problems.*[5]

In fairness, it should be noted that *most* software is sold on an "as-is" basis; check the first few pages of the user-manual of your favorite PC software, and you'll find a similar disclaimer. The reason is quite simple: Except for very simple computer programs that operate on a narrow range of well-known computer hardware/software "platforms," most software is too complex for today's software organizations to test completely. The Fed is being honest in its statement about the possible existence of "software defects" in its Y2000-version of Fedline. And if you press any responsible corporate officer in any company or government agency around the world, you're almost certain to get a similar disclaimer with regard to the correctness of their Y2000 efforts.

Obviously, that doesn't mean that the software *will* fail on January 1, 2000. It simply means that you have to take any bland, optimistic Y2000 assurances with a grain of salt. Indeed, it's fairly difficult to avoid becoming distrustful and suspicious when you have a conversation along the following lines with a company official:

> *You*: "Is your company going to be fully Y2000 compliant by December 1999?"
>
> *Official:* "Sure, don't worry about it. We're working on the problem, and we're confident that everything will be fine."
>
> *You:* "Well, that's great—but the ability of your company to provide products and services is really important to me, and I have to be sure. Can you provide a written warranty, signed by an officer of your company, that you'll be Y2000-compliant?"
>
> *Official:* "Well, no, we can't do that. But don't worry: we'll definitely be Y2000-ready."
>
> *You:* "Y2000-ready? What does that mean?"
>
> *Official:* "It means we're ready for Y2000, and we stand by our commitment to pro-

vide superior quality and excellent service to our customers."
You: "But no warranty? No written guarantee?"
Official: "Ummm... er, ah, well... no, we can't do that."

This could lead to another series of questions: If the company's products or services turn out *not* to be Y2000, can you turn it in for a refund? Can you get a replacement product? If the answer to these questions is "no," then the company is effectively saying to you, "We don't *really* know if our product/service will function correctly on January 1, 2000—and we won't take responsibility if it doesn't. *You* take the risk." Since this is likely to be the case with almost *all* products and services, the real question is: How much risk are you willing to take? What are the consequences if the products and services that you now take for granted stop working on January 1, 2000?

Even with a written guarantee, you may still be taking a risk. If you buy a product or service from a company that goes bankrupt because of its Y2000 problems, you might not be able to recoup your losses. Even worse, if it's a safety-critical system, a Y2000 failure may cause personal injury—the consequences of which might render the manufacturer's written guarantee irrelevant.

With or without a written guarantee, you'll need to judge the credibility of any Y2000 claims that you hear throughout 1999. If the FAA, or the IRS, or your local bank, or the local utility company, announces with great confidence, “We *are* Y2000 compliant!”, you still need to ask yourself, “How do I know I can trust this statement?” The answer is surprisingly simple: Ask for an independent validation/verification by an unrelated, unbiased third-party testing or consulting organization.

The situation is analogous to an organization that tells you it has just finished its financial year with surprisingly large profits; the CEO announces the great news, and invites the public to buy shares of stock in his company. An astute investor will ask to see the company’s *audited* financial statement before making such an investment—and he will check to ensure that the auditor is a recognized, unaffiliated firm, such as one of the Big-6 accounting firms. If the audit has been performed by the CEO’s cousin, or if it’s an unaudited financial statement, there’s no reason an investor should trust it. Indeed, without audited financial statements, a company cannot trade its shares on the U.S. stock exchanges.

Similarly, if a CEO says to you, “We’ve finished our Y2000 project, and we’ve repaired all of our systems!”, a savvy computer expert might say, “Show me the test data that you used, so I can be confident that you thoroughly tested all of the Y2000 modifications you made to your systems.” Most companies will balk at this request, which raises some questions about the credibility of the claim. And of course, a non-computer-oriented person wouldn’t know how to read the test reports, just as many of us would have trouble analyzing and interpreting the financial details of a company's operations. That's why we want an independent, third-party audit.

Alas, we're not likely to see very many such audits; it's an expensive, time-consuming process, and most organizations are simply hoping that you'll take their word for it when they tell you they've finished their work. At the very least, look for caveats and weasel-word qualifiers like "we're substantially finished with our Y2000 renovations," or "we've repaired all of our key systems." Question: What's a "key" system? Answer: Any system the organization managed to finish repairing. If they didn't finish it, then it's not "key."

Make Your Own Assessment of Y2000 Consequences

While attempting to explain the possible consequences of Y2000 computer failures to one of our friends, we used the following metaphor: It's equivalent to the experience of being bitten by as many as a thousand gnats, a hundred mosquitoes, ten bumblebees, and one rattlesnake—possibly all at the same time. The gnats will be annoying and unpleasant; and the discomfort caused a hundred mosquito bites is sufficient that most of us would be willing to invest the time and money to buy mosquito repellent. Bee stings are *far* more unpleasant—and in some cases, a dozen bee stings could be fatal. As for rattlesnake bites: The prospect is sufficiently frightening that any sensible person would either take proactive steps to eliminate the possibility, or would ensure that he had an ample supply of the appropriate anti-toxin.

The whole point of this book has been to suggest a wide range of Y2000-related "what if?" questions for you to consider. But we don't know the specifics of your life, nor do we know what's important and what's not important to you. Now it's time for you to do some homework, quite possibly the most important homework of your adult life. For each aspect of the social infrastructure that we've discussed—jobs, telephones, banking, government, and so forth—it's crucial for you to ask yourself, "What would happen to me if this part of society was disrupted by the Y2000 bug?"

Some of the potential Y2000 consequences are so unpleasant that the easiest course of action is to ignore them—on the theory that perhaps we'll be lucky enough that we won't have to deal with them. This is roughly akin to the reaction that teenagers have when informed of the dangers of smoking: Intellectually, they understand the medical warnings about smoking, but they'd like to think that they'll be one of the lucky ones who can avoid cancer and emphysema. And even if they do understand and accept the health risks on a personal level, the power of nicotine addiction makes it extremely difficult to change one's behavior. It's not much of an exaggeration to suggest that most of us are addicted to the comforts of our high-tech, computer-supported lives in today's world; breaking that addiction (if it turns out to be necessary to do so) will be one of the most painful things we've ever experienced.

The risk of denial is particularly high for many of today's American adults, simply because we're so busy coping with the demands of life. Many of us work 12-hour days, and then spend the evenings and weekends raising a family and squeezing in shopping and the laundry and other personal errands. We're bombarded with news alerts, overwhelmed with email and voice-mail, and utterly frazzled by the pressure and chaos of modern life. In the midst of all this, someone comes along and warns us that it might all collapse because of an obscure computer problem that most of us don't understand—and it's no surprise that most of us shrug and say, "They'll fix it somehow. Meanwhile, I've got more pressing problems to worry about." As Henry Kissinger once said, "There can't be a crisis next week. My schedule is already full."[6]

But ignoring the problem isn't going to make it go away—it simply changes the situation to one of Russian roulette, where we put our lives in the hands of companies and government agencies who may or may not be able to minimize the effects of Y2000 disruptions.

As the Big Day approaches, it's conceivable that we may begin to see some concrete, tangible evidence that massive Y2000 disruptions are unavoidable. And this may lead to another kind of denial on the part of some citizens: A gloomy denial that there is any way at all of surviving the Y2000 crisis. As British novelist Iris Murdoch observed:

> *The notion that one will not survive a particular catastrophe is, in general terms, a comfort since it is equivalent to abolishing the catastrophe.*[7]

This kind of despair is more likely, we believe, if the bad news comes suddenly and unexpectedly. The "news" in this book may have been unexpected and gloomy, but at least you have a couple years left to plan and prepare. If nothing else, you have time to prepare yourself psychologically for the likelihood that survival in post-Y2000 society may not be as easy and automatic as it is today. As George Orwell put it in his recollections of the Spanish Civil War:

> *To survive it is often necessary to fight and to fight you have to dirty yourself.*[8]

Most Important: Maintain Flexibility

If it turns out that the overall impact of Y2000 bugs is of the two-day or one-month variety, then it won't go down in the history books as a major disaster. Those who have planned for the disruptions by stockpiling a modest amount of cash, food, and other essentials, will get through the disruptions with a modicum of inconvenience; and those who have not made such preparations will find it an extremely unpleasant experience—but then it will be over.

But if the Y2000 problems disrupt society for a year—or, in some areas, as long as a decade—then many of us are going to find that it's a new ball game. In addition to finding that our savings and stock-market portfolio has been wiped out, we may find that old rules, old skills, old careers, and old assumptions about cause-and-effect consequences in society, are no longer true. The specific problems and disruptions could well turn out to be completely different than the scenarios we've painted in this book; we've used our knowledge of computer technology and economics to postulate what *might* happen, but we make no claims that our crystal ball can peer into the future with complete precision.

Similarly, we would be extremely wary of anyone else's crystal ball, if it purports to show a *specific* Y2000-related scenario with great precision. A Y2000-related crisis in banking and finance, for example, might lead to the familiar phenomenon of hyper-inflation; but one can also construct a plausible scenario in which massive deflation is the result.[9] And if it turns out that the telecommunications system and the Internet remain intact after 2000, it's even possible that the collapse of traditional banking could lead to an entirely new scenario, in which economic transactions are conducted through Internet-mediated, gold-backed "digital cash." And there are probably a dozen other scenarios that are equally plausible; gambling all of one's current financial assets on any one of these scenarios is risky indeed.

Thus, if you're worried—as we are—about the possibility of severe Y2000 disruptions in one or more aspects of the social infrastructure that we currently depend on, then flexibility and mobility and liquidity are likely to be the most important criteria for survival. By analogy: If your house catches on fire in the middle of the night, your first priority is to get yourself and your family out of the building. You may not have time to save anything else; but ultimately, everything else can be replaced. And if you waste too many precious moments trying to save all of your clothes, all of your books, and your stamp collection and your high school yearbook, you may not survive at all.

A Final Thought

We are optimists at heart, and we agree with the late Mary McCarthy's assessment:

> *The happy ending is our national belief.*[10]

But we are also deeply concerned about the potential impact of Y2000 software problems in every aspect of our lives. The more we've investigated the situation during the course of preparing this book, the more worried we have become. We would like to believe that the actions by computer technicians, business executives, and government leaders during 1999 will give us cause for optimism—but we are reminded of Oscar Wilde's observation in *The Picture of Dorian Gray*:

> *The basis of optimism is sheer terror.*[11]

In the final analysis, we believe that it's better to be terrified now and take appropriate actions, even if it turns out that the Y2000 problems are no worse than a few mosquito bites. The alternative—being complacent now and facing the possibility of severe

Y2000 problems without any fallback plans—could turn out to be the equivalent of a fatal rattlesnake bite. As many of the computer professionals in the Y2000 community are prone to say, "Hope for the best, but plan for the worst."

Consequently, we're making our fallback plans now—and we hope this book has convinced you to begin making yours.

Endnotes

1. On a personal level, we *have* begun making our own fallback plans, including some significant lifestyle changes in 1997 and 1998. As a father-daughter coauthor team, we have different families to look after, different careers, and different personal preferences—but our respective plans are very much based on the possible risks to key infrastructure services (utilities, transportation, banking, telecommunications, etc.), as well as a possible economic decline resulting from the Y2000 problem.
2. There are some exceptions: In particular, the *Washington Post* and *USA Today* have both published frequent, detailed articles on Y2000. These articles, as well as the articles from most other American, Canadian, British, and Australian newspapers, are available on the Internet. Two good sources of Y2000 "press clippings" are http://headlines.yahoo.com/Full_Coverage/Tech/Year_2000_Problem/ and http://www.y2knews.com.
3. We *strongly* recommend that you back up any important data on your computer before you try this—just in case the act of inducing a Y2000 rollover creates some obscure problem that can't be easily remedied. Also, if you're operating a computer system in your office, make sure that you get the assistance of a professional computer person. Some of the commercial software packages in office environments have an expiration date, beyond which the software won't function. Thus, if you "fool" the package by resetting the hardware clock on the computer, you may create permanent damage.
4. You may also be able to find some useful information in the annual statements and quarterly 10-Q statements filed with the SEC. You may or may not own any shares in XYZ Motor Com-

pany, but if you're about to buy one of their cars, it would be nice to know if they're going to survive the Y2000 problem. The SEC began requiring publicly traded companies to disclose "material" expenditures on Y2000 at the beginning of 1998; by the summer of 1998, the disclosure requirements were expanded significantly. You won't be able to obtain *proof* that a company will succeed with its Y2000 efforts, but you should be able to get enough information to make an informed judgment.

5. This information was posted on the Internet at http://www.frbsf.org/fiservices/cdc/fedline.html, but by mid-August 1997, the Web link had been removed.
6. *New York Times Magazine*, June 1, 1969 from *The Message to the Planet,* part 6 (1989).
7. From *The Message to the Planet*, part 6 (1989).
8. "Looking Back on the Spanish War" (reprinted in *Collected Essays,* 1961).
9. Indeed, we could even have a combination of inflation and deflation simultaneously. Since the demand for "necessities" (food, shelter, etc.) is likely to remain relatively constant, and since the supply of those necessities could be disrupted by Y2000, prices could go up. But the same supply-vs.demand lessons of traditional economics could lead to a different outcome for "optional" items. You might already have three pairs of jogging shoes in your closet, but you're tempted by the constant barrage of television commercials to buy a fourth pair. Maybe the company that builds the jogging shoes is completely successful in repairing its computers, and thus continues to churn out large numbers of shoes. But if the company *you* work for has not repaired its computers, then you may be out of a job. With no income, the likelihood of buying that additional pair of jogging shoes drops sharply. And if demand drops, traditional economics argues that the producer will have to lower his prices into order to maintain the same volume of sales.
10. Mary McCarthy, *On the Contrary,* part 1, "America the Beautiful: The Humanist in the Bathtub" (1962; first published Sept. 1947).
11. Oscar Wilde, from remarks by Lord Henry, in *The Picture of Dorian Gray,* chapter 6 (1891).

What the Y2000 Problem Is All About

The Vice President discussed the design flaw in millions of the world's computers that will mean they will be unable to recognize the year 2000. And if they can't, then we will see a series of shutdowns, inaccurate data, faulty calculations.

The consequences of the millennium bug, if not addressed, could simply be a rash of annoyances, like being unable to use a credit card at the supermarket, or the video store losing track of the tape you have already returned—has that ever happened to you? It really is aggravating. (Laughter.) It could affect electric power—I just want to remind you that I used to have a life and I know about things like that. (Laughter.) It could affect electric power, phone service, air travel, major governmental service.

As the Vice President said, we're not just talking about computer networks, but billions of embedded chips built into everyday products. And it's worth remembering that the typical family home today has more computer power in it than the entire MIT campus had 20 years ago. An oil drilling rig alone may include 10,000 separate chips.

President Bill Clinton, Speech at the National Academy of Sciences, *July 14, 1998*

Introduction

In a nutshell: The Y2000 problem exists because most computer systems have been programmed to record and manipulate dates with only the least-significant two digits of the year; thus "1999" is represented as "99" and "2000" is represented as "00". Once we reach January 1, 2000, most computer systems will produce incorrect results whenever "date arithmetic" is carried out. In some cases, the results will be amusing, but nonetheless grossly incorrect behavior or output from the computer; in other cases, the results could have serious economic or life-threatening consequences.

Here's a simple example: You borrow $1,000 from your neighborhood bank on January 1, 1998, and repay it on January 1, 1999. The bank's computer system recorded the details of the loan transaction, and probably represented the date of the loan as "980101" (a compact, shorthand notation for "98th year, 1st month, 1st day") and the date of the repayment as "990101". In order to calculate the amount of interest that must be paid for the privilege of having borrowed the money, the computer system subtracts the loan-creation date from the loan-repayment date:

```
          990101
minus     980101
          0100000
```

This is an oversimplification of the way computers actually work, but in essence, the result of the calculation above tells the computer that the duration of the bank loan was 1 year, 0 months, and 0 days—at which point the interest calculation can be carried out.

Now imagine what happens to a loan that was created on January 1st, 1999 and repaid on January 1, 2000 (ignoring the fact that January 1, 2000 is a Saturday and that most of us will be too hung over to stagger down to the bank to repay a loan!). If the bank's computer tried to calculate the interest in the same manner shown earlier, it would attempt to carry out the following arithmetic:

```
        000101
minus   990101
       -9900000
```

Thus, the computer decides that the loan existed for a "negative" time period, i.e., a period of *minus* 99 years. In the real, physical world that all of us live in, this makes no sense at all; in the world of computer logic, it's clearly incorrect, and will almost certainly lead to an undesirable result. The actual behavior of the computer will depend on the technical details of the hardware, the operating system (e.g., software like Windows 95 for personal computers), the programming language used to write the banking software (e.g., COBOL, RPG, Visual Basic, and so forth), and whatever programming logic was created by the people who developed the banking system. Here are some, but by no means all, of the possibilities that could occur:

- The negative time period could be used, without any modification, to calculate a "negative interest"—i.e., the bank system could end up deciding that it owes you interest. This would be a pleasant surprise, but is certainly not what the bank intended!

- Because of the way numbers are stored internally in computer systems, the negative number could "wrap around" or "roll over" and appear to be an extremely large positive number—e.g., 990101. Thus, the computer could decide that you had borrowed the money for 99 years rather than one year; and the interest charges, with compound interest calculations, could be substantially larger than the principal of the loan.

- The computer system could decide that, since dates were intended to be stored as a positive number, it will replace any negative numbers with zero. Thus, the interest calculation decides that you borrowed the money for zero years, zero months, and zero days—and thus charges no interest at all. This is good for you, of course, but bad for the bank.

- The computer system might have been programmed in such a way that if a negative result ever occurred in an arithmetic operation that was intended to produce a positive result, it would abort all processing and halt. (This kind of behavior is relatively rare for arithmetic operations involving addition and subtraction, but it's very common when a computer attempts to divide a number by zero, because the results are mathematically undefined.) Thus, the banking system screeches to a halt every time it processes a loan that extends across the Year-2000 boundary; you never receive any statement of the interest charges due, and the bank never collects any interest payments. Again, good for you, but bad for the bank.

- In a few rare cases, the banking system might have been programmed to ignore any unexpected negative values by computing the "absolute value" of a numerical calculation; in this case, the result of "-010000" shown above would actually be stored as "0100000", and everything would proceed normally.

It's important to emphasize that some banking systems would have no problems with any of this, because they were programmed from the beginning to be "Year-2000 compliant." It isn't a great surprise that the turn of the century is coming, after all, and some computer systems have been programmed with *four*-digit representations of the year. In this case, the date-calculation shown above would look like this:

```
          20000101
minus     19990101
          00010000
```

This example is admittedly simplistic, but it's enough to illustrate the fundamental nature of the Year-2000 problem. If it were as simple as this, we might have a chance of fixing the problem; but as we'll illustrate below, there are several more computer-oriented anomalies related to dates; and there are some *enormous* problems associated with finding all these quirks and fixing them within the computer systems of large organizations. Indeed, almost all of the computer professionals who are working on the Year-2000 problem today regard the technological aspects of the problem as relatively trivial; it's the management and logistics problem of finding and fixing *all* of the date calculations, all at once, that is proving to be so overwhelming.

Additional Anomalies and Quirks of the Year-2000 Problem

For a computer programmer reading through the hypothetical banking system described above, it's fairly obvious that a date involving year, month, and day could cause problems if the year is represented with two digits. But sometimes dates are "hard-coded" and embedded within the computer program in a more subtle fashion; suppose, for example, that the programmer found the following piece of program logic within the banking system:

```
IF GEEZER > 65
    THEN INTEREST_RATE = 0.05
ELSE
    INTEREST_RATE = 0.09
```

Here's the question: Is "65" a reference to the calendar year 1965, or is it intended to be the literal number 65? It's very difficult to answer this question without knowing the "context" in which this calculation is being carried out; in particular, we need to know what "GEEZER" really means. When programmers write computer programs, they use symbolic names to refer to an area of the computer's memory that will be used to store a piece of information; a good programmer will use a mnemonic name that helps other computer programmers understand what's going on. Unfortunately, smart-ass programmers use the names of their pets, their favorite foods, or their girlfriends/boyfriends. If the small piece of computer logic shown above had been written by a good programmer, it might have appeared thusly:

```
IF AGE_OF_BORROWER > 65
    THEN INTEREST_RATE = 0.05
ELSE
    INTEREST_RATE = 0.09
```

Or it might have looked like this:

```
IF YEAR_OF_LOAN_ORIGINATION > 65
    THEN INTEREST_RATE = 0.05
ELSE
    INTEREST_RATE = 0.09
```

In the first case, "65" is a literal constant, and should *not* be changed to 1965 during a Year-2000 project; in the second case, the bank has apparently decided that any loan granted after 1965 should be given a preferential interest rate.

There are three things worth noting about this example:

- The person who has to examine the computer program to see if it requires changing is almost certainly *not* the person who wrote the program in the first place. Indeed, many of the computer programs that are associated with the Year-2000 problem were first written 25 years ago by people who have retired, died, or moved on to greener pastures at some other company. In the rare case where the same programmer is still working on software that he/she created, it's very difficult to remember the details of intricate program logic that was written years ago. By analogy, take a look at your checkbook from three years ago: Can you remember why you wrote that check to "cash" for $43.98?

- The details of a computer program are sometimes explained in separate documentation—memos, manuals, flowcharts, and the like—created while the program was first being developed. Thus, in the best of all cases, we might be able to find a document for our cryptic example above, in which the original programmer wrote "I used the name 'GEEZER' to refer the age of a person taking out a bank loan, simply because my Dad always used to refer to people who had retired as 'geezers'." Unfortunately, in many computer projects, the documentation was never written at all; or it was lost; or it became obsolete because subsequent generations of maintenance programmers changed the program logic without updating the associated documentation. By analogy: Can you even find the checkbook for those checks you wrote three years ago? Did you even bother making an entry for that $43.98 check to cash? Was it perhaps a surprise birthday gift for your spouse, in which case you might have written an entirely misleading entry in the checkbook?

- While it's difficult to guess the underlying meaning of a cryptic name like GEEZER, sometimes it can be inferred by looking at other portions of the same program. In our banking example, for instance, a careful scrutiny might have uncovered another section of computer logic that read

```
        SUBTRACT BIRTHDATE_OF_ BORROWER FROM
TODAYS_DATE AND
        STORE RESULT IN GEEZER.
```

- This would obviously lead us to conclude that GEEZER was intended to be used as an "age" field, and so the literal reference to "65" should not be changed. While it's almost impossible for a human to scan through all of the complex interdependencies of a large program (some of which contains millions of computer instructions) to draw such conclusions, an automated analysis can be carried by another computer program. An entire industry of software vendors has emerged in the past few years with automated tools to scan through programs like the hypothetical banking system and find both the obvious and the not-so-obvious references to dates.

This example of "embedded" dates is just one of the problems; here are two more:

- Many computer programs were written in the 1960s, 70s, or 80s with the implicit assumption that they would be scrapped or replaced within 10 years; as a result, many computer programmers assumed that "99" and "00" would never represent legitimate values for a date-year. And because of this assumption, they would sometimes use these two values to assign a special status to a customer, or an invoice, or similar pieces of information.[1] A birth-year of 99, for example, might be used in a banking system to indicate that an account-holder has deceased, and therefore should not be sent any marketing literature. A birth-year of 00 might be used to indicate that the account-holder has declared personal bankruptcy, and is therefore ineligible for loans or certain other banking transactions. Note that this could lead to problems for the bank's computer systems before January 1, 2000; indeed, some organizations are bracing for possible problems on September 9, 1999 because of the tendency of programmers to use "9/9/99" as a special value in some of the older computer systems.

- 2000 is a leap year, but some computer systems fail to recognize this fact. Everyone knows that any year divisible by four is a leap year; and many computer programmers also know that there is an exception: a year divisible by 100 is *not* a leap year. But some programmers are unaware that there is an exception to the exception: If the year is also divisible by 400, then it *is* a leap year. Thus, 1900 was not a leap year, nor is 2100, but 2000 is. All of this is relevant for the computer programs that carry out a straightforward calculation to determine whether February 29th exists in the year 2000; note that this is a problem that may not be recognized in some business organizations until two months after New Year's Eve at the turn of the millennium.

- January 1, 2000 will be a Saturday (as you can easily confirm by looking at your own calendar), but January 1, 1900 was a Monday. Thus, a non-compliant computer that bases its decisions on the day of the week (e.g., an elevator system in a high-rise office building, which has one operating schedule for weekdays, and a different one for weekends) may not function correctly.

Consequences of the Problem

What happens when a computer system incorrectly interprets the date after December 31, 1999? Unfortunately, there's no single, simple answer to this question; we can't make a simple public announcement to the entire human race that says, "Whenever you have an encounter with a computer system that overcharges you by $3,141,592.65 after December 31, 1999, just ignore it. It's a minor problem, and it will fixed as soon as the computer experts can get to it."

As we've seen, many of the common Y2000 problems *do* involve incorrect calculations within business-oriented computer systems (e.g., computers associated with a bank, insurance company, phone company, and the like); but here are a few more of the typical things that can go wrong:

- *Incorrect decisions resulting from erroneous date calculations:* There have already been reports of computer systems sending notices to 104-year old grandmothers that they should report to kindergarten; and the British department store, Marks & Spencer, has reported that its inventory control systems have already begun rejecting incoming arrivals of perishable items whose expiration date is beyond January 1, 2000. As illustrated in the examples above, there will also probably be numerous cases, in the early part of the next decade, where a computer system incorrectly decides that a person is dead. If the bank's marketing department stops sending you junk-mail advertising based on that incorrect decision, you probably won't object; but if the electric company shuts off your electricity and the IRS fails to send your tax-refund check, you'll be pretty annoyed. Stop for a moment and think about the situations you're likely to encounter with a computer-controlled bureaucracy that thinks you're dead...

- *Incorrect decisions, one step removed*: Suppose you open your monthly credit-card statement on January 3, 2000 and find an interest charge of $3,141,592.65 for last month's unpaid balance. By itself, that's bad enough—but imagine what happens next. Your first reaction might be to ignore the bill on the basis that it's clearly incorrect; or you might decide to call the customer service department to complain about the bill. But if a million other customers also got an incorrect bill, then the phone line will be permanently busy (assuming it works at all), and you won't be able to rectify the situation. A month later, you'll get another bill; this time it's for $3,188,716.54 because the credit-card company charges you an additional 1.5 percent per month for unpaid balances. You won't pay this bill either, of course, but the next thing that happens is that the credit-card company cancels your card because of the large delinquent balance. Then it will send you a dunning notice threatening to sue you if you don't pay the entire amount ...

- *Corruption of internal databases:* Computers not only make decisions and generate bills and invoices "on the fly," they also store information for subsequent processing. Thus, if the credit card system sends you a monthly statement for $3,141,592.65, it also stores that information in a "record" or "file"—the electronic equivalent of a paper-copy of that statement, which a 19th century clerk would have placed into a file folder and stuffed into a file cabinet. But the file storage area on many computer systems is often designed in a very rigid, constrained fashion, with an allowance of a specific number of characters, or digits, for each piece of information. The person who designed the credit-card system, for example, may have decided that a storage area of only 20 characters will be assigned for the customer's name, and 30 characters for the customer's street address; that's why you sometimes find that your name or address has been truncated in a bizarre fashion in the computer-generated statements and invoices you receive. Suppose that the same programmer has decided (with or without approval and knowledge of his managers) that no customer will ever get a credit-card statement involving an amount greater than $99,999.99—so he allocates enough space in the computer's file-storage area to hold seven numerical digits. Now, because of the Year-2000 bug, the computer program tries to store a 9-digit number ($3,141,592.65) into that seven-digit space. What happens? Possibly the high-order two digits, or the low-order two digits, will be truncated, which will lead to further confusion if you ever do manage to talk to a customer service representative to complain about your bill; the representative will retrieve the record from the computer file and assume that you're complaining about a credit-card bill of $41,492.65. But here's a worse scenario: The extra two digits of the invoice amount over-writes the first two digits of whatever information was stored "adjacent" to the invoice amount. For example, the computer programmer might have decided that it would be a good idea to store your home address in the file-storage area immediately adjacent to the invoice amount. Because of the Year-2000 bug, the first two digits of your street address are now "65".

- *Aborts, abends, and halts*: In some cases, a computer system will make an incorrect decision, or generate an incorrect output, or store some incorrect information in a file or database; and then it will keep chugging along, carrying out a similar (incorrect) activity for the next customer, the next invoice, or the next "transaction" that it's supposed to process. But there will be numerous cases where a Year-2000 problem causes the computer to stop all subsequent processing and come to a halt; computer professionals sometime refer to these situations as an ABEND (particularly for older mainframe computer systems), or an "abort". For a business computer system that's trying to send out thousands of invoices or credit-card statements, there won't be any immediate consequences of an ABEND; it may cause some middle-of-the-night phone calls to the computer programmers, but it will take a while for the bank's customers to notice that they haven't received their monthly statement. The situation is far more serious, though, for the vast number of "embedded" systems that permeate society: "Process control" computers are used for refineries, nuclear reactors, air-traffic control, traffic signals, and dozens of other systems in which a sudden halt could have life-threatening consequences. This is discussed in Chapters 3 and 4.

How the Year-2000 Problem Came to Be

When our car malfunctions, what do we do? For most of us, the answer is simple: Yell at it, as if it were an unruly child. When the word-processor on our home-computer or office-computer somehow deletes the document we were working on, we're likely to snarl, "You stupid computer! How could you do that to me?" We *anthropomorphize* complex mechanical and computerized devices, and treat them as if they were living, sentient creatures; even veteran computer professionals have a tendency to behave in this fashion, and the behavior has been popularized with examples like HAL in the movie *2001*.

But there's an important point to remember in our discussion of the Year-2000 situation: *Computers* aren't responsible for all these problems, people are. Aside from transient hardware failures (e.g., from an overheated circuit, or the effect of a piece of dust in a disk drive), computers behave or misbehave in whatever fashion they were instructed by the computer programmer. In general, programmers try to design and implement a computer program to produce the behavior specified by their managers, or by the customers for whom the system is being developed. But in other cases, particularly when it comes to low-level technical details, programmers make their own decisions—either because customers and managers trust the technicians to make the right decisions, or because they're uninterested in the details, or because they're overwhelmed by the technical nature of the situation.

Thus, sometimes the managers of a computer department, and the business managers within the organization, were aware of the conscious decision to represent dates with a two-digit year, and sometimes they weren't. If this sounds sloppy and irresponsible, think about *yourself* as a "customer." When you bought your home, did you ask the architect whether the plumbing hardware and electrical wiring had been designed and implemented to last for any specific period of time? If this had resulted in a lengthy conversation with the plumber and the electrician, would you have understood the nuances of what they were telling you? Probably not.

Of course, you might have responded, "I don't have to worry about such details. I trust the architect, because I know that he's licensed. And I trust the plumber and electrician to do the right thing, because there's an independent building inspector who must certify that my new house has been constructed according to standard building codes."

Unfortunately, there's no such parallel in the software industry. Most computer programmers, systems analysts, software engineers, database designers, and other specialists have college degrees, but there's no such thing as a "license" in the field. And while the software systems in a few safety-critical industries *do* have to be "inspected" before they are allowed to operate, there's no equivalent of a "building code" regarding the proper way to represent a date—although the U.S. government has recently adopted a standard definition of what it means for a computer program to be "year-2000 compliant." For the vast majority of business-oriented computer systems, though, and for a reasonable majority of embedded systems and control systems, there has been no oversight, review, or inspection at all.

If the legendary cartoon figure, Pogo, were a computer programmer, he might say, "We have met the Year-2000 enemy, and he is us... and our managers." It's fair to say that, in most cases, the business managers—e.g., the vice president of the credit-card division of a bank—had no idea that the computer systems being developed for them had a Year-2000 time-bomb ticking away. But even if they did, they probably would have been susceptible to the same mistakes and weaknesses of the technical computer specialists.

But *why* did the technical specialists get us into this problem? After all, you don't have to be a rocket scientist to understand the potential problems we've outlined in this appendix. And most computer programmers *are* rocket scientists, in one fashion or another, so how could they have been so dumb? Here are the most common explanations:

- *Casual sloppiness.* Depending on how you count such things, four or five generations of people have been born in this century. The 20th century is the only thing we've known, and that our parents and their parents have known. In our written and verbal communications, we naturally truncate the first two digits of the year: "Where were you back in '63 when Kennedy was shot? Were you in San Francisco during the '89 earthquake?" The assumption that only the low-order two digits are relevant permeates much of what we do; and though they're usually fairly careful about details, computer programmers suffer from this same casual assumption. It simply didn't occur to them, when they wrote their computer programs, that it would be a good idea to use all four digits of the year.

- *Computer hardware was expensive when most business computer systems were first developed*. As we pointed out earlier, many of the business computer systems that are most vulnerable to Year-2000 problems were designed 20 or 30 years ago. In those days, computers were several thousand times larger, and slower, and more expensive. Today, we casually buy a home computer with 32 megabytes (millions of characters) of memory, and 2 gigabytes (billions of characters) of disk storage, and we expect to pay about $1,000. Thirty years ago, business organizations had to spend a million dollars to buy a computer with 32 kilobytes (thousands of characters) of memory, and 2 megabytes of disk storage; instead of sitting on a desktop, the old computers filled an entire room. In the 1960s and 1970s, programmers were expected to use every trick they could think of in order to save a few precious characters of storage; if a bank had a million customers, and each customer's banking record had a dozen different dates (e.g., the customer's birthdate, the date the account was opened, the date of the last deposit, the date of each of the checks written during the past month,and so forth), then eliminating the high-order two digits of the year could save a few dozen characters for each customer, and a few hundred million characters of aggregate storage requirements. Today, we would shrug our shoulders at the prospect of a few hundred million characters of storage; Microsoft's new Office97 software gobbles up 300 million characters when it's installed on our home computer. But in the 1960s or 1970s, numbers like that could represent the difference between success and failure. So the Year-2000 problem was, in a sense, created deliberately by well-intentioned programmers who were coping with the economics of the times.

- *Nobody thought computer systems would last so long.* Thirty years is a long, long time in the computer industry; the speed, power, storage capacity, and cost of computer hardware has improved by a factor of approximately one million. This is not just an academic notion: If you bought one of IBM's first PC computers in 1981, you've seen five subsequent generations of Intel-based PC hardware: the 286, 386, 486, Pentium, and Pentium II. In this kind of environment, the natural assumption is that software will be replaced quickly, too; indeed, some of the computer systems designed in the 1960s and 1970s used a one-digit representation of the year, on the assumption that the software would almost certainly be replaced or rewritten before the end of the decade. The situation was sometimes exacerbated by business managers who yelled at the programmers, "Don't waste your time trying to design the system to last for 20 years—we only need to run the system once or twice to produce some reports for the government, and then we'll never need it again." True, some software does get used only once or twice; and some software does get rewritten and replaced after four-five years, in order to take advantage of more powerful hardware capabilities. But to everyone's surprise, many of the largest and most complex systems have survived (albeit with extensive modifications, enhancements, and repairs) for 20-30 years.

- *Nobody thought of the "system-level" consequences.* In the cases where computer programmers did think about the consequences of a Year-2000 problem, they typically thought about it only in the context of the particular system they were working on, e.g., "Uh oh, what's going to happen to the insurance billing system that I'm responsible for when we reach New Year's Eve in 1999?" And in the rare cases where a higher-level computer manager contemplated the problem, the attention was focused only on that manager's organization, e.g., "I sure hope I'm retired when it comes time to fix all the Year-2000 problems in our systems!". But until a year or two ago, it didn't occur to anyone that every computer program in every company in every industry in every country was going to face the Year-2000 problem at the same time. As we'll explain in Appendix B, it's the "system dynamics" aspect of the Year-2000 problem that's most difficult to anticipate or control.

- *Nobody wanted to be the victim of "shoot the messenger" politics.* Though it might appear that computer professionals have been unbelievably short-sighted with regard to the Year-2000 problem, a few individuals began thinking about the problem in 1990. A new year, a new decade, the last decade of the century... a few forward-thinking computer managers began muttering to themselves, "Uh, oh ... it may be 10 years away, but it's pretty obvious that our systems won't work at the beginning of the next decade." And it became a little more obvious in 1995, when a few companies began to notice that their five-year financial forecasts were blowing up, because of the Year-2000 problem. But the politics of dealing with the situation are pretty difficult, especially when (a) most organizations have a planning horizon of one year or less, (b) computer budgets are being scrutinized more and more carefully, and (c) a Year-2000 project provides no new functionality or "business value." Imagine what it's like for the manager of a computer department at the XYZ bank, who finds himself saying to the vice president of the credit-card division: "You know that new credit-card billing system that we developed a couple years ago, for a cost of $10 million? Well, I'm sorry to tell you that we're going to have to spend another $3 million to make it Year-2000 compliant.

> You won't get any additional benefit from that $3 million expense, except for the fact that, five years from now, the software will still run correctly. Oh, and by the way, this project will require all of our best programmers, so we won't be able to work on any new computer projects for the next two years."

What to Do?

In the rare cases that senior business managers were made aware of the Year-2000 problem in 1990 or 1995, they generally ignored it. The typical response was, "We'll worry about it next year, when we have more time and more money in the budget." Or, "I'm going to be transferred next year, and it's crucial for me to achieve all of my revenue and profit and cost-reduction objectives this year. I'll let my successor worry about this problem." Indeed, this continues to be a common reaction: "Hey, we still have a whole year left—we can take care of this over the weekend in late 1999."

But the widespread discussion and debate about the Year-2000 problem within the computer industry has gradually made it evident that it will be far too late to solve the problem in 1999; indeed, for many organizations, it was already too late when the first edition of this book was written in the summer of 1997. Throughout the United States, computer departments have been gradually shifting more and more of their people and computer resources to Year-2000 projects, which usually involves one or more of the following strategies:

- *Retiring the systems that are no longer needed:* Even though some 30-year-old systems are still being used on a daily basis, and are considered "mission-critical," there are other business computer systems that have fallen into disuse. More important, there are computer systems that run daily, weekly, or monthly to produce reports that nobody bothers looking at any more. Obviously, the best Y2000 strategy here is euthanasia of the old systems; however, this requires a careful analysis and assessment of the organization's "portfolio" of software systems, as well as a consensus among the senior business managers as to which systems are mission-critical and which ones are irrelevant. The time required for this kind of analysis and consensus-building can take longer than the technical work to fix the programs—and there's not much time left to do it!

- *Replacing old systems with a commercial "package":* Imagine the scenario of a medium-sized company that runs a weekly payroll system, which was developed 20 years ago by a programmer that has vanished. The software is not Year-2000 compliant, and nobody can figure out how it works, because the documentation has disappeared. Finding and fixing all the date occurrences will be time-consuming, tedious, expensive, and error-prone; an obvious alternative is to scrap the program and replace it with a commercial "package" or payroll service. The same is likely to be true for accounts payable, accounts receivable, general ledger, inventory control, and a wide variety of common business applications. However, for large Fortune 500 companies, it typically takes two-three years to customize, configure, and install a large, complex commercial package from vendors such as SAP, Peoplesoft, and Baan. It was often an attractive, practical alternative in 1995; by the beginning of 1998, it was too late for many companies; and by the beginning of 1999, it will be too late for all but the smallest companies.

- *Changing two-digit year fields to four digits:* This is the "obvious" correction, of course, and it's one of the more common approaches taken by companies today. But it has two problems: First, the extra two digits take up additional space on printed reports and on computer display screens. And second, it requires updating and expanding of date fields on database records and files. The first problem is likely to be a minor one, though you would be surprised how many computer systems have every conceivable piece of "real estate" on such reports and screens — in some cases, it's not possible to cram in an extra two digits without a major redesign of the report or screen layout.

The required modifications to the database are far more problematic. Again, there's the problem of "real estate": As mentioned earlier in this Appendix, some of the older computer systems are designed so that the information in a database record takes up all of the available space within the storage area of the hard disk or magnetic tape; adding two more digits (or, more likely, several instances of double-digits, since a typical business database record will have multiple instances of date fields) could mean redesigning the entire database. And even without this nuisance, there's the enormous logistics problem of updating (and expanding) the database while the organization attempts to continue running its day-to-day business operations. Many large organizations now have databases consisting of several terabytes (trillions of bytes), and it would require weeks or months of uninterrupted computer time to update the database.

- *Using a "windowing" approach:* Because of the database and report-expansion problems mentioned above, many organizations have decided to use a programming approach known as "windowing" to deal with the Y2000 problem. Essentially, this involves defining a century-wide "window" with which to interpret the real meaning of a two-digit year. For example, an organization might decide to define a window that extends from 1920 to 2019; this means that whenever its computer programs encounter a two-digit year field of, say, "43", it will be interpreted as 1943; a two-digit year field of "03" will be interpreted as "2003", and so forth. Of course, if such a computer program is dealing with birthdates of people, then it's going to make the wrong decision if it encounters someone born before 1920, and it's going to run into far more serious problems if the same program is still being used in the year 2020. Thus, it's crucial for companies to choose a window carefully, depending on the nature of their business applications; unfortunately, this is a concept that has not been standardized, so if company A's computers send date-related information to company B's computers, there's going to be a lot of confusion unless both companies have chosen the same window, or have some way of translating between one window and another.

Year-2000: The Biggest Computer Project of All Time

While we've over-simplified some of the technical details in this Appendix, the essence of the Year-2000 problem is not very difficult to understand, from a technical perspective; nor is the solution. While the concept of a Y2000 problem might have taken you by surprise when you first picked up this book, and while the whole thing might seem a bit overwhelming, most computer professionals tend to downplay the problem when they first hear about it. An eminent computer consultant, who is now *very* aware of the magnitude of the Year-2000 problem, commented to one of the authors in early 1996:

> *Who can believe we are about to be undone by such a nothing problem? The mighty software monolith brought to its knees by diddly squat. It's like reading through 900 pages of Gibbon only to be told that the decline and fall of the Roman empire was really due to a bad case of head lice.*

Technologically, the Year-2000 problem *is* diddly squat—so why is everyone making such a big deal of it? The answer is simple: Industrialized society is now filled with millions of computers, which contain hundreds of *billions* of program instructions. All of these computers, and the "portfolios" of software systems they contain, must be examined and updated appropriately. And, with minor exceptions, they all need to be updated at the same time, with proper synchronization, in order to avoid what we'll describe in Appendix B as a "ripple effect" problem.

In 1996-97, several consulting and research organizations began "sizing" the Year-2000 problem; in addition to the rather crude approximations that have been widely publicized by the Gartner Group, more careful estimates have been prepared by Dr. Howard Rubin (Chairman of the Computer Science department at Hunter College in New York City), Dr. Edward Yardeni[2] (Chief Economist of Deutsche Morgan Grenfell), and by Capers Jones (CEO of Software Productivity Research). Of these, Jones has the most detailed figures, and the ones that appear to be the mostly widely accepted by other professionals and researchers in the field. Here are just a few snippets of data from his recently published book, *The Year-2000 Software Problem:*[3]

- The United States has a total, aggregate portfolio of approximately 1.57 billion "function points" of software. A function point is a language-independent way of measuring the size of a computer program, and is approximately equal to 100 COBOL statements. Thus, if all of the computer software in the U.S. had been written in COBOL (which was largely true for the business computer systems of the 1960s and 1970s, but is definitely not true as an overall characterization), we would have 157 billion program statements to deal with.[4]

- The effort to perform Y2000 repairs on this software is estimated by Jones to involve approximately 9.3 million person-months, or slightly more than 750,000 person-years, of work. The cost of this effort, given typical salaries and overhead, is approximately $74.6 billion.

- While the U.S. has more than twice as much software as the next largest country (which turns out to be Japan), the overall global figures for the 30 most significant industrialized countries are astounding: 7 billion function points (approximately equal to 700 billion program statements), 3.5 million person-years of effort, and approximately $297 billion in repair costs.

- None of these figures include the cost of likely lawsuits and post-Y2000 repair efforts associated with software that was not fixed correctly.

All of these figures must be taken with a large grain of salt, for at least two reasons:

- The vast amount of software that companies run on their mainframe computers is gradually being dwarfed by the even vaster amount of software on millions of PCs. In addition to professionally developed software on the PCs (e.g., the copy of Microsoft Word and Excel that you might have on your own computer), there are millions upon millions of hand-crafted spreadsheets and database programs that have been developed by amateurs over the past 15-20 years.

- While it's no surprise that the amateurs have typically never documented anything they've done, many large companies are discovering the humiliating fact that the same can be said of their professional programmers. A company might have a payroll system, for example, that was written 20 years ago, and is still running on a weekly basis today. Unfortunately, the program that actually runs inside the computer is a "binary" or "machine language" program that's almost impossible for a human to read and understand. The original "source program," typically written in a language like COBOL or BASIC or FORTRAN (and from which the binary program was produced by "compiling" the source program) has been lost; or it was compiled by an ancient version of IBM's compiler, which no longer exists. Or... well, the problems go on and on here, but the "bot-

> tom line" is that many organizations are now discovering that their "legacy" programs are completely out of control.

So, in short, the Y2000 problem is an enormous one, by far the largest software project any company has ever undertaken. To complicate matters, *every* company will be working on it at the same time, leading observers like Capers Jones to suggest that "the costs of fixing the 'year 2000 problem' appear to constitute the most expensive single problem in human history." President Clinton echoed this assessment in his July 14, 1998 speech with the suggestion that "With millions of hours needed to rewrite billions of lines of code and hundreds of thousands of interdependent organization[s], this is clearly one of the most complex management challenges in history."

Problems that are large and messy and expensive have a tendency to be postponed or avoided within many organizations—both from a governmental/political perspective, and also within the bureaucracy of business organizations. The situation is complicated further because, in most cases, there is no "added business value" associated with a Y2000 repair effort. Computer departments in most organizations are routinely criticized for spending lavish sums of money on advanced computer systems that fail to provide a tangible "return on investment" (ROI); consequently, the political climate in many such organizations prevents anyone from even suggesting a multi-million dollar Y2000 project, because the resulting software won't do anything bigger, better, faster, or sexier than the old system ... the only difference is that two years from now, it will continue to function correctly. For the vice president who worries about *this* year's budget (and the personal bonus or stock options that may be associated with it), the temptation to postpone the Y2000 effort for another year has been a powerful one all through the decade of the 1990s.

The problem is compounded further in many government agencies, because once a computer project has been justified and approved, *then* the necessary tools and contractors have to be acquired—typically through a procurement process that can last months or years. The notion that some state and federal government agencies won't have their personnel and Y2000 software tools in place until 2001 would be enormously amusing were it not for the fact that millions of citizens could be affected; we discuss this situation in more detail in Chapter 11.

As already noted, most organizations will need to overlap the Y2000 conversion efforts with their ongoing day-to-day business affairs. This is going to cause four additional problems:

- Additional hardware resources will be required for all of the scanning and analysis of old legacy programs, conversion efforts, compiling, and testing of Y2000 programs. Some of the work can be done on PCs and workstations, but additional mainframe resources will be required. This will not only add a large cost item, but introduces a logistics problem of its own: You can't order a mainframe from an overnight mail-order company the way you can with PCs.

- The personnel assigned to Y2000 projects will, to some extent, have to be taken from other software development projects the company would normally be working on. By mid-1998, surveys of U.S. organizations conducted by several research organizations indicated that approximately 20-25 percent of the software staff had already been thus diverted. In 1999, according to an estimate produced by the Gartner Group, many organizations will be forced to devote 50 percent of their IT resources to the Y2000 problem, which will necessitate a moratorium on all other new software development work.

- Even if all the personnel could be obtained from outside the organization (from consulting firms, big vendors like IBM, or "outsourcing" firms in India, for example), it would still represent a significant expense. If Capers Jones' worldwide Y2000 cost of $297 billion is at all accurate, that money has to come from somewhere—and the first place it will come from is the "normal" software budget of the organization.

- The demand for Y2000 personnel is going to exacerbate a shortage of software professionals estimated in early 1998 to be 300,000 professionals in the U.S. alone. It typically takes 5-10 years for universities and educational institutions to respond to marketplace shortages like this, which means that for the remainder of this decade, the shortage will probably get worse. One of the most obvious consequences of such a shortage is rising labor costs; many researchers are already predicting that the costs of Y2000 conversion projects in 1998-99 will be 50-100 percent more expensive than they would have been in 1996-97.

- While all of this is going on, the business will have a demand for ongoing changes, corrections, and improvements of the business applications that are simultaneously being reviewed and corrected for Y2000 compliance. The trivial solution to this problem is to "freeze" all existing computer programs in their current state, and to disallow any changes until the Y2000 corrections have been made. For obvious reasons, this will turn out to be unpopular, expensive, impractical, and in some cases, downright impossible. Thus, the organization will have the added burden to coordinating two entirely different categories of "maintenance" projects: a massive Y2000 effort with a bare-minimum of "ordinary" enhancements.

- The same problem exists with the database, as noted earlier in this Appendix. Indeed, even if the programs could be "frozen" for the duration of the Y2000 projects, the databases would continue to change on a daily, hourly, or even continuous basis—reflecting the orders and invoices and payments and other business transactions that are the very heartbeat of the business organization. For a medium-sized organization with a modest-sized database, the solution is to halt normal business operations early on a Friday afternoon, and tell the Y2000 project team to work around the clock through the weekend, in order to have an updated, Y2000-compliant database ready to resume normal operations on Monday morning. This sort of thing has happened before, and it's always stressful and problematic; for large organizations, it's simply impossible to accomplish all of the database conversion within a limited time-frame of 48 hours.

As you can see, the logistics and project-management aspects of the Y2000 project are daunting, to say the least. There's one last discouraging item:

The software industry, as a whole, has *never* been very good at completing projects on time, within budget. The situation varies by industry, by programming language, and by size of project — but in general, only 15-20 percent of software projects are finished within the budget and timeframe originally allocated. About 15-20 percent of projects are canceled, and the most common scenario is a project that exceeds both its budget *and* its schedule by 50-100 percent. Whether a budget overrun is acceptable depends on the specific circumstances, of course; but the obvious constraint of a Y2000 project is that it *cannot* overrun the deadline of December 31, 1999.

When software-project schedule delays first began to be noticed 30 years ago, there was a common tendency to add more programmers to the project, in the optimistic hope that the additional personnel could help speed things up. But in a classic software engineering book, first published in 1975, Dr. Fred Brooks articulated what has come to be known as "Brooks' Law": Adding more people to a late software project just makes it later.[5] Like trying to produce a baby in one month by assigning nine women to the task, there are some things you just can't speed up.

Producing software isn't quite like producing babies, of course, and you *can* produce software somewhat more quickly by adding more people to the project team, asking everyone to work double overtime, for example; but the law of diminishing returns sets in very quickly, and the *negative* effect of Brooks' Law occurs much sooner than the layman would think. Every professional programmer and project manager is well aware of this fact, but it probably won't prevent senior management in large organizations and government agencies from attempting to refute Brooks' Law by throwing large numbers of programmers at the project as the December 31, 1999 deadline looms nearer and nearer.

The likelihood of any software project finishing on time is dependent on many different variables, including such obvious things as the competence of the programmers working on the project. But if all other factors are fixed (because of the shortage of programmers, the finite amount of dollars and other resources that can be allocated to Y2000 projects, and the like), it's likely to turn out that the biggest single determinant of Y2000 success will be *how much calendar time is available for the project.* Imagine, for example, that an organization developed a "rational" estimate, devoid of any political bias, of its Y2000 software efforts and determined that it requires three years of calendar time to finish the job properly (an estimate that usually includes the need to spend most of calendar year 1999 on testing all of the modified software to ensure that it runs correctly). Now assume that because of politics and bureaucracy, the Y2000 project doesn't actually begin its efforts until January 1, 1998; not only will the costs escalate, but the odds of finishing the project successfully by the (non-negotiable) deadline drop sharply. If additional politics and bureaucracy prevent the project from beginning until January 1, 1999, the odds of successful completion are perilously low; indeed, this is exactly the situation that many small businesses will find themselves in.[6] As Capers Jones argues, "October of 1997 is the last month and year in which there is a reasonably possibility of finding and repairing all year 2000 instances before the end of 1999 as a normal business activity."[7]

Summary

During the summer and fall of 1998, when the second edition of this book was being written, various surveys and estimates suggested that approximately 10 percent of large organizations had not yet begun their Year 2000 projects, and that approximately 75 percent of the small businesses around the world had not yet begun. It's impossible to determine precisely what the final outcome will be, but it's not unreasonable to assume that 15-25 percent of the date-sensitive computer systems in the United States will *not* be repaired in time; a survey conducted by Cap Gemini in August 1998, for example, found that 88 percent of large organizations expected to have at least 75 percent of their computer systems repaired by December 31, 1999. The situation is likely to be somewhat worse in Europe, and considerably worse in Africa, South America, and Asia—simply because these countries have gotten a much later start on their Year 2000 projects.

As you can imagine, the problem could be annoying—or worse—if the non-compliant computer systems happen to be associated with *your* bank or *your* telephone company, or *your* employer. But as we'll demonstrate in Appendix B, the problem is likely to be magnified by the "ripple effect" caused by interdependencies between organizations. If 15 percent of the banks fail to convert their software in time, for example, the simplest scenario we could imagine is that *only* those banks would fail—that would be a problem you could ignore with a sympathetic shrug of your shoulders, unless your bank was one of the unlucky 15 percent. But the problem is that some of the non-Y2000-compliant banks won't cease operations as of midnight on December 31, 1999; instead, they'll start spewing out incorrect inter-bank transactions to other banks, the Federal Reserve, and the U.S. Treasury. And if the non-compliant banks *do* fail, they not only consume the deposits and savings of their immediate customers, but also the deposits and loans of other Y2000-compliant banks. What happens then?

One last item: Many business organizations and government agencies that began focusing on their Year-2000 problem in 1996-1997 have already concluded that they simply *cannot* fix all of their software in time; if the October 1997 deadline suggested by Capers Jones is accurate, then it's a virtual certainty that any organization beginning its Y2000 efforts after January 1, 1998 will be forced to admit that complete success is no longer possible. That doesn't mean that the organization will give up and declare bankruptcy right away, though one of the authors has heard an apocryphal story of a company whose owners concluded in 1996 that successful Y2000 conversion was no longer financially and logistically possible—so the owners sold the business.

What most organizations will do, if and when they face up to the impossibility of complete Y2000 conversion, is simple and obvious: *triage*. A careful assessment of their software portfolio will reveal that there are some systems and applications that are so critical that the business will halt immediately if they're not fixed; there are other systems for which a Y2000 failure would be painful and expensive, but that would not put the company out of business (or at least, not right away). And finally, there are some systems that are already "dead," in the sense that they're not being used, or nobody cares about them; those systems can be ignored, and the precious Y2000 resources can be diverted elsewhere.

Year-2000 guru Peter de Jager offers an intriguing example of the triage decision: If you're an airline, and you only have enough time and/or Y2000 technical personnel to fix *either* your airline reservation system *or* your aircraft maintenance/repair system, which one should you choose? The manager in charge of airline reservations (which might be a marketing function, or perhaps something reporting directly to the finance/accounting department, depending on the airline) would obviously argue that reservations are critical to the success of the airline: No reservations, such a manager might argue, means no tickets, and thus no revenue, and thus a very quick death of the business. But "shuttle" airlines like Delta and U.S. Air and Southwest

Airlines have demonstrated that customers *will* show up at the airport, pay their money, and get on the flight even if they don't have a reservation or ticket. On the other hand, a failure in the maintenance/repair system means that engines will fail, tires will blow out, and airplanes will fall out of the sky. *That* would be terminal.

Unfortunately, the fact that most organizations will find a way to limp along by sacrificing some of their non-critical systems does *not* mean that individuals like you and me will be shielded from the problem. To offer one trivial example, consider the ticket agents and airline reservation clerks who work for the hypothetical airline mentioned above. Given the scope of its problems, the airline could easily decide that it will take six months to repair the airline reservation system, and furlough the appropriate employees without pay for that period. For the airline's customers, the lack of a reservation system is an annoying nuisance; for the furloughed employees, it's a much more serious problem.

And while this is only a small—and admittedly hypothetical—example, it illustrates the perspective that you'll see throughout this book. We don't expect large, responsible organizations to ignore the Y2000 repairs on their most critical systems; consequently, we don't expect airplanes to fall out of the sky, nor do we think that Western civilization will come to a screeching halt. But we do think that there will be serious, visible, widespread problems not only at the corporate level (as in the case of our hypothetical airline, which will presumably lose some revenue because of the faulty reservation system) but also at the personal level.

Endnotes

1. Computer consultants Joe Celko and Jackie Celko have reported on the situation in a prison system, where the "prisoner release date" field was coded in such a way that "999999" was used for prisoners on death row, and "888888" was used for those with a life sentence. See "Double Zero," *Byte*, July 1997.
2. Dr. Yardeni's Web site—located at http://www.yardeni.com—is one of the most important resources for those concerned with the economic consequences of the Y2000 problem. When the first edition of this book was being prepared in the summer of 1997, Dr. Yardeni estimated that there was a 35-percent chance of a Y2000-induced global recession; by the time we began working on the second edition in the summer of 1998, Dr. Yardeni had raised his estimate to 70 percent.
3. Capers Jones, *The Year-2000 Software Problem: Quantifying the Costs and Assessing the Consequences* (Reading, MA: Addison-Wesley, 1998).
4. It should be emphasized that these figures vary dramatically depending on the programming language involved—which is the main reason that Jones and others prefer to express the Y2000 economic data in terms of language-neutral function points. While the older business applications are typically programmed in COBOL, newer applications are programmed in a variety of so-called "fourth generation" languages such as PowerBuilder, Visual Basic, and Delphi. But of more concern is the category of embedded systems and military systems that have been programmed in "low-level" languages such as assembler. Jones estimates that approximately one-third of the Y2000-sensitive software in the U.S. is written in COBOL, but there are approximately 500 specialized, obscure, and proprietary programming languages that have been used for software applications over the past 50 years.
5. Frederick P. Brooks, Jr., *The Mythical Man-Month,* revised 20th anniversary edition (Reading, MA: Addison-Wesley, 1995).
6. In many cases, the problem does not involve repairing software, but rather upgrading and replacing equipment that contains non-compliant embedded systems. Many small business organiza-

tions, for example, will discover in mid-1999 that their PBX telephone switchboard is non-compliant—but when they call their telecommunications vendor to order an upgrade, they're likely to find that the backlog is 12 months long.

7. Capers Jones, *The Year-2000 Software Problem: Quantifying the Costs and Assessing the Consequences*, page 1.

The Ripple Effect of the Y2000 Phenomenon

The millennium bug is a vivid and powerful reminder of the ways that we are growing ever more interdependent as we rise to the challenges of this new era.

President Bill Clinton, Speech at the National Academy of Sciences, *July 14, 1998*

No man is an island entire of itself; every man is a piece of the Continent, a part of the main. . . . Any man's death diminishes me because I am involved in Mankind; and therefore never send to know for whom the bell tolls; it tolls for thee.

John Donne, Devotions Upon Emergent Occasions, *Meditation 17 (1624).*

Six Degrees of Separation, a popular Broadway play written by John Guare, suggests an intriguing concept: if you communicate a message to all of the people you know, and each of these people passes on the same message to all of the people they know, and each of those people does the same thing—then after six levels, or "degrees," of communication, you will have reached everyone in the world.[1]

When it comes to the Year-2000 problem, the same principle applies. No person stands alone; no computer system stands alone; no company stands alone; no industry stands alone. *Everything*, as computer expert Tom DeMarco humorously puts it, is deeply intertwingled.[2] Thus, even if you feel that you've fixed or avoided *your* Year-2000 problems, you may be at the mercy of others who have not done so.

Here's a visual representation of the situation. Suppose, notwithstanding John Donne's observations, that you were an "island," independent of everything else in society. As we discussed in Appendix A, you probably have a dishwasher, VCR, microwave oven, and a few other appliances that might possibly be affected by the roll-over from 1999 to 2000; perhaps you have a home computer, too, which is also likely to be vulnerable to the Year-2000 phenomenon. We've represented these items as small circles within the larger circle shown in Figure B.1.

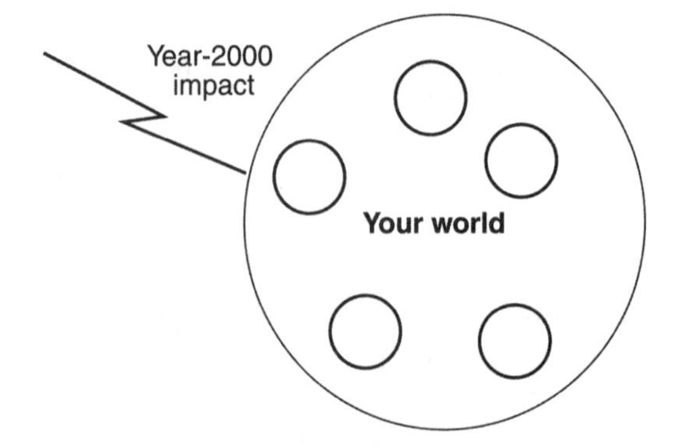

Figure B.1 The impact of Year-2000 on an individual person.

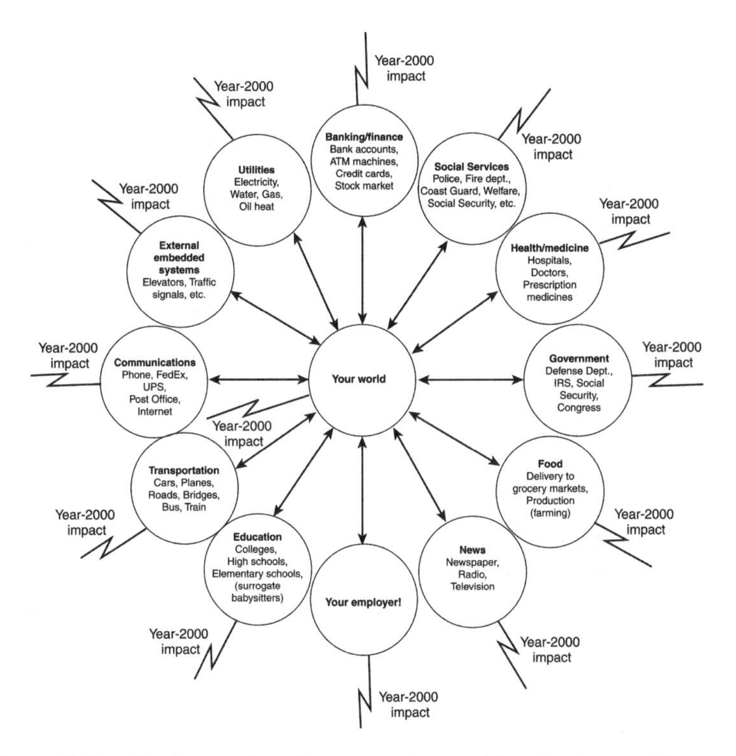

Figure B.2 The interactions between your world and other worlds.

If this is your perspective, then the Year-2000 problem is like a lightning bolt; it threatens to disrupt or destroy a number of important items in your world. Interestingly, this is the same perspective that most companies have, too—except that the little circles in their world are not simple household appliances, but large computer systems they use to run their day-to-day operations. Nevertheless, the typical corporate reaction is likely to be the same as your personal reaction: get rid of the Y2000-sensitive items that you're not using any more, fix or replace the ones that are important to you, and figure out how to survive without the other ones.

Unfortunately, it's not as simple as that. Unless you're a hermit, or marooned on a desert island, your personal world is interconnected with a number of other "worlds." We're not talking about your family members (all of whom could conceivably be *inside* the circle shown in Figure B.1), but rather the Y2000-sensitive systems that exist outside your world. If you consider only the first-level interactions, it might look something like Figure B.2.

Note that we've drawn an arrow in both directions between your world and the various other worlds that you interact with. You interact with your employer, for example, and your employer interacts with you; if the Year-2000 problem prevents interactions in either direction, it could cause a problem. Note also that we've shown the Year-2000 problem impacting *each* of the various worlds, including your own; it's unlikely that anyone will go unscathed. Furthermore, the Year-2000 impact hits everyone at the same time, aside from the minor issue of time-zone differences around the world; within 24 hours after the first part of the world celebrates New Year's Eve in 1999, everyone else will too. And so will their computers.

Although the situation in Figure B.2 looks fairly complicated, it omits an obvious point: In addition to the various worlds interacting with your world, they interact with each other. Thus, a more realistic scenario is shown in Figure B.3.

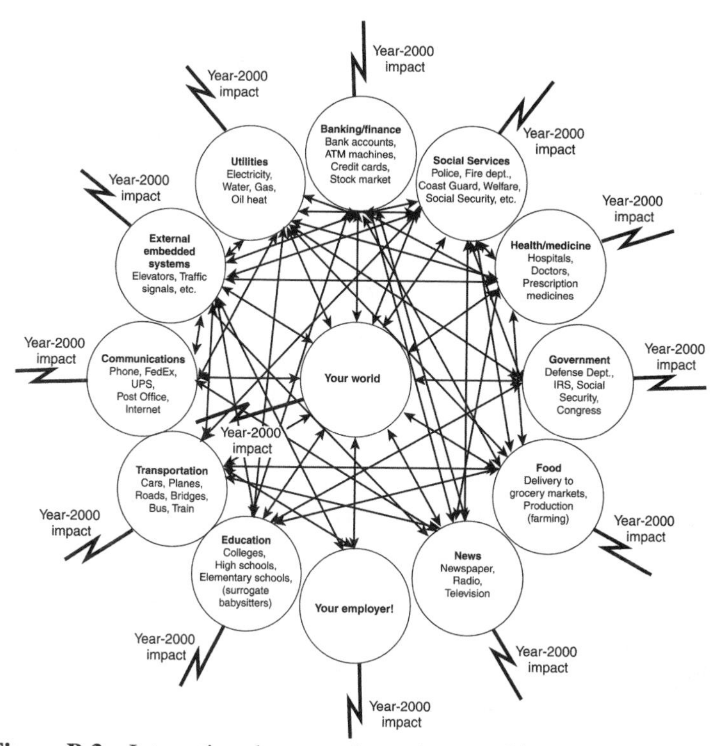

Figure B.3 Interactions between the various worlds.

Some simple examples will illustrate the point. If the electrical generators fail and the lights go out because of the Y2000 problems discussed in Chapter 3, it will be pretty difficult for your employer to conduct business; as a result, you're out of work. If the phone lines don't work (for reasons we'll discuss in Chapter 13), then most of Wall Street will be unable to conduct business. If schools are closed because of Y2000 problems (a possibility we'll discuss in Chapter 12), a lot of parents will find that they've lost a surrogate baby-sitter; they'll have to stay home to keep track of their kids.

Now let's make the situation even more realistic: Each of the "worlds" that we've shown in Figure B.3 depends on a complex network of suppliers, vendors, subcontractors, customers, employees, and others. Some of these are already represented in the two-way interactions shown in Figure B.3, but there's much more involved. If a newspaper company doesn't receive its regular supply of paper and ink, it can't produce newspapers even if the lights are on and the phones are working and the employees show up for work. Similarly, if the feed stores and fertilizer suppliers are closed, the farmers can't feed their animals or plant their crops. We've represented all of this in the fashion shown in Figure B.4.

All of these secondary worlds are potentially impacted by the Year-2000 phenomenon; and they not only have interactions with the primary worlds, but also with each other. We haven't drawn the appropriate arrows to represent this in Figure B.4, for it would result in a completely unreadable spider's web.

In some cases, these secondary worlds might consist of individual people; thus, they might view their world in the same way you do—i.e., as a small circle in the middle of a complex universe. But when you consider the secondary worlds that "feed" General Motors[3] or Citibank or the U.S. Government, it's more likely that you're dealing with medium-sized companies—which have their own network of suppliers, subcontractors, vendors, and so forth. Thus, we're likely to find that the Year-2000 interactions involve a situation as shown in Figure B.5.

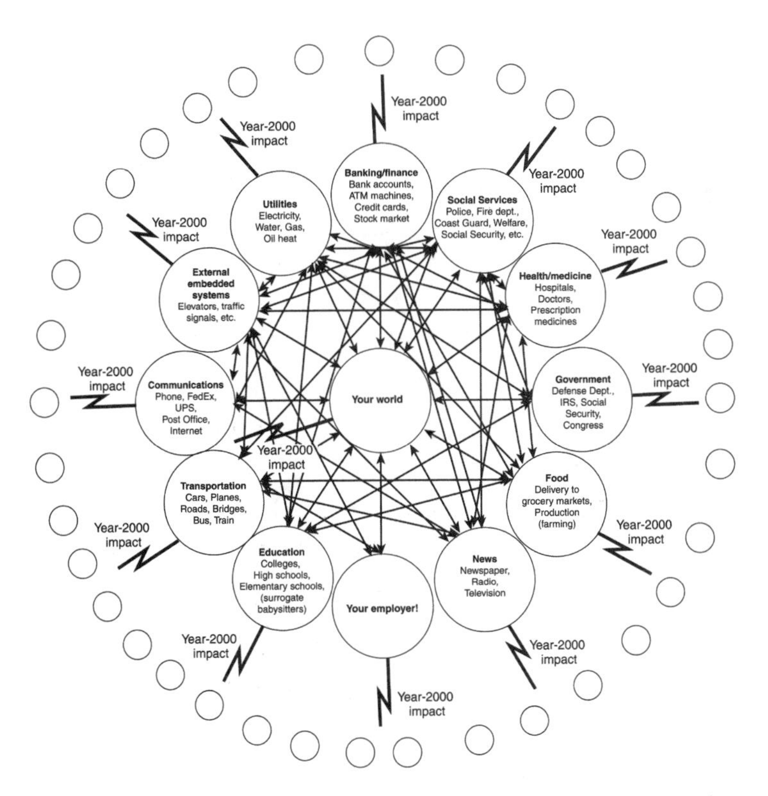

Figure B.4 The Interactions between primary worlds and secondary worlds.

You can tell what's coming next: The tertiary worlds have their own network of suppliers, vendors, and subcontractors. And those fourth-level worlds have their own network, and so forth; and if we extend this notion to the level where each "world" consists of a person, or an individual computer system, we may indeed be dealing with "six degrees of separation."

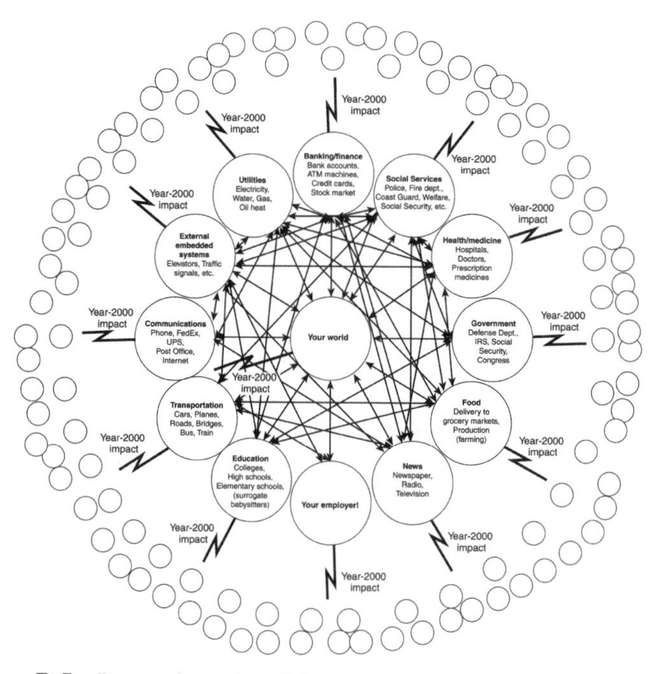

Figure B.5 Interactions involving secondary worlds and tertiary worlds.

While we firmly believe that the fundamental concept illustrated in Figure B.5 is correct, we have no way of knowing whether the Y2000 problem will have a noticeable impact on three, four, five, or six levels. But the precise number hardly matters: The point is that your day-to-day life in today's society depends on the smooth operation of at least a dozen other "primary worlds," and that those worlds depend, in turn, on the proper functioning of each other as well as the proper interactions with one or more additional levels of worlds.

Some of these interactions might not involve computers: They could consist of person-to-person conversations, or hand-delivered pieces of written correspondence. You might leave a handwritten note for the manager of the neighborhood liquor store, asking him to have a case of beer delivered later in the day; and you might then walk down to the neighborhood branch of your bank, and complain to the branch manager that you think the bank's mortgage interest rates are outrageous, and that you're considering moving your account elsewhere. Those interactions don't involve computers, and they'll function just as well after January 1, 2000 as before.

But for business-to-business interactions, the situation is quite different. As far back as the early 80s, studies indicated that 50-75 percent of the interactions between company A and company B consist of "transactions" (purchase orders, payments, inquiries,and the like) generated by a computer system in A, and processed by a computer system in B. Many, if not most, of those transactions involve Y2000-sensitive dates: the date of the transaction itself, the date of a purchase order, the date that the ordered items are expected to be shipped, the date that payment is due, and so on.

Note that this situation already exists today; it has nothing to do with the Year-2000 phenomenon per se. Amazingly, this "system of systems" works, and it manages to maintain a fairly steady equilibrium. Economists and politicians have argued for centuries whether a complex socio-economic system like the one illustrated in Figure B.5 can operate with an "invisible hand," or whether it requires a Soviet-style centralized planning mechanism to keep it from getting out of whack. We're not trying to argue in favor of socialism, capitalism, or communism here, but we do want to emphasize that if this system receives a sudden jolt—e.g., a stock-market crash, a hurricane, an earthquake, an oil embargo, or an epidemic—it can cause a massive set of ripple-effect interactions before everything settles down to a new equilibrium. The Year-2000 phenomenon is clearly such a jolt, and we believe that it will be much more pervasive and serious than most of the ones we've experienced in modern history.

Year-2000 and the Concept of System Dynamics

Back in the 1960s, MIT Professor Jay Forrester began developing the field of *system dynamics*, based on earlier work in the field of operations research and cybernetics. Forrester's work led to a "world model"[4] that attempted to extrapolate the current trends in energy consumption, population growth, food production, and so forth to see what conditions would be like 20 or 30 years in the future. Though the model was probably overly ambitious, and while it was severely criticized by economists and systems researchers for both political and theoretical reasons, it nevertheless set into motion the development of a number of "micro-world" models that have proven to be enormously useful in various companies and government agencies around the world. The field is too elaborate and too technical to discuss here, but we highly recommend Peter Senge's wonderful book, *The Fifth Discipline*,[5] as a very readable and entertaining discussion of what system dynamics is all about.

There are two key system dynamics concepts that are relevant when thinking about the Y2000 problem: feedback loops and time delays. They can be explained simply, and we'll use a non-computer metaphor to get the point across. Suppose you wake up tomorrow morning in a foul mood, and you happen to encounter your next-door neighbor as you leave home for the office. Having no one else to vent your bad feelings upon, you shout at this innocent soul, "You're the most pig-headed idiot of a neighbor I've ever known. I don't know how I got stuck living next door to you!"

What happens at that point? Probably nothing: Your neighbor is too stunned by the outburst to do or say anything. Both of you then get in your cars and drive off to work; having reached the office and having had a cup of coffee, you find yourself in a better mood, and the entire episode is forgotten.

Unfortunately, your neighbor also happens to be your spouse's supervisor—and he has *not* forgotten the insult. Six months later, when it comes time for your spouse's annual review, the neighbor/supervisor unexpectedly yells at your spouse, "You're the most pig-headed idiot of an employee I've ever seen in my entire career! I don't know how they hired you in the first place, and you're certainly not getting a raise this year!"

Stunned and shaken, your spouse stews about this all afternoon, becoming ever more frustrated and angry. You're not aware of this, of course, because you work in a different company; but when you get home from work that evening, you're flabbergasted when your spouse shouts at you, "You're the most pig-headed idiot of a spouse I could ever imagine! I don't know how I could have married you in the first place—I want a divorce!"

Obviously, this is a bit melodramatic, but you get the point. To paraphrase of one of Newton's laws, every action has a reaction—but in situations like the one described above, it may not be an "equal and opposite reaction." And more importantly, the reaction isn't necessarily immediate, nor is it necessarily aimed back at the source of the original action. Your neighbor doesn't yell back at you when you insult him, and he doesn't take *any* immediate action.

If we were to pursue our metaphor a little further, we would encounter what the system dynamics experts call a *causal loop*, one version of which is known in popular terms as a "vicious circle." Because your spouse has asked for a divorce, you're in an unbelievably bad mood the next morning when you encounter your neighbor on the way to work; of course, it never occurs to you that the entire situation was caused by your insulting remark six months earlier. All you know is that you're in such a bad mood that you can't stand the sly, mischievous grin that your neighbor is aiming in your direction. Enraged, you punch your neighbor in the nose; and a week later, your neighbor retaliates by firing your spouse. Your spouse is both furious and frightened at the prospect of being unemployed, and thus decides to accelerate the divorce process, suing your for all your worldly possessions.

What's this got to do with the Y2000 crisis? In a nutshell: the problems won't all occur at the stroke of midnight on December 31, 1999; and the problems won't consist of direct, "one-time-only" interactions between the "source" of the Y2000 problem and the "victim" of the Y2000 problem. In some cases, the consequences of the Y2000 problem will be delayed by a week or a month or a year; and in some cases, the consequences will "ripple" from the source to victim A, who then causes problems for B, which creates larger problems for C, when then "feeds back" an even larger problem to the original source. Here are a few examples:

- Some of the problems will occur before January 1, 2000 because of its anticipated effects. If you thought that there was a good chance your bank's ATM machines wouldn't work for the entire month of January 2000, you would probably withdraw a few hundred dollars of spare cash; you might even close your account and withdraw all of your money. What if all of the bank's customers did the same thing?[6] Here's a better example: If you thought there was a good chance the IRS would shut down in January 2000, would you bother making your estimated tax payments in the last quarter of 1999?

- Some of the problems will occur on January 31, 2000, when computer systems generate invoices, statements, and other monthly reports for the month of January. Other problems will occur at the end of February, because a few computer systems will mistakenly decide that 2000 is *not* a leap year. Other problems will occur at the end of the first quarter, or the end of the calendar year.

- Some of the problems will occur during the spring and summer of 2000 because of contingency plans that were *not* put into place in 1999. For example, disruptions in fuel supplies and distribution of seeds and fertilizers could cause problems with the spring-2000 planting activities throughout the Northern hemisphere. The problem won't manifest itself for consumers until the late summer and fall of 2000, when the harvest produces inadequate results. But rather than blaming all of this on the failures occurring on January 1, 2000, we could blame it instead on the poor planning by government officials—i.e., those officials who could have been subsidizing larger-than-normal "bumper crops" in 1999, so that wheat, corn, rice, and other basic foodstuffs could be stockpiled.

- Some of the problems will occur at random intervals during the first year or two after the roll-over date, because of subtle, insidious computer errors that corrupt the organization's database. Imagine, for example, a billing system associated with your credit-card company: In January 2000, it calculates the interest on your unpaid credit-card balance, and because of a Y2000 bug, it does so incorrectly. As we illustrated in Appendix A, this might not only involve sending you an outrageously high invoice, but it might also "clobber" another database record—e.g., the database record of another customer, Mr. Jones, of the credit-card company. Suppose Mr. Jones has no unpaid balance in December 1999 or in January 2000; but he buys a new television set in February, and has an unpaid balance in March. When the monthly billing system runs in March, it retrieves Mr. Jones's record, computes the interest payment, and sends him a statement. Even if the Y2000 bug has been fixed, it might not have been evident that the *address* in Mr. Jones's record has been clobbered. Thus, Mr. Jones's statement is sent to the wrong address, and a complete stranger throws the statement away after muttering about "those damn computers." After three months of nonpayment and increasingly nasty warning letters sent to the wrong address, Mr. Jones's credit card is canceled.

- The feedback loops are potentially the most serious aspect of the Y2000 problem, because of the vast numbers of people that may be involved. If Mr. Jones has problems with his credit card, as in the example above, society won't notice or care. But suppose the credit card company has the same problem with a *million* of its customers; what happens then? It's reasonable to assume that a substantial percentage of those people will get on the phone (assuming it works) and call the toll-free, hot-line customer-service number. A few people may get through, and may receive a plausible reassurance that everything will be fixed, but the majority won't. What happens to the disgruntled customers who couldn't get through? Chances are that a lot of them will cancel their credit card (before or after the credit-card company does the same thing!) and take their business elsewhere (assuming they can find another credit-card company whose computers work). Along the way, they tell all of their neighbors and friends to avoid their original credit-card company, because of its lousy computer systems. Conclusion: The original card company loses a substantial number of customers, and thereby loses a substantial amount of revenue (from the interest charges it would have collected), and could conceivably go bankrupt.

- If you want to think about some *serious* feedback loops, try these scenarios: The Social Security System (which, by the way, continues to be further along in its Y2000 conversion efforts than most other federal government agencies) fails to send out its monthly retirement checks to a few million retired citizens. And the state welfare agencies and unemployment agencies fail to send out their monthly welfare and unemployment checks. Or food stamps get lost because of a Y2000 computer bug. When electric power failed in the eastern United States for a couple days in 1977, riots broke out. What happens if the problems extend for a month? Or a year?

Indeed, we could continue this list of examples indefinitely. To those of us who work on Y2000 problems on a full-time basis, it's like an onion: every time you peel off one layer of the problem, there's another layer beneath it. For example, there has been a great deal of discussion about potential Y2000 problems in the FAA air-traffic control systems. But as we'll discuss in Chapter 4, the FAA is just the tip of the iceberg if you're concerned about the operation of a stable, reliable air-transport business. Even if the U.S. air-traffic control system works, global travel will be severely disrupted if other countries don't manage to get their systems fixed; and while we might have cause to be optimistic about some of the European countries, there is definite cause for concern about the Y2000 air-traffic problems in Africa, South America, and some Asian countries. Then there are the airlines, of which there are nearly 300 in the U.S.; and we have to worry about the airports, of which there are over 500 in the U.S. The typical airline has between 10,000 and 20,000 suppliers and vendors; the airports also have thousands of vendors and suppliers. Two of the most critical vendors in this discussion are the airplane manufacturers (e.g., Boeing, Airbus, McDonnel Douglas, and other such companies) and the insurance companies whose casualty policies allow the airports to stay open, and the airlines to risk sending their planes into the sky. *All* of this has to work, smoothly and reliably, and all of it is threatened by Y2000 computer problems.

One of the reasons we're particularly concerned about all of this is because of the "triage" strategy discussed in Appendix A. In the case of a telephone company, for example, it's obviously critical to produce a dial tone when customers pick up the phone; and all of the other computer systems that effectuate a phone call from person A to person B are critical. Without these systems, there is effectively no phone company; and for what it's worth, the major telephone companies swear categorically that these systems *will be* Y2000-compliant, hopefully by mid-1999.

What about the telephone company's billing systems? Arguably, the phone company won't shut down if it can't generate bills on January 2nd; however, the volume of billing is so high that most phone companies have to distribute the billing for all of their customers across the entire month, in order to finish an entire "cycle" by the end of the month. But let's assume, for the sake of argument, that all of the bills are generated on the last day of the month; and let's assume that a Y2000 bug made it impossible for the phone company to generate those bills on January 31, 2000. Would the company declare bankruptcy on February 1st? Not likely—but if the billing systems failed again in February and March, the company's cash flow situation would become rather precarious. So the billing systems are extremely important, or "mission-critical," even if they don't cause a total collapse at the stroke of midnight on December 31, 1999.

What systems are *not* critical? Perhaps some of the *internal* systems used by the phone company to manage its affairs. Any large organization typically has dozens of internal management and reporting systems to keep track of what it's doing; these include scheduling, inventory, human-resource, financial accounting systems, and on and on. All of these are typically considered "important," but in a severe emergency, the business could probably continue to function, at least for a while.

Whether the phone system keeps track of its internal affairs may or may not be of interest to you; but what about the important-but-not-critical *external* systems? One possibility is the computer systems that generate all of the marketing and promotional literature that seems to be stuffed into every piece of junk-mail that comes to your house. Think about this for a moment: You would probably be delighted if you didn't receive that kind of junk mail, but what about the advertising agencies, graphic artists, printers, paper-supply companies, and delivery organizations that carry out the marketing/ promotional activities? Many of these are likely to be small organizations for whom the phone company is their largest (and perhaps *only*) customer. Thus, when the phone company casually announces, "We won't be sending out the usual 10 million pieces of junk mail per month in 2000, because it's one of the non-critical systems that we didn't have time to fix," the result could be that half a dozen small companies eke out an existence for a few months, but then go bankrupt.

While this particular example involving the phone company may or may not actually occur, we hope that you see the point: What one company deems a non-critical system may well turn out to be a *very* critical system to one of its suppliers, subcontractors, vendors, or customers. And the corollary point is that some of these company-to-company interactions are going to be terminated deliberately and consciously on January 1st (quite possibly without any advance warning) as a matter of expediency.

As we discussed in Appendix A, vintage-1998 estimates by software metrics experts indicate that roughly 15-25 percent of the computer systems in the United States will *not* be Y2000-compliant by January 1, 2000. Some of those non-converted systems will be the "dead" or "dormant" ones that are of interest only to the most moribund of bureaucrats within the organization; but it's inevitable that there will be many non-converted systems that fall into the category of the phone company's marketing system discussed above. And this doesn't count the critical systems that didn't get converted because the organization simply ran out of time, or the critical systems that were *incorrectly* fixed (i.e., additional bugs were innocently and unconsciously injected into the systems as the programmers frantically tried to fix the Y2000 problems) or *incompletely* fixed (i.e., the programmers overlooked some subtle occurrences of date-related activities within some of the programs).

Bottom line: The interactions shown in Figure B.5 are virtually certain to receive a series of "jolts," ranging in size from moderate to massive. The initial series of jolts will occur on or about January 1, 2000 and there will be a series of after-shocks that last for at least a full year, if not longer. Though it's stretching a point, the situation could be compared to the meteor impact that occurred in the midst of the dinosaur age. Some scientists argue that within a matter of days, the entire earth was covered by a dense cloud of ash and dust that effectively blocked all sunlight for a period of time. Debates continue as to whether this was indeed the "jolt" that killed off the dinosaurs, either directly (through short-term loss of plant life) or indirectly (through long-term changes in the weather and climate), but one thing is indeed clear: It was sudden and massive and pervasive.

Scientists don't really know, with absolute certainty, what happened when the meteorite hit, and whether it really killed off the dinosaurs. Similarly, we don't really know what the impact of the Y2000 meteorite will be, nor can anyone else predict the outcome with certainty. The feedback loop, time-delay, and ripple-effect consequences of a pervasive series of Y2000 jolts upon the complex sauce-economic system shown in Figure B.5 is beyond anyone's ability to predict in a precise, mathematical fashion.

By the way, at least one species *did* survive the age of dinosaurs: the cockroach. Hopefully, we'll do better!

Endnotes

1. Actually, this depends heavily on the size of each person's circle of friends. If each person knows 40 other people, with no overlaps (e.g., you and I have no friends in common), then after six levels of communication, a total of 4,201,025,641 people will have received the same message.
2. Careful readers of the first edition of our book have pointed out to us that while Tom DeMarco popularized the unofficial term "intertwingled," it was actually created by computer pioneer Ted Nelson.

3. General Motors is reported to have approximately 100,000 suppliers. As of early August 1998, only half of the "critical" suppliers had responded to GM's written queries to determine if they would be Y2000-compliant. Of those who did respond, approximately 25 percent provided an unacceptable response. Naturally, this raises serious questions about GM's abilities to function even if it does manage to repair its own vast portfolio of software, estimated to be 2-3 billion lines of code. And if GM has problems with its suppliers and vendors, it's not unreasonable to imagine that large firms such as Ford, Chrysler, Toyota, BMW, Mercedes, and Honda might have similar problems. For more details, see "Automakers prep for year 2000," by Bob Wallace, *Computerworld*, July 27, 1998 (available on the Internet at http://www.computerworld.com/home/print.nsf/all/9807275D36)
4. See *The Limits to Growth: A Report for the Club of Rome's Project on the Predicament of Mankind* by Donella H. Meadows, Dennis L. Meadows, Jorgen Randers, and William W. Behrens III (1972)
5. Peter M. Senge, *The Fifth Discipline: The Art and Practice of the Learning Organization* (New York: Doubleday, 1990)
6. Of course, this is the classic "bank run" we've all heard about, and it's easy to imagine that it requires *all* of the bank's customers showing up at the same time for the crisis to occur. But as we discuss in Chapter 7, that's not the case in a fractional-reserve banking system, in which the bank maintains only a small percentage of its deposits on hand. Here are two statistics with which you can assess the U.S. banking situation: There are approximately 100 million families, and there is approximately $17.9 billion in cash circulating in the U.S., according to Patrick K. Barron, chief operating officer of the Federal Reserve Bank of Atlanta, and senior official in charge of the Federal Reserve's nationwide Year 2000 project (see "Y2K dilemma no problem for Fed, exec says," by Rob Chambers, *Atlanta Journal and Constitution*, July 15, 1998, also available on the Internet at http://web.lexis-nexis.com/more/cahners/11370/3523624/4). That works out to approximately $179 per family, which is considerably less than the approximately $2,833 median U.S. monthly family income. Thus, if 10 percent of the nation's families decide to withdraw approximately a month's income, the banks will run out of cash—unless the Federal Reserve system substantially increases the cash in circulation in the months prior to January 1, 2000. The situation may not be quite so bleak if one uses statistics from the Federal Reserve

Bank of St. Louis, which reports that in July 1998, there was $442.7 billion in circulation (see http://bos.business.uab.edu/charts/cgi-bin/data.exe/OKfedstl\currns+1 for current figures). Even if all of this cash was physically located inside the United States—and more particularly, inside the bank vaults—a withdrawal of a month's cash by the entire country would consume approximately 64 percent of all available currency.

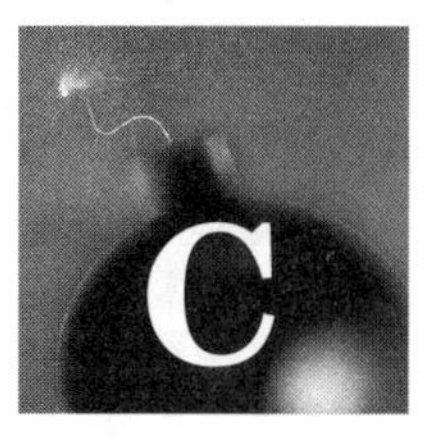

Additional Sources of Information

Technical Y2000 Books

Year 2000 Fixes for Dummies, Bourne, Kelly C. (IDG Books Worldwide, September 1997).

Practical Methods for Your Year 2000 Problem, Chapman, Robert B. (Manning Publications Co., November 1997).

Meltdown 2000: 25 Things Your Must Know to Protect Yourself and Your Computer, Cleenewerck, Lawrence (Robert Reed, May 1997).

Electric Utilities and Y2K, Cowles, Rick (self-published, March 1998; see URL for Cowles' web site below).

Managing 00: Surviving the Year 2000 Computing Crisis, de Jager, Peter, and Richard Bergeon (John Wiley & Sons, June 1997).

Year 2000 Compliance: A Guide to Successful Implementation, Fairchild, Alea (Computer Technology Research, May 1997).

Finding and Fixing Your Year 2000 Problem: A Guide for Small Businesses and Organizations, Feiler, Jesse (AP Professional Books, April 1998).

2001 Questions and Answers About the Year 2000 Problem, Franklin, William N. (Metro Information Systems, March 1997).

The Millennium Bug: How to Survive the Coming Chaos, Hyatt, Michael S. (Regnery Publishing, May 1998).

Year 2000: Best Practices for Y2K Millenium Computing, Lefkon, Dick, editor, (Prentice Hall, October 1997).

The Year 2000 Problem: Quantifying the Costs and Assessing the Consequences, Jones, Capers (Addison-Wesley, 1998).

The Year 2000 Computer Crisis: Solutions for IBM Legacy Systems, Jones, Keith (International Thomson Computer Publishers, June 1997).

Year 2000 Problem: Strategies and Solutions from the Fortune 100, Kappelman, Leon (International Thomson Press, August 1997).

Surviving the Year 2000 Problem, Keogh, James Edward, and Stephen C. Ruten (AP Professional Books, January 1997).

The Year 2000 Computer Crisis: An Investor's Survival Guide, Keyes, Tony (The Y2K Investor, July 1997).

Solving the Year 2000 Crisis, McDermott, Patrick (Artech House, May 1998).

Year 2001: Reaching Y2K Compliance After the Deadline, Miller, Stewart S. (Digital Press, November 1998).

The Year 2000 Computing Crisis: A Millennium Date Conversion Plan, Murray, Jerome T., and Marilyn J. Murray (Computing McGraw-Hill, March 1996).

The Year 2000 Problem Solver: A Five-Step Disaster Prevention Plan, Ragland, Bryce (Computing McGraw-Hill, December 1996).

Evaluating the Success of a Year 2000 Project, Robbins, Brian, and Howard Rubin (Information Systems Press, April 1998).

How To 2000, Sims, Dean, and Raytheon E-Systems (IDG Books, January 1998).

The Year 2000 Software Systems Crisis: Challenge of the Century, Ulrich, William M., and Ian S. Hayes (Prentice Hall, March 1997).

The Year 2000 Software Crisis: The Continuing Challenge, Ulrich, William M., and Ian S. Hayes (Prentice Hall, April 1998).

The Computer Time Bomb: How to Keep the Century Date Change from Killing Your Organization, Zetlin, Minda (AMACOM, January 1998).

Non-Technical Books

None of the books in this list are technical computer books intended to help explain the Y2K problem, or to provide specific solutions for it. The works of fiction may provide some insights into the reactions of society before, during, and after a serious crisis. The non-fiction books provide advice and guidance in the areas of health, gardening, food preparation, and other traditional skills that may prove helpful if there are serious disruptions in today's highly automated products and services.

Fiction

Nightfall is the novel-length version of a short story first published by Isaac Asimov in 1941; it describes a mythical world in which sunlight is always provided by one of six suns—except once every 2049 years, at which point total nightfall occurs, and civilized society collapses. *Alas, Babylon* is a classic story of the aftermath of nuclear war in a small community in Florida; substitute Y2K in place of atomic bombs and you'll find a lot to think about in this story.

As for Ayn Rand's *Atlas Shrugged*—well, you probably read it in college, but you've probably forgotten all about it. You probably don't remember John Galt's famous line, "I will stop the engine of the world." Read the book again now, with Y2K-colored glasses, and remember that computer programmers are reading it, too. The question you need to ask them is whether they intend to stay on the job if the lights go out on January 1, 2000, and whether they feel sufficiently motivated to re-start the engines of the world. If you don't think that's a question worth asking, then you haven't read *Atlas Shrugged*.

Nightfall, Asimov, Isaac and Robert Silverberg (Bantam/Doubleday, 1990).

Alas, Babylon, Frank, Pat (HarperCollins, 1960).

Y2K: It's Already Too Late, Kelly, Jason (JK Press, June 1998).

Atlas Shrugged, Rand, Ayn (Penguin Books, 1957).

Y2K: The Millennium Bug, Tiggre, Don L. (Xlibris, 1998).

Non-Fiction

Some of the books on this list, as you can tell from the titles, are concerned with preparedness, self-help, and so forth. But we would particularly like to recommend *The Fourth Turning* by William Strauss and Neil Howe; its theme is that major world events (e.g., World War II) hit different generations at different stages of their lives, which strongly influences everything they do thereafter. If Y2K does turn out to be a disaster, it will hit the baby-boomer generation at a point where they're seriously thinking about easing up and getting ready for retirement; if the world ends up having to be "saved" by a generation ready to go to war, it will be the generation born in 1980... and so forth. There's a lot of debate and controversy about this book, and you may not completely agree with its overall premise; but if nothing else, it's extremely thought-provoking. The one major irony is that while the authors are convinced that a major "turning" is almost certain to hit us in the next few years, they don't seem to recognize Y2K as a possible cause of the crisis.

If you're interested in seeing how government and business leaders respond to the possibility of impending crisis, read Galbraith's history of the 1929 crash. Assuming that human nature hasn't changed much in the past 60 years, it does make one wonder how forthright we should expect today's leaders to be if there is indeed a serious Y2K problem looming ahead of us.

Square Foot Gardening, Bartholomew, Mel (Rodale Press, 1981).

Live off the Land in the City and Country, Benson, Ragnar, with Devon Christensen (Paladin Press, 1982).

Life After Doomsday, Clayton, Bruce (Paladin Press, 1980).

Where There Is No Dentist, Dickson, Murray (The Hesperian Foundation, 1983).

The Encyclopedia of Country Living (9th Edition), Emery, Carla (Sasquatch Books, 1994).

The Great Crash 1929 (reprint edition) Galbraith, John Kenneth (Houghton Miflin, 1997).

Back to Basics: How to Learn and Enjoy Traditional American Skills (Readers Digest, 1981).

We Had Everything But Money: Priceless Memories of the Great Depression, Mulvey, Deb, editor, (Reiman Publications, L.P., 1992).

The Fourth Turning: What the Cycles of History Tell Us About America's Next Rendezvous With History. Strauss, William, and Neil Howe (New York: Broadway Books/Bantam Doubleday Dell, 1997). For more on the concept of "fourth turning," visit the authors' Fourth Turning Web site (http://www.fourthturning.com).

Making the Best of Basics: Family Preparedness Handbook (Tenth Edition), Steves, James Talmadge (Gold Leaf Press, 1997).

Where There Is No Doctor: A Village Health Care Handbook (Revised English Edition), Werner, David with Carol Thuman and Jane Maxwell (The Hesperian Foundation, 1992).

Web Sites

These are the key Y2K sites that we've bookmarked in our own Web browsers. Obviously, it's not an exhaustive list of every document or report or Y2K Web site, but it's the collection of sites that we usually visit at least once a week. In general, we're less interested in listing the technical computer sites—if you're a programmer, you might want to visit IBM's or Microsoft's Y2K site on a weekly basis, but we're more concerned here with the personal aspects and ramifications of Y2K.

Our own Web site (http://www.yourdon.com), contains a collection of essays, pointers, Powerpoint slides, and other materials about Y2K.

The President's Y2K Council (http://www.y2k.gov) site provides details of National Y2K Action Week, which took place on October 19-23, 1998. It also provides details of the Y2K strategy outlined in President Clinton's July 14, 1998 speech. We were very disappointed with President Clinton's speech—but whether it was a good speech or a bad speech, it's important for American citizens to know that the president did utter some words on the topic.

The Y2000 Personal Preparation site (http://www.readyfory2k.com). Articles, quotes, checklists, advice, and links to various vendors of books, food, and other materials. This site is the result of a collaboration between Y2K Solutions Group, Inc, which produces a series of Y2K videos; James Talmadge Steves (author of *Making the Best of Basics: Family Preparedness Handbook*); and Ed Yourdon.

Sanger's Review of the Millennium (http://www.cruxnet.com/~sanger/y2k/), a daily summary of the news about Y2K by Larry Sanger. Updated and archived daily, it provides a succinct, one-paragraph abstract of various Y2K articles, as well as a link the article itself. The abstracts are "neutral," without the editorializing and "spin" that, for example, Gary North puts on his links.

Community planning sites: More and more people have been contacting us to ask about information resources for community-level awareness and Y2K planning (particularly since the official city, county, state, and federal governments seem to be clueless, in a state of deep denial, or utterly overwhelmed by their own bureaucracies). We've listed about 10 items below; by the time this book is published, there will probably be several more.

"Year 2000 contingency planning for municipal governments" (http://www.angelfire.com/mn/inforest/capersj989.html), a paper by software metrics guru Capers Jones.

Bill Bole's article about Y2k community organizing (http://www.americannews.com/Recent/ans-000580.html).

The Cassandra project Web site (http://www.millennia-bcs.com/casframe.htm), mentioned below for personal contingency planning, is also a good source for community planning.

Lowell, Massachusetts' Web site (http://www.lowellonline.org/bna/y2k) on community Y2K preparation.

Napa Valley (California) Web site (http://www.y2knapa.com/) on Y2K community planning, with a good section on Family Preparation.

year2000@efn.org is a community preparedness listserv hosted by Oregon Public Networking in Eugene, Oregon. The list discusses community preparedness issues resulting from potential century-date-change (CDC) complications impacting the nationally and internationally shared infrastructures of power, fuel, food, telecommunications, currency, and community services through several means. To subscribe to the Regional Preparedness Listserv, send an email to: listproc@efn.org with the body of your message containing the following text (without the quotes): "subscribe year2000 [type your name in here]"

The Y2K Fellowship League founded by Steve Baldwin: (http://www.geocities.com/Eureka/Enterprises/7336/index.html).

"What Local Governments Should be Doing about Y2K" (http://www.erols.com/steve451/whatgov.htm#What), a paper by Steve Davis.

The Co-Intelligence Institute's Y2K Home Page (http://www.co-intelligence.org/y2k breakthrough.html), with lots of sections and links to community-related resources.

Santa Cruz, California's draft document for Y2K community planning (http://www.co-intelligence.org/y2k communityplan2.html). An excellent, detailed document with a great deal of involvement on the part of Y2K guru Bill Ulrich, co-author of *The Year 2000 Software Crisis: Challenge of the Century* and *The Year 2000 Software Crisis: The Continuing Challenge.*

y2ksurvive (http://www.y2ksurvive.com), a survivalist Web site. You may not consider yourself a survivalist, but it wouldn't hurt to peek at this site from time to time, especially if you're thinking that it might be a good idea to stockpile a modest amount of food and other essentials. The site owner, Ron Courtney, says that it's aimed at ordinary people (not computer programmers, not religious millennialists, not militia members) who believe they have good reason to fear the effects of Y2K. He does his best to discuss various aspects of Y2K survival in a fairly conversational tone.

Y2Ktoday (http://www.Y2Ktoday.com), a new Web site created on September 14, 1998 by the former CEO of United Press International, James Adams.

Adams describes the site as "the world's largest Y2K Web site" in order to "sound a public wake-up call." Y2Ktoday features a daily feed of some 500 stories from a special reporting team, plus wire reports.

The Senate Special Committee on the Year 2000 Technology Problem (http://www.senate.gov/~y2k/priorities.html), chaired by Senator Robert Bennett (R-Utah). Senator Bennett's hearings on the Y2K situation in transportation, utilities, telecommunications, and other aspects of society have been among the most thorough and wide-ranging of the various government activities in 1998. Until recently, the proceedings were not published by the Committee, and we were forced to rely on various other media sources to find out what was going on. This site is worth checking periodically, because the Committee plans to continue holding hearings through the remainder of 1998, and presumably throughout 1999, to track progress and identify problems in various infrastructure areas and industry sectors.

The Joseph Project (http://josephproject2000.org), which focuses the impact of Y2K on charities. You can also find an article by the President of this group on the Westergaard Web site (http://www.y2ktimebomb.com).

The Mitre Y2K Web site (http://www.mitre.org/research/y2k), which provides a detailed, comprehensive discussion of several aspects of Y2K. Consider it as an alternative to the ITAA Web site cited below.

U.S. State Y2K sites (http://www.state.or.us/IRMD/y2k/other.htm) and Y2K coordinators (http://www.nasire.org/year2000/coordinators.html): sooner or later, it occurs to us that we should find out what's going on within our own state (unless, of course, you don't live in the U.S., in which case you should be concerned about the province, state, or local region of your own country). Anyway, the two sites listed here provide contact information for the various agencies and coordinators for Y2K activities within the states; an alternative site (http://www.y2k.gov/java/abouty2k6.html) provides a graphic image of the U.S., which you can click-through to reach information about various states. For information about cities and counties, see Public Technology, Inc.'s site (http://pti.nw.dc.us).

For small businesses who are just getting started on y2k, check out the support2000 site (http://www.support2000.com). An alternative is the Small Business Administration's site (http://www.sba.gov/y2k/), which many feel is a less user-friendly site.

If you're looking for a Y2K technical job, check out the America job bank site (http://it.jobsearch.org).

The GOP (Republican Party) Y2K site (http://www.freedom.gov/y2k) on what the government is doing about Y2K. This is not to suggest that the Republicans are necessarily any more competent, honest, or forthright than the Democrats about the Y2K situation, but since Y2K has already become a political football, it's probably worth seeing who's saying what about whom within the major political parties.

Heath's Links to Y2K Congressional testimony (http://home.swbell.net/adheath/testimony.htm)—this is an amazing resource for anyone who wants to know what kind of testimony is being presented to various House and Senate committees about Y2K. Many thanks to Roleigh Martin for passing it on to us!

Peter de Jager's Web page of daily Y2K press clippings (http://www.year2000.com/y2karticles.html): Peter de Jager created the first serious Web site for Y2K discussions and announcements a few years ago, and it continues to be one of the most heavily visited Y2K sites. There are interesting book lists, announcements, and discussion groups, but the majority of the site is devoted to vendor announcements and advertisements. We visit the press clippings section of the site almost daily; it's not too hard to spot the articles in your own local publications, but de Jager's site covers U.S., Canadian, British, and Australian media, among others.

Yahoo Web page of daily Y2K press clippings (http://headlines.yahoo.com/Full_Coverage/Tech/Year_2000_Problem/): This is an alternative source of press clippings on Y2K. We find it more impersonal than de Jager's, and we don't visit it quite as often—but it's nice to know it's there.

Gary North's Web site (http://www.garynorth.com): Love him or hate him, but don't ignore him. Gary has strong opinions on Y2K, which you may agree or disagree with; but his site has become one of the pre-eminent sources of material on Y2K, covering a much broader area than the Yahoo and de Jager sites mentioned above. As of late October 1998, North had accumulated nearly 3,000 articles, grouped into such categories as "power grid," "government," "banking," and so forth. Most of the material consists of newspaper or magazine articles, but he has also tracked down a variety of other documents, reports, memos, email messages, and the like; with very rare exceptions, he provides a direct link to the document on the Internet, as well as his summary and interpretation of the significance of the document. If you're lazy or curious about his opinion, you can simply read his summary and opinion; if you want to see the original material, he's got a hyperlink to click on. One section of his site summarizes the new entries that he has posted within the past few days; he typically adds 5-10 entries each day. We visit this site daily.

Westergaard Y2K Web site
(http://www.y2ktime-bomb.com/): John Westergaard claims to have introduced Senator Daniel Patrick Moyhnihan to the Y2K problem in 1996, which may be one of the reasons the Congress and Senate eventually began paying attention to the problem. The Westergaard site tends to provide a Washington-centric perspective on Y2K, with interesting assessments of the government's actions and inaction, as well as the political ramifications of Y2K. The site now has half a dozen

different "columnists," many of whom are recognized authorities within the Y2K computer industry; in the course of a week, you're likely to find two or three really interesting articles and columns from these folks. Worth visiting at least once a week.

Roleigh Martin's Web site (http://ourworld.compuserve.com/homepages/roleigh_martin/): If the lights go out, it won't matter whether your home PC is working or not. More and more attention is beginning to be focused on the electric utilities, but most of the coverage is spotty—e.g., an occasional series of Senate hearings, followed by ominous silence. There are two individuals who have been tracking the utility industry since the beginning, and who continue to update their sites with recent reports and developments associated with various agencies and regulatory bodies. Roleigh is one of those individuals, and his efforts to raise awareness and generate action in the state of Minnesota (where he lives) are a good example of efforts we all could, and should, be making in our own neighborhood. Roleigh also has an excellent collection of recommended books on different aspects of Y2K. Worth visiting at least once a week.

Rick Cowles' Web site (http://www.euy2k.com/index.htm): Another excellent source of material on the utility industry. Rick has also written a book on the subject, which I've included in my list of recommended Y2K books. Worth visiting at least once a week.

The Cassandra project Web site (http://www.millennia-bcs.com/casframe.htm): This is *the* site to visit if you have begun asking the question "What kind of personal preparations should I be making for myself and my family?" Among other things, the site contains a detailed checklist of items you might want to consider stockpiling—not only food, but also medical supplies, and other important items. The Cassandra project is also very heavily involved in community-awareness projects; thus, if you've been thinking of organizing a Y2K awareness seminar for your school, church, or neighborhood, you're likely to pick up some good ideas from this site. Definitely worth visiting once a week, if not more frequently.

ITAA Web site (http://www.itaa.org/year2000.htm): ITAA is one of the most influential of the professional computer societies in the Y2K area; by contrast, we believe that the Association of Computing Machinery (ACM) and IEEE computer society has basically abdicated any useful role it could have played (we're less aware of the activities of the professional computer societies in England, Canada, and Australia; hopefully they're somewhat more active). It does have to be emphasized that ITAA (which stands for Information Technology Association of America) is basically a consortium of computer vendors; so it might be a bit more commercial and self-serving than one would want; but the organization has played a major role in helping to promote awareness and concern about Y2K problems within the U.S. federal government, as well as the private-sector organizations that are likely to be heavily impacted by Y2K failures.

Y2K for women (http://www.y2kwomen.com): For those who are finding that Y2K is one of those "Mars/Venus" situations, this site might help. We've already received numerous email messages from men who complain that their wives just don't "get it" when they express concern about Y2K—but that may be because the man comes home from work one evening and announces that (a) Y2K is going to cause the end of civilization, (b) he has decided to sell the house, (c) he's going to withdraw all of the money from the family savings account the next morning, (d) he's going to buy a collection of submachine guns, and (e) he intends to move the entire family into a fortified bunker somewhere in the mountains of Montana, where they will camp out and wrestle grizzly bears. No matter how intelligent, supportive, and open-minded the wife might be, this is a somewhat overwhelming message. Karen Anderson, a professional sociologist and therapist, has created this site to communicate the basic issues and concerns about Y2K in a somewhat less confrontational, end-of-the-world fashion; it's worth taking a look at. (By the way, we do realize that in many families, it's the wife who raises the alarm, and it's the husband who stubbornly refuses to acknowledge the potential danger of Y2K disruptions; but we don't know of any sites aimed at pigheaded husbands.)

Edward Yardeni's Web site (http://www.yardeni.com). Contrary to rumor, Dr. Yardeni is not related to the authors, even though our names are suspiciously similar. Yardeni is arguably the most prominent American economist offering a commentary on the Y2K problem (he is the Chief Economist at Deutsche Morgan Grenfell), and his site contains a wealth of Y2000 information, updated frequently. Well worth a weekly visit.

Index

B

C

D

G

J-K-L

M

S

T

U